THE LETTERS OF
KING HENRY VIII

UNIFORM WITH THIS VOLUME

THE LETTERS OF QUEEN ELIZABETH I
edited by G. B. Harrison

THE LETTERS OF KING CHARLES I
edited by Sir Charles Petrie

THE LETTERS OF KING CHARLES II
edited by Sir Arthur Bryant

THE LETTERS OF QUEEN ANNE
edited by Beatrice Curtis Brown

THE LETTERS OF KING GEORGE III
edited by Bonamy Dobrée

King Henry VIII
A painting on copper after Holbein

(National Portrait Gallery)

THE LETTERS OF KING HENRY VIII

A Selection, with a few other Documents

Edited by

M. ST. CLARE BYRNE

FUNK & WAGNALLS
NEW YORK

First published 1936

This edition first published 1968

Library of Congress Catalog Card Number: 68-25019
Published by Funk & Wagnalls, A Division of Reader's Digest Books, Inc.,
by arrangement with Cassell & Co. Ltd.
Printed in Great Britain.

CONTENTS

INTRODUCTION TO THE FIRST EDITION

There are about a thousand documents which may properly be described as the letters of Henry VIII. Their total bulk is enormous, and there are many single letters which run to between thirty and forty pages. To print in their entirety even a preliminary selection of just over a hundred of the more important of these letters would require a book more than half as long again as this: and even then they would be entirely unequipped with comment or annotation. For this reason, and for the others that follow, a somewhat different plan from that already established by the other volumes in this series has had to be adopted.

Henry's letters, even when the term is used to include signed and unsigned instructions drafted for him by secretaries and ministers, do not tell the story of his reign. There are facts and events of the utmost importance which find no place in them. There is very little in Henry's letters to indicate the extent of the power wielded by Wolsey: similarly, Wolsey's fall would pass almost unnoticed if they were the only source of information. They are equally inadequate for the rise, the amazing achievement, and the eventual fall of Thomas Cromwell; nor do they in any way indicate the tremendous importance of the work of the Parliament of 1529. Printed *in extenso* even the thousand documents would not give a comprehensive and satisfactory history of this very important period.

For this reason, then, in selecting a small volume of letters and a few other documents, I have not attempted to illustrate the whole of the reign. I have concentrated, instead, upon the more or less coherent interest that can be found in following the development of Henry's personality as a monarch, and in watching how that personality finds expression in letters connected either with certain outstanding events or with certain important lines of policy. That the selection should not be able to deal with every aspect of Henry's activities was inevitable. It does not, for example, tell us anything of the Henry VIII who founded the English navy, nor of the practical and personal interest that he took in his ships. It should give, nevertheless, a reasonable idea of the bulk and quality, the range and scope of the available material.

Fortunately for such a plan the letters provide an admirably detailed and comprehensive history of what the ordinary reader generally regards as the pivotal event of the reign—namely, the divorce from Katharine of Aragon. While realizing that it was a momentous event with momentous results, it is, however, not unusual for such a reader to find a text-book account of the *process* of the divorce both intricate and dreary; so that he is tempted to skip as quickly as possible to the *event* itself, and to ignore the rest as something beyond the layman's comprehension. Hence the frequent assertion, repeated by many people who ought to know better, that England forsook the Catholic faith simply because Henry VIII was tired of his elderly wife, and wanted to marry Anne Boleyn, and could not get the Pope to grant him a divorce. Difficult as it is to thread a way through the tangle of chicanery and intrigue of the negotiations, their story, nevertheless, becomes a thing of absorbing interest as soon as we have access to the documents in the case, and I believe that the letters in this section should prove both exciting and illuminating even to those who have hitherto found this long-drawn-out process a trifle wearisome.

Domestic policy is represented only by two sections—a few documents dealing with religion, and the extremely adequate and self-contained group of letters dealing with the Pilgrimage of Grace. This latter gives a comprehensive account of the one great domestic crisis of the reign; and some of the letters show as clearly as any he wrote, Henry's real practical ability, his methods of statesmanship, and his capacity for handling a state of emergency.

To illustrate Henry's dealings with the kingdoms he was trying to unite with England I have chosen his Scottish policy. As a group these letters suffer from the defect common to all which are concerned with a policy extending over the whole period of the reign: that is to say, letters written by Henry himself are comparatively few in number and tend to be of second-rate importance until after Wolsey's fall. The Scottish correspondence as a whole is one of the most voluminous belonging to the reign and certainly one of the most exciting. Nowhere, perhaps, can the real quality of Henry's methods and his diplomacy be more fully realized; and though by confining ourselves to his letters only, we lose the subtle interplay of mind and mind, and much of the direct impression of the extraordinarily vivid personalities with whom he was contending, nevertheless the story which can be followed in the one-sided correspondence still makes amazingly good reading.

To attempt to follow Henry's foreign policy throughout the reign was obviously impossible. Here, as in the Scottish correspondence, any one who becomes really interested is bound to be tantalized almost beyond bearing by not being able to read the replies. Moreover, during the long period of Wolsey's ascendancy his letters are generally more important and more interesting than the King's. I have therefore represented foreign policy only by two groups of letters, chosen not arbitrarily, but because they seem to me reasonably self-contained and complete, as well as characteristic. Although both are based on the inevitable three-cornered diplomacy of England, France and the Empire, I have simplified as far as possible by making the one group (III, 2) illustrate an episode in Henry's dealings with the Emperor Charles V; and by making the other (III, 5) more directly concerned with the French war of the last years of the reign.

If we are to see Henry himself at work, to catch unmistakable glimpses of the typically Tudor bent of mind, we are bound to turn to the later years, the period of his personal rule and of his full maturity. Moreover, if we want as far as possible to read English letters and avoid translations from the Latin, we must avoid concentrating on the earlier period covered by the lifetime of Ferdinand of Aragon and the longer one during which Henry was still on corresponding terms with the Papacy. The material itself has, in fact, more or less forced a choice such as I have made, practically ignoring the letters of the years before the divorce, except for the sake of contrast with those that come after.

There is no easy or superficial interest in Henry's letters, with the exception, perhaps, of those to Anne Boleyn. And even these, when not written in the key of courtly compliment, are the letters of a business man. Genuine affection is adequately but briefly stated. Their very existence says almost more for the ardour of his love than do the terms in which they are couched. That the busy man of affairs, occupied with the detail of state policy and administration, the Englishman to whom hunting and sport were part of the serious business of life, the man to whom writing with his own hand was a tedious matter, should have made time to pen them, is the suggestive thing. They are concerned with simple facts—the sending of a gift, his desire for her presence, a request she has made, his fears for her health, the progress of his divorce. They give us, in consequence, an extraordinarily vivid impression of the simple, direct, vigorous, downright and attractive side of his personality, which is in every way as real, as fundamental, and as important to our understanding as are its other and sometimes less attractive aspects.

Even these love-letters, however, for all the directness of their appeal, gain enormously as soon as they are placed in some reasonable order, set in their attendant circumstances, and generally annotated for the sake of a completer grasp of the details and incidents to which they refer. The story, in fact, has to be 'produced', even when the material has an obviously popular appeal. When it is realized that the bulk of what remains is business and not personal correspondence, it will be obvious that here the need for substantial commentary will be even greater. Like most business letters in any age, these letters are dull, unless the reader knows what they are all about. A letter that describes a well-known event as a rule needs little beyond identification to evoke the reader's knowledge and the associative values that he attaches to it. Business letters seldom describe events: as often as not they are just so much talk—interminable preparations for events that never happen, and plans that come to nothing. There is something inherently romantic in the very idea of a king's letters; but actually, when a king conducts the business of his kingdom—as Henry VIII did for a large part of his reign—his letters are just as likely as any other man's to contain the waste products of history-making, the stuff that was eliminated in discussion and by contact with circumstances and reality.

The reader, in consequence, may find more comment in this volume than the rest of the series will have led him to expect. It is, I believe, a bare minimum of comment; and it has been determined throughout by the amount of explanation that I have found myself in need of, in order to understand these letters, either as human or historical documents.

The only way to get any satisfaction out of these letters of Henry VIII is to read them. Dipping, skimming, gutting, tasting, and the various other processes that the skilled reader is accustomed to employ to circumvent Tudor long-windedness, will only produce boredom. There is nothing for it but to submit oneself to the intolerable wordiness, immerse completely in the alien element, accept the whole preposterous convention. Read, word by word, and gradually ear and mind alike grow accustomed to the unendingly sustained rhythms, and the unfamiliar idiom begins to please. Despite their bewildering ramifications, sentences drive on and thrust through, with the strength and solidity of tree trunks half hidden beneath their abundant leafage. Apparent repetitions resolve into distinctness, impacting like hammer-blows.

All the vigour, the determination, the relentless pertinacity and the sheer force of the man speak eloquently in his style when it comes to its maturity. If some of the earlier letters are colourless and unremarkable, the later ones more than compensate in interest—especially, perhaps, those concerned with the Pilgrimage of Grace and the last phase of Scottish policy. There is an almost terrifying quality in the steady battering of the marshalled phrases, as week by week, month by month, year by year, these Scots letters, grim with implacable purpose, reiterate their demands.

Opinions vary about Henry's ability as a ruler. About the fixity of his aims, the strength of his will, and his capacity for concentration and hard work there can be no dispute. It is possible to dispute his wisdom, impossible to deny the power of the mind. And it is this power, this ' maistry ', this concentrated will, that expresses itself more clearly than anything else in the style of his prose, and even in his very handwriting—highly individual, totally uncompromising, large, clear, steady and always unmistakably the same.

Power. Break it up into its components, and in Henry's case they will be energy and control. Look at his handwriting, and find them dominating the structure of every letter. Look at his alterations in a draft, and see the one breaking forth in long insertions, the other cutting down a superfluity of ambages with one ruthless stroke of the pen. Watch the vigorous exploration of fact and hypothesis throughout the intricacies of subordinate and co-ordinate clauses, and wait for the ramming home of the inexorable conclusion half a page away. Listen to the dignity and balance of the compacter sentence:

> This is no fashion for subjects, but rather after the fashion of war between prince and prince, which maketh us to marvel that they would thus blind us with fair words, calling us their natural and most dread sovereign lord under God, with desire of our mercy and pity, when nevertheless the effect of your said letters, in sundry points (as, in desiring hostages, a place indifferent, and abstinence of war for fourteen days after the meeting) showeth the contrary.[1]

For us to-day 'eloquence'—so-called—too often connotes emptiness. Men fight shy of the complex and of the periodic sentence, having little skill in their construction and less confidence in the powers of concentration that may be looked for in their hearers or readers. But Tudor England loved and cultivated 'eloquentia' for all the graver concerns of life. It admired the sustained flight of declamation, found weight and purpose in the devices of rhetoric. Caught up in the excitement of discovering the magnificent possibilities of their own language, Tudor Englishmen are to be envied rather than patronized for the more extravagant delights of their prose. They *felt*

[1] The light punctuation of this and other passages may, at first, seem inadequate to those unaccustomed to Tudor rhythms; but anything heavier destroys the fluency, the speed, and the drive, which must be kept if the style as well as the meaning is to be fully appreciated.

about words. One word was not as good as another, and two were generally better than one. When his secretary presents him with 'Mahometans' Henry crosses it out and writes 'Turk'. His secretary writes 'A friend seeth sometimes in his friend's causes more than him that the matter toucheth.' Henry finds this bald, and emends to 'A friend seeth sometimes in his friend's causes, when they consist in diversity of matters, more, peradventure, than he to whom the matter toucheth near.'[1]

Very few of Henry's letters are written in his own hand, with the exception of brief notes to Wolsey and the letters to Anne Boleyn. How far, in consequence, the language of diplomatic letters may be that of the ministers and secretaries who actually penned them, is open to dispute. No one, however, who consults the original documents, can fail to realize the concentrated attention and the personal supervision of detail that he gave, day by day, to his official correspondence.[2] The nature and the extent of the alterations and additions that he was accustomed to make in his own hand demonstrate the close scrutiny to which even the most apparently formal draft was subjected before it was allowed to go forth under his bold signature. The man who alters small formalities of phrasing in a letter to the Queen of Hungary,[3] who handles a draft as Henry handles the one illustrated in facsimile in the frontispiece to this volume, is a man who is fastidious about the way his meaning is expressed. Those who frequently wrote either for him or at his dictation, soon, I believe, caught 'the hang' of Henry's own style. Wriothesley writing for the King is not the same as Wriothesley writing personally.

I doubt if any one who is interested in such things can read

[1] The habit of drafting and re-drafting, even unto a third or fourth version, is normal throughout the century with most writers of diplomatic correspondence. The really remarkable thing about letters or passages in Henry's own hand is the ease and decision with which he gets the wording right at once, so that an absolute minimum of correction is required when expressing his own thought.

[2] See particularly Part III, Chapter 2, p. 203 ff.: also Chapter 3.

[3] It is a mere eight lines of credentials for his ambassadors, but in it Henry makes seven alterations, and even goes to the trouble of altering 'Ma mieulx aime soeur' into 'Madame ma bonne soeur'. (MS. Cotton Galba B.X, f. 42.)

even this small and rather mixed selection of the letters without becoming definitely conscious of the individual manner that time and again stamps a letter as indubitably Henry's. It would be unwise, however, to lay too much stress on tricks of style and turns of speech, cherished phrases and choice of words. The soundest evidence for their authenticity as the utterances of his mind is to be found in their clear and consistent revelation of an unmistakable personality—the personality of the real Henry. And the real Henry is not the popular Bluebeard, whose tendencies to matrimony have been greatly exaggerated; nor yet the bullying tyrant who muddled through, somehow, because he had the luck to secure clever ministers; but the King who has been described by his finest biographer as ' the most remarkable man who ever sat on the English throne '.

In making my selection I have had to be guided not so much by the absolute value of single letters as by the cumulative value of grouped letters and by their value for my set purpose. The descriptive symbols used in Appendix I will enable readers to ascertain at a glance the exact nature of each letter printed—whether holograph, or a draft, or a fair copy made for reference, or whatever it may be. There is only one instance of a letter, hitherto accepted without question, which I am unable to describe with any certainty. This is the letter from Henry to his secretary, William Knight, printed at p. 49. The manuscript belongs to Corpus Christi College, Oxford, and was first printed by the Rev. E. L. Hicks in *The Academy* in 1879, afterwards by James Gairdner in his *New Light on the Divorce*, in *The English Historical Review* for 1896. It is an important letter, as it shows us Henry trying to work secretly, and independently of Wolsey, in the matter of his divorce from Katharine of Aragon; and it also shows us that by the end of the summer of 1527 he had determined to marry Anne Boleyn.

This letter has hitherto been accepted as an original signed by Henry. It is definitely not a holograph letter; and since examining the MS., and comparing the signature with 130 other specimens, I am convinced, on palæographical grounds, that the

'H.R.' is not genuine. Henry's signature, throughout his life, remains as uniform and constant as the rest of his handwriting. In no single instance that I have seen—and I have examined a great many more than the 130 check specimens—does Henry's H agree in formation or appearance with the H of the Corpus letter, and the R, when closely scrutinized, is equally suspect. Whatever the size of the writing, whatever the nature of the pen used, the constancy and conformity of Henry's signature is as remarkable and as characteristic of the man as is the constancy of his purpose. His H is simple and bold, always properly formed, with the various strokes all made in their natural order. In the Corpus signature the H has either been drawn with two or three separate strokes, or else has been made by a not-very-skilful copyist who was not sure of the right order of the various strokes and has got them wrong. For a detailed description of the two letters, however, reference should be made to p. 51.

If I am right in my belief that this is not Henry's signature, the question arises, What does the Corpus MS. represent? There are certain obvious possibilities. In the first place, it is not a draft, and it may be the fair copy made for filing, to which some one—possibly a collector—has at some period added an imitation of Henry's signature. Secondly, it may be a later contemporary or an Elizabethan copy of the original document,[1] to which the copyist has appended as good a reproduction of the signature as he could manage. This is not an unusual occurrence in Elizabethan copies of letters from important people. Thirdly, there is the possibility that the whole letter might be an Elizabethan fabrication; but whether this last is a reasonable conjecture it is for the historian rather than the bibliographer to determine. For a note on the style of the letter, reference should be made to p. 52.

On palæographical grounds I do not think it is possible to choose between the first and second possibilities. The evidence offered by the secretarial hand in which the letter is written is quite inconclusive. It looks much more like an Elizabethan than an early Tudor hand, but I have found hands of roughly

[1] Or even an Elizabethan copy, plus 'signature', of the original *unsigned* copy of the original document.

equal 'modernity' as early as the fifteen-twenties. The most I can safely say is that I have not been able to identify it with any of the hands of those who were doing secretarial work for Henry round about 1527.

Palæographical evidence apart, it is, I think, the signature that provides one of the biggest problems; for the simple reason that, in checking through hundreds of Henry's letters, I have come upon no single instance of the signature 'H.R.', except in the seventeen love-letters written to Anne Boleyn. Henry's style throughout his reign, in personal letters (e.g. to Katharine Parr, p. 365), in letters of state, warrants, and other documents, is 'Henry R.' Even in his intimate letters to 'mine own good Cardinal', written in his own hand, it is still 'Henry R.' And I can see no reason why to William Knight, confidential secretary, but not *friend*, as Wolsey was (see pp. 49, 76-79, 81), he should use the 'H.R.' that, with this only exception, he kept for the woman he loved, and to whom he was writing these very letters at this very time.

It is for the historian to say whether or not his belief in the authenticity of the letter is in any way weakened by the palæographical case against the genuineness of the signature. When printing the letter I have given the facts, such as they are, and have added a few comments; but from the bibliographical point of view I do not think it is possible to describe this document with any certainty, and to me, therefore, its value and importance remain doubtful.

I have been privileged to discuss the palæographical problem with Mr. Hilary Jenkinson and Dr. W. W. Greg. Both confirmed my suspicions from the start. Mr. Jenkinson suggested that the check provided by an examination of a really considerable number of signatures would constitute evidence, and considers that, taken in conjunction with the wrong order of the strokes used in forming the H, it gives me 'a very distinct case'. Dr. Greg considers the palæographical evidence I have given at page 51 is 'absolutely conclusive', and is in complete agreement with my belief that the signature is not genuine.

To the many friends who have helped me I owe what Henry would have described as 'inestimable thanks'; and first to Miss G. Scott-Thomson, who read the whole book before it went to press, and to whom I have always been able to turn for advice and criticism and stimulating discussion. I have to thank Professor A. W. Pollard, Miss E. D. Monro and Miss A. M. Huntington for having, when necessary, tempered with syntactical discretion the Tudor exuberance of my translations from Latin, French and Italian; also Professor M. K. Pope, Miss B. M. Daunt and Miss Dorothy L. Sayers who have helped me with some linguistic problems. I have to thank Dr. W. W. Greg, to whom I have been able to refer palæographical difficulties: Miss M. M. Barber, who, after enduring Henry's giant bulk and overwhelming personality in the house for over two years, has corrected my proofs: Miss G. Murphy and Miss M. A. Cullis for loans of books: Miss Hazel Barkley and Miss Joan Watson for invaluable secretarial help: Mrs. Murrie for correcting the proof of one of the letters by the earliest known copy: and Miss N. O'Farrell who has helped me with various queries. To each and all, my thanks for the graces they have added to my book: for its deficiencies, and for errors of fact, text or reference, I alone am responsible, as my own checker.

My grateful acknowledgements are due to the Society of Antiquaries for permission to reprint a proclamation from the unique copy in their library; and to Corpus Christi College, Oxford, for permission to print Letter No. III (Part II, Ch. I) from the original manuscript, and to reproduce the signature in facsimile.

It is, as always, a pleasure to acknowledge the help so freely given by the officials and staff at the British Museum and the Public Record Office. I also owe special thanks to the Librarian and staff of Dr. Williams's Library.

M. St. Clare Byrne.

London.
March, 1936.

THE TEXT

THE text of these letters is a selected and edited one. Spelling, punctuation and paragraphing have been modernized, and in most cases a word like *owght* or *ought=owes* has been similarly treated. When, however, a word is definitely characteristic of Henry's style the old form has been retained: e.g. *arbitre=arbitrament.* If a small portion only of a letter is printed it is described as an extract. If the greater part of a letter is printed the positions of omitted paragraphs or sentences are indicated by dots in the usual manner. Henry's own additions and alterations are indicated by the words being printed in CAPITALS.

The sources from which the letters have been taken are fully described in Appendix I. While reading the text it may be assumed, unless otherwise stated, that letters have in every case been taken from whatever I believe to be the best source available.[1] This is generally a manuscript, though not often holograph. In a considerable number of cases, however, it is a draft with corrections in Henry's own hand. These corrections I have printed in capitals; and because it is interesting to see him at work I have given a few examples of what it was he deleted.

I have made no attempt to explore foreign archives for new material. The results of such work—if any—would not be suitable for a selection of this kind. In consequence, most of the important letters and papers I have used have already been printed—some of them several times. As, however, this is not a critical text I have made no attempt to collate existing printed versions. I have only indicated variants if and when my own reading differs from that of a first-rate printed authority, as e.g. *The Hamilton Papers*. Lacunæ in the Cotton MSS. have been indicated by square brackets, except in the cases where I believe these may properly be supplied from such authorities as Harpsfield or Rymer.

I have re-translated all the letters in Latin or French, and a certain number are, I believe, here translated for the first time.

[1] But letters in foreign archives I have, regretfully, printed from transcripts or printed sources.

In some cases I have re-done the translations simply because I felt it was possible to work out a version that would be nearer to Henry's in point of style; in others, because I felt that greater accuracy could be obtained. In particular, I found the translations of the Anne Boleyn love-letters made by Hearne and Halliwell at times both inaccurate and inadequate. For the history of the text of these Anne Boleyn letters reference should be made to Appendix B. I have printed from G.-A. Crapelet's edition, which I believe to be reliable.

ABBREVIATIONS

B.M.	British Museum.
P.R.O.	Public Record Office.

Manuscript sources.

Harl.	Harleian.
Addit.	Additional.
Calig., Cleo., Vesp., Vitell., etc.	Cotton MSS. Caligula, Cleopatra, Vespasian, Vitellius, etc.

Printed sources and references.

L.P.	*Letters and Papers, Foreign and Domestic, of the reign of Henry VIII.* 21 vols. Ed. J. S. Brewer and J. Gairdner.
S.P. (in text)	*State Papers of Henry VIII.* 11 vols. Record Commission. (See *Bibliography*.)
S.P. 1 (in list of MSS.)	Public Record Office classification number of Henry's state papers preserved there.
S.P. 49	P.R.O. classification number of Henry's state papers referring to Scotland.
Span.Trans.	P.R.O. transcripts from original MSS. in Spanish archives.
Ven.Trans.	P.R.O. transcripts from originals in Italian archives.

Square brackets round words or letters indicate that they are not to be found in the original, either because the MS. has been damaged or mutilated, or by reason of omission.

PART I

'VIRTUE, GLORY, IMMORTALITY'

CHAPTER I
PROLOGUE

'These kingdoms of your Highness are in great tranquillity.'
KATHARINE OF ARAGON TO HER FATHER (1509)

ONLY two letters written by Henry VIII before he came to the throne have been preserved. One is addressed to the great European scholar and humanist, Erasmus: the other to Philip, Archduke of Burgundy and King of Castile. Unimportant as their contents are, these two letters form, nevertheless, a significant prologue to the story of his reign. The letter to Erasmus, written when he was a youth of fifteen, reminds us at the outset that Henry was one of the best educated monarchs who ever ascended the English throne, and a man of unusual character and attainments. The letter to the Archduke, the brother-in-law of Katharine of Aragon, establishes the fact of the alliance between England and Spain, accomplished by the marriage of Henry and Katharine. Between them these letters indicate, therefore, the two vital factors that were to affect so momentously the future course, not only of English, but of European history. The first is the character of the individual; and the second, that particular circumstance which was to provoke the full and determinate expression of his remarkable personality.

The letter to Erasmus, though the later of the two, merits attention first. It is significant of the King who, years later, was to single out for his friend that light of English learning, Sir Thomas More, that as a boy-prince he should make choice of the learned Erasmus as a correspondent upon whom to try his prentice hand. Erasmus was greatly impressed by Henry's Latin style—so much so that he suspected there had been help from others in the matter of ideas and expression. One of the prince's companions, however, William Lord Mountjoy, assured him this was not so; and finally, to convince the still-doubting scholar, showed him various other letters written by Henry, in which second, third and even fourth corrections had been made, but always in his own hand. The fact that Henry has nothing to say in the letter does not matter; it is the way in which he says it that is important, as Erasmus realized. That at fifteen he should deliberately set himself to meet a great stylist, a master of eloquence, on his own ground, with no fear of cutting a poor figure, is prophetic of the future—of the royal theologian who was to challenge, first Luther, and then the Pope: and of the royal statesman who was to see in himself the only final arbiter of peace and war in Europe.

1. To Erasmus

[1507.]

Jesus is my hope.

I am greatly affected by your letter, most eloquent Erasmus, which is at once too elegant to be taken as written in haste, and at the same time too plain and simple to seem premeditated by a mind so ingenious. For in some way those epistles which by a mind thus endowed are brought forth with the more designed elaboration, in like manner carry with them a more studied difficulty. For while we apply ourselves to a purer eloquence, that apert and clear manner of speech escapes us almost unawares. But this your epistle is to be esteemed as much for its evident perspicuity, so that, in fine, you seem to have achieved every point. But wherefore do I determine to laud your eloquence, whose renown is known throughout the whole world? Nothing that I am able to fashion in your praise can be enough worthy of that consummate erudition. Wherefore I pass over your praises, in the which I think it the more fit to keep silence than to speak in manner too niggard.

The news of the death of the King of Castile my wholly and entirely and best-beloved brother, I had reluctantly received very long before your letter. Would that the report thereof had either reached us much later or been less true! For never, since the death of my dearest mother, hath there come to me more hateful intelligence. And to speak truth, I was the scanter well-disposed towards your letter than its singular grace demanded, because it seemed to tear open again the wound to which time had brought insensibility. But indeed those things which are decreed by Heaven are so to be accepted by mortal men. Continue, therefore, if in your parts there be any occurrents, to advertise us by letters, but may they be of happier sort. May God bring to a fortunate issue whatsoever may happen that is worthy thus to be remembered. Farewell.

From Richmond, the 17th day of January.

It is endorsed by Erasmus ' the whole of the letter enclosed he wrote when a youth with his own hand '.

The letter to the King-Archduke, which establishes the Spanish connection, makes some account of Henry's marriage to Katharine of Aragon an essential preliminary. Henry was born June 28, 1491, the second son and third child of King Henry VII and Elizabeth of York. In 1502, when he was only ten, his elder brother Arthur, Prince of Wales and heir to the throne, died at the age of fifteen. Five months earlier Arthur had married the Spanish princess Katharine, the daughter of Isabella of Castile and Ferdinand of Aragon. Though each had done his diplomatic best to conceal from the other his eagerness for the match, both Henry VII and Ferdinand had been anxious to secure the alliance. To Henry it meant the friendship of Spain, which had become, under its joint rulers, one of the greatest of European powers, had triumphantly run the French out of Naples, driven the Moors out of its own territory, captured Granada, and sent its ships to America. To Ferdinand and Isabella it meant yet another outlying kingdom which might be more or less effectively acquired by the house of Spain.

And then, unfortunately, Arthur died. Unfortunately, that is to say, for Ferdinand and his daughter Katharine. For Henry VII, however, whatever private grief it may have occasioned him, the death of his son was in no sense a political disaster. He had the magnificently healthy, handsome, clever and popular child Henry to supply the loss of his heir. He had the young Spanish princess and half of her dowry safe in England; and there, as Ferdinand soon realized, both were doomed to remain. In any further negotiations with Spain

Henry had obviously the whip-hand. Knowing that he still had one considerable asset as a basis for a new bargain, namely the as yet unpaid half of the young widow's dowry, Ferdinand immediately suggested that she should marry the new heir. True, the canon law forbade marriage with a brother's widow; but dispensations could be obtained from Rome, where the principles which governed dynastic marriages were accepted and understood.[1] Ferdinand was assured that the marriage between Arthur and his daughter had never been consummated—no need for any one concerned to harbour even the shadow of a scruple, whether real, imaginary, or politic. Henry VII, for his part, was anxious to make sure of that extra hundred thousand crowns. So on June 25, 1503, two months after Arthur's death, Henry and Katharine were formally betrothed, and on December 26 the papal dispensation arrived. It was arranged that they should marry when Henry was fourteen.

Royal betrothals could mean little or much, according to the intentions of those who arranged them. The last thing ever considered was the feelings of the contracting parties. While betrothed they were spoken of as husband and wife. Henry, in the letter to the King-Archduke, refers to Katharine as 'the Princess, my wife', and in documents her style is Princess of Wales. But for all that, six unhappy years of poverty, anxiety and neglect were to be the lot of Katharine of Aragon before the marriage was finally ratified and consummated—years during which the unfortunate young princess was callously utilized by the two mean-minded monarchs who were her father and her father-in-law, as a useful pawn in the diplomatic game of treaties and alliances they were playing against each other. In letter after letter she

[1] As recently as August, 1907, in the debate in the House of Lords on the Deceased Wife's Sister bill, the late Duke of Norfolk made a very clear statement describing the position of the Roman Catholic Church. It applies to Henry's case, as well as to the modern instance. 'The Church of Rome does not uphold the theory that this particular act of which we speak is in itself an immoral one. It does not maintain that it is against the law of God, but that it is against the enactment of the Church; and that being so, the same power that has granted those enactments can also grant dispensations, if it should consider that such dispensations are on the whole less of an evil than the enforcement of the enactment to which I have referred.' (Hansard, *Parliamentary Debates*, 4th ser., vol. clxxxi, col. 377.)

implores her father for money, and the payment of the remaining half of her dowry. Henry VII seems to have housed and fed her, but she writes to Ferdinand that all her attendants have to serve her for no wage, and that she has not even the means to reward the bringer of a letter. To try to keep up appearances she was eventually reduced to selling her jewels. The worst mortification of all, however, was the formal refusal to carry out the contract of marriage, made by Henry—presumably at his father's command or instigation—on the eve of his fifteenth birthday, June 27, 1505.

Whatever might be the underground diplomacy in which both Ferdinand and Henry VII indulged, on the surface the relations between England and Spain were amicable enough, and are aptly expressed in the younger Henry's letter which follows. On the death of Isabella of Castile the crown of that kingdom passed to her daughter Juana, the wife of the Archduke Philip of Burgundy, son of the Emperor Maximilian. In January, 1506, they left the Netherlands to travel by sea to Spain. Driven by a storm on to the English coast they were received and entertained at the English court. In the interchange of compliment and courtesy Philip was made a Knight of the Garter, and Prince Henry received from him the Order of the Golden Fleece. Juana and Philip left England towards the end of March: Henry's letter was written a few weeks later.

II. To Philip, King of Castile

[1506.]

Right excellent, right high and mighty Prince,

I commend myself unto you in most hearty and affectuous manner. And because the Chamberlain of my dear and best-beloved consort, the princess my wife, goeth presently to you, for certain matters which, as he says, concern him there, he has besought and required me that I should write to you in his behalf. Right excellent, right high and mighty Prince, very cordially I pray you that you will hold him recommended in these his affairs; and that from time to time you will ascertain me and let me know of your good health and prosperity, the which most singularly and with all my heart I do desire to be of long continuance as in manner mine own. And for my part, whensoever I may find fit bearer, I am entirely resolved to do the like for you.

Furthermore, on your signifying if there be anything here, in the which I may do you honour and pleasure, I will take the pains to satisfy you therein with all my heart, with the help of our Lord, whom I pray, right high, right excellent and mighty Prince, give you good life and long.

Written at the manor of Greenwich, the 9th day of April.

Your humble cousin,

HENRY, PRINCE OF WALES.

Henry VII died in April, 1509, having on his death-bed advised his son to complete his marriage with Katharine of Aragon. On May 14 Ferdinand wrote to say that the remainder of her dowry should be paid in coin in England on bills of exchange. By the thirtieth the greater part had been received, and on June 11 the marriage was privately solemnized by Warham, the Archbishop of Canterbury and Chancellor of the realm. On the twenty-fourth they were crowned at Westminster, and Henry announced his marriage to Europe.

III. TO MARGARET OF SAVOY[1]

[*June* 27, 1509.]

RIGHT HIGH AND EXCELLENT PRINCESS, our very dear and well-beloved cousin, We commend us unto you in most hearty manner, letting you wit that we have written at this present a letter to our most honoured brother and cousin, the Emperor your father, by the continue whereof we signify unto him that, for the love and singular affection which we know he truly bare towards the late Prince of worthy and noble memory, the King our lord and father, whom God pardon, and which we unfeignedly hope he beareth towards us, that we desire him to be advertised of our news and affairs and to inform you thereof,

[1] Daughter of the Emperor Maximilian, and Regent of the Netherlands during the minority of her nephew Charles, afterwards Emperor.

the which we send to you specially for that we are assured both he and you will take joy and pleasure therein.

True it is, right high and excellent Princess, our very dear and best-beloved good cousin, that for the consideration which we are bound to have for the treaty and appointment that was of long time made, promised, accorded and sworn between the late King our lord and father and our father-in-law and mother-in-law the King of Aragon and the Queen of Spain his consort, concerning the marriage of ourself to the Lady Katharine their daughter, and considering also the betrothals that were afterwards made between us and her *per verba praesenti*;[1] we being come to full age, as well among divers wise counsels, honourable instructions and behests that the King, our said late lord and father, gave us when he summoned us before him, he being then upon his death bed, he gave us express command that we should take in marriage the Lady Katharine, in fulfilment of the said treaty and appointment of the said betrothals. Now, therefore, in obedience to his command and instruction, which we would not, neither in this nor in a thousand other things whatsoever they be, disobey nor infringe: considering also the worthy, great and honourable alliance and affinity that there is between our most honoured brother and cousin the Emperor your said father, our cousin and brother-in-law the Prince of Spain your nephew, your house of Burgundy and us and our realm of England, by reason of the marriage concluded and accorded between our said cousin and brother-in-law your nephew and the Lady Mary our sister,[2] as well for that it seems to us that in view of the said betrothals, promises and oaths made on our part, and on the other the dispensation obtained from our holy father the Pope, as well by the King my said late lord and father as by the said King of Aragon

[1] There is no English phrase for the French 'par parolles de present'; but cf. Webster, *Duchess of Malfi*, I, i, 'I have heard lawyers say, a contract in a chamber *per verba presenti* is absolute marriage'. The actual legal phrase is *per verba de praesenti*, and means a contract of marriage by words.

[2] In the MS. there follows the phrase, 'et nous maintenant à son ante,' meaning, presumably, 'and now us to his aunt'. This does not make sense in the context. Though true, as a statement of fact, it cannot be included with the other preliminary 'causes and considerations' which lead up to this very statement in l. 6, p. 10. It reads like a hasty interpolation.

and the late Queen of Spain, we could not, according to God, right, reason and good conscience take any other party whatsoever, if we would not offend our creator and charge our conscience, which we would not do in this nor in any other matter of what sort soever, whatsoever thing may chance thereof.

For the which causes and considerations aforesaid, on the 11th of this present month of June, the espousals were performed between us and the said Lady Katharine now our consort. And on the feast of the nativity of St. John Baptist last past we were together consecrated and crowned in the Abbey of our monastery of Westminster, in our city of London, which is always the place ordained and accustomed where are consecrated and crowned all our progenitors, Kings of England. There were present all the great princes, nobles and lords of our realm, in great honour and triumph.

And thanks be to God, our said kingdom is in as good obedience, peace and tranquillity as it was in the time when the King my said late lord and father was still alive. Of the which, and of these things, we have been greatly desirous thus to advertise you, knowing that, as our said good cousin, you for your part will take therein all joy, felicity and pleasure, as is said. If, moreover, we pray you, right high and excellent Princess, our very dear and well-beloved good cousin, to do us this honour and pleasure to have our said letters that we have written to him conveyed by the posts to our very honoured brother and cousin the Emperor your father; and often to advertise us of his good news, health and prosperity, whensoever these may come to your knowledge, and equally of your own; you will do us great and singular pleasure. As knoweth our Lord, who, right high and excellent Princess, our very dear and well-beloved good cousin, give you good life and long, with the accomplishment of your desires.

Written at our palace of Westminster, in our said city of London, the 27th day of the said month of June.

Your good and loyal cousin,

HENRY R.[1]

[1] A summary, but not a translation, of this letter, is given in *Court and Society from Elizabeth to Anne*, and in Mumby's *The Youth of Henry VIII*.

To his father-in-law's letter of felicitation Henry replied in an elegant Latin epistle, patting himself on the back for having 'so liberally' completed the marriage, and having rejected all other ladies in the world. In it he also assured Ferdinand that

> 'as for that entire love which we bear to the most serene queen, our consort—day by day do her inestimable virtues more and more shine forth, flourish and increase, so that even if we were still free, it is she, nevertheless, that we would choose for our wife before all other. [*July* 26, 1509.]'[1]

The Spanish match, so long debated, haggled over, bargained with, was at last accomplished; and the most magnificent princeling in Europe had succeeded peacefully to his throne, secure in the loyalty and affection of his people, and desirous only—in the words of his friend Lord Mountjoy—of 'virtue, glory, immortality'. Banquets, jousts and courtly pastime were the order of the day. England had a full treasury, and peace at home and abroad. Her young king could indulge himself to the full in the delight of music and masques and revels, could display his unrivalled prowess at tennis and with the long-bow. Katharine wrote to her father of their 'continual feasting', and reported that 'These kingdoms of Your Highness are in great tranquillity'. And Henry himself wrote the letter of a dutiful son-in-law to inform Ferdinand of the way in which he passed his time, diverting himself with 'jousts, birding, hunting, and other innocent and honest pastimes', and also with visiting different parts of his kingdom; taking care to add that he did not 'on that account neglect affairs of state'.

On November 1 Henry wrote to his father-in-law to tell him that Katharine was expecting a child. The following is the pertinent extract.

IV. To Ferdinand of Aragon

[*Nov.* 1, 1509.]

. . . Your daughter, her Serene Highness the Queen, our dearest consort, with the favour of heaven has conceived in her

[1] Egerton MS. 616, f. 44. Latin.

womb a living child, and is right heavy therewith, which we signify to your Majesty for the great joy thereof that we take, and the exultation of our whole realm, and because it will be thus received by your Majesty and her Serene Highness the Queen of Castile, to whom be pleased to give our hearty greeting. . . .

From our palace of Greenwich, 1 November, 1509. . . .

Your good son,

HENRY R.

Ferdinand replied to them both just four weeks later, and in his letter to his daughter gives her much wise advice. She must be careful of her health, and must avoid all exertion, and especially she must remember not to write with her own hand. But in spite of the hopes of England and Spain the news that Katharine herself broke to her father on May 27, 1510, was that some days earlier she had been delivered of a still-born daughter.

In the meantime the comments of the Spanish ambassador in England are worth noting. The first year of the new reign has come and gone. The King still devotes all his time to jousts, tournaments and martial exercises. The festivities of the court are unceasing, everything in England is terribly expensive, his own outlay is, perforce, enormous . . . and, in fine, His Excellency cannot hope to keep pace with all this extravagance unless Ferdinand will increase his allowance so that it at least equals that received by the ambassadors of other countries!

CHAPTER II

DIPLOMACY AND WAR—FIRST ROUND

'et dicere Regem Maiestatem esse iuvenem, nec quicquam praeter puellas ac venationes curare.'

SYLVESTER, BISHOP OF WORCESTER
(Vitell. B. II, f. 221v).

i. 1509-1519

The European scene—the Empire, Spain and France: the dramatis personæ—the Emperor Maximilian, Ferdinand of Aragon, Louis XII, past masters in the arts of diplomatic trickery, promise-breaking and downright deception.

Their common battle-ground—Italy.

Their common aim—power: ultimately, the hegemony of Europe.

Their common method—territorial aggrandizement, achieved by military aggression and conquest, diplomatic bargaining, matrimonial alliances.

In the background—Rome—the spiritual and temporal might and claims of the Papacy.

A factor to be reckoned with—England, and the military and financial aid to be gained by alliance with her wealthy, guileless and honest young king.

The letters belonging to this decade are amongst the least interesting of the whole reign. Only a few representative episodes are treated, therefore, and no attempt is made to trace the history of the period.

1509

Henry made his first appearance in European politics as a diplomatic peacemaker. Surveying the field of European intrigue, he found Louis XII of France, Pope Julius II, the Emperor Maximilian, and his own father-in-law Ferdinand of Spain, all leagued together to despoil Venice—' Venice, the eldest child of liberty ', Venice the nurse of scholarship, the ancient ally of England. To his well-regulated conscience, and well-trained constitutional mind, the notion was quite shocking; and like a youthful but discreet paladin he advanced into the fray, armed with dignified letters of protest. The following is an extract from the one written to his father-in-law.

To Ferdinand of Aragon

(*Continued from p.* 12)

[*Nov.* 1, 1509.]

. . . Next we understand that your Fatherly Goodness after your territories had been recovered from the Venetians had been urged and required by certain princes to the intent that you should join with them for the extermination of the Venetians, and had nevertheless refused to agree to such request, doubtless because such a business seemed to you to be unjust; in which we greatly recommend your Majesty as both Catholic and just, and judge also that you have taken the wisest course in your own interest.

For we do not think that it would in any way help the safety of Christendom that the State of Venice, which in former times has always stood as the strongest bulwark and obstacle against the Turks and other infidels, and which, if at any time an expedition be undertaken against Turks or Saracens will bring incalculable protection and help to faithful Christians, should be destroyed or abolished.

Moreover, it is to be remembered that there are certain Christian princes who, if Venice were conquered and destroyed, might recover too large shares in the rest of Italy, and this might bring, peradventure, some danger or hurt to your Majesty, nor would it be possible either by the Venetians or by the other Italian powers to resist such immoderate ambition. We greatly approve, therefore, your Majesty's decision in this, and we beg that you will receive into your protection the state of Venice, which for so long in former times has been joined with us in friendship. . . .

1512

Henry in his boyhood had received an admirable theological education, and was nothing if not a good son of the Church. When, therefore, a 'Holy League' was formed in 1511, between Ferdinand, Julius II and Venice, England found herself a member of the League, pledged to war against her ancient enemy France. The aim of the League was to drive the French out of Italy, to restore her lost possessions to Venice, to recover Bologna and Ferrara for the Pope, and to defend the unity of the Church. Henry, superintending the embarkation of his troops at Southampton, writes in the most exemplary manner to Cardinal Bainbridge, his emissary at Rome.

1. To Cardinal Bainbridge

[*May* 6, 1512.]

. . . Nevertheless, in this reverse of fortune,[1] and amid these contradictory rumours, we have not changed our intention of defending the Church and protecting our Holy Father; but as

[1] The defeat of the allies at Ravenna (April 11) made France momentarily supreme in North Italy.

we have begun so verily do we mean to persevere, and therefore signify to your Reverence that our fleet of six thousand men is now at sea, well and truly supplied with victual and ordnance, which fleet has already captured twelve ships of the French and the Bretons; and that another army of twelve thousand men is prepared to set forward against Guienne and Gascony, there to join with the larger force levied by our father the most Catholic King. . . . We believe that never, its numbers considered, has there been seen a finer army, nor one more ready to die in defence of the Church and of our Holy Father, as the indulgence which our Holy Father has sent to us has marvellously roused them against the enemies of the Church, whom they deem Turks, heretics and infidels.

We therefore believe that by the grace of God this our army will acquit itself right nobly, and confound the warfare and tyranny of those who by fair means or foul seek to oppress the Church of God and uphold the great schism which will be effected unless the Catholic rulers resist it. . . .

He finishes up by telling Bainbridge to exhort the Pope to trust in God 'and the help of the greater number of good Christian monarchs . . . for we ourselves in person, with all our power, will attack the enemies of the Church'.

The English arrived in Spain on June 7, expecting to join with a Spanish force of equal strength in an attack on Guienne. Ferdinand, however, had other plans. The idea of a campaign to restore Guienne to the English crown had been nothing but a bait. What Ferdinand wanted was a useful English force, to act as a screen and occupy the attention of France while he himself set about his real objective, which was the conquest of Navarre. With apparent reason he urged that he could not possibly advance till he had secured his rear. The English, unable to take the offensive without Ferdinand's support, idled the months away in camp, till dysentery and mutiny drove everyone desperate, and in October they returned home without orders. Ferdinand secured Navarre, as he had intended: but the English expedition was a complete and discreditable fiasco.

1513
The Spurs and Flodden

The Guienne expedition was a blow to national prestige, and it had to be avenged. Ferdinand made it quite plain that he had no intention of helping Henry to make war on France, and advised his son-in-law to join him in a truce with Louis. This was more than either Tudor or national pride could stomach. England should carry the war into the enemy's country, and the King in person would lead his army out from Calais, while his fleet swept the Channel and blockaded the French ports.

An advance force besieged Thérouenne on June 27. The main army under Henry came up on August 1, to be joined by the Emperor Maximilian, who chivalrously offered to serve with the English and whose experienced advice postponed a direct assault and outwitted the French strategic move to get supplies to the town. Their expedition from Guinegatte was attacked in front by English and Burgundian cavalry and cut off from its base by a large force in its rear. Seized with panic the French were completely routed in the Battle of the Spurs and on the 22nd Thérouenne capitulated. The loss of Guienne in 1453 was avenged, and the more recent loss of military prestige was wiped out.

Henry's next objective was Tournay, 'the wealthiest city in all Flanders'. In the meantime, however, Scotland, true to its ancient tradition of friendship with France, had seized the opportunity of Henry's absence to invade England. On August 13 Katharine, writing to Wolsey, says that all Henry's subjects 'be very glad, I thank God, to be busy with the Scots, for they take it pastime. My heart is very good to it, and I am horribly busy with making standards, banners and badges.' Henry wrote from camp to protest against the treacherous behaviour of the Scots.

11. To James IV of Scotland

[1513.]

Right excellent, right high, and mighty prince, etc.

And have received your writing, dated at Edinburgh the sixteenth day of July, by your herald Lyon this bearer, wherein, after rehearsal and accumulation of many surmised injuries, griefs, and dangers done by us and our subjects to you and your lieges, the specialities whereof were superfluous to rehearse, remembering that to them and every of them, in effect, reasonable answers, founded upon law and conscience, hath heretofore been made unto you and your council.

Ye not only require us to desist from farther invasion and destruction of your brother and cousin the French king, but also certify us ye will take part in defence of the said king; and do that thing which ye trust may rather cause us to desist from our pursuit of him; with many contrived occasions and communications, by your counsel sought, made and imagined, sounding to the breach of the perpetual peace passed, and concluded, and sworn betwixt you and us; of which your imagined quarrels, causeless devised to break with us, contrary to your promise, all honour and kindness, we cannot greatly marvel, considering the ancient accustomable manners of your progenitors, which kept never longer faith nor promise than pleased them.

Howbeit, if the law or dread of God, nighness of blood, honour of the world, law or reason, had bound you, we suppose ye would never have so far proceeded, specially in our absence. Wherein the Pope and all Princes christened may well note in you dishonourable demeanour, when ye, lying in await, to seek the ways to do that thing in our absence which ye would have been well advised to attempt, we being in our realm and present. And for the evident approbation hereof, we need none other proofs ne witness, but your own writing heretofore to us sent, then being within our realm; wherein ye made never any mention of taking part with our said enemy the French king, but passed the time with us till after our departure from our said realm. And now, percase, ye supposing us, so far from our realm, to be destitute of defence and against your invasions, have uttered the old rancour of your mind, which in covert manner ye have long kept secret.

Nevertheless, we remembering the brittleness of your promises, and suspecting, though not wholly believing, so much unsteadfastness, thought right expedient and necessary to put our said realm in a-readiness for the resistance of your said enterprises, having firm trust in our Lord God and the rightwiseness of our causes, with the assistance of our confederates and allies, we shall be able to resist the malice of all schismatics and their adherents, being by the general council expressly excommunicate and interdict; trusting also in time convenient to remember our friends and requite you and our enemies, which by such unnatural demeanour have sufficient cause to the dishersion of you and your posterity for ever from the possibility to that ye think to have to the realm which ye be now attempted to invade.

And, if the example of the king of Navarre being excluded from his realm for the assistance given to the French king, cannot refrain you from this unnatural demeanour and dealing, we supposing ye shall have like assistance of the said French king, as the king of Navarre hath now, who is now a king without a realm; and so the French king suffereth him to continue: whereunto good regard would be taken.

And like as we heretofore touched in this our writing, we need not to make any further answer to the manifold grieves by you surmised. Ye have been many and oftentimes sufficiently answered to the same, except only to the pretended grieves touching the denying of our safe-conduct to your ambassador to be last sent unto us: whereunto we make this answer, that we had granted the safe-conduct, and if your herald would have taken the same with him, likewise as he hath been accustomed to solicit the safe-conducts for merchants and other heretofore, he might as soon have had that as any other; for we never denied safe-conduct to any your lieges to come unto us, and no further to pass. But we see well, that like as your herald had heretofore made sinister report contrary to truth; so he hath done now in this case, as it is manifest and open.

Finally, as touching your requisition to desist from further attempting against our enemy the French king, we know you for no competent judge of so high authority to require us in that behalf. Wherefore, God willing, we purpose with the aid and assistance of our confederates and allies to prosecute the same; and as ye do unto us and to our realm, so shall it be remembered and acquitted hereafter, by the help of our Lord God and our patron Saint George, who, right high and mighty prince, etc.

[Given under our signet in our camp before Tyrwin,[1] the 12th day of August, in the fifth year of our reign.][2]

[1] i.e. Thérouanne. [2] For note on text see Appendix I, Notes.

Under the leadership of James IV the Scottish forces crossed the Border on the very day that Thérouanne surrendered. Katharine as regent met the crisis magnificently. The seventy-year-old Earl of Surrey, experienced in Border warfare, advanced against the Scots, and offered battle on the fourth of September. On the ninth, at Flodden, he won an overwhelming victory, and the flower of Scottish chivalry perished on the field with their ill-fated monarch. On the sixteenth Katharine wrote to Henry: 'My husband, for hastiness with Rouge Cross I could not send your Grace the piece of the King of Scots' coat, which John Glyn now bringeth. In this your Grace shall see how I can keep my promise, sending you for your banners a King's coat. I thought to send himself unto you, but our Englishmen's hearts would not suffer it.' Henry himself sent the news to Maximilian Sforza, Duke of Milan, in a Latin letter from which the following is the pertinent extract:

III. To the Duke of Milan

[*Sept.* 16, 1513.]

. . . Since our entry into France we have in every encounter been victorious over our common enemies: we have captured a great number of them and some of their chief nobles, and have taken their strongly fortified city of Thérouanne. From thence we moved towards Tournay, before which city we arrived on the 20th day of this month, invested it; and ordered our artillery to be disposed for the assault. We greeted the inhabitants thereof with some shots: and conceded them, at their request, a two days truce for the negotiation of a surrender. So much for our affairs in France to this present.

As to English affairs—the king of Scots utterly unmindful of the bond of his affinity in blood, and of a most sacred treaty between us, has betaken himself to the side of the French, which he seems to account of more importance than the observance of any law, human or divine, and has permitted an inroad of ten thousand of his Scots into our realm of England, who were for the most part captured or destroyed by a force of our men not exceeding a thousand. The king of Scots himself, with a great army invaded our aforesaid realm of England, and first took a little old town, belonging to the Bishop of Durham, already nearly in ruins and practically unfortified, and on that account almost deserted. He then advanced four miles into our realm. There the noble lord, the Earl of Surrey, to whom we had committed the charge of repelling the Scots, having advanced against them, on the eighth day of the aforesaid month met with them in a battle which was long and fiercely contested on both sides. Nevertheless, with the Almighty avenging the broken league and aiding the better cause, our forces emerged victorious, and killed a great number of the enemy and many of their nobles, and put the rest to flight. We took all their artillery, and finally spoiled them of all their camp, having lost none of note amongst our own forces, as far as we yet know. Of the king of Scots himself, what fortune befell him in that battle, there is as yet no certain news. The said lord, the Earl of Surrey, hastily and when wearied by the long fight, sent this news to her Serene Highness the Queen, our most dear consort, to whom we have committed the charge of our whole realm of England. He promises to write more exactly a little later. . . .

From our camp at Tournay, 16th September, 1513.

HENRY.

PS. Since these were written we have received certain news that the King of Scots himself was killed in the aforesaid battle, and his body found and recognized, and taken to the nearest church: so that he has paid a heavier penalty for his treachery than we would have wished.

On September 24th Tournay surrendered: a new treaty against France was signed at Lille by Ferdinand, Maximilian and Henry; and in October Henry returned to England. Parliament granted a subsidy of £160,000 in recognition of the victorious campaign. English prestige was more than restored. Instead of figuring as a wealthy dupe England had become a power to be reckoned with, whenever any schemes of aggrandizement were to be set on foot.

1514-1519

Peace with France

With her enemy England now a formidable power, France stood in need of an ally. This, needless to say, was more than obvious to Ferdinand, who realized that if he could be first in the field, before the same idea occurred to Maximilian, France might be prepared to give him Milan and Genoa as the price of his friendship. Within six months he had made a truce with Louis; and almost immediately afterwards Maximilian followed suit. England had been tricked again. 'I do not see any faith in the world, save in me,' Henry protested with some justice to the Venetian ambassador.

It had taken four years, and two of Ferdinand's neatest bits of trickery, to open Henry's eyes and spoil his temper; but in 1514 he was ready to meet his father-in-law on his own ground. Now that honour had been satisfied by the campaign of 1513 he, too, could make peace with France. Moreover, at fifty-two, Louis XII was once more in the marriage market, and Henry had a marriageable sister. The bait was dangled, and proved attractive. Mary Tudor was a beautiful girl of eighteen; and Henry, so far, had proved himself a more formidable enemy in the field than either Ferdinand or Maximilian. Henry waited until May, and for the date fixed in the treaty of Lille for the marriage of Mary and Prince Charles. The date passed, with Maximilian's promise unfulfilled: and the game was in Henry's hands. The Emperor had broken the treaty. Within three months Henry and Louis had bound themselves to assist each other against their common enemies, and in October Mary became Queen of France. It was altogether a most successful diplomatic move. With England as his ally Louis could afford to break off the negotiations about Milan, and take the offensive by discussing with Henry a scheme for the conquest of Castile. England had been used as a cat's-paw in the Guienne affair, had been tricked after Tournay, but in the third trial of wits had called stalemate to her opponents.

The only letter in which Henry himself discusses the match has an added interest, in that it is addressed to Wolsey, who is thus for the first time introduced to our notice. 'The Duke' referred to in the letter was the Duc de Longueville who had been captured in the Battle of the Spurs and had helped during his captivity in England to further the Anglo-French alliance.

IV. To Thomas Wolsey[1]

My Lord of Lincoln,

I recommend me unto you, and let you wit that I have spoken with the Duke, which in the beginning was as ill afraid as ever he was in his life lest no good effect should come to pass. Nevertheless, in further communing, we went more roundly to our matters, insomuch that I said to him: Seeing that the King, your master, hath sought so gently unto us for both amity and marriage, I assure you (our honour saved) we could be well content to give hearkening thereto; and if the offers were reasonable, to agree upon those same. But these be not reasonable, except the amity should no longer continue than the payment of money; and yet not so, except there were a reasonable sum of money to be paid in hand by and by. If his master will have the marriage I cannot see how it can be conveniently, except the amity be made during our lives, and one year after, to the intent that all suspicion of both sides may be set apart. Which marriage and amity your master may have under this manner: that is to say, paying yearly one hundred thousand crowns; and at his request I not to stick for no ready money in hand, but I to stand content therewith, for recompense of all things. Which thi[ngs][2] if your master consider what heritance[3] he holdeth from me, and what good my amity may do to help forth his matter in Italy, I think he will not greatly stick at.

This furthermore I said to the Duke: surely I cannot see how the amity made for years can any longer endure than the payment, which expired should be occasion of new breach and demands, whereby neither he nor we should live quietly; which,

[1] Although the original MS. (Calig. E. VI, f. 119) from which I have printed is much mutilated I have not indicated the lacunæ, as these may properly be supplied from Rymer, *Foedera*, XIII, p. 403.
[2] Rymer omits.
[3] i.e. the crown of France. cf. p. 31 ff.

if there fall alliance, I would be loath to see; wherefore I see no way to eschew all dangers and perils, and to recompense me for withholding of mine inheritance[1] (which, if I would be slack in, my subjects would murmur at), but to make this amity during our lives, and one year after, paying yearly as above rehearsed: which amity once granted, the alliance should not be refused, nor no other thing which, with my honour saved, I might do. Saying furthermore to him, that if I might demand, with my honour, any less, or take any less offer (seeing his master is so well minded to the foresaid alliance and amity), I would be glad to do it[2] at his request; but less than this it cannot stand with my honour, nor my subjects will not be content that I should take.

My lord, I showed him furthermore, that if he thought we might trust to have this end, I would be content that you and they should commune on all other articles concerning the amity and marriage, till we might have absolute answer[3] in that behalf for lessening of time. To which he answered, that he could not assure me thereof, but that he trusted, seeing my demands were so reasonable, that his master would agree thereto. On trust hereon we will that you begin to pen the residue of the articles as soon as you can. And thus fare you well.

Written with the hand of your loving master,

HENRY R.

The successful prosecution of the war of 1513 and the achievement of the peace of 1514 were mainly due to the ability and exertions of Henry's chief adviser Thomas Wolsey, who had first emerged into prominence in 1511, and was already in 1514 Bishop of Lincoln and Archbishop of York. From 1514 until 1529 he was supreme in church and state, in foreign and domestic policy. In 1515 he was made a cardinal, and became Lord Chancellor of the realm. Henry, it is true, supervised personally all the political business of his kingdom, but administrative power, as also the power to guide and influence his ideas and decisions, was concentrated in Wolsey.

[1] i.e. the crown of France. cf. p. 31 ff.
[2] Rymer reads *that*
[3] Rymer reads *assurance*

The first check to Wolsey's policy was the death of Louis XII on January 1, 1515, and the accession of his twenty-year-old nephew, Francis I—a monarch in every way as ambitious, as incalculable, as crafty and as capable of double-dealing as even Ferdinand and Maximilian. In April, 1515, having diplomatically secured his rear by an Anglo-French treaty, Francis was ready to march his army into Italy to recover Milan. Followed, his magnificent crossing of the Alps, with all his artillery, and then on September 13 and 14 the victory of Marignano, which meant the conquest of the whole of northern Italy. In one great battle, within nine months of his accession, Francis at the age of twenty had proved himself a brilliant military commander. Before this new glory Tournay and the Battle of the Spurs dwindled into insignificant little skirmishes. At one blow he had annexed Milan: the Pope recognized his claim and made a treaty with him, in return for French support for his own Medici family's claim to Florence. Never had French dominion in Italy appeared a more likely prospect.

Hardly had the accession of Francis I and his military achievements become accepted facts, however, before another important event took place, which again altered the European situation. On January 23, 1516, Ferdinand of Aragon died, and his grandson Charles succeeded, at the age of sixteen, to the throne of Spain. The new king had for many years been ruler of the Netherlands, where the policy of his chief advisers was definitely pro-French. Francis and Henry bid simultaneously for his friendship, and the result, in August, 1516, was the Treaty of Noyon, by which Charles was betrothed to an infant daughter of the French King, in return for the ceding by France of its claim to Naples. England was left out in the cold.

In 1517 another bid was made—this time for alliance with France. Francis wanted to buy back Tournay, and Henry was quite ready to sell. In October a treaty was signed, including not only England and France, but Spain, the Empire and the Papacy. Tournay was to be ceded: and Henry's daughter, the Princess Mary, aged two, was betrothed to the seven-months-old Dauphin. Moreover, Henry and Francis pledged themselves to a personal meeting near Calais for the following spring.

England had not managed affairs so badly in 1517. The sale of Tournay brought six hundred thousand crowns into the exchequer: and a treaty of international scope had been engineered and accomplished in London. The usual *sine qua non* of a crusade against the Turks had, of course, been included as one of the articles.

And then, at the beginning of 1519, Maximilian died. In June Charles V, ruler of Spain and of the Netherlands, was elected Emperor.

1519-1529

In Europe power has shifted, has compacted, has distributed itself in two main blocks of control. Two rival dynasties confront each other—Hapsburg and Valois. The three-cornered struggle resolves into a duel between Charles and Francis: and of itself, power balances. But the equilibrium is delicate: a small mistake, a miscalculation, outside interference, and one of the scales knocks the beam. The loser pays—in cash, in pensions, in promises; weight is thrown into his scale, and the balance readjusts. That is where England comes in.

Geographically, the redistribution means that Charles V, Emperor by election of the German states, rules Spain, Austria, the Netherlands, Burgundy Franche Comté, Naples and Sicily, by inheritance: while Francis is master only of a diminished France, the Duchy of Burgundy, and Milan. Actually, however, they are much more equally matched than their territorial possessions suggest. Francis rules a kingdom well adapted either for defence or attack: the Emperor's dominions are so widely scattered that there is sure to be trouble in one kingdom or another all the time. Keeping the peace within his own boundaries leaves him little opportunity for vast schemes. Nor is he as ambitious as his rival. His wants are moderate—the Duchy of Burgundy as his hereditary right, Milan in self-defence. He does not dream of great conquests. Francis wants adventure, military glory: and he dreams of the conquest of Italy.

In the background there is still the Papacy. Charles, Francis, and their brother Henry of England are still, nominally, the Christian warrior kings, ready to unite in the defence of Christendom. Actually, Henry's paladin days are over, and Charles and Francis are much too preoccupied with power to have any intentions of leading crusades, unless to their own political advantage. The Turk may overrun Syria and Egypt, may threaten Hungary and Rhodes and the whole of Christian civilization—Charles and Francis are debating their rights in Milan. It is for Henry of England to make what he can of the situation—to estimate the characters and intentions of his brother monarchs, to realize the true nature of the European equilibrium, and to manipulate, upset, or adjust it, when possible, for his own advantage. But it will not do to imagine him, as the popular phrase has it, 'preserving the balance of power in Europe'. Let him speak for himself, in the year 1522: 'And glad His Grace is to hear and understand of the base exile and poor estate of the French king, being destitute of men and extenuate of substance, so that there was never better time to set upon him than now, *as the Emperor's espy reporteth.'*[1]

[1] Henry VIII to Sir Thomas Boleyn and Dr. Sampson, his ambassadors to the Emperor. *S.P.* VI, p. 101.

ii. 1523-1525

'By just title of inheritance.'
HENRY VIII (1525)

As statesman-ruler Henry VIII matured slowly. During the first decade of his reign he was well content to allow first his Council and then Wolsey to guide his administration and to get the actual work done. He himself was more concerned with watching the doing of it, with learning what he could from his advisers, with pitting his brain and his ideas against theirs in discussion. For the rest, he persisted in taking a keen interest in his navy: he pursued his theological studies: and managed to persuade most people that his main interests in life were sport and amusement. Hence what might be called the ornamental nature of the few letters already quoted—suitable, dignified, princely compositions, but otherwise not displaying any very particular signs of diplomatic ability.

Of his personal regard for Wolsey at this period we get a pleasant glimpse in the brief note that follows.

v. To Cardinal Wolsey[1]

Mine own good cardinal, I recommend me unto you with all my heart, and thank you for the great pain and labour that you do daily take in my business and matters, desiring you (that when you have well established them) to take some pastime and comfort, to the intent you may the longer endure to serve us, for always pain cannot be endured. Surely you have so substantially ordered our matters both of this side the sea and beyond, that in mine opinion little or nothing can be added. Nevertheless, according to your desire, I do send you mine opinion by this bearer, the reformation whereof I do remit to you and the remnant of our trusty councillors which I am sure will substantially look on it.

As touching the matter that Sir William Sandys brought

[1] Dated 1521 by *S.P.*, and 1518 by *L.P.*

answer of, I am well contented with what order soever you do take in it.

The queen my wife hath desired me to make her most hearty recommendations to you, as to him that she loveth very well, and both she and I would know fain when you will repair to us. No more to you at this time, but that with God's help I trust we shall disappoint our enemies of their intended purpose.

Written with the hand of your loving master,

HENRY R.

In so far as foreign policy was concerned the second decade of the reign opened with England pledged to that friendship with France which was so picturesquely and so aptly symbolized by the elaborate and useless pageantry of the meeting of Francis and Henry at the Field of the Cloth of Gold. In spite of French pensions and the French marriage for the Princess Mary, Wolsey and Henry were ready to throw over the French alliance the moment that friendship with the Emperor should seem to promise greater profits. By 1523 the change-over had been accomplished, and England committed to the Emperor's war against France—committed neither for right nor justice, patriotism nor profit, but for the sake of a dream, a dream of power.

Wolsey hoped to attain the Papacy through the alliance with Charles: Henry, according to his own statements, and those of his contemporaries, hoped to get either the crown of France or else a substantial part of what had once been the English kings' French territories. In modern times much scorn has been cast upon such an absurd pretension. It has been suggested that neither Henry nor Wolsey can have been so foolish as to treat the English claim to France seriously. Exactly what alternative motive for the alliance with the Emperor is to be regarded as genuine I do not know; but on the evidence of their letters both Wolsey and Henry took the claim in all seriousness, as did other Englishmen, and amongst them two no less intelligent than Sir Thomas More and Thomas Cromwell.

More writes to Wolsey in 1522 that 'the King's Grace said that he trusted in God to be their governor [i.e. of France] himself, and that they should by this means make a way for him as King Richard [III] did for his father.' Cromwell, speaking in Parliament in 1523, asks who would not spend life and goods 'to recover again by the sword the realm of France, belonging to our most redoubted sovereign by good and just title, and to change the sums of money which we have in sundry years received from thence into the whole and just revenues that might there from year to year be levied if we did peaceably enjoy the same?' His question was rhetorical, for he himself saw all too clearly the folly of such aspirations in the sixteenth century; but he goes on to say that the question of the King's claim, and of the war that should assert it, has been 'ripely digested, debated, yea, and finally concluded' by the King and his Council, as 'not only possible but also very apparent and likely'.

Moreover, it is very obvious from the diplomatic correspondence of 1523 and 1524 that England during this period was making every effort to gain the Duke of Bourbon, the Constable of France, as an ally in the cause. Bourbon was the most powerful man in France, and quite ready for any such treasonable practices. There are various letters dealing with the proposal that he shall 'recognize the King's Grace his supreme and sovereign lord, making oath and fidelity unto him as to the rightful inheritor of the said crown of France.'[1] Pace, writing to Wolsey in 1524,[2] says, 'I do see in the Duke of Bourbon so faithful and steadfast mind without vacillation to help the King to his crown of France, that if he be assuredly entertained the King shall assuredly obtain his crown in France, considering his intelligences and the favour he hath universally in that realm, like as the French King is universally hated.' Pace also gives an account of how Bourbon, 'very religiously,' after confession and communion, promised him upon his faith 'that I will, by the help of my friends, put the crown of France upon the King our common master's head, or else my (han)ds shall be cut off, if his Grace will (attempt) the same.'

In 1524 there was a papal election. Charles wrote his

[1] *S.P.* VI, p. 137. cf. also Nos. LIX and LXII.
[2] *Ibid.*, p. 313.

promised letter in favour of Wolsey's candidature, detained his own messenger until the election was concluded, and saw to it that his own candidate, Cardinal de Medici, was elected as Clement VII. In 1525 the war between Charles and Francis came to a spectacular conclusion, when the Imperial victory at Pavia revenged Marignano. Francis himself was taken prisoner, and the French army was practically wiped out. Charles was master of Europe. All Henry had done was to throw away money and men upon futile though destructive raids on French territory. But in spite of what it is easy for us to describe to-day as the crass stupidity of his policy throughout, he still believed that he was going to share in the gains of his victorious ally.

On March 26, 1525, Henry wrote to his ambassadors to congratulate Charles, and to ask outright for what he wanted. It is an amazing letter, and one of the longest he ever dispatched—thirty-six pages in manuscript, twenty-five as printed *in extenso* in the *State Papers*. The following brief extracts give a reasonable idea of his 'seriousness' about the crown of France.

VI. To Tunstall and Wingfeld

[1525.]

. . . The said Ambassadors, at the delivery of the King's letters to the Emperor, shall first, with as good and hearty words as they can devise, make unto him the King's most cordial and affectuous recommendations, with congratulations, not only of the good recovery of his health, and convalescence from the danger of the quarteyn, wherewith the King's Highness, to his great ingrete and heaviness, understood that His Majesty was right lately visited, but also for the fortunate and prosperous success ensued by overthrow of the French army in Italy, and taking of the French King prisoner; wherein, after lauds and thanks to be given unto Almighty God, the said ambassadors shall greatly commend the prudence, order and provision taken and devised by the said Emperor and his Council, with the valiant acquittal, virtue and strenuity of the faithful and good captains, servants and subjects, in the honourable defence of the affairs and enterprise of Italy, showing the inward rejoice and consolation that the King's Highness doth take for the same; which, for the honour ensued unto the said Emperor thereby, with the surety of the matters in Italy, and the great benefit like to follow thereupon unto the common causes and generally unto all Christendom, hath been as much to the King's high comfort and gladness as could be thought or devised: trusting verily that, since Almighty God of His infinite grace hath thus provided for the repressing of the inordinate pride and insatiable ambition of him which was the common enemy and general disturber of all peace, rest and tranquillity, there is now evident appearance that the Emperor and the King's Grace, taking good and substantial ways by conformity, shall conduce and bring their common causes unto high and notable effect, to their great honour and benefit, and to the repose and quiet of all Christendom. . . .

There follow instructions to try to find out the Emperor's mind at this point, before they say anything more. If, however, he and his Council insist on knowing Henry's mind first, then they are to proceed as follows:

[1] First, they shall say that the King's Highness, who since the time that Almighty God called him unto his crown and dignity royal hath affixed and established the foundation of his intent and purpose, like a most virtuous Prince, to do some notable service unto Christ's religion, groundly pondering and devising with himself, and the most profound and discreet folks of his Council upon the present state of the same; having also due consideration and respect to the infinite troubles, dissensions, discords and contentions, which of a long season have depended between Christian princes, potentates, seignories and countries in Christendom, by reason whereof, the same being in so great division within itself, not only innumerable occasions, destructions, devastings and depopulations of countries, with other infinite inconveniences, have ensued to the high displeasure of Almighty God, but also thereby commodity hath been given to the Turks, enemies of Christ's faith, marvellously to encroach, extend and ampliate their usurped empire and dominion, to the

[1] fol. 91.

notable diminution of Christ's said religion; having, besides other their excellent conquests, now lately subdued and acquired into their dominion the two chief and most sure propugnacles of Christendom, by reason whereof not only the realms of Naples, Sicily, and other parts of Italy on the one side, but also the realms of Poland, Hungary, and other parts of Germany, on the other side, lie open, ready in manner to the prey and entry of the said infidels to destroy and vanquish all the rest of the same; remembering furthermore the damnable heresy of the Lutheran sect, sustitate and brought up in the time of this division, tending principally and chiefly to the withdrawing of the obedience of the Church of Rome, and also of the governance, regiment and supreme dignity of princes and all nobility; in such wise, as, if by the special grace of Almighty God some direct, perfect and most prudent way be not taken and remedy adhibited unto these great inconveniences in time, not only greater and more sore punishment, adversities, slanders, wars, hostilities, with general trouble, dissension and division, not able to be remedied by the heads and princes, are like to arise in brief time, but also, if God put not His help hereunto, the whole Christendom is in evident danger of utter perdition and ruin.

The King's Highness therefore, having most tender remorse and respect unto the premises, knowing furthermore that the high orgule, pride and insatiable ambition of the French Kings, which of many days have contended by usurpation upon the countries, patrimonies and rights of all other bordering upon their confines, to aspire unto the monarchy of Christendom, hath been the chief, principal and in manner only ground, cause and occasion of all the said inconveniences, cannot think, imagine or believe otherwise, but that by the thraldom, captivity, overthrow and taking of the said French King, who of his own nature is inclined to as much arrogance and extreme ambition as ever was King of France; it is the pleasure of Almighty God to ordain and provide a way, mean and introduction, how the tyranny, oppression and excess of those that, directly or indirectly, be enemies of Christ's faith, may be suppressed and extinct, and the religion of Christendom again to flourish, increase and augment; which occasion offered by Almighty God, if by the proceeding of other Christian

Princes at this time, into whose hands it seemeth this matter is by God put and committed, the same should not be duly amplected, embraced and followed, it is to be feared that God should take high indignation against them, executing His terrible sword of correction and dreadful punishment upon them for the same.

For which cause it hath been thought unto his Highness, that, in accomplishment of his duty unto God and the world, his Grace oweth and is bounden first to search, examine and inquire where should rest the culpe, blame, default, and occasion of so many evils, to the intent that, the cause once removed and extirped, the effects of the same may also be disappointed. And verily his Grace, revolving with himself and his said Council as much as may or can be by them thought or studied herein, cannot find or perceive but that as long as the realm of France, situate and constitute in manner in the heart and midst of all Christendom, shall remain in the hands of those which cannot, ne never will, cease to apply their wits, powers, thoughts, and studies to ampliate and extend their limits and dominion, never satiate ne contented with enough, there can never be rest, quiet ne tranquillity in Christendom, but that only the ambition of France shall be always an occasion to bring all Christian princes and countries unto war, hostility and division. For it is facile and easy to consider that a tyrant, usurping and encroaching upon his neighbours' and other men's rights, cannot think to conserve, defend and maintain his unjust quarrel, unless than he seek ways and means how to sew discord and dissension amongst them; and what great patrimonies, countries and dominions the French King and his ancestors have detained hitherto from others, is well known.

For first it is notorious and manifest that the King's Highness pretendeth by just title of inheritance to have the whole crown of France, as that which ought to descend unto him of very right and succession; as largely may be proved and justified by sufficient matter of truth and record, over and besides particular treaties, whereby his Grace is justly entitled unto the same. Besides that, if his Grace had never had any such title of inheritance to the whole crown of France, yet it cannot be by no man rightfully denied but that the Duchies of Normandy, Gascony, Guienne, Anjou, Maine, Poitou, and other great patrimonies unjustly detained by the French King, ought of right to belong unto the King's Highness by like lineal descent and succession.

Furthermore, what noble countries and great dominions the French King wrongfully hath and keepeth from the Emperor, His Majesty and his Council do best know; and semblably what other pieces he hath, belonging to divers persons pretending title and interesse in the same. (f. 94[v]) Over this, not contented with all the premises, it is not unknown how long the realm of France hath contended to have the Duchy of Milan, Asti, Genoa, the realm of Naples, with other great territories in Italy; and drawing unto their devotions the Venetians, the Florentines, the Lucchese, with other potentates of the same, hath studied nothing more than how they may aspire to the said monarchy. . . .

First, how it may be feasible and conducible, utterly to extinct the regiment of the French King and his line, or any other Frenchman, from the crown of France: the said ambassadors shall say, that it may well be known the same can never be conduced or brought about by any composition or consent, either of the French King, or of the peers and estates of that realm; and therefore to speak or treat with France thereof were but vain and superfluous.

Wherefore to bring that matter to effect there is no way to be devised, but only by force, violence and puissance; which thing, the said French King now remaining in captivity, his noblemen, captains, and whole army vanquished, slain, destroyed or taken prisoners, and consequently the realm of France remaining without an head, destitute of courage, good counsel, ability or power, is more facile to be done at this time, than at any other that ever hath been known or heard of; and specially if the King's Highness and the Emperor, according to the conventions and treaties passed between them, do make their personal invasion into France this summer, as they be bounden to do; which, if it were thought sufficient to attain the intended purpose for vanquishing of the French King or attaining the overhold on the realm of France when the French King with his nobility and puissance was within the same, must needs now be thought to be much more able and of power so to do.

And in this matter the said ambassadors may say that, the Emperor being contented to make the said personal invasion on that side, such ways may be taken, leving fortresses and strongholds, that the Emperor may come with his army unto Paris, where the King's Highness will not fail, God willing, to meet him; supposing verily that there shall be none impediment, by any power of France, whereby either of them should be impeached thus to do. At which Paris, after the said personal meeting, the King's Grace may in this case take the crown of France; and the same had, His Grace, to show mutual correspondence of kindness unto the Emperor, shall give unto him all effectual assistance for attaining of his crown Imperial: wherein the said ambassadors shall use these degrees:

First, they shall say the King's Highness can in this case be contented to give the Emperor 5,000 archers at the King's charges, for five, or, rather than fail, for six months, or in the lieu and stead thereof, the sum of 100,000 crowns.

The second degree is, that the said ambassadors shall grant thereunto the sum of 150,000 crowns.

Thirdly, 200,000 crowns: and finally, if by none of these offers the Emperor can be induced to invade in person, meeting the King at Paris as afore, they shall say, as of themselves, that they doubt not but, the crown of France once had, the King's Highness will be contented in his own person to accompany the Emperor unto Rome. And if such general words will not satisfy the Emperor and his Council, the said ambassadors shall not let, all the residue of the King's desire in this point concurring with the same, to conclude the King's personal accompanying of the Emperor unto Rome, there to see the crown Imperial set on his head,[1] giving his best assistance as well thereunto, as to the recovery of all such droits and rights as appertain to the Empire, whereof Italy is the chamber: of which glorious voyage the said ambassadors shall say is like to ensue unto the Emperor the whole

[1] This was the crown of the world, which had to be received at Rome. For the Emperor's titles and four crowns see Bryce, *Holy Roman Empire*, App. C.

monarchy of Christendom; for of his own inheritance he hath the realm of Spain, and a great part of Germany, the realms of Sicily and Naples, with Flanders, Holland, Zeeland, Brabant, and Hainault, and other his Low Countries; by election he hath the Empire, whereunto appertaineth almost all the rest of Italy, and many towns imperial in Germany and elsewhere; by the possibility apparent to come by my Lady Princess[1] he should hereafter have England and Ireland, with the title to the superiority of Scotland, and in this case all France with the dependencies: so as the said Emperor, performing this voyage, and taking this way, should in process be peaceable lord and owner in manner of all Christendom; which the King's Grace can be contented the Emperor shall have, he concurring effectually with the King for recovery of his crown of France. . . .

[2] As to the second, who should succeed in the realm of France, the French King and his line removed? The King's Highness verily trusteth that, his just title and right thereunto remembered and considered, the Emperor, since the treaties and alliances passed between the King's Grace and him, was never, ne is, of other mind but firmly to join with His Highness for recovery of the said crown; wherein the said ambassadors may, apart unto himself, put him in remembrance of his secret promise made, as well unto the King's Highness as to my Lord Legate, at sundry places and times: wherefore in this matter there is no question or ambiguity which may insurge, but that the French King taken or not taken, his army vanquished or not vanquished, one of the chief and principal things intended and convented by their confederation hath always been to expel the French King from his usurped occupation of the crown of France, and to conduce the King's Highness, as right requireth, unto the same. . . .

[3] Albeit, if they shall make any such allegation, whereby it may be perceived that all the premises cannot reasonably satisfy them, ne induce the Emperor to come unto the personal invasion, and to help the King actually and really to attain the crown of

[1] It was proposed that Charles should marry Henry's daughter Mary, then aged nine. They had been betrothed in 1522.

[2] fol. 97.

[3] fol. 99.

France, without delivery of my said Lady Princess; then the said Ambassadors shall say, that the Emperor proceeding to this personal invasion, and meeting the King at Paris, His Grace will be contented to transport my Lady Princess thither; and, the King's Highness once crowned in Paris King of France, to deliver her unto the Emperor according to his desire: and so His Grace to pass to Rome, or concur with the Emperor for attaining his Crown Imperial, as is aforesaid. Which thing if the Emperor refuse to condescend unto, it is a sign that neither he intendeth to come unto Paris, ne to help the King's Highness to be crowned King of France. . . .

By the premises the said ambassadors be sufficiently instructed, what they shall say and do touching the personal invasion this year to be made, and for inducing the Emperor to be content to forbear ransoming of the French King, or making any composition with him or his realm, but utterly to exclude him and his line with all other from the crown of France except only the King's Highness, to whom the same rightfully doth appertain and belong. . . .

It is an amazing document, and not the least remarkable thing about it is the pertinacity with which no less than seven alternative schemes are worked out, for the ambassadors to propound in succession, if one after another Henry's proposals should fail. They descend by degrees from the claim to the whole of France to a claim to the whole duchy of Normandy and a perpetual yearly pension of 100,000 crowns. The ambassadors were empowered to conclude on any of the seven, and commissions were drawn up for that purpose.[1] In May Henry also wrote to the Regent of the Netherlands in precisely the same strain, and at considerable length.

Out of the whole business England got exactly nothing. Charles, in effect, never even answered Henry's letter. He communicated with him, many times, at much length: but he made it quite plain that he had no intention whatever of invading France in person, and simply ignored Henry's references to the crown of France. A miscalculation, it might be said: so

[1] See especially Vesp. C. III, f. 150, 153.

much for England's first large-scale attempt at upsetting the European equilibrium. A political miscalculation: which could be, and was, retrieved financially by a prompt alliance with the loser, which yielded a sum of no less than 2,000,000 crowns to be paid in yearly instalments of 100,000 crowns.

There are dreams which are at once prophecy and inspiration, and dreams which are illusion. Wolsey's dream of the Papacy and Henry's dream of the crown of France were both illusions. They belonged to a vanished past—meaningless for the future, and out of touch with the actuality of the moment. Both meant power; but what neither Wolsey nor Henry managed to realize, during the years when they were still hoping to achieve them, was the fact that they could never, in the sixteenth century, be brought to mean power for England. The Papacy was too hopelessly embroiled with the block of temporal power that was Italy, where the usurping French and Spanish interests would never have tolerated the intrusion of an Englishman. The disrupted France of the Middle Ages, where Anglo-Norman kings could successfully lay claim to vast hereditary dominions, was a thing of the past, that had given way to a kingdom as conscious of nationalism as England. Moreover, as Thomas Cromwell's realist mind demanded, 'Suppose that Almighty God sent our Sovereign his desired purpose, how should we be able to possess the large country of France, which have our own realm so marvellous rarely stored of inhabitants and able men?'

For Henry the shattering of the illusion came at just the right moment. It pulled him up sharply, and in time. From henceforth we hear no more of impracticable pretensions. Essentially a realist, he turns, instead, to the dream which is inspiration and prophecy—the dream of his own imperial power, founded on a united kingdom—a manageable block of control, an integral whole, racially, nationally, geographically.

In the light of modern historical knowledge Henry's pretensions were absurd, and out of date. But to say that therefore he cannot have entertained them seriously seems to me as logically inadmissible as to say that because a scene or passage in a Shakespeare play is to modern taste bad, *therefore* Shakespeare cannot have written it. It is worth while to remember that in 1535

Henry was still using his 'just title of inheritance' as an asset for bargaining with Francis. If Francis will obtain from the Pope a revocation of Clement's 'unjust and slanderous' sentence on the divorce Henry will *consider* giving up the title of King of France,[1] which remained incorporated in the style of the Kings of England until 1800. It is also as well to remember that in the last years of his life Henry obviously regarded the retention of Boulogne as of great practical value (see III, 5). To him, the English possession of Calais and Boulogne meant the 'keeping' of the Channel; and no one questions the genuineness or the sincerity of the English belief that the loss of Calais in Mary's reign was a national disaster, although it is the modern verdict that we were well rid of it.

In consequence, I am prepared to believe that Henry's letter to the Emperor after Pavia is a genuine—though to us, futile—expression of policy. His whole life was a continuous expression of the Tudor will to power. In 1525 he had not begun to tap what were, for him, its real sources. He was looking abroad when he should have looked homewards. Not until 1529, when he summons his own Parliament, does he begin to realize that both the material and spiritual sources of power were to be found within his own realm. To Professor A. F. Pollard the net result of the foreign policy of the first two decades is that in 1525 England counted for less in the councils of Europe than she did in 1513, while at home the statute book 'may be searched in vain for an act of importance'. An ironic prelude on the theme of 'virtue, glory, immortality'!

[1] See *S.P.* VII, pp. 586-7. And it might also be remembered that it was only seventy years since the English had been driven out of France at the end of the Hundred Years War.

PART II

'THE KING'S GREAT MATTER'

CHAPTER I

'NO SON OF MINE SUCCEEDING'

. . . a barren sceptre in my gripe,
Thence to be wrench'd with an unlineal hand,
No son of mine succeeding.

SHAKESPEARE

IN 1503, when Ferdinand of Aragon sought the papal dispensation to enable his widowed daughter to marry her brother-in-law, some at any rate of the parties concerned had obviously been troubled in their minds about the validity of such a dispensation. Katharine herself had had doubts and scruples, suggested, possibly, and certainly encouraged, by her confessor, whom Ferdinand promptly removed as a dangerous adviser. Isabella, Katharine's devout mother, was not too happy about the proposed remarriage of her daughter, though a brief[1] from Julius II calmed her doubts before her death. What is more, the Pope himself, though eventually granting the necessary dispensation, had expressed doubt as to his own powers in the matter. When, however, on Henry's accession it became politically convenient for the marriage to take place, nobody mentioned such things as religious scruples: the dispensation of the common father of Christendom, the supreme spiritual authority, was enough.

For the greater part of eighteen years Henry and Katharine lived contentedly as man and wife. Katharine was devoted to her husband and his interests. There had, it is true, been occasional dissensions. In 1514, when Ferdinand was still shocking and outraging all Henry's decent instincts of loyalty and friendship, Peter Martyr, recording the gossip of the Spanish court, writes that they hear Katharine has given birth prematurely to a child, as a result of her grief at the misunderstanding between her father and her husband, and at the way Henry in his wrath had turned on the daughter of Spain. Martyr says that Henry 'conquestus suos in eam expectorabat'—had, in plain terms, boasted of and cast in her face the fact of his own infidelity.

[1] That is, a formal but private letter, embodying the intent of a bull, but not, like the latter, a public document.

An even more significant bit of gossip is retailed by one Vetor Lippomano, a Venetian, who writes from Rome on August 28 in the same year, and reports that it is said 'that the King of England means to repudiate his present wife, the daughter of the King of Spain and his brother's widow, because he is unable to have children by her, and intends to marry a daughter of the French Duke of Bourbon. *Si dize* the King of England means to annul his own marriage, and will obtain what he wants from the Pope as France did.'[1]

A more serious cause of unhappiness to both Henry and Katharine was provided by the successive deaths of no less than five children in four years. There had been a still-born daughter in May, 1510: a son, Henry, born on January 1, 1511, who lived barely two months: a still-born son in September, 1513: a son, who died at birth, in June, 1514: and another, prematurely born, in December of the same year. On February 18, 1516, however, the Princess Mary was born. In contrast to these other ill-fated Tudor babies she seemed a healthy child. Henry was as delighted as any other father with his daughter, boasted to the Venetian ambassador that she never cried; boasted also that he and Katharine were both young, and that, by the grace of God, sons would follow. A genuine affection for his wife, as well as care for the succession, speaks through the letter he wrote to Wolsey in July, 1518, when Katharine was again pregnant.

1. To Cardinal Wolsey

[*July*, 1518.]

My lord cardinal, I recommend unto you as heartily as I can, and I am right glad to hear of your good health, which I pray God may long continue. So it is that I have received your letters, to the which (because they ask long writing) I have made answer by my secretary. Two things there be which be so secret that they cause me at this time to write to you

[1] i.e. Louis XII, who for political reasons secured a divorce from his wife, in order to marry Anne of Brittany, and so absorb Brittany into the French crown. Quoted from *Venetian Calendar*, II, 479; from *Sanuto Diaries*, V, xix, p. 1.

myself; the one is that I trust the queen my wife be with child; the other is chief cause why I am so loath to repair to London ward, because about this time is partly of her dangerous times, and by cause of that, I would remove her as little as I may now. My lord, I write thus unto not as a ensured thing, but as a thing wherein I have great hope and likelihood, and by cause I do well know that this thing will be comfortable to you to understand; therefore, I do write it unto you at this time. No more to you at this time, *nisi quod deus velit inceptum opus bene finire.* Written with the hand of your loving prince,

HENRY R.

It is generally thought that Henry's mention of Katharine's 'dangerous times' refers to various miscarriages that had happened after the birth of Mary. In the following November their last child was still-born, and by 1525 even Henry, always reluctant to believe that the world was going to deny him something upon which he had set his heart, realized that Katharine, then aged forty, could never give him the son he so passionately desired. Mary was his acknowledged heir, but, like everyone else, Henry believed that the succession of a woman would mean a disputed succession. He and his Council saw James V and various claimants, all waiting to plunge England into civil war, with the crown as the prize. There were several nobles with claims of descent, the foremost being the Duke of Buckingham, a descendant of Edward III. In 1521 he had been tried and sentenced to death, ostensibly for high treason, actually because as a potential claimant to the throne he was a potential danger to Henry's line. It was a drastic move, and shows clearly enough that the question of the succession had already made Henry both nervous and ruthless years before the divorce was begun. Nor is it fantastic to see, in his treatment of his illegitimate son, yet further evidence of his concern. In 1525 he created the six-year-old boy Duke of Richmond—his own father's title before he came to the throne; and soon afterwards conferred on him the offices of Lord-Lieutenant of Ireland and Warden of the Scottish Marches, which he had himself held when a child. The boy had lived in complete obscurity till

1525—the year in which Henry finally realized he would have no more children by Katharine. If proof is needed that Henry was deeply concerned about the succession long before he fell in love with Anne Boleyn, we need hardly look any farther than the execution of Buckingham in 1521, and then this shower of honours—the prelude to further advancement—that fell with such unexpected suddenness upon his hitherto unregarded son.

At what precise moment Henry decided he must divorce Katharine of Aragon and wed Anne Boleyn it is impossible to say. Anne's elder sister, Mary, the wife of Sir William Carey, had been Henry's mistress, probably between the years 1522 and 1525; and although he may have been attracted to the younger sister as early as 1526, there is nothing in the earliest letters he wrote to her to enable us to be certain of their dates. They may belong to the year 1527: they may be earlier, or even later. The only thing we know for certain is that the first move to procure a divorce was made in the spring of 1527, and that the first allusion to Anne Boleyn and the King's determination to marry her belongs to September of the same year. Henry himself gave the date of his estrangement from Katharine as 1524. Lord Rochford, Anne's brother, deposed on July 15, 1529, that it had begun 'about two years since', i.e. in 1527.

Shakespeare, whose account tallies with those of Holinshed and Cavendish, makes Henry explain how he was moved to sue for the divorce:

> My conscience first receiv'd a tenderness,
> Scruple, and prick, on certain speeches utter'd
> By the Bishop of Bayonne, then French ambassador;
> Who had been hither sent on the debating
> A marriage 'twixt the Duke of Orleans and
> Our daughter Mary. I'the progress of this business,
> Ere a determinate resolution, he
> (I mean the bishop) did require a respite;
> Wherein he might the king his lord advertise
> Whether our daughter were legitimate,
> Respecting this our marriage with the dowager
> Sometimes our brother's wife.

The Bishop's embassy arrived in February, 1527. Whether Wolsey and Henry both lied when they said the Bishop suggested these doubts we do not know. But though not the cause, it may likely have been the occasion that served as the match to the fuel, as the following extract suggests, written after Wolsey had sounded Fisher, Bishop of Rochester, on the subject of the King's 'scruples'.

[*July* 5, 1527.]

. . . I repeated unto him the whole matter of France, and of the marriage intended between the French King and my lady Princess. . . . The Bishop of Tarbes, one of the said ambassadors, wrote unto me from his lodging . . . they were compelled to demand likewise, that, on Your Grace's behalf, it should be showed and opened unto them what had been here provided for taking away the impediment of that marriage whereof my Lady Princess cometh; and that although he doubted not but Your Grace's Council had well foreseen that same, yet, for discharge of their duties towards their master, they must needs require a sight thereof, fearing lest upon such altercation on both sides little effect should succeed. Whe(reupon) Your Highness had commandment to make ensearch for such dispensations as were obtained therefore, to show unto them when they should require it. And, finally, for the said Bishop's satisfaction, showed unto him the bull of dispensation; which, after he had deliberately perused and read, noting and marking every material point thereof, although he said, for the first sight, he supposed the said bull was not sufficient, as well for that this impediment was *de juro divino,* wherewith the Pope could not dispense *nisi ex urgentissima causa*, as for other things deprehended in the same.[1]

Before this, however, between February and June, various measures had been secretly concerted by Henry and Wolsey. It was, apparently, a propitious moment, in so far as European politics were concerned. Pope Clement VII wanted to clear the foreigner out of Italy by means of an anti-Spanish league. For this he needed the help of England—a good moment, then, for England to rely upon the help of the Pope in a spiritual cause. In May the Cardinal summoned the King to appear before him, to answer the charge of living with his brother's wife. Henry

[1] Quoted from *S.P.* I, 199.

replied with a justification: the suit was terminated, and the ground prepared. The plan was that Wolsey should declare the King's marriage invalid, the plea being the insufficiency of the brief of Julius II: Henry was to remarry: and the Pope was then to confirm the Legate's sentence, thereby confirming the second marriage and ensuring the legitimacy of the confidently-expected heir. It was exactly what had been done for Charles Brandon, Henry's own brother-in-law: then why not, argued Henry, for the Defender of the Faith? Unfortunately, however, before the preliminary divorce plot was well under way, an event occurred which profoundly affected this apparently English domestic project. On May 6 Rome was sacked by the Imperial troops—an event which shocked the whole of Christendom.

When the idea of the divorce was first mooted the Pope was a free man, at enmity with the Emperor. Within a month he was the Emperor's captive in the Castle of St. Angelo: and the Emperor, as Katharine's nephew, was bound to oppose the divorce. Such was the political situation with which Wolsey and Henry at once found themselves confronted. So far, Wolsey and the King were acting together. It was at the specific point of Henry's second marriage that their plans diverged, as each soon became aware. Henry meant to marry Anne Boleyn: Wolsey meant his master to marry Renée, the daughter of Louis XII of France. To bind yet closer the kingdoms of France and England was at this juncture the basic aim of the Cardinal's foreign policy: to secure his succession, at the same time gratifying his own desire, had, for the moment, become the sole and fundamental aim of the King. In July Wolsey went to France on a diplomatic mission, ostensibly to settle the treaty which included the marriage of the Princess Mary, and to arrange for war against the Emperor. Actually, his real project was a daring bid for power made on his own behalf and his master's, being nothing less than an attempt to have himself appointed Vicar-General for the Pope during the period of the latter's captivity. It came to nothing; but had it succeeded 'the King's matter' would have been dealt with at once, and as the King wished, as the appointment would have conferred on Wolsey the power to act on behalf of Clement.

In the meantime, while he pursued his own designs in France, Wolsey dispatched Ghinucci, the Bishop of Worcester, Salviati and Gregory Casale to Rome to forward the King's cause with the Pope. Henry, however, was not trusting his affairs entirely to Wolsey's skill, and in September he himself sent his personal secretary, William Knight, on the same mission, but armed also with secret instructions. He gave him a letter to Wolsey, who was to send him on his way to obtain a dispensation for the divorce. Knight, unknown to Wolsey, was at the same time to secure a dispensation for the King to marry Anne Boleyn, with whom—according to the canon law—he had already contracted affinity in the first degree, by reason of his illicit relations with her sister, Mary. This dispensation is the second, and secret, commission referred to in the letter to Knight (No. III). The first matter, which was countermanded as 'unreasonable to be granted', was a request for a dispensation to take another wife without divorcing Katharine.

II. To Cardinal Wolsey

[1527.]

My Lord, this shall be to thank you of your great pains and travail which you have sustained since your departure hence for our business and causes, wherein you have done to us no little honour, pleasure and profit, and to our realm an infinite goodness, which service cannot be by a kind master forgotten, of which fault I trust I shall never be accused, specially to your warde, which so laboriously do serve me. Furthermore, because as yet since the Pope's captivity we never sent to salute him, nor have no man resident there to advertise us of the affairs there, and also lest the Queen should prevent us, by the Emperor's means, in our great matter, we think it meet to send this bearer thither, of whose truth and sincerity we have had long proof. Praying you to give him such instructions and commissions as shall be for our affairs there requisite, and that with convenient diligence, to the intent our affairs there may have some stay. No more at this time, but that greatly I desire your return home, for here we have great lack of you, and that you may give full credence to my secretary this bearer. Written with the hand of your loving sovereign lord and friend.

HENRY R.

III. TO KNIGHT

[*? Oct.-Nov.*, 1527.]

MR. SECRETARY, this shall be to advertise you that the secret bull I sent you for is at this hour known perfectly to my lord cardinal, by whose means I know well enough, but I advertise you thereof because I am sure that (though my lord cardinal do write unto you that he know it) you would not yet be a-knowen thereof; whereby mayhap he should suspect that you were sent (as you be indeed) for things that I would not he should know. Wherefore if he either write or send to you in that matter I will your answer be that truth it is I sent after you such a one, but that it was no part of your commission when you went from me, and that therein you will nothing do but as I and the said lord cardinal shall command you. For my pleasure is indeed (as peradventure you shall be advertised by the said lord cardinal hereafter) that you shall make no further labour touching that bull. Nevertheless I do now send to you the copy of another which no man doth know but they which I am sure will never disclose it to no man living, for any craft that the cardinal or any other can find; willing you both to keep it secret and to solicit that it may be made in due form, keeping the effect and tenor thereof and·with all diligence (it once impetrate) to send it to us. Surely to be plain with you, we are of the opinion that the cardinal is of touching the first bull, for surely we think it is too much to be required and unreasonable to be granted, and therefore he and I jointly shall devise another, which hereafter we shall send to you (and that or it be long), willing you to make all diligence to you possible for impetrating of this first which presently I send you for, that is it which I above all things do desire, and if you cannot attain it, then solicit the other which my lord cardinal and I shall send you, which, peradventure, shall not be much discrepant from this, but that shall be made *pro forma tantum*—and so to cloak other matters if you possible [*sic*] may attain this, desiring you heartily to use all ways to you possible to get access to the Pope's person, and then to solicit both the protestation and this bull with all diligence; and in so doing I shall reckon it the highest service that ever you did me. And if peradventure the Pope do make any sticking at this bull, because peradventure it is not yet to him known but that the marriage between the Queen and me is good and sufficient, you may show him that I doubt not but if he ask the dean of his Roote,[1] which hath deeply seen the matter, he will show him the truth thereof, and this bull is not desired except I be *legittime absolutus ab hoc matrimonio Katherinae.* Wherefore I must humbly desire him (in consideration of such service as I have done or hereafter may do to his holiness and the church) that he will grant me the same, making as few privy thereto as is possible, causing the plumary[2] to seal it in his presence without further sight thereof, which I hear say he may lawfully do. Good Mr. Secretary, solicit these causes with all both celerity and dexterity you can, and with the best counsel, so they be secret, that you can get. I do send you this bearer by whom you may assuredly send me whatsoever you will, for he will with diligence bring it me and wisely enough too. I fear me sore that if you find not some by ways beside them that my lord cardinal did devise with you to have access to the Pope's presence it will be long or you attain the same. Wherefore I instantly desire you to seek all means possible. *Pauca sapienti*, and thus fare you well. By your loving master and sovereign.

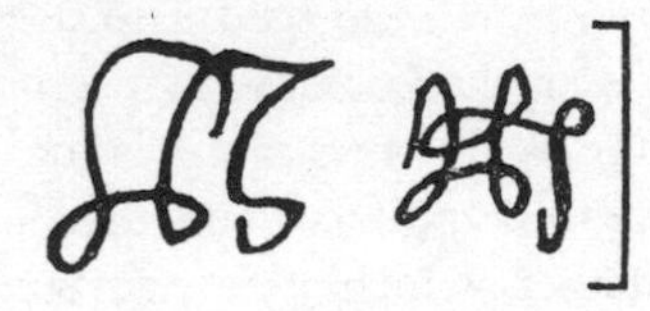

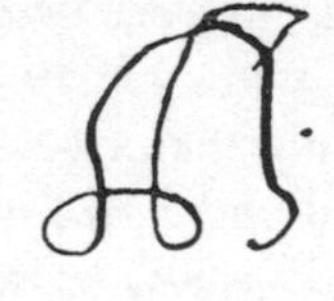

[1] i.e. of the Rota, the supreme ecclesiastical and secular court.

[2] *N.E.D.* records only *plumbator* in a unique 1677 example. Maigne d'Arnis, *Lexicon mediae et infimae Latinis* gives *plumbator, plombateur,* ' l'officier de la chancellerie romaine qui scelle les bulles en plomb '. This is obviously the meaning of *plumary*, but it does not explain why the writer assimilated *plumbator* with *plumarius.*

The signature of this letter is reproduced above, with typical specimens of Henry's H and R at the left for comparison. (cf. also specimen on cover.) As already stated in the Introduction (p. xvi ff.), I do not believe that this signature is genuine. The H is abnormally formed, and differs very markedly from the hundred and thirty signatures I examined as a check, all of which are perfectly regular and true to type. Henry's genuine H is made without lifting the pen. He starts with the top curve of the left-hand upright, makes his first down-stroke, and the loop at its base, then the horizontal crosspiece and the bottom loop of the second upright, and then the upright itself (an up-stroke). He then makes a preliminary horizontal stroke, ending in a sharp angle, before the last vigorous down-stroke of the third limb, with its distinctive curve, and final hook. The abnormal specimen may have been formed in several ways. It may have been drawn in two, or even three, strokes: or it may simply have had the strokes made in the wrong order—i.e. the copyist has started with the angled loop of the medial upright, and made the second of the three before the first. Personally, I incline to think it has been drawn in two strokes: i.e. that the copyist began correctly with the curve of the first upright, but realized he had gone wrong when he came to the angled horizontal preliminary to the third limb, gave it up, and joined the third limb on to the first at the top of the curve where a slight thickening may be noticed. Perhaps the most obvious signs of the copyist are: (1) the way in which the first upright falls feebly over on to the second, instead of maintaining a nicely proportioned distance; (2) the queer angled loop that has been substituted for Henry's characteristic link between the second and third uprights, and (3) the altogether wrong shape of the final curving down-stroke. Whether the 'two strokes', or the 'wrong order' explanation is correct, either is equally destructive of belief in the genuineness of the signature.

The R, though properly formed, is also untrue to type. Henry's R is invariably made with a long or longish, nearly straight, vigorous preliminary up-stroke, starting just above the lower left-hand base loop. The suspect R has a preliminary curve instead; and where Henry's R tends to have a slightly flattened and angled top loop to the right-hand upright, this R has a regular writing-master's rounded loop. The loop forming the crosspiece between the two uprights is even more suspicious. In none of my test specimens does it cross the left upright with anything like the same length and lavishness of looping. In genuine examples there is a decided tendency in the bottom cross-stroke to slope up slightly from left to right. Moreover, the final flourish in this R is apparently unique. It is a free, large, curving stroke, finishing seven-twelfths of an inch below the bottom crosspiece. Henry's final stroke invariably resembles a pothook, and finishes either just underneath or slightly to the right of the right-hand base loop. I am also suspicious of the stop after the R. In only two out of the 130 specimens have I found a stop used, and in both cases it occurs just below the loop of the pothook and very near to it.

Without suggesting that I consider style constitutes evidence, I think the following points may be noted. In so far as obvious tricks of style are concerned the letter is authentic enough: for example, the 'surely', the use of brackets, the opening (cf. No. 11, above), and the '*pauca sapienti*' (cf. a letter to Wolsey, not printed here, in Addit. 19398, f. 644, 'no more to you at this time, but *sapienti pauca*'.) Whether this last touch is too 'authentic' to be true is perhaps disputable. As used in the letter to Wolsey it has point, in that it concludes a brief and very cryptic note. Here it follows a somewhat lengthy and perhaps over-elaborate explanation. I am also a little inclined to think the 'good Master Secretary' more like a reminiscence of Elizabeth's familiar style than of Henry's; nor am I quite happy about the phrases 'which I hear say he may' and 'I fear me sore'. On the question of substance, my impression is that, although I see no reason why anyone should need to fabricate this letter, it would have been possible to put it together from the information given by Knight in his letter of September 13 to Henry (see *S.P.*, VII, 3; *L.P.*, IV, 3422), and in his later letter of December 4 (*L.P.*, IV, 3688). This second letter posits the existence, if not of the actual Corpus letter, at the least of a letter similar in its contents.

CHAPTER II

'FROM ALL OTHER ONLY TO HER I ME BETAKE'

Now unto my lady
  Promise to her I make,
From all other only
  To her I me betake.

HENRY VIII

THROUGHOUT the spring and summer of 1527 Henry had endeavoured to cloak his designs from Katharine, the world in general, and the Emperor in particular, by making it appear that all his proceedings were merely concerned with the investigation of the validity of his marriage, to the end that if there were any defects in the dispensation they might be remedied, for the sake of removing any doubts as to the legitimacy of Princess Mary. He told Katharine, however, on June 22, that he no longer considered her his lawful wife; and that he had already determined to marry Anne is amply attested by Knight's secret commission for the Mary Boleyn dispensation. It is evident, therefore, that the earliest of his letters to Anne must belong either to these summer months of 1527, or even earlier. It is impossible to arrange them in order of time with any absolute certainty, and neither the Vatican arrangement nor that of the *Letters and Papers* is entirely satisfactory.[1] All one can safely say is, that they tell us that Henry has been in love with Anne for a whole year, and has declared his affection: that they belong to a period when she had withdrawn from Court; and that Henry can already assure her that he is going to cast off all others out of his thought and affections for her sake (p. 57).

The most interesting thing of all, however, is something which comes through quite clearly—so clearly that it makes us impatient of details of such secondary importance as exact dates. It is the fact that Henry was simply and whole-heartedly in love.

[1] These differing orders are given in Appendix I. See also *Bibliographical List*, p. 439, for the history of the MSS., which belong to the Vatican.

I. TO ANNE BOLEYN

MY MISTRESS AND FRIEND,

I and my heart commit ourselves into your hands, beseeching you to hold us recommended to your good favour, and that your affection to us may not be by absence diminished; for great pity it were to increase our pain, seeing that absence makes enough of it, and indeed more than I could ever have thought, remembering us of a point in astronomy, which is this: that the longer the days are, the farther off is the sun, and yet, notwithstanding, the hotter; so is it with our love, for we by absence are far sundered, yet it nevertheless keeps its fervency, at the least on my part, holding in hope the like on yours; ensuring you that for myself the annoy of absence doth already too much vex me; and when I think upon the increase of that which of necessity I must needs suffer it is almost intolerable to me, were it not for the firm hope that I have of your ever-during affection towards me; and sometimes to put you in mind of this, and seeing that in person I cannot be in your presence, I send you now the thing most nearly thereto appertaining that it is possible to me to send, which is my picture set in a bracelet, with the whole device which already you know. Wishing myself in their place, when it should please you. This by the hand of your loyal servant and friend.

H.R.

From the point of view of Tudor etiquette in this matter of present-giving it would be suitable that Henry's gift should be answered by one from Anne; and the next letter suggests that it was appropriately requited.

II. TO ANNE BOLEYN

For so beautiful a gift, and so exceeding (taking it in all), I thank you right cordially; not alone for the fair diamond and the ship in which the solitary damsel is tossed about, but chiefly for the good intent and too-humble submission vouchsafed in this by your kindness; considering well that by occasion to merit it would not a little perplex me, if I were not aided therein by your great benevolence and goodwill, for the which I have sought, do seek, and shall always seek by all services to me possible there to remain, in the which my hope hath set up his everlasting rest, saying *aut illic aut nullibi.*

The proofs of your affection are such, the fine posies of the letters so warmly couched, that they constrain me ever truly to honour, love and serve you, praying you that you will continue in this same firm and constant purpose, ensuring you, for my part, that I will the rather go beyond than make reciproque, if loyalty of heart, the desire to do you pleasure, even with my whole heart root, may serve to advance it.[1]

Praying you also that if ever before I have in any way done you offence, that you will give me the same absolution that you ask, ensuring you that henceforth my heart shall be dedicate to you alone, greatly desirous that so my body could be as well, as God can bring to pass if it pleaseth Him, whom I entreat once each day for the accomplishment thereof, trusting that at length my prayer will be heard, wishing the time brief, and thinking it but long until we shall see each other again.

Written with the hand of that secretary who in heart, body and will is

Your loyal and most ensured servant,

H autre (AB) ne cherce R.

After the opportunity for letters provided by this exchange of presents we may conjecture a pause in the correspondence. Then the lover finds another plausible pretext to enable him to write again to the beloved.

III. To Anne Boleyn

To MY MISTRESS,

Because the time seems to me very long since I have heard of your good health and of you, the great affection that I bear

[1] 'Si loyaute du ceur, desire de vous complaire, vous sans autre racine en ceur le peut avancer.' The French is slightly obscure, and previous translators have got over the difficulty by omitting it. Though the construction is muddled I have no doubt, however, that the phrase which Henry is attempting to use is 'even with my whole heart root', which is to be found in various other familiar English letters of this period.

you has prevailed with me to send this bearer to you, to be the better ascertained of your health and pleasure; and because since I parted with you I have been advised that the opinion in which I left you is now altogether changed, and that you will not come to court, neither with my lady your mother, if you could, nor yet any other way; the which report being true I cannot enough marvel at, seeing that I am well assured I have never since that time committed fault; and methinks it is but small recompense for the great love I bear you to keep me thus distanced both from the speech and the person of that she which of all the world I most do esteem; and if you love me with such settled affection as I trust, I assure me that this sundering of our two persons should be to you some small vexation, though in truth this doth not so much pertain to the mistress as to the servant.

Bethink you well, my mistress, that your absence doth not a little grieve me, trusting that by your will it should not be so; but if I knew in truth that of your will you desired it, I could do none other than lament me of my ill fortune, abating by little and little my so great folly. And thus, for lack of time, I make an end of my rude letter, praying you to give credence to this bearer in that which he will tell you from me.

Written with the hand of your entire servant,

H.R.

Anne was cautious, and knew how to keep the King still in love, and, at the same time, uncertain of his hold upon her. She had no mind to succeed her sister as Henry's mistress. Her answer to the above letter must have been ambiguous, non-committal and discreet, but also tantalizing and provocative. It roused Henry to immediate and vehement reply, and—more important—to definite promises of what he could and would do, if only he might be assured of her love.

IV. To Anne Boleyn

Debating with myself the contents of your letters, I have put myself in great distress, not knowing how to interpret them, whether to my disadvantage, as in some places is shown, or to advantage, as in others I understand them; praying you with all my heart that you will expressly certify me of your whole mind concerning the love between us two. For of necessity I must ensure me of this answer, having been now above one whole year struck with the dart of love, not being assured either of failure or of finding place in your heart and grounded affection. Which last point has kept me for some little time from calling you my mistress, since if you love me in none other sort save that of common affection that name in no wise belongs to you, for it denotes a singular love, far removed from the common. But if it shall please you to do me the office of a true, loyal mistress and friend, and to give yourself up, body and soul, to me who will be and have been your very loyal servant (if by your severity you do not forbid me), I promise you that not only shall the name be given you, but that also I will take you for my only mistress, rejecting from thought and affection all others save yourself, to serve you only. Beseeching you to make me answer absolute to this my rude letter, how far and in what I may put trust; and if it does not please you to make me answer by writing, assign me some place where I may have it from your own mouth, and with well-willing heart I will be there. No more, for fear of wearying you. Written with the hand of him who would willingly remain your

H.R.

The two brief notes that follow place themselves neither by tone nor yet by any detail. They might belong to any month of the summer of 1527. Like all the preceding letters, however, they are written in French, and serve prettily enough to conclude the story of the King's courtship in 1527. One and all, they are the letters of a man grown young again, and ardent, and fired with a genuine affection, in which devotion and respect and the capacity for idealizing the woman he loves show as plainly as if the letters were those of any of his subjects.

v. To Anne Boleyn

Although, my mistress, it hath not pleased you to remember the promise that you made me when I was last with you, which was, to hear good news of you, and to have answer to my last letter; nevertheless, methinks it is the part of a true servant (seeing that otherwise he can hear nothing) to send to understand of the health of his mistress, and so, to acquit myself of the office of a true servant, I send you this letter, praying you to advertise me of your well-being, the which I pray God may endure as long as I would mine own. And to the intent that you may the more often remember me, I send you by this bearer a buck, killed by my hand late yesternight, trusting that as you eat of it you will have in mind the hunter. And thus, for lack of space, I will make an end of my letter. Written with the hand of your servant, who oft and again wisheth you in your brother's room.

H.R.

This and the following are both attributed by the *Letters and Papers* to July, 1527, but with the warning that they may well be earlier.

VI. To Anne Boleyn

Although it doth not appertain to a gentleman to take his lady in place of servant, nevertheless, in compliance with your desires, I willingly grant it to you, if thereby you can find yourself less unthankfully bestowed in the place by you chosen, than you have been in the place given by me. Thanking you right heartily for that it pleaseth you still to hold me in some remembrance.

6.n.A.I.de A.o.na.v.e.z.
Henry R.

Personally I believe that with these 1527 letters there should be grouped also the one that follows. By the *Letters and Papers* it is attributed to July, 1528; but it does not seem to me possible to insert it between Nos. XVI and XVIII. It is written in French, and the formality of its tone links it as surely with these early letters as it separates it from those belonging to 1528; for which reason I have assigned it conjecturally to September, 1527.

VII. To Anne Boleyn

The drawing near of that time which has for me been so long deferred so much rejoiceth me that it is as if it were already come. Nevertheless, the perfect accomplishing thereof cannot be until the two persons are together met, the which meeting is on my part the more desired than any earthly thing; for what joy in this world can be greater than to have the company of her who is the most dearly loved, knowing likewise that she by her choice holds the same, the thought of which greatly delights me.

Judge, therefore, what that very person shall do, whose absence hath so grieved my heart that neither tongue nor pen can express the hurt, which no other thing excepting that[1] can ever cure. Praying you, my mistress, to say to my lord your father on my part that I beg of him to hasten by two days the time appointed, that he may be at court before his former promise,[2] or, at least, on the day already agreed. For otherwise I shall think he will not serve a lover's turn, as was his promise, nor will not allow of mine expectation.

No more at this present, for lack of time, trusting soon to tell you by word of mouth the residue of the sufferings that I by your absence have sustained. Written with the hand of that secretary who wishes himself at this time private with you, and who is and always will be,

Your loyal and most assured servant,

H. autre (AB) ne cherche R.

Since the sack of Rome in May, 1527, the Pope had been imprisoned in the Castle of St. Angelo. Rome was in the hands of the Emperor's forces, and the Emperor, in spite of Henry's precautions, had heard from Katharine of the King's intentions. Then, on December 9, the Pope escaped to Orvieto. Knight followed him and eventually secured his audience. No difficulty was made about the 'secret matter' of the dispensation

[1] i.e. her return in person.

[2] In the French the phrase Henry uses is 'devent le vieill terme'. Halliwell translates this as 'before the old term', as does the eighteenth century version.

for Henry's marriage with Anne. In granting it Clement committed himself to nothing, as it could only become valid if and after Henry's marriage with Katharine was declared null and void. But the other dispensation, which was to declare that he had never been lawfully married, was a very different matter. Knight presented the Pope with a draft commission drawn up by Wolsey. Had it been granted as a 'decretal commission' it would have delegated to Wolsey the Pope's absolute power to decide the case and pronounce the marriage a nullity, on an examination of the facts. Clement did his utmost to shelve the responsibility. He suggested that Henry should obey his own conscience, and wed again, if he considered it lawful. He could do it on the legatine authority of Wolsey, and settle the whole affair in England. Neither Henry nor Wolsey would accept this solution; so finally, before granting it, the Pope gave the draft to Cardinal St. Quattuor, to be amended and drawn up in strict accordance with canon law. Had Knight been a more expert diplomatist he might have realized that by the time that experienced canonist had dealt faithfully with the draft he had rendered it quite harmless from the Pope's point of view, and useless from Henry's. Being more eager than able, he was completely taken in, and posted back to England with his commission and dispensation; only to realize, when it was presented to Wolsey, that the former was completely inadequate, and 'of no effect or authority'. A full decretal commission meant one in which the Pope undertook to ratify and confirm any and every decision made by Wolsey, without any question of revocation of the cause to himself as the supreme authority. This he could not and would not give: and anything less than this was not enough for Henry's plans.

At the beginning of 1528, therefore, King and Cardinal returned to the attack. The next step was to dispatch to Rome the ablest ambassadors who could be found, and early in February Dr. Stephen Gardiner, Wolsey's own secretary, and Edward Foxe, also in the Cardinal's service, set out. On their way to the coast they stopped at Hever to pay their respects to Anne Boleyn. As their credentials they presented the following letter from Henry, hopeful and vigorous, and written in English, not

French—the almost business-like English of the lover who, though no less ardent than before, has now for the moment done with the terms of courtly fantasy, and has fully determined to get what he wants at whatever cost.

VIII. To Anne Boleyn

[*Feb.*, 1528.]

Darling, these shall be only to advertise you that this bearer and his fellow be dispatched with as many things to compass our matter, and to bring it to pass as our wits could imagine or devise; which brought to pass, as I trust, by their diligence, it shall be shortly, you and I shall have our desired end, which should be more to my heart's ease, and more quietness to my mind, than any other thing in this world; as, with God's grace, shortly I trust shall be proved, but not so soon as I would it were; yet I will ensure you there shall be no time lost that may be won, and further can not be done; for *ultra posse non est esse.* Keep him not too long with you, but desire him, for your sake, to make the more speed; for the sooner we shall have word from him, the sooner shall our matter come to pass. And thus upon trust of your short repair to London, I make an end of my letter, mine own sweet heart.

Written with the hand of him which desireth as much to be yours as you do to have him.

H.R.

Henry's relations with Rome at this time may be judged from the tone of the two items that follow—both, apparently, rough drafts in Latin of letters accrediting Gardiner and Fox to the Pope.

IX. To Clement VII

[*Feb.* 11, 1528.]

MOST BLESSED FATHER,

Partly by your letters written in your holiness's own hand to us and to the Cardinal Archbishop of York, partly by your discourse held with, and assurance given to, the Right Reverend the Elect of Tortona,[1] we have learnt with the utmost pleasure not only how great the good will and affection is that you bear us, but also how ready and disposed you are to favour our wishes and requests, and how courteously you have promised to gratify our yearning desire. Since we were long halting in doubt whether this would be conceded by your holiness, and now promise ourself that the affair of your kindness is (as it were) accomplished, we return, as far as we can, thanks unbounded to you, who, in this cause alone, as urgent as it is upright, will forever bind most closely to you, ourself, our resources, our kingdom, and all our friends. . . . (*Vitell. B. X, 79.*)

Most blessed father, our fidelity and reverence towards your holiness and the Apostolic See is more firm and sure than ought to be expressed by messengers and the testimony of letters. Now, at this time, we, wholly confiding in your holiness's goodness and affection, which you have ever shown to be truly paternal, fly to you as a suppliant, and most reverently beseech you; and more strenuously implore we the favour of the Apostolic See (which ought to be open to every Christian man, much more to a prince), that it deign to show itself compliant and forward in conceding our just and sacred cause; a cause, truly, wherein is at stake the continuation of our succession, the quiet (as the ruin) of our kingdom, and safety of our being. This is the favour, which alone, and now for the first time, we ask of your holiness and the holy see, and which ought not, cannot justly be denied to our piety and our efforts and endeavours for the Catholic cause.

Wherefore, from our very heart we pray your holiness that, if you love us, if you have ever held any services of ours acceptable—if, in short, our welfare, or even salvation concerns you, that you deign to relieve this so heavy anxiety of ours, and to lend a kind ear to these most just and proper entreaties; and by this benefit to bind us to you for ever. . . . (*Vitell. B. X, 80.*)

[1] i.e. the protonotary Gambara, Bishop Elect of Tortona, *not* 'the Reverend E. Terton' as Halliwell translates. I have used Halliwell's translation of these two notes (which he treats as one letter), but have made one or two minor corrections.

Forced by now to accept the fact of Anne, Wolsey sent with the new ambassadors precise instructions as to what they might say on the subject. The Pope, he fears, has been labouring under some misapprehension,

> as if the king had set on foot this cause, not from fear of his succession, but out of a vain affection or undue love to a gentlewoman of not so excellent qualities as she is here esteemed.

Further they may assure His Holiness that Wolsey would not

> for any earthly affection to his prince, or desire of reward, transgress the truth or swerve from the right path, nor would he have consented in any way to have reported to his Holiness otherwise than his conviction, which was of the insufficiency of the marriage.

He 'dare put his soul' that the King's desire

> is grounded upon justice, and not from any grudge of displeasure to the Queen, whom the King honours and loves, and minds to love and to treat as his sister, with all manner of kindness. Also as she is the relict of his dearest brother he will entertain her with all joy and felicity. But as this matrimony is contrary to God's law, the King's conscience is grievously offended. 'On the other side the approved, excellent virtuous [qualities] of the said gentlewoman [i.e. Anne], the purity of her life, her constant virginity, her maidenly and womanly pudicity, her soberness, chasteness, meekness, humility, wisdom, descent of right noble and high thorough regal blood, education in all good and laudable [qualities] and manners, apparent aptness to procreation of children, with her other infinite good qualities, more to be regarded and esteemed than the only progeny,'[1]

are the grounds of the King's desire, and Wolsey regards it as honest and necessary.

They were also told to say that there were deeper causes than

[1] From the Hatfield MSS. Quoted from *L.P.* IV. ii. 3913.

his love for Anne Boleyn at work in Henry's mind, and that moreover his will would assuredly be executed, whatsoever the reply from Rome.

Foxe and Gardiner reached Orvieto on March 21, 1528. In spite of all their efforts it was not until June 8 that a commission was finally secured, by which Wolsey and Cardinal Campeggio were to try the case in England and pronounce sentence. Appeals from their jurisdiction were forbidden, but the Pope still kept his power of revoking the case to Rome. While refusing the decretal commission, however, he gave the King a private and personal pledge in writing that he would not revoke the cause, and would not reverse the decision of Wolsey and Campeggio. What was even more important, he was finally persuaded to give Campeggio a decretal bull, on the strict understanding that no one should see it save Henry and Wolsey.

This was, in fact, the very thing for which they were striving—a declaration of law given by the Pope. In spite of all the political forces at work to confuse the issue, Henry's case was one which admitted of genuine doubt. Admitted that the Pope had power to dispense, necessity had to be shown. The English case was, that Julius II had been deceived as to the necessity for the original dispensation. It had been asserted, for example, that without it there was danger of war between England and Spain, when actually there was none, as was amply proved by the fact that no use was made of the dispensation until six years after it had been granted. Opinions, in fact, could and did honestly differ, both in Rome and England, as to the validity of Henry's marriage. In the decretal given to Campeggio, however, the Pope declared the circumstances in which his predecessor's dispensation must be held valid. It was valid only if it could be proved that Ferdinand was telling the truth when he declared that his daughter's marriage with Prince Arthur had never been consummated.[1]

While these concessions were being wrung from the Pope during April and May, Henry's agents were helped by a series of French victories in Italy, which for the moment served to over-

[1] See Lord Acton: *Wolsey and Henry VIII.* (*Historical Essays and Studies.* 1907.)

shadow the Emperor's power. By August the situation had been reversed, and by the time Campeggio arrived in England the Pope had gone over to the Emperor in order to save himself.

In the meantime, however, before following up the disastrous results for Henry which arose from this change in the European situation, it is interesting to listen to the defender of the Seven Sacraments lecturing his sister Margaret, the Scottish queen of errant amorous fancy. In March, 1527, Rome had granted her a divorce from her second husband, the Earl of Angus. The grounds given were ridiculously slight—a precontract (entirely unproven) on the part of Angus, and a preposterous story to the effect that James IV had not been killed at Flodden, and had still been alive when she married again. She was known to be living in adultery with Henry Stewart, who had already secured his divorce in order to be able to marry her. Nevertheless, Clement VII made no difficulty about annulling Margaret's marriage with Angus. This 'shameless sentence from Rome' outraged Henry's sense of decency. He believed in 'the divine ordinance of inseparable matrimony'. He was moved by the spectacle of his niece, the young Margaret Douglas, who was to be rendered baseborn, illegitimate, by the action of her own mother. His own case, obviously, was no just parallel, nor does he at any time appear to have been affected by his own daughter's similar misfortune. His conscience was fully convinced that he had been living in sin with Katharine, his brother's wife. Their so-called marriage was a nullity, had never existed. Fully conscious of his own right-mindedness, secure in his own unassailable position, he sends, through Wolsey, his brotherly rebukes and admonishments to the erring Margaret, beseeching her to avoid 'the inevitable damnation threatened against adulterers', and to be reconciled to her 'true married husband, for during his life ye may have none other by the law of God'.

To Queen Margaret

Most gracious and high renowned Queen,

Pleaseth your excellent goodness benignly to advertise, with favourable acceptation, the cause of my most necessary message unto your Grace from your only especial and entirely beloved Brother, my sovereign lord King of England, much concerning the wealth of your soul, and fame of your honourable estate; wherein, to persuade (your Excellency considered) no marvel if my unworthy rudeness may abash at such enterprise; albeit regarding the majesty of his Highness that hath sent me his goodly prepensed purpose and Christian desire so fervent toward your Grace, also the cause most reasonable, and so greatly urgent, hath somewhat strongly encouraged me to utter the matter. Trusting that the same undisceyvable spirit of God *qui operatur omnia in omnibus*, which moved his Highness to send unto you, shall effectually work. And in this your Grace may be assuredly persuaded, the mindful memory of love towards you, deeply to be engraved in the bottom of his breast, whose Highness, so far off by distance of place, so endued with felicity which oftentimes might cause oblivion, and continually busied with manifold weighty matters concerning the governance of his realm, yet nevertheless among such exceeding occasions of impediment hath never suffered the remembrance of your Grace to be absent from his heart, as well appeareth by his liberal readiness always in a preparement with diligent succour to condescend unto your necessity, not only in things behovable to the use of this mortal life, but also with godly advertisement to the increase of your immortal felicity, for the which his Highness looketh no further recompense than furtherance of your honour, correspondent to the nobility of your estate, agreeable with God's laws, which in this life he accounteth his chief glory, delight and comfort.

Wherefore it may please your Grace at the instant motion of his Highness (all disteynable persuasions of false flattering fautors and carnal affections put apart) to turn the sight of your soul unto God's word, the vyvely doctrine of Jesus Christ, the only ground of salvation, 1 Cor. iii. *no man can lay none other foundation than that is laid ready, which is Jesus Christ, he is the Rock,* Math. vii. Whereupon any building immoveably abideth. And unto this foundation behoveth your Grace to fashion the estate of your life, advertising the divine ordinance of inseparable matrimony first institute in Paradise between man and woman. Genesis ii. now for no cause to be sundered except alone for adultery.[1] And our Saviour confirming the same sayet'. Mat. xix. *truly I say unto you that whosoever forsaketh his wife except for adultery, and whosoever marrieth her that is forsaken committeth likewise adultery. . . .*

Your Grace should soon perceive how synystrally they seduced you with damnable delusion, which persuaded you to an unlawful divorce from lawful matrimony, directly against the ordinance of God, and utterly repugnant with man's law, as some of them which at that time were of your counsel have since acknowledged. For it is more manifest than can be denied, how that the causes alleged against the right noble Earl of Angus were untruly surmised of malice. Notwithstanding, in case they had been of verity able to be instesyed,[2] yet were they of no such urgent importancy reasonable to make a divorce between him and your Grace, inseparably knit together by the fast bond of just matrimony. *Quod deus coniunxit homo(non) separet.* Math. xix. Furthermore, the shameless sentence sent from Rome plainly discovereth how unlawfully it was handled, without order of justice, which sentence was given against the party neither personally present, nor in absence admitted to answer by a proctor.

Finally, if the Scriptures cannot move her

yet the natural love, the tender pity, and motherly kindness towards the fruit of your own body, your most dear child and natural daughter, cannot but provoke your Grace unto reconciliation, whose excellent beauty and pleasant behaviour, nothing less godly than goodly, furnished with virtues and womanly demeanours, after such a sort that it would relent and mollify a heart of steel, much more a motherly mind,

[1] *Marginal note.* So it be once lawfully and according to the truth of God's word contracted, consummated and established.

[2] Instesyed = ? instanced, i.e. urged, cited as proof.

which in your Grace, nature enforcing the same, ought largely to be showed. Moreover, what charge of conscience, what grudge and fretting, yea, what danger of damnation should it be to your soul, with perpetual infamy of your renown, slanderously to distain with dishonour so goodly a creature, so virtuous a lady, and namely your natural child, procreate in lawful matrimony, as to be reputed baseborn, which cannot otherwise be avoided, unless your Grace will (as in conscience ye are bound under peril of God's ever lasting indignation) to relinquish the adulterer's company with him that is not nor may not be of right your husband. . . .[1]

In the middle of June there was a very bad outbreak of the disease known as the 'sweating sickness', from which England had been free for some twelve years. People died like flies, especially in London and the home counties, and the Court kept moving from place to place to avoid the risk of infection. Even so, however, the disease claimed its victims from the King's household, and on June 16 one of Anne Boleyn's maids succumbed to the infection. It was the day the Court was due to remove to Waltham. Henry kept to his plan, taking with him only a few attendants, to lessen the danger of infection, and Anne was sent to Hever, in Kent, her father's household. After a few days at Waltham Henry removed to Hunsdon, from whence he wrote the following, sometime before June 22.

x. To Anne Boleyn

The unquietness I had from doubt of your good health troubled and distressed me not a little, and I should have had no rest had I not been ascertained thereof, but since as yet you have felt nothing I trust and am indeed well assured that it will cease where you are, as I trust it is doing here; for when we were at Waltham two ushers, two grooms-of-the-chamber, your brother and Master Treasurer sickened, and are now wholly

[1] Calig. B. VI, f. 225.

restored; and since then we have returned to our[1] house at Hunsdon, where we are right well bestowed without a single sick person at this hour, God be praised; and I believe that if you would retire from the parts of Surrey as we did you will pass it without danger. And there is also another thing that may comfort you, for in truth, as they say, few women or none have this malady, and, what is more, none of our court and but few elsewhere have died thereof. Wherefore I implore you, my entirely beloved, to have no fear at all, nor to let our absence too much vex you, for wheresoever I may be I am yours; and notwithstanding one must sometimes submit to such ill-fortune, for whoso will struggle against fate at such a point is full often the further off from his desire, nevertheless comfort yourself and take courage, and banish this distemper so far as you can, and then I trust full soon to make us exult in its dismissal.[2] No more at this present, for lack of time, but that I wish you in my arms, that I might a little relieve your inutile and vain[3] thoughts.

Written with the hand of him who is and always will be your

Im HR mutable.

Anne's brother, referred to in the letter, was George Boleyn, afterwards Viscount Rochford, who was finally to be involved in his sister's ruin, and executed on the charge of incest. Master Treasurer was Sir William Fitzwilliam, afterwards Earl of Southampton, who had been brought up with the King from childhood, and was always one of his most intimate associates.

On June 23 Heneage wrote to Wolsey from Hunsdon saying, 'This morning is told me that Mistress Anne and my Lord of Rochford had the sweat and was past the danger thereof.' It does not tell us on what day she and her father had sickened, but taken in conjunction with the letter from Henry which follows it looks as if the King had received the news on the evening of June 22. The physician whose absence Henry regrets was

[1] *The Pamphleteer's* reading *nostre* seems preferable to Crapelet's *vostre*.

[2] I believe this is a more probable translation of 'chanter le renvoi' than the usual 'sing the return'.

[3] *Déraisonable.* I have translated by Henry's own phrase in Letter No. XXI.

Dr. Chambers; to Anne he sent Dr. Butts, one of those Tudor personalities with whose countenance Holbein has made us familiar.

XI. To Anne Boleyn

News has come to me suddenly to-night, the most displeasant that could be brought, for the which for three reasons I must needs lament. The first, to hear of the illness of my mistress, whom I do esteem more than all the world, whose health I desire as much as mine own, and the half of whose malady I would willingly bear to have you healed thereof. The second, for the fear I have to be yet again longer oppressed by absence, mine enemy, which to this present hath done me all possible annoy, and in so far as I can judge is determined to do worse, though I pray God to rid me of such an importunate rebel. The third, because the physician in whom I put most trust is now at this time absent when he could most do me pleasure, for by him and his assistance I should hope to obtain one of my chief joys in this world, which is, to have my mistress healed. Nevertheless, for lack of him, I send you the second, who alone remains, praying God that he may soon restore your health, and I shall accordingly hold him even more closely in my affection. Beseeching you to be governed by his advices in all things concerning your malady, by which doing I trust soon to see you again, which to me will be more sovereign remedy than all the precious stones in the world. Written by that secretary who is and always will be

Your loyal and most assured servant,

H (AB) R.

Anne evidently recovered quickly, as there are no further allusions to her sickness in the letters. The one that follows belongs apparently to the end of June or the beginning of July.

XII. To Anne Boleyn

The cause of my writing at this time, good sweetheart, is only to understand of your good health and prosperity; whereof to know I would be as glad as in manner mine own, praying God (that and it be his pleasure) to send us shortly together, for I promise you I long for it. How be it, trust it shall not be long to; and seeing my darling is absent, I can no less do than to send her some flesh, representing my name, which is hart flesh for Henry, prognosticating that hereafter, God willing, you must enjoy some of mine, which, he pleased, I would were now.

As touching your sister's matter, I have caused Walter Welche to write to my lord mine mind therein, whereby I trust that Eve shall not have power to deceive Adam; for surely, whatsoever is said, it cannot so stand with his honour but that he must needs take her, his natural daughter, now in her extreme necessity.

No more to you at this time, mine own darling, but that with a wish I would we were together an evening.

With the hand of yours,

H.R.

By 'your sister's matter' the King means the death of his attendant, William Carey, the husband of Mary Boleyn, which took place on the twenty-second, a few days after the move to Hunsdon. Henry removed again, on June 26, to Wolsey's house of Tittenhanger near Bishop's Hatfield; and it is quite evident from the tone of the following letters that, as yet, the Cardinal stood as high as ever in the royal favour and esteem. Though actually penned by secretaries both letters are personal and friendly, and show clearly the genuine regard which had hitherto always been the note of their relationship.

To Wolsey

[1528.]

. . . This morning, at 7 of the clock, I delivered Your Grace's letters to the King's Highness; wherewith I assure Your Grace, His Highness was greatly comforted, and giveth unto Your Grace hearty thanks for the same, and especially for the good news he hath out of Italy from Mr. Doctor Stevyns.[1] And this morning he hath word that my lady Marquess of Exeter is sick of the common sickness, which causeth His Highness to appoint to remove, upon Saturday, from hence to Ampthill, and hath commanded that all such as were in my said Lord Marquis' company and my said Lady, to depart in several parcels, and so not continue together; and so he desireth Your Grace to do, if any such case shall fortune, as God forbid. And glad he is to hear that Your Grace hath so good a heart, and that you have determined and made your will, and ordered your self anenst God, as you have done, as His Highness hath semblable done; which will he intendeth shortly to send unto Your Grace, wherein Your Grace shall see and perceive the trusty and hearty mind that he hath unto you above all men living. And also, this morning, His Highness hath knowledge of the death of one of his Chapel, which had divers promotions of his gift, and of yours by reason of the Chancellorship, which he desireth you to forbear the gift of any of them, unto such time that Your Grace have knowledge of his further pleasure in them. And also he desireth Your Grace that he may hear every second day from you, how you do; for I assure you, every morning, as soon as he cometh from the Queen, he asketh whether I hear any thing from Your Grace. . . . Written at Your Grace's house at Tittenhanger this Thursday, the 9th day of July, by your humble and most bounden servant,

THOMAS HENEAGE.[2]

Heneage, afterwards Sir Thomas, was one of various likely men originally chosen by the Cardinal for his own service, and later, when his usefulness had been proved, ' transferred ' to the King's. Bryan Tuke, who wrote the letter from which the following extracts are taken, was one of Henry's secretaries

[1] i.e. Stephen Gardiner.
[2] Quoted from *S.P.* I, p. 312.

whom the King kept constantly with him at this time, and who afterwards suffered from the sickness and recovered.

So most humbly thanking His Highness, I read forth till it came to the latter end, mentioning Your Grace's good comfort and counsel given to His Highness for avoiding this infection, for the which the same, with a most cordial manner, thanked Your Grace; and shewing me, first, a great process of the manner of that infection; how folks were taken; how little danger was in it, if good order be observed; how few were dead of it; how Mistress Anne and my Lord of Rochford both have had it; what jeopardy they have been in, by returning in of the sweat before the time; of the endeavour of Sir Butts, who hath been with them, and is returned; with many other things touching those matters and, finally, of their perfect recovery. His Highness willed me to write unto Your Grace, most heartily desiring the same, above all other things, to keep Your Grace out of all air where any of that infection is, and that if in one place any one fall sick thereof, that Your Grace incontinently do remove to a clean place; and so, in like case, from that place to another, and with a small and clean company: saying, that that is the thing whereby His Highness hath purged his house, having the same now, thanked be God, clean. And over that, His Highness desireth Your Grace to use small suppers, and to drink little wine, namely that is big, and once in the week to use the pills of Rasis; and if it come in any wise, to sweat moderately the full time, without suffering it to run in; which, by Your Grace's physicians, with a possetale, having certain herbs clarified in it, shall facilly, if need be, be provoked and continued; with more good wholesome counsel by His Highness in most tender and loving manner given to Your Grace than my simple wit can suffice to rehearse; which his gracious commandment I said I would accomplish accordingly. . . .

The letter of my Lady, the French king's mother, to Your Grace, the King's Grace thought also very prudently, well, and truly couched. All which things read, being then 11 of the clock at night, His Grace said he would see the news of Spain this day. Howbeit, His Grace is not yet come down, for His Highness cometh by my chamber door, and doth for the most part, going and coming, turn in, for the devising with me upon his book, and other things occurrant.

As I was at this word, His Highness came down, and straight into my chamber, asking me how near I had done; and I showed His Highness how far forth I am; and thereupon did put His Grace in remembrance to see the news of Spain, and to sign the King of Scots' letter, which His Grace saith he will do soon, and is gone a walking.[1]

The three letters that now follow, all belonging to the early days of July, make an interesting group. 'The matter of Wilton', to which Henry at once refers in his letter to Anne, is really the occasion of all three. The Abbess of Wilton Priory had died in April, and John Carey, Mary Boleyn's brother-in-law, seconded by Anne, had asked for the vacant appointment for his sister Eleanor, who was one of the Wilton nuns. The King, naturally, was eager to please his beloved; Wolsey, to whom the election had been committed, had been approached by the Boleyn-Carey group, and was ready to befriend them. Then came the discovery that Dame Eleanor was a woman of unchaste life: whereupon Henry at once wrote to Anne to explain the impossibility of such an appointment. Like most of the love-letters in which he happens to deal with practical matters, it is written in English. It is generally only for courtship and compliment that he finds French preferable.

XIII. To Anne Boleyn

[*July*, 1528.]

Since your last letters, mine own darling, Walter Welshe, Master Brown, John Carey, Yrion of Brearton,[2] and John Cocke,

[1] Titus B. I, f. 305-306.

[2] Walter Welsh, John Carey, and Yrion (or Urien) Brereton were all grooms of the King's Chamber, whose business it was to assist the Gentlemen of the Privy Chamber who were the King's personal attendants. Master Browne was Sir Anthony Browne, one of the Gentlemen of the Chamber.

the apothecary, be fallen of the sweat in this house, and thanked be God, all well recovered, so that as yet the plague is not fully ceased here, but I trust shortly it shall. By the mercy of God, the rest of us yet be well, and I trust shall pass it, either not to have it, or at the least, as easily as the rest have done.

As touching the matter of Wilton, my lord Cardinal hath had the nuns before him and examined them, Mr. Bell being present; which hath certified me that, for a truth, that she had confessed herself (which we would have had abbess) to have had two children by two sundry priests; and further, since hath been kept by a servant of the Lord Broke that was, and that not long ago. Wherefore I would not, for all the gold in the world, clog your conscience nor mine to make her ruler of a house, which is of so ungoodly demeanour; nor, I trust, you would not that neither for brother nor sister I should so distain mine honour or conscience. And as touching the prioress, or Dame Eleanor's eldest sister, though there is not any evident case proved against them, and that the prioress is so old that of many years she could not be as she was named; yet notwithstanding, to do you pleasure, I have done that neither of them shall have it, but that some other good and well-disposed woman shall have it, whereby the house shall be the better reformed (whereof I ensure you it had much need), and God much the better served.

As touching your abode at Hever, do therein as best shall like you, for you know best what air doth best with you; but I would it were come thereto (if it pleased God), that neither of us need care for that, for I ensure you I think it long. Suche is fallen sick of the sweat, and therefore I send you this bearer, because I think you long to hear tidings from us, as we do in likewise from you.

Written with the hand de votre seul,

H.R.

The Convent itself, as Wolsey knew, favoured their own Prioress, Isabel Jordan. Scandal was promptly set on foot to ruin her reputation, as Dame Eleanor's had been ruined: and the Carey party put up another candidate, Dame Eleanor's elder sister. To settle the matter Henry decided that neither of the rivals should have the appointment, and apparently informed Wolsey of his desire. For some reason, however, Wolsey proceeded to appoint Isabel Jordan, and sent the appointment to the King to be confirmed. The following is Henry's rebuke to the Cardinal—dignified and measured, and combining the relations of monarch and friend without injury to either. Dr. Brewer describes it as 'not less honourable to the King than the Cardinal'; and it is in every way one of the most sincere and candid of Henry's utterances that has been recorded.

XIV. To Wolsey

[*July*, 1528.]

The great affection and love I bear you causeth me (ensuing the doctrine of my Master, saying *Quem diligo castigo*) thus plainly as now ensueth to break to you my mind, ensuring you that neither sinister report, affection to my own pleasure, interest parts, nor mediation of any other body beareth place in this case; wherefore whatsoever I do say, I pray think it spoken of no displeasure, but of him that would you as much good both of body and soul as you would yourself.

Methink it is not the right train of a trusty loving friend and servant, when the matter is put by the master's consent into his arbitre and judgement (specially in a matter wherein his master hath both royalty and interest) to elect and choose a person which was by him defended; and yet another thing which much displeaseth me more, that is, to cloak your offence made by ignorance of my pleasure, saying that you expressly know not my determinate mind in that behalf. Alas, my lord, what can be more evident or plainer than these words (specially to a wise man), 'His Grace careth not who, but referreth it all to you; so that none of those who either be or have been at any time noted or spotted with incontinence (like as by report the Prioress hath been in her youth) have it'; and also in another place of the letter which sayeth, 'and therefore his highness thinketh her not most meet for that purpose'. Thirdly, in another place of the said letter by these words, 'and though his grace speaketh it not so openly, yet meseemeth his pleasure is that in no wise the Prioress have it, nor yet Dame Elinor's eldest sister for many considerations, the which your grace both can and will best consider'. And, my Lord, it is a double offence both to do ill, and colour it too, but with men that have wit it cannot be accepted so; wherefore, good my Lord, use no more that way with me, for there is no man living that more hateth it; these things being thus committed, either I must have reserved them *in pectore*, whereby more displeasure might happen to breed; or else thus roundly and plainly to declare them to you, because that I do think, that *cum amico et familiari sincere semper est agendum*, and specially the Master to his best beloved servant and friend. For in so doing, the one shall be the more circumspect in his doing, the other shall declare and show the loathness that is in him to have any occasion to be displeased with him. And as touching the redress of religion, (if it be observed and continued) undoubtedly it is a gracious act, notwithstanding if all reports be true, *ab imbecillis imbecilla expectantur*; howbeit Mr. Benet hath informed me that her age, personage, and manner *prae se fert gravitatem.* I pray God it be so indeed, seeing that she is preferred to that room. I understand furthermore, (which greatly to my comfort), that you have ordered yourself to godward as religiously and virtuously as any prelate or father of Christ's Church can do; wherein so doing and persevering there can nothing more be acceptable to God, more honour to yourself, nor more desired of your friends, amongst the which I reckon not myself the least.

Since hitherto I have played both the part of a master and friend me-thinketh, yet once more I must occupy the same, desiring you to take it in good part; for surely I do it upon no other ground but for the wealth of your soul and mind; and because I dare be bolder with you than a great many that mumble it abroad, and to the intent that I would that the foundation by you meant and begun, should take felice and prosperous success. Surely it is reckoned that much of the good that buildeth the same should not be the best acquisite and gotten, reckoning it to come from many a religious house unlawfully, bearing the cloak of kindness toward the edifying of your College; which kindness cannot sink in many a man's heart to be in them, since that those same religious houses would not grant to their Sovereign in his necessity, not by a great deal, so much as they have to you for building of your College. These things bear shrewd appearance, for except they have accustomed to have some benefit for it, they nor no other that ever I heard of have used to show that kindness, *tam enim est aliena ab eis ipsa humanitas*; but of this case your conscience can be best judge *semota affectione* and substantial scrutiny made of the endeavour of those which you put in trust, in meddling with the religious houses, for I trust verily that if anything be amiss, it is more long of them than of you. Notwithstanding I am sure you know that *in talibus ignorantia non excusat peccatum*; wherefore I doubt not but that you will make such ensearch and reformation and need be, that it shall be to the exoneration of your conscience before God. I pray you, my Lord, think not that it is upon any displeasure that I write this unto you. For surely, it is first for my discharge afore God, being in the room that I am in; and secondly for the great zeal I bear unto you, not undeserved of your behalf, wherefore I pray you take it so; and I ensure you, your fault acknowledged, there shall remain in me no spark of displeasure. Trusting hereafter you shall recompense that with a thing much more acceptable to me; and thus fare you well; advertising you that, (thanked be God), both I and all my folk be, and have been ever since we came to Ampthill, which was on Saturday last,[1] in marvellous good health and cleanness of air. Written with the hand of him that is, and shall be, your loving Sovereign Lord and friend.

HENRY R.

Wolsey must have replied immediately, with full explanations and apologies, the tenor of which can be gathered from the beginning of Henry's next letter. Wolsey's enemies had already begun to set abroad discreditable rumours about his methods of raising money from the religious houses for his college at Oxford. That the suspicion had stuck in Henry's mind is evident from this second letter, which concluded the episode, and which again shows Henry at his best, dealing, as he himself believed, ' an entire loving friend and master should do to another '.

[1] July 11, 1528.

XV. To Wolsey

[*July*, 1528.]

As touching the matter of Wilton, seeing it is in no other strain than you write of, and you being also so suddenly (with the falling sick of your servants) afraid and troubled; I marvel not that it overslipped you as it did. But it is no great matter, standing the case as it doth; for it is yet in my hand, as I perceive by your letter; and your default was not so great, seeing the election was but conditional. Wherefore, my Lord, seeing the humbleness of your submission, and though the case were much more heinous, I can be content for to remit it, being right glad, that, according to mine intent, my monitions and warnings have been benignly and lovingly accepted on your behalf, promising you that the very affection I bear you caused me thus to do.

As touching the help of Religious Houses to the building of your College, I would it were more, so it be lawfully; for my intent is none but that it should so appear to all the world, and the occasion of all their mumbling might be secluded and put away; for, surely, there is great murmuring of it throughout all the realm, both good and bad. They say not that all that is ill gotten is bestowed upon the College, but that the College is the cloak for covering all mischiefs. This grieveth me, I assure you, to hear it spoken by him which I so entirely love. Wherefore methought I could do no less than thus friendly to admonish you. One thing more I perceive by your own letter, which a little methinketh toucheth conscience, and that is, that you have received money of the exempts for having of their old Visitors. Surely this can hardly be with good conscience. For, and they were good, why should you take money? And if they were ill, it were a sinful act. Howbeit your Legacy herein might, peradventure, *apud Homines* be a Cloak, but not *apud Deum*. Wherefore, you, thus monished by him who so entirely loveth you, I doubt not, will desist, not only from this, (if conscience will not bear it), but from all other things which should tangle the same; and, in so doing, we will sing, *te laudant angeli atque Archangeli, te laudant omnis Spiritus*. And thus an end I make of this, though rude, yet loving letter; desiring you as benevolently to take it as I do mean it, for I ensure you, (and I pray you think it so), that there remaineth, at this hour, no spark of displeasure towards you in my heart. And thus fare you well, and be no more perplexed. Written with the hand of your loving Sovereign and Friend, HENRY R.

During July, while the King was at Ampthill, Anne still kept away from court; but the letter which follows indicates that Henry was expecting soon to be with her again.

XVI. TO ANNE BOLEYN

Darling, I heartily recommend me to you, ascertaining you that I am not a little perplexed with such things as your brother shall on my part declare unto you, to whom I pray you give full credence, for it were too long to write. In my last letters I writ to you that I trusted shortly to see you, which is better known at London than with any that is about me, whereof I not a little marvel; but lack of discreet handling must needs be the cause thereof. No more to you at this time, but that I trust shortly our meetings shall not depend upon other men's light handlings, but upon your own.

Written with the hand of him that longeth to be yours,

H.R.

This and the note which follows were both written in English, and the latter helps us to date their next meeting. Heneage, in a letter to Wolsey dated July 21, writes, 'My Lady Rochford and Mrs. Anne cometh this week to the court', and they were obviously together when the next letter was written, as Henry's note is really only the postscript of a letter from Anne to Wolsey. The reference to the arrival in France of the legate Campeggio means that the letter itself must belong to the last few days of July or the first week of August. Campeggio left Cornuto to cross to Provence on July 24 or 25, and by August 22 had travelled through Provence and reached Lyons.

XVII. To Cardinal Wolsey[1]

[*July-Aug.*, 1528.]

The writer of this letter would not cease till she had [caused me likewise] to set to my hand; desiring you, though it be short, to t[ake it in good part.] I ensure you there is neither of us but that greatly desire[th to see you, and] much more rejoice to hear that you have scaped this plague s[o well, trusting] the fury thereof to be passed, specially with them that keep[eth good diet,] as I trust you do.

The not hearing of the Legate's arrival in [France causeth] us somewhat to muse; notwithstanding, we trust by your diligе[nce and vigilancy] (with the assistance of almighty God) shortly to be eased out [of that trouble.] No more to you at this time; but that I pray God send you [as good health] and prosperity as the writers would.

By your loving so[vereign and] friend,

Henry [R.].

After this meeting early in August another parting intervened, this time, apparently, brief. The next letter—again in English—suggests that a new stage in their relationship had been reached. It is much more intimate than any of those that precede it. Knowing that Campeggio was well started on his journey to England Anne had probably begun to feel more secure. She had ceased to be the solitary damsel, tossed in seas of doubt. Henry was no longer held at a distance. It would probably, however, be a mistake to infer from his frank expressions that she had already become his mistress. She and her family were playing for high stakes, nothing less than a crown; and there is everything to show that at no stage was any precipitate action allowed to endanger the ultimate achievement. And though it may not altogether fit in with the popular idea of Henry VIII, it is reasonable to surmise that, at this period of his courtship, he was as much the protector of Anne's 'virtue' as she herself. He had made up his vigorous Tudor mind that she was to be

[1] Vitellius B. XII (4). Badly damaged. Lacunæ, in square brackets, supplied from Burnet, *History of the Reformation* (ed. Pocock) I, ii, 55.

his wife, and the mother of the heir of England. The tenacity with which he fought for a sanction which could admit no possibility of after-doubts concerning the validity of his divorce and the legitimacy of that heir, suggests that his idealism and his practical sense both combined to dominate the situation.

xviii. To Anne Boleyn

Mine own sweetheart, this shall be to advertise you of the great elengeness[1] that I find here since your departing; for I ensure you methinketh the time longer since your departing now last than I was wont to do a whole fortnight. I think your kindness and my fervency of love causeth it; for otherwise I would not have thought it possible that for so little a while it should have grieved me. But now that I am coming towards you, methinketh my pains be half released, and also I am right well comforted in so much that my book maketh substantially for my matter; in looking whereof I have spent above four hours this day, which caused me now to write the shorter letter to you at this time, because of some pain in my head; wishing myself (specially an evening) in my sweetheart's arms, whose pretty dukkys[2] I trust shortly to cusse.[3]

Written with the hand of him that was, is, and shall be yours by his will,

H.R.

It looks as if this letter and the one which follows both belong to the same ' gap of time ' at the end of the summer, just before Henry lodged her at Greenwich some time in the autumn.

xix. To Anne Boleyn

Darling,

Though I have scant leisure, yet, remembering my promise, I thought it convenient to certify you briefly in what case our affairs stand. As touching a lodging for you, we have gotten one by my lord cardinal's means, the like whereof could not have been found hereabouts for all causes, as this bearer shall

[1] Elengeness = loneliness. [2] Dukkys = breasts. [3] Cusse = kiss.

more show you. As touching our other affairs, I ensure you there can be no more done, nor more diligence used, nor all manner of dangers better both foreseen and provided for, so that I trust it shall be hereafter to both our comforts, the specialties whereof were both too long to be written, and hardly by messenger to be declared. Wherefore, till your repair hither, I keep something[1] in store, trusting it shall not be long to; for I have caused my lord, your father, to make his provisions with speed; and thus, for lack of time, darling, I make an end of my letter, written with the hand of him which I would were yours.

H.R.

The book to which Henry refers in the earlier of these two letters was the treatise in defence of his divorce which he was at this time composing, and with which he frequently busied himself in the evenings. (See above, p. 73.) The days were devoted to hunting; and business was much left to Wolsey; though here again it is obvious, from Tuke's letter quoted above, that Henry himself looked closely into all matters of foreign policy.

His relations with Wolsey were still extremely cordial, as is evident from a letter written for him by Heneage, from which the following is a brief extract:

Sept. 25, 1528.

> Humbly showeth unto your Grace, The King's Highness commendeth him heartily unto you, and glad he is that you liked your pastime in hunting so well as ye did at your last being with his Grace; and of his own mind hath devised that your Grace shall come hither upon Monday next, to the intent that he and you may have pastime together for two or three days. . . .[2]

Meanwhile, Cardinal Campeggio was on his way to England. Although the commission appointing him to act with Wolsey had been granted in April, it was June before his illness allowed him to start. He suffered greatly from bad attacks of gout, which genuinely incapacitated him for the conduct of business;

[1] *The Pamphleteer* reads *that thing*

[2] Quoted from *S.P.* I, p. 325.

and although any and every delay was exactly what the Pope wanted, and had, indeed, enjoined, nevertheless by September 18 he had left Paris to start on the final stage of his journey. A few days earlier Henry sent Anne news of the legate's progress.

XX. To Anne Boleyn

[*Sept.*, 1529.]

The reasonable request of your last letter, with the pleasure also that I take to know them true, causeth me to send you now these news. The legate which we most desire arrived at Paris on Sunday or Monday last past, so that I trust by the next Monday to hear of his arrival at Calais; and then I trust within a while after to enjoy that which I have so longed for, to God's pleasure, and our both comforts.

No more to you at this present, mine own darling, for lack of time, but that I would you were in mine arms, or I in yours, for I think it long since I kissed you.

Written after the killing of an hart, at eleven of the clock, (minding, with God's grace, to-morrow, mightily timely to kill another) by the hand[1] which I trust shortly shall be yours.

HENRY R.

During the last few months of 1528 no secret of their relationship was made any longer. He lodged her first at Greenwich, in what was practically royal state, probably early in the autumn. The French ambassador, writing on December 9, informs his master that 'Mademoiselle Boleyn' has come to London, and 'the King has lodged her in a very fine lodging, which he has furnished very near his own. Greater court is paid to her every day than has been for a long time paid to the Queen'. It is, therefore, to some time subsequent to Campeggio's arrival on October 8, and prior to Du Bellay's letter of December that the following letter to Anne must be assigned.

[1] *The Pamphleteer* reads *hand of him*

XXI. To Anne Boleyn

[*Oct.*, 1528.]

To inform you what joy it is to me to understand of your conformableness to reason, and of the suppressing of your inutile and vain thoughts and fantasies with the bridle of reason. I ensure you all the good in this world could not counterpoise for my satisfaction the knowledge and certainty thereof. Wherefore, good sweetheart, continue the same, not only in this, but in all your doings hereafter; for thereby shall come, both to you and me, the greatest quietness that may be in this world.

The cause why this bearer tarrieth so long is the business that I have had to dress up gear for you; which I trust, ere long, to cause you occupy; and then I trust to occupy yours; which shall be recompense enough to me for all my pains and labours.

The unfeigned sickness of this well-willing legate doth somewhat retard his access to your presence; but I trust verily, when God shall send him health, he will with diligence recompense his demur. For I know well where he hath said (lamenting the saying and bruit that he should be imperial) that it should be well known in this matter that he is not imperial. And thus, for lack of time, sweetheart farewell. Written with the hand which fain would be yours, and so is the heart.

H.R.

Anne's return to court was permanent this time; and this, written in English, is the last of the love-letters. They provide a unique personal interlude in the midst of the King's otherwise unfailingly business-like correspondence. The letters which now follow, and which tell the rest of the story of the divorce, tell it in the language of official documents.

CHAPTER III

'THE HIGHEST AND SUPREME COURT'

Though the law of every man's conscience be but a private court, yet it is the highest and supreme court for judgement or justice.

HENRY VIII.

CAMPEGGIO arrived in London on October 8, and the letter he despatched on the twenty-eighth to Salviati, the Pope's secretary, shows clearly the position of affairs, as also the Pope's intentions. It is of such vital interest at this point of the story that no excuse need be made for translating two substantial extracts. In his interview with the King, so he writes:

> Secondly, we argued and discussed whether the prohibition belonged to Divine law, or whether it was possible for the Pope to dispense therein; and, given the possibility, whether such dispensation would be good and valid. And in effect His Majesty has studied this matter with such diligence that I believe in this case he knows more about it than a great theologian or jurist: and he told me briefly and in the plainest terms that he wanted nothing but a declaration whether the marriage was valid or not, he himself presupposing always its invalidity; and I believe that if an angel was to descend from heaven he would not be able to persuade him to the contrary. We then discussed the proposal to persuade the Queen to agree to enter some approved religious house. And this solution was extremely pleasing to him, for which, indeed, there are the strongest arguments; and amongst others, the Queen will only lose the use of the King's person thereby, which she has already lost these two years, and he will not return to her, however things may fall out. In everything else His Majesty will allow her whatever she would like to demand, and above all will settle the succession upon her daughter, in the event of his not having male heirs by another marriage.

He then discussed the situation with Katharine, and admitted the truth of her accusation that they were anxious to persuade her to enter some religious order:

Which I did not deny, and tried to persuade her that it rested in her hands, by doing this, to settle the whole matter in such a way that it would be satisfactory to God and her own conscience, to the glory and fame of her own name; and that she would by this means secure her honours and worldly possessions, and above all would secure the succession of her daughter: while at the same time she would lose nothing by it, as she had already lost the King as a husband and I knew she could not recover him. It would be better, I suggested, to yield to his displeasure rather than risk the danger of a sentence—considering how great her grief and trouble would be if it went against her, and how derogatory it would be to her honour and reputation. She would lose her dowry, because in her matrimonial treaties it was concluded that the dowry was not recoverable on the dissolution of the marriage, in whatever way. She should consider also the scandals and enmities that were bound to ensue. On the other hand, instead of all these inconveniences which ought to be avoided, she would preserve her dowry, her jewels, the guardianship of her daughter, her own rank of Princess, everything, in short, that she wished to demand from the King, without offending either God or her own conscience. And I alleged the example of the former Queen of France, who did the same thing, and still lives in the greatest honour and respect before God and that whole kingdom.[1]

Although Henry and Wolsey saw the decretal bull (p. 64) brought by Campeggio its actual utility was nil. In December Clement sent orders for its destruction, which the Cardinal presumably obeyed; and about the time of Campeggio's arrival (October, 1528) a document was discovered which served as yet another cause of delay.

Katharine was informed that in Spain there was a brief of Julius II,[2] much fuller than the original bull of dispensation,

[1] Translated from Laemmer's *Monumenta Vaticana*, p. 25. Campeggio to Sanga (actually, Salviati), 17 Oct. 1528. *L.P.* IV. 4858. For date see *E.H.R.* XII. p. 11.

[2] According to Gairdner (*The English Church in the Sixteenth Century*) this was the brief originally sent to Isabella by Julius II. He also states that Ferdinand sent it on, at the time, to Henry VII.

which supplied any and all of the bull's defects. Neither Wolsey, Campeggio, Henry nor the Pope had heard of its existence, nor, without seeing it, could any one know if it was genuine. Once its nature had been clearly stated, however, it became imperative for Henry to have it pronounced a forgery, for the simple reason that it was free from all the technical flaws upon which he had grounded his case.

Campeggio having entirely failed to move either Henry or Katharine, Wolsey tackled the question of the brief at the end of 1528. Fresh instructions were dispatched to Rome for the English ambassadors to explore all other possibilities, supposing the worst, in the shape of the brief's undoubted authenticity, should have, ultimately, to be faced.

1. To Bryan and Vannes[1]

[*Dec.* 1, 1528.]

. . . In which meantime the King's said orators shall secretly retain of the best advocates that they can get in the Court of Rome, to be of the King's counsel, and on his Grace's part making them sure by secret rewards, pact, and convention that afterwards they shall not be allured or drawn to the adverse part; by whose learning, experience and knowledge they shall instruct themselves perfectly and substantially against the coming of the King's said principal secretary. Whether if the Queen, for the great and manifold benefits that may ensue thereof, can be moved and induced to take vow of chastity, or enter into lape [*sic* i.e. lax] religion, the Pope's holiness may, *ex plenitudine potestatis* dispense with the King's Highness to proceed thereupon, *ad secundas nuptias*, and the children to be procreate in the same to be legitimate.. And though it be thing that the Pope percase may not do, stonding such laws as be already written, both divine and human, and using his ordinary power, yet whether his holiness may do it of his mere and absolute power, as thing

[1] A 6-page extract from a 24-page letter, beginning f. 172. Lacunæ caused by burns are not noted when they may properly be supplied from Harpsfield.

that the same may dispense in above the laws, must perfectly and secretly be understanden and known. And what precedent hath been seen of like matter, or how the court of Rome shall define and determine. And what it doth use, or may do therein, so that it may perfectly and assuredly appear that none exception, no scruple, question or doubt can or may be found or alleged hereafter in any thing that may or shall be affirmed, to be in the Pope's power touching that matter.

Semblably, forasmuch as it is like that the Queen shall make marvellous difficulty and in no wise be conformable to enter religion or take vow of chastity, but that to induce her thereunto there must be ways and means of high policy used, and all things possible devised to encourage her to the same, wherein percase she shall resolve that she in no wise will condescend so to do, unless than the King's Highness also do the semblable for his part. The King's said orators shall therefore in likewise ripe and instruct themselves by their secret learned counsel in the court of Rome, if for so great a benefit to ensue unto the King's succession, realm and subjects, with the quiet of his conscience, his Grace should promise so to enter religion or vow of chastity for his part, only thereby to conduce the Queen thereunto, whether in that case the Pope's holiness may dispense with the King's Highness for the same promise, oath or vow, discharging his Grace clearly of the same, and thereupon to proceed *ad secunda vota cum legitimatione prolis* as is aforesaid.

Furthermore, to provide surely to all events, as well *propter conceptum odium*, as for the danger that may ensue to the King's person by continuance of his Grace in the Queen's company, whose body his Grace for marvellous great and secret respects is utterly resolved and determined never to use; if it shall be found and appear assuredly that the Pope may in no wise dispense with the King to proceed *ad secunda vota,* the Queen being alive in religion, but that she, being in religion or without, shall still be reputed as his wife. Then shall the King's said orators perfectly inquire and insearch whether the Pope's holiness may dispense with his Grace, upon the great considerations that rest herein, to have *duas uxores*. And that the children of the second matrimony shall be as well legitimate as those of the first; wherein some great reasons and precedents, specially of the Old Testament appear. So that the King's said orators, thus secretly riped[1] what the Pope's holiness may do herein, may be in the better readiness at the coming of Sir Secretary and Dr. Benet to inform them of the same. And thereupon to do further as the instructions to be given to the same Sir Secretary and Dr. Benet shall purport. In which meantime they shall not also let to advertise the King's Highness and the said Lord Legate by post and in ciphers what they shall may know and understand in all and singular the premises. So handling the same with secrecy, dexterity and policy as they shall perceive by their wisdoms to serve best to the conducing of the King's purpose. Foreseeing always, principally and above all other things, that in making of any privy search, conducting of advocates or learned counsel, offering of rewards or entertainment, or otherwise, they use such high circumspection as the King's cause be not thereby published or known, to the hindrance, slander or empeachment of his Grace's intent, using and proponing always the King's case as it were another man's, by mean whereof they shall know and perceive the likelihood of the same, and have them without fear or respect of the Emperor to speak the more frankly and liberally therein.

At the ' best opportunity ' they are to assure the Pope of the King's entire love, and his care for the dignity of the Holy See, as a prince who from the beginning of his reign has done everything he could for the Pope, and who

besides all his study, good will and travail, hath expended more great sums of money and treasure than all the princes christened have done, worthy, therefore, of thank reward, of the grace of the Church, and of due respect and consideration to be had thereunto accordingly. That is to say, like as the merits of his Grace towards the See Apostolic be incomparable above the same of any other prince; so the treasure of the same See and Church ought in the highest and most abundant manner to be liberally and bountifully extended to his Highness before any other prince.

[1] Instructed.

And not to be restrained or minced with the quiddities and discrepant opinions of the laws. And since the Pope's holiness hath been by [ ] ways assuredly ascertained, how much to heart his Highness hath this matter of the insufficiency of matrimony between his Grace and the Queen, as the thing that more near and highly toucheth his Grace, and doth pierce the bottom of his mind than anything that ever [succeeded] or may succeed to his Highness and Realm, whereupon a [ ] depend so great and notable consequences. They shall say his Holiness well counselled, profoundly examining with himself, and substantially weighing the premises, cannot do too much for so noble, gentle, great and so loving a prince, specially in so great and weighty a matter. And that surely of good congruence and obligation his Holiness oweth all in due respects [ ] and put apart to show unto his Majesty a special and singular grace herein, such one as may correspond to the excellence of his acts, deserts, and merits. Beseeching therefore his Holiness, on my Lord Cardinal's behalf, most humbly and in most affectuous wise upon his knees, to have that thing in his special recommendation. Resolving with himself to do therein for comprobation of the due respect and consideration that his Holiness hath to the King's said merits, according to his Grace's trust, confidence and expectation. As the King's Highness and other princes, his friends and confederates, their nobles, realms and subjects, may thereby be encouraged to do for his Holiness and the said See, thinking their acts therein well collocate and employed. And the said Sir Peter, as of himself, shall apart say unto his Holiness, Sir, I being an Italian cannot but with a more fervent zeal and mind than any other study and desire the weal, honour and surety of your Holiness and the See Apostolic, which compelleth me to show unto your Holiness frankly what I see in this matter. Surely, Sir, in case your Holiness continuing this particular respect of fear of the Emperor, do thus delay, protract and put over the accomplishment of the King's so instant desire in this matter, and not impart unto his Majesty therein bounteously of the treasure and grace of the Church and See Apostolic *quantum potestis ex thesauro ecclesiae, et ex plenitudine potestatis auctoritate a Deo vestrae sanctitati collata*, I see assuredly that it will be a mean so to aliene the fast and entire mind which his Highness beareth to your said Holiness, as not only thereby his Grace, nobles and realm, but also many other princes, his friends and confederates, with their nobles and realms shall withdraw their devotion and obedience from your Holiness and the See Apostolic, studying how they may acquit this your ingratitude in the highest cause that can be devised, showed and so long continued with the semblable. And therefore Sir, at the reverence of Almighty God, cast not from you the heart of this noble virtuous prince, who finally cannot fail, the peace had which Christendom may not long forbear, to have in his puissance such a stay as may be able in the highest and largest manner to recompense his friends and acquit the contrary.

HENRY R.

Having thus provided for the worst, Wolsey and the King turned their attention to the brief itself. If it should prove authentic it was absolutely essential to prevent it being used at the trial; the original, therefore, must be secured. But the original was safe in the Spanish archives; and it was not to be expected that Charles would allow it to go out of his possession. Presumably by Wolsey's advice, but certainly with Henry's concurrence, Katharine herself was to be made the author of her own undoing. She was to be persuaded into writing to the Emperor to say that the production of the original was essential for the success of her case. The following are the instructions for this piece of chicanery, labelled 'A device to be given to the Queen's Grace by her counsellors'. (P.R.O., S.P. I., § 50, f. 212.)

Forasmuch as your Grace now late did show unto us of your counsel the copy of a bull and a brief concerning your marriage . . . which after his Grace and his Council had seen and considered, forasmuch as after due search made in his treasury no like brief can be founden, but a bull only, they by many presumptuous moving them in that behalf do think the said brief whereof ye show the copy, to be but forged and counterfeited;

which thing, if the original were seen, and well and duly examined, they think would so appear. And whensoever process shall begin against you the bringing forth and exhibiting only of the seen copy can little or nothing help you . . . Wherefore seeing the King's Highness cannot nor yet ought not to be satisfied with the said copy ye must endeavour yourself by all good means to you possible, both for his satisfaction, and chiefly for the advancement of your cause, and as ye tender the continuance of love between the King's Highness and your Grace, to attain the original of your said copy, now being in the Emperor's custody which is thought ye may facilly obtain of him, if ye will apply your good mind and will thereto.

She is to explain the King's 'great scruple', the unsatisfactory replies of the learned doctors consulted, and the referring of the cause to the Pope and the appointment of the legatine commission.

Wherefore ye most humbly desire his Majesty as he tendereth your honour, wealth, and continuance of the marriage betwixt the King's Highness and you, and for the love of God and the advancement of justice to be ministered to you in your cause; and on the otherside as he would be both to see you divorced from your husband, and your child thereby greatly prejudiced . . . to condescend to your humble petition, the which is that he would cause the original of the said brief . . . to be sent hither into England. . . . And the lacking thereof might be the cause of extreme ruin and decay in your affairs, and no little danger to the inheritance of your said child. . . .

She must also explain that she has promised to exhibit the original in England within three months, and if unable to do this will probably find that the sentence will go against her.

For if we ourselves were judges in this matter, and should lawfully find that where ye might ye did not do your diligence for the attaining of the said original, surely we would proceed further in that matter as the law would require, tarrying nothing therefore, as if never any such brief had been spoken of.

Finally, in the event of the Emperor refusing, she is to say that she will ask the Pope to insist on its surrender; ' and to the intent the King's Highness and his Council shall not think your Grace doth move and mind herein any frivole delay, it shall be expedient that ye in the presence of a notary do depose and declare that ' she has done everything suggested by this amazing ' device '.

It makes a nasty story, even allowing for the fact that Katharine was not taken in by this advice of her so-called ' counsellors '. She wrote the required letter, but her chaplain, Thomas Abel, who was sent for the brief, managed to write to the Emperor to let him know that the Queen had written under compulsion, that she could expect no justice in England, and that she begged her nephew to persuade the Pope to revoke the cause to Rome.

Such, then, was the state of affairs at the end of 1528. Campeggio had been in England for two months. He had found both Henry and Katharine equally immovable. The King would not have anything less than the divorce, and he would have it sanctioned by the Pope. The Queen would accept no compromise, such as entering a nunnery, and was determined to fight the cause to the bitter end. The King and the Boleyn faction were getting restive, and blame for the delay was accumulating, ready to fall on Wolsey's head. Du Bellay reported to Francis that the King had had some bitter words with the Cardinal. Gardiner was again sent speeding to Rome, to urge matters on with his uncompromising and fiery attack. But before he could reach his destination the Pope fell ill, early in January, 1529; and almost immediately rumours of his death flew about Europe. The news reached England at the beginning of February, and was believed by Henry and Wolsey. The matter of the election was vital to their cause. Hence the following letter, which explains the situation very fully, and throws interesting light on what occurred behind the scenes at a papal election.

11. TO GARDINER, BRYAN, CASALE AND VANNES

. . . His Highness, pondering and profoundly considering the present state of Christendom, miserably and piteously afflicte with the intestine wars, dissensions and disorders reigning amongst the princes of the same; and how the dignity of the see Apostolic, by such trouble and persecution as hath been inferred thereunto these years passed, is not a little diminished and impaired, like to come into total ruin, if by the help and assistance of good and virtuous princes the ambition of those which study the extermination thereof be not in time repressed. Considering furthermore, that as well to conduce rest and tranquillity in Christendom, as to restore, repair and reintegrate the state, authority and reputation of the said see Apostolic, nothing is more requisite and necessary than that such an head and common father be now, at this time of vacation of the dignity papal, provided and elected to succeed in the same, as both may, can, and will purvey to the restoration of the said See: and that hath and may have the assistance of such virtuous and puissant princes as tender the defence, maintenance and increase of the dignity aforesaid: and that may meet with the inordinate ambition of the Emperor, who nothing more studieth than for his own exaltation to suppress the Church and See Apostolic. Remembering also the high importance of the King's great and weighty cause of matrimony committed to the charge of his said orators, and how manifold dangers and irreparable damages depend upon the tract, delay, or disappointment thereof, which by no way or mean can be conduced to the King's purpose and desire by the authority of the Church, but only by the special, assured and perfect favour of the head of the same Church, being also his Highness as loath as any living prince or person may be to recur unto other refuge, succour or remedy, in his said cause, than to the authority of the See Apostolic, if his Grace may there find the favour and benignity that to his merits towards the same be correspondent: of which favour his Highness should be clearly deprived and frustrate in case the election of the future pope should pass upon any person of whom his Grace were not perfectly assured.

His Highness, for the respect and considerations before specified, perceiving his good brother and perpetual ally the French King in the said intention to be unite, knit and in all occasions and doings of importance assuredly combined unto his Grace, proceeding together in one will, mind, purpose and conformity, hath by good and mature deliberation, studied, devised and excogitate with himself who were and might be the most able, meet and convenient person, having the qualities before specified, to be advanced at this time unto the said dignity papal. And finally, when his Grace hath well resolved with himself all the aspects and considerations beforesaid, noting also all things meet to be regarded in every of the Cardinals of the Church of Rome, both present now in the Court there, and absent from the same; it cannot be found that there is any person sufficiently furnished with the requisites before specified, but only the most reverend father in God, and his most trusty counsellor, the lord legate, Cardinal Archbishop of York, Primate and Chancellor of this realm, who, being well known to have as fervent zeal, study, mind and desire to the universal weal, respect and tranquillity of Christendom, to the reintegration and restoration of the dignity, authority, reputation and rights of the Church and See Apostolic, to the surety, weal and exaltation of the King's highness, the French King and other their confederates, and finally to the prosecution of the King's said great and weighty cause, whereupon dependeth the surety of his royal person, succession, realm, people and dominions, as any person living can or may have. And that the said most reverend father hath the fast assured favour herein of the said French King, who of his own mere motion hath frankly and liberally assured unto him all that by himself, his friends, his power, his dignity or otherwise he may or can possibly do for his advancement to the said dignity papal, is the person who for his singular virtue, his entire devotion to peace, and restoration of the said See, the excellency of his wisdom, learning and experience, the magnanimity in his occasions and doings, the dignity wherein he is already constitute, the promotions which he hath attained, the substance that he is of, his reputation, his conduct, his diligence, his dexterity, his discretion, his policy, and finally the notable and high favour that the King's highness and the said French King bear unto him, is only he that, called to the said dignity papal, may, can, and will meet with the inordinate ambition of the said Emperor. And consequently with establishment of tranquillity among Christian princes, is, by the assistance of his friends, meet, convenient and able to succour, relieve, and clearly to repair the piteous jacture and decay that the Church and See Apostolic hath so long suffered and taken, and to defend the same from the imminent dangers now apparent to ensue thereunto if the said Emperor (who, as the King's Highness is credibly ascertained) determined in the beginning of January now past to take his journey towards Rome should, upon this vacation of the said See, chanced as it is upon many evident presumptions to be thought by some detestable act committed for the said late Pope's destruction, now by force, violence, cautele, blandishing promises, or otherwise, have the election to proceed at his will, favour and devotion. Whereby, having a Pope at his arbitre, either he should not fail to usurp and take from him the right provinces and patrimony of the Church, using him as his chaplain and vassal, as well by little and little utterly to exclude and extinct him and his authority.

For this cause, if ever it were expedient that good Christian princes should look to the tuition, maintenance, defence and continuance of Christ's church, faith and religion, now is it the time above all other to provide and beware by all ways possible, lest the same, neglected, forgotten and not in time relieved, be brought unto extreme ruin. And therefore the King's highness, having singular and special trust and confidence, in the wisdoms, discretions, fidelities, diligence and circumspections of his said orators, to whom no part of the premises is unknown, ne how necessary and in any wise expedient it shall be for prosecution of the King's said good and weighty matter to them committed to have the said Lord Legate of York and none other advanced to the said dignity papal, willeth, desireth, ordaineth and expressly chargeth and commandeth his said orators and every of them no less to employ, endeavour and determine themselves to solicit, set forth, further, procure, labour and conduct the advancement of the said Lord Legate of York to that dignity, than they would that thing which the King's Highness most highly, next God and his soul, with all earnestness and fervent mind doth above all other things covet and desire, ne also less than they would the speedy obtaining and prosecution of all such things touching the King's said good and weighty matter committed to their charge, the making or marring whereof, being now the said late pope deceased, consisteth only in the advancement of the said Lord Legate of York to the dignity papal. For, as the King's said ambassadors may by their wisdoms well think and consider, the same must of necessity come and fortune either to one that is an assured friend to his Grace and the French King, or to one that is a manifest enemy to them, favouring the Emperor's part, or to one indifferent and mean between both. And if it should chance upon a manifest enemy it is evident that the King's desire at his hand were merely impossible to be had, and never were to be attempted that way. If it should come to one being indifferent and mean between both, it is more than notorious that his Grace, at the best, should be contained with fair words and promises, and yet such respect should be had to the Emperor that finally, under hope of attaining something, there should be no more but to act delay, and finally no more fruit or effect, whereof experience hath already been seen in one that had cause to be more friendly to the King than indifferent or mean between both. And yet how the matter hath depended is to the King's said ambassadors well known, so that of necessity this thing must be conduced to one that is an assured friend.

. . . And for the better introduction of the ways and means how this thing shall be solicited, they shall receive herewith a schedule, wherein is mentioned and noted by name how many and what cardinals of likelihood shall be present at the election, and how many and which of the other shall be absent. Semblably, how many of them that be like to be present may be thought to be friends to the King's Highness and the French King, whose names in the said schedule be noted with A. And how many be thought to be Imperial, whose names be noted with K.[1] In the said schedule be also set out the number and names of those that be thought to be neutral or indifferent, noted with

[1] It is doubtful whether this letter is really *k*, but it is more like a *k* than a *b*, or an E.

N. And furthermore, they be first mentioned therein which be thought most like to aspire unto that dignity. Herein be many things well to be regarded. First, the number of the cardinals that are like to be present, which, as is thought here, shall not exceed 39. Secondly, that to have election to the King's purpose, shall be requisite to have two parts of the three of the said number, which two parts must be 26. Then is it to be noted that they which be thought to be friends to the King's Highness and the French King be in number 20. So that if they may be made sure to the King's devotion there shall lack but six of the number which shall suffice to make the election, which number the King's said ambassadors shall move, win and attain, either of them that be thought to be indifferent, or some other.

In the conducing thereof, two ways be to be specially to be remembered. One is, if the cardinals present, having God and the Holy Ghost before them, shall be minded, as to their duty appertaineth, to have respect unto the present calamity of the Church and all Christendom, intending the relief, succour, and restoration of the same, and to preserve themselves and the dignity of the See Apostolic; then, looking profoundly upon the state of the things they cannot fail facilly of themselves to find and perceive that to conduce their purpose there is only the said Lord Legate of York. And in this case it is verily to be thought that the very reason's self and their own conscience shall lead them like virtuous fathers to have their principal respect hereunto, and all particular affections set apart, to accord and agree without difficulty to that which so manifestly is known to be the thing above all other expedient. Nevertheless because percase human fragility suffereth not all things to be pondered, trutynate[1] and weighed in just balance, but that as we be men, errors may run unless their remedy be provided, it appertaineth in matter of so high importance to the comfort and weal of all Christendom to succour the infirmity that may chance, not for corruption or to any perverse, unlefull or evil intents, but rather to help to the lack and defaults which by such fragility might else take place: and therefore expedient shall it be that the King's said orators to

[1] Estimated, considered.

so notable a purpose, where they shall perceive the consideration and respect, whereunto reason leadeth, to be in any particular aided or supplied, do the same with pollicitations[1] of promotions special, offices, dignities, rewards of money or other thing such as they shall seem meet to the purpose. Inculking into the minds of such persons as shall be requisite first what things the said Lord Legate of York shall leave, if he should be advanced to the said dignity, which be such as, the establishment of his state considered, be far more to his commodity if he should regard his private weal than to enter into this dangerous storm and troublous tempest for the relief of the Church and all Christendom, whereunto, his said private weal set apart, he is totally devowed and dedicate, to the exposition of his body, blood and life, glad and ready with the sacrifice thereof to do service to God, his Church, his faith and religion, which said promotions, the King's Highness, finding cause given unto him by the gratitude and conformity of his friends, will not fail to bestow to their benefit, besides large rewards, to have this so virtuous an act brought to perfection, for pollicitation[1] whereof the King's said ambassadors be furnished at this time with ample commission, as by the same they shall perceive the effect, whereof they shall execute without exception as by their wisdoms shall be thought convenient, so always as it may be done with such circumspection as may be appearance of good fruit to ensue. And semblably they be furnished with letters as well to the College of Cardinals in general as to them all that be like to be present in particular, which they shall now deliver to the best furtherance and advancement of their purpose, not sparing to declare unto them the liberality of the said Lord Legate of York, the substance that he is of, the assured assistance that he shall have of these princes and their confederates, whereby he shall be able, above any other that they can devise, to reward, promote, advance and recompense his friends to the uttermost, assuring them that these two princes will not fail also highly and in the best sort to consider their gratitude with any thing that may be excogitate to their profits and promotions, or any of their friends. So that by this mean, and with such good pollicitations,[1] grounded upon a leful,

[1] Promises, or documents conveying promises.

honourable, and just cause, and not upon any corrupt or undue intent to conduce thing to sinister purpose, the King's said orators shall, by their good policies, attain the perfect and sure good will of a great many of them, and by that way shall, with good dexterity, combine and knit those which will adhere hereunto in a perfect fastness and in an indissoluble knot, firmly to stick and hold together, without variation or declining from their purpose, for any persuasion, practice, or mean that can be made to the contrary: which thing surely to be provided, and such a knot of twenty, eighteen, or at the least, if it may be, of sixteen cardinals to be had, is in anywise expedient. For they, persisting in their determination, shall not fail to empeche that no adverse part can have a full number to make a due and lawful election; and yet they, being found in a constantness to this good purpose, shall by little and little allure and bring other unto them, so as the residue, perceiving so great a towardness, and fearing a sufficient number to accede without them, and thereby the election to pass against their wills, shall percace be the more prone and ready to come unto that party: whereunto nothing should of reason sooner move them than the very respect to the infinite goodness that thereby to themselves in particular, and the universal Church and religion Christian in general, is apparent to ensue.

Nevertheless, if leaving the direct way, they will be abused with any other incantations, or, for private ambition, persist in contending for themselves, then is it evident they search nothing more than the ruin of the said See Apostolic. In which case other ways be to be devised, and their undue demeanour to be remedied and resisted, for this cause; and to be sure in all events, the King's said orators shall by their wisdoms find the means to have some fast and sure persons in the conclave, such as may not only practise and set forth things there to the purpose, but also give such knowledge outward as the King's said orators may thereby the better know how to order their proceedings. And, amongst other, it is thought that Monsieur de Vaulx, one of the French ambassadors, whom the French King hath commanded expressly to further this matter by all the means to him possible, should be one to enter the said conclave, not as an ambassador, but as the minister of some cardinal, friend of the French king.

And, semblably, Sir Gregory de Cassalis, who for his wisdom, conduct, language, acquaintance, and other good qualities, may do excellent good in that behalf. . . .

And to the intent the cardinals may be the better animated to finish the said election to the king's desire, the king's said orators shall, as they see good, offer them a presidye[1] of two or three thousand men to be in the city of Rome for the time of the same election, which, if they will accept, the said orators shall see furnished, taking money by exchange and otherwise for their entertainment as shall be requisite: which money, or any other, that they shall take for conducing this the king's purpose, shall be truly repaid with interest and all requisites as they shall assign. And, semblably, lest terror or dread of the imperials in Naples should induce the cardinals to any error, the French king hath ordained that Seignior Renzio shall lie in a presidye, between the army of Naples and the city of Rome, like as the Viscount of Turenne is also commanded to lie on the other side, and semblably the Venetians. So that, [by] those means, not only they shall be out of all fear of the imperials, but also in the more devotion of these two princes, which shall much confer to the king's purpose, and embold the cardinals favouring the desire of these two princes, both to persist in their deliberation and also, in time of extreme despair, to protest and depart as is aforesaid.

And because nothing should withdraw the minds of the cardinals from this purpose, who percase might think that the said Lord Legate of York, being elected, would not repair to the court of Rome, but demeur in Avignon or some other place out of Italy, the king's said ambassadors shall remove all such suspicion by two evident arguments and reasons: one is, that the said Cardinal of York, advanced to that dignity, must thereby leave all other his promotions, and consequently should be dispurveyed of any habitation, place, or convenient living, if remaining in another strange country, he should defer to come unto Rome, where should be the place of his See and entire living; wherefore it were far from reason to think that he, which hitherto for his estate hath lived in such abundance, should be so pusillanime for this promotion, to bring himself into condign penury

[1] i.e. an armed guard.

and poverty, or to live in place private, to the hindrance of his honour, profit, or reputation. Secondly, the thing principally moving him to be contented at these princes' requests to change his state present is the fervent zeal he hath to expone his study, travail, labour, substance, wit, body, blood and life in the quarrel of God's Church, faith, and of Christendom, which is too high and a ground to be taken to remain and lie in a corner or private place; but that rather than he would suffer so high an exception to be found in him, he would expone all that he might do: who, having the assistance of these two princes, should not fail (God willing) to pass directly to his See with honour and comfort unto all Italy, and the discourage of the party that would be adverse thereunto; and therefore the cardinals should not need to fear of any such thing, but might be well assured to have his presence there to their comfort in all celerity and diligence possible. . . .

Even if the news of Clement's death had been true there would not have been the remotest likelihood of Wolsey's election; but by the time both letter and ambassadors had arrived at Rome the Pope had recovered, and when he was able to give audience he explained quite clearly that he could do nothing for the King. Eighteen months had gone by since Knight had sped post-haste and hopefully to Rome, and 'the King's matter' was no whit advanced. Henry's irritation was only held in check by his almost childlike belief that in his just cause he *could not* fail, eventually, to receive justice at the hands of the 'common father' of Christendom. Mistakes in diplomacy and the machinations of the Imperialists might set back his cause: but in the spring of 1529 his mind still could not admit the possibility of failure.

Sir Francis Bryan, holding a watching brief for Henry's and the Boleyn interests, saw as clearly as the ambassadors that the Pope would do nothing for them. His position of privileged intimacy, however, enabled him to put the truth to his master more bluntly than Gardiner, Vannes and Casale could dare to do; and on April 21 he wrote it, with a plainness that must at last have carried some conviction even to the unwilling Henry. Everything possible they have 'done and caused to be done'. 'Plainly he will do nothing for your Grace.' If he wrote otherwise he would put the King 'in a hope of recovery where none is to be had. There is not one of us but that hath assayed him, both by fair means and foul, but nothing will serve. And whosoever hath made your Grace believe that he would do for you in this cause hath not, as I think, done your Grace the best service.' 'There is no man living,' he concludes, 'more sorrier to write this news to you than I am; but if I should not write this I should not do my duty.' With exemplary discretion he adds: 'Sir, I write a letter to my cousin Anne, but I dare not write to her the truth of this, because I do not know whether your Grace will be contented that she should know it so shortly or no; but I have said to her in my letter that I am sure your Grace will make her privy to all our news.'[1]

In February the Emperor had required the Pope to revoke the cause to Rome; and when, later on, Katharine herself succeeded in lodging her protest against the proceedings in England, Clement allowed the protestation, and promised the revocation. The news filtered through to England quickly enough. Even so, Henry still tried to refuse to believe that ultimately Rome would thwart his will. The Pope was merely playing for time, keeping the Emperor quiet by a promise which he did not mean to fulfil. He could not betray such a steadfast friend to the Papacy as Henry had always been. The trial was hurried on in England, and a court prepared in the Great Hall of Blackfriars. For years English interests and English money had been sacrificed to the papal policy. Henry had received from the Pope the cap and sword, and any number of golden roses. And he had the Pope's written promise. Bryan and the rest must be mistaken.

On Monday, June 21, Henry and Katharine both appeared before the Court, and this is the occasion which has been so vigorously dramatized by Shakespeare in *Henry VIII*, Act II, Sc. iv, when the Queen threw herself at her husband's feet and made her moving appeal to his love to do her right and justice. The following letter is the account sent by Henry to his ambassadors at Rome, denuded of all the pity and the poetry with which Shakespeare has vitalized the scene.

[1] Quoted from *S.P.* VII, p. 166.

III. TO BENET, CASALE AND VANNES

[*June* 23, 1529.]

. . . The said legates [i.e. Wolsey and Campeggio] all due ceremonies first observed, have directed citations both to us and to the Queen for our and her appearance before them the XVIIIth day of this month, which appearance was duly on either part kept and performed and all requisite solemnities accomplished. At which time, the Queen, trusting more in the power of the Imperialists than in any justness of her cause, and thinking of likelihood by frustratory allegations and delays to tract and put over the matter to her advantage, did protest at the said day, putting in libels, recusatories[1] of the judges, and also made a provocation[2] alleging the cause to be avoked[3] by the Pope's holiness *et litis pendentiam coram eodem*,[4] desiring to be admitted for probation thereof and to have a term competent for the same. Whereupon day was given by the judges till the XXIst of the same month for declaration of their minds and intentions thereunto, the Queen in person, and we by our proctor enjoined to appear the same day to hear what the said judges should determine in and upon the same; at which time both we and the Queen appeared in person, and notwithstanding that the said judges amply, and sufficiently declared as well the sincerity of their minds directly and justly to proceed, without favour, dread, affection or partiality, as also that no such recusation, appellation, or term for proving of *litis pendentiam* could or might be by them admitted, yet she nevertheless, persisting in her former wilfulness, laid in her appeal, which also by the said judges was likewise recused. And they minding to proceed further in the cause, the Queen would not longer make her abode to hear what the said judges would fu[lly] discern, but incontinently departed out of the court, wherefore she was thrice precognisate[5] and called eftsoons to return and appear, which she refusing to do was denounced by the judges *contumax*,[6] and a citation discerned for

[1] Containing a rejection or refusal.
[2] An appeal, especially to a higher ecclesiastical court.
[3] Revoked.
[4] Pending its hearing before the same.
[5] Erron. for *preconizate*, summoned by proclamation.
[6] Contumacious.

her appearance on Friday next, to make answer to such articles and positions as should objected unto her. So as now it is not to be doubted but that she will use all ways and means to her possible to impetrate[1] and attain such things, as well by her own pursuit as by her friends, as may be to the empeachment of the rightful process of this cause, either by advocation, inhibition or otherwise.

Wherefore, seeing now in what state this our matter standeth and dependeth, necessary and requisite for the grave consequences hanging upon the same, not only for the exoneration of our conscience, but also for the surety of our succession and the weal of this our realm and people, to be with all celerity perfected and obsolved: it was thought convenient to advertise you of the premises to the intent you being before well and sufficiently instructed in all things concerning the same, shall, by your wisdoms and diligence have special regard that nothing pass or be granted there by the Pope's holiness which may either give delay or disappointment to the direct and speedy pass to be used in this cause, neither by advocation of the cause, inhibition nor otherwise. But that if any such thing shall by the Cæsarians,[2] or by her agents, or other, be attempted or desired, ye likewise of wisdom, good zeal, learning and experience, diligently procure the stopping thereof, as well upon such reasons and considerations as before have been signified unto you as by inferring the high and extreme dishonour and intolerable prejudice that the Pope's holiness thereof should do to his said legates, and also the contrariety both of his bull and commission and also of his promise and pollicitation[3] passed upon the same, besides the notable and excellent displeasure thereby to be done by his holiness to us and our realm, clear contrary to our merits and deserts; extending also the other damages mentioned in the said former writings apparent to ensue thereby to his holiness and the See Apostolic, with the manifold and in manner infinite inconveniences like to follow of the same to all Christendom, and all other such reasons, introductions and persuasions as ye can made and

[1] To obtain by applying to authority.
[2] Imperialists.
[3] A document conveying a promise.

devise for that purpose. Putting him also in remembrance of the great commodity coming unto his holiness herein, by reason that this cause being here decided the Pope not only is delivered from the pain that he should, in this his time of disease and sickness to the extreme peril of his life sustain with the same, seeing that it is of such moment and importance as suffereth no tract or delay, but also his holiness shall by such decision here eschew and avoid all displeasure that he should not fail to have if it were or should be passed elsewhere; which matter is no little wisdom well to foresee and consider. And not only to forbear to do or pass anything derogatory or prejudicial to his said commission, but also by all means possible to corroborate and fortify the same and all such acts judicial as shall pass by his said legates by virtue thereof, like as we doubt not but that the Pope's holiness, of his uprightness, virtue and perfect wisdom, will do. And rather, like a most loving father and friend, tender and favour our good, just and reasonable causes and desires, putting thereunto all the furtherance he may do, than to do, or consent to be done, anything hurtful, prejudicial, damageable, or displeasant unto us or this our said cause.

And finally, if need shall be, we will ye also infer as the case shall require, how inconvenient it were this our matter should be decided in the Court of Rome, which now dependeth totally in the Emperor's arbitre, having such puissance near thereunto that as hath been written by the Pope's own letters, their state and life there is all in the Emperor's hands, whose armies may famish or relieve them at their pleasures. And semblably ye shall not forget the prerogative of our Crown and jurisdiction royal, by the ancient laws of our realm, which admitteth nothing to be done by the Pope to the prejudice thereof; and also what danger they should incur that would presume to bring or present any such thing into the same, as in our last letters sent by Alexander was touched at good length. Wherein, since ye be already so well and amply instructed, knowing also how much the matter importeth, and toucheth us, and what perfect and agreeable service ye may do unto us herein, with the high thanks that ye may deserve for the same, we shall not be more pro[li]x but refer the substantial, perfect and assured handling hereof to your circumspections, fidelities and diligences, not doubting but that ye will now above all other things look vigilantly hereunto, and so acquit yourself in the same as it may well appear that your acts shall be correspondent to our firm trust and expectation, and no less tender this thing than ye know it to be imprinted in the bottom of our heart, ne than as ye know both the importance and high moment, and also the very necessity of the matter doth require. In which doing, besides the laud and praise that you shall consecute thereby of all good men we shall so have your acquitailles in our remembrance as ye shall have cause to think your travails, pains, and studies herein in the best wise collocate and employed. Given under our signet at our palace of Bridewell, the twenty-third day of June.

Katharine had made her appeal to Rome, and left the Court:

> I will not tarry: no, nor ever more,
> Upon this business, my appearance make
> In any of their courts.

Nevertheless the proceedings took their inexorable course. Fisher, Bishop of Rochester, defended the validity of the marriage, and declared himself willing to lay down his life for his opinion. But by June 13 Wolsey had managed so to accelerate matters that, as Campeggio complained, he had no moment's breathing time and could not possibly defer sentence any longer. On July 23 the judgement was expected: the Court met: Henry appeared in person: ministers, courtiers, nobles thronged the hall: and Henry's proctor demanded sentence. Campeggio rose to reply: and speaking in fluent Latin, in a few brief words, shattered the King's hopes, and sealed the fate of his greatest minister. He announced that the court was adjourned till October 1, that is to say for the two months' vacation observed by the court in Rome.

On the face of it, merely another instance of 'the law's delays': but Henry and Wolsey—and indeed every one else—knew that in reality it meant that Henry would never get his divorce in this or any other papal court. The King retired to

Greenwich, and on July 28 Stephen Gardiner became chief secretary. Wolsey was denied access. The King went hunting. And then, at last, came the news from Rome. The English ambassadors wrote on July 16 that they had found out secretly that, the day before, the Pope had signed the revocation of the cause. He had definitely allied himself with the Emperor by the Treaty of Barcelona. He was bound, therefore, to revoke the cause of the Emperor's aunt to Rome, where Katharine would find the 'justice' denied her in England, and where Henry would find himself in what had formerly been Katharine's predicament. The stubborn fact could no longer be denied. The Pope could not do for Henry what he had done for his sister Margaret, and his brother-in-law Charles Brandon. Rome had failed the Defender of the Faith: so on August 9, 1529, the writs were issued by which the King of England summoned his Parliament, the first that had been summoned since 1523. The third decade of the reign was over, and with it went the 'full meridian' of the glory of the great Cardinal.

1529

In Europe—Pope and Emperor reconciled, formally leagued by the Treaty of Barcelona: and Charles and Francis, through the medium of their womenfolk, preparing for a reconciliation.

In England—three years of negotiations for the royal divorce ended suddenly when the Pope revokes the cause to Rome, and cites Henry and Katharine to appear before the curia.

On the face of it—momentous alliances in the making, for Charles, Francis and the Papacy: for Henry, a personal and domestic crisis. Actually—the setting of the match to the train, that by its explosion was to shatter the whole fabric of the established order of things.

A momentous year for the future history of Europe and England—momentous, not because it saw the reunion of Pope and Emperor, but because it saw the fall of Wolsey, the summoning of the English Parliament, and the beginning of the breach with Rome.

The summoning of Parliament spelt the doom of Wolsey. Wolsey had helped Henry to do without Parliament: now the King had made up his mind that Parliament was to be his chief weapon. Rome and its legate had failed the King's need, and Wolsey himself had prophesied that if this happened 'the speedy and total ruin would follow', not only of himself but of 'the Church's influence in this kingdom': and in October, 1528, Campeggio had written to Sanga, 'He often impresses upon me that if this divorce is not granted the authority of the See Apostolic in this kingdom will be annihilated.'[1]

Wolsey's fall came first. A bill of indictment under the Statute of Praemunire was brought in against him. He pleaded guilty, was deprived of the Great Seal, and of most of his possessions. He was not, however, deprived of his Archbishopric of York, and it was in the exercise of his duties in that See that he spent the last six months of his life.

IV. To Lord Dacre

By the King

HENRY R. [1530.]

Right trusty and well beloved, we greet you well. And forasmuch as the most reverend father in God our right trusty and right entirely well beloved the Lord Cardinal Archbishop of York doth now repair into those parts, minding to reside in that his Province for the better administration of the cure to him committed, which now of a long season hath been orbate and destitute of an Archbishop there resident, and consequently it shall be the more needful unto him to have the favourable and loving assistance of the noblemen and other in those parts. We therefore will and desire you not only to show yourself unto him from time to time, of toward and benevolent mind, using, entreating and accepting him as to his dignity doth appertain; but also in such things as shall concern either the administration of his said cure, or the furtherance of his own reasonable causes, with the good order of his church and things appertain-

[1] Du Bellay, the French ambassador, gauging the temper of the country, wrote: 'I expect the priests will never have the Great Seal again'

ing to the same, ye will be to him comforting, aiding, helping, and assisting, as we specially trust you.

Given under our Signet, at our Castle of Windsor, the 28th day of March.

With this last letter written on his behalf by Henry, Wolsey passes from the story. On November 4, 1530, he was arrested at York on the charge of treason. He died at Leicester on his journey towards the Tower, ' an old man broken with the storms of state '.

To return, however, to the Parliament which was to be known to history as the Reformation Parliament, and was to sit for those seven years which H. A. L. Fisher describes as ' one of the few epoch-making periods in the history of English legislation'. Unpropitious as the moment might seem, when the country as a whole was sympathizing with Katharine as the injured wife, actually it was the precise moment for Henry's purpose. By revoking the King's cause to Rome the Pope turned a moral into a national and political issue, and so focused to a point the English anti-clerical feelings which had been steadily accumulating for more than a century, and which Wolsey alone had held in check. Henry himself, in various letters, does not scruple to threaten the Pope with the secession of his realm. Writing to Benet on April 23, 1531, he instructs him :

> as of your self privily say to the Pope, that ye be advertised from your friends out of England, such as be learned in the laws and of our counsel, that it were the plainest entry the Pope might make to the destruction of his whole authority here, to strike upon this point, to call us to Rome, for that will in no man's ears sound well, and that the lawyers indeed think and will counsel us, to the defence thereof.

He is instructed also to say that

> here lieth a great number in wait to hear of open dissension between the Pope and us; and as soon as that trumpet blow-

eth, they will think a most propice occasion to strike at his power, which is in all points abhorred, as he and other his predecessors hath used it; and thus putting the Pope in good hope, that we may hap to condescend to indifferent judges and place, ye shall percase work much in the delaying of the process: wherein ye must use all policy to make them to give credit unto you, and abuse them as they have abused us, for they have been to us always like willow tree, shewing fair buds and leaves without any fruit.[1]

The grievances which the laymen who came to the Parliament of 1529 wanted to reform were the wealth, power and privileges of the Church. It is probably safe to say that no questions of faith or dogma entered their minds or the King's. At the same moment, though for different reasons, both King and people were thoroughly angry with Rome. As Professor A. F. Pollard says, 'Englishmen are singularly free from the bondages of abstract ideas, and they began their Reformation not with the enunciation of some new truth, but with an attack on clerical fees.'

In sum, Henry answered the Pope's revocation by refusing to appear in person at Rome and by giving more or less free rein to the anti-clerical feeling of the country. If justice could not move the Pope pressure might be more effective. The cry of the Commons, unprompted by their sovereign, was 'Down with the Church'. Very well. Let them cry: their voices might be heard in Rome. But if heard, they went unheeded, for early in 1531, Clement issued two bulls—the one prohibiting Henry from a second marriage, under ban of excommunication, the second forbidding all written or spoken support of Henry's cause by ecclesiastics, advocates and others. These were followed up by a prohibition preventing the Archbishop of Canterbury from taking cognizance of the King's suit, and another to prevent universities, courts of law, and parliaments, from giving a decision.

Clement had played straight into Henry's hands. Nothing could have been better calculated to rouse national indignation

[1] Quoted from *S.P.* VII, pp. 297-8. Original in cipher.

on the King's behalf, to make Parliament ready to help him, and also to press on with the attack against the Church. In December, 1530, the King's attorney had issued a writ of Praemunire against the whole body of the clergy of England. Technically guilty, by reason of having accepted Wolsey's legatine powers, they had no choice but to buy themselves off, and to submit to Henry's demand that they should acknowledge him as the Supreme Head of the Church—which they did in February, 1531. In March, 1532, Parliament passed an Act to prohibit the payment to Rome of Annates, that is, the first fruits of benefices; leaving Henry moreover, for about a year, the power to give or withhold his assent, as he should think fit; thereby putting into his hands an extremely useful weapon. According to the King, the bill was 'moved by the people, who hate the Pope marvellously'. Actually Henry 'managed' the affair very skilfully for his own benefit. That the following letter 'means mischief' is very obvious: and the actual results will soon appear.

v. To Ghinucci, Benet and Casale

[*March* 21, 1532.]

Right Reverend Father in Christ, and trusty and well-beloved our other orators, we greet you well. Since we are not ignorant that some men's natures are so given to malice that they studiously seek every occasion of calumniating even what has been done holily and rightly, we have thought it good to write to you more at length of the matters recently discussed and carried in our Parliament concerning the abrogation of the payment of Annates which has so long been heavy and (to speak plainly) burdensome, and of which everyone, of every sort and condition, has vehemently complained and with our agreement resented. In the which matter, albeit the knowledge of our own upright dealings should suffice us, nor are we compelled to reply to the calumnies of others, nevertheless as at this time we hear that the Pope and Cardinals, whom this cause seems nearly to concern, are likely to be somewhat more favourable to us than before, we have thought fit to come to agreement with those whom we either have or hope to have as our friends, not on the basis of legal strictness but in friendship, and to set forth to them the very truth and so to explain the reason of what has been done, that after being instructed in the truth in order to refell the calumnies of others, they shall find no ground of offence in what has been honestly and rightly done.

We send you, therefore, a copy of the said statute, that you may understand all the circumstances of the case: we send it to you, let it be understood, for your own use, not that it shall be communicated to others. For we neither do permit, nor will we permit that it should be communicated to others, until a case shall occur where it may take effect. For as you will easily perceive, it is so framed that the Pope and Cardinals who wish us well, and who in justice and truth wish to favour us, ought to rejoice at it, and equally be grieved and saddened if without cause they go about to endamage us.

A benefit deserves thanks, an injury retaliation: and although for Christian charity we abhor retaliation in ill-doing, nevertheless we are not so encompassed in an inordinate patience that while we are bearing with equanimity the harms inflicted by others we are doing nothing to cast off those which we have incurred gratuitously of our own will and accord: of which sort is the payment made from Annates, wantonly taken upon ourselves in the deepest darkness of ignorance. Wherefore taking note of the changes in the disposition of Pope and Cardinals, who measure all things by their own advantage and are driven to the same end by varying passions, so that at one time they are moved by love and prayers, grace and favour; at another, on the contrary, by fear and threats to do their duty and note what should be done: your labour, dexterity and prudence will most especially find scope in interpreting to them the force and effect of this statute, and the gain and loss it may bring to the Curia. To the end that if in the Pope or in the Cardinals you shall see any inclination at work in favour of us and our cause, and it seems expedient that their goodwill should not be broken by lack of hope or by fear, and you note that already the Pope or Cardinals are beginning to complain and expostulate because the question of Annates has been brought under public discussion, you shall reply with the truth, that discussion is free in our

Parliament and we cannot prevent them from talking and determining of everything, and especially from commenting on matters where some advantage to the common weal is involved, or some misfortune threatens it. Again you must reply that the question of Annates is an old one, and the payment thereof reprobate at the Council of Basle; lastly, that with the new officials created at Rome and the increased value of money, the sum involved has grown and increased to such an intolerable exaction that all the Bishops have bitterly complained of it to us, and recently much discontent was aroused among the people because the Bishops of York and Winchester were both obliged to borrow money from their friends, they not having it to hand, arousing much talk and not a little indignation that so large a sum of money should be paid for Bulls, to no purpose, and as it seemed to them without legal obligation. This was reported to Parliament and so reported as forthwith it is to cease as iniquitous, to save us from shedding the blood of our people without cause, that is, from rashly squandering money which is the blood of the state.

In our desire that neither the Pope nor the Cardinals should have occasion of complaint against us, far from falling away from truth and justice we have sought means of friendship, for it seemed good that we should not despise the advice of our Parliament, and also agreeable to our friendship with the Pope and Cardinals that neither at once nor yet of a sudden, they being ignorant and unware nor yet in friendlywise given warning, should we promulgate any statute that might be to their hurt. Therefore our foresight and prudence have brought it to pass that the question of Annates, which was being bandied about in the mouths of the people, and in the opinion of all good men was rightly being taken up, is wholly referred to our judgement and arbitre, and with the mouth of Parliament closed, our decision alone stands and is valid, to be inviolably observed by all. By which discreet and proper ordering we have satisfied the people, and can be seen to have worked for the Pope and the Cardinals, if they in reason will consider what has been done. For as our people trust to our judgement, so ought not the Pope and the Cardinals to distrust it; nor think that we wish to depart from what is just. First, as is right, place shall be given to justice and truth; next, to friendship; and assuredly whatsoever shall by us be done in that matter, it will be in perpetuity firmly observed; which thing should carry much weight. Of nothing will we define rashly, but regarding the intent of the Statute, and examining the truth, both as to what should and what can be done, we shall diligently consider how far justice might extort, how far friendship might demand.

It rests with the Pope and the Cardinals in justice and truth to earn our friendship, which with us has never been an idle one; nor, if they will well discern, can it escape notice that in this our Statute nothing is accounted as more to be desired than that for the determining of controversy the arbiter to be appointed should be one whom honourable friendship doth well incline, and who will with all zeal strive to turn away from extreme severity, and to bring all things to just issue. It is for you, therefore, to see that from the power entrusted to us by this Statute, as from our mind expressed in your words, they neither hope too much nor yet too much despair. Which hope, nevertheless, or which despair, as the time prescribes, you must so augment and on such grounds given, that we may be free, when the time comes, freely to make known our decision. We have no stomach to deceive them and feed with vain hope, but to point out to them what this matter means; namely, that this Statute will turn to their benefit, if only they will show themselves worthy of being benefited; and, on the other hand, will rightly bring loss to them if that is what they shall have deserved. Desert dependeth first upon justice, then upon friendship: the case is free from all malice and resteth upon justice, which is to them both owed and will be granted, even though they themselves prove utterly inimical. The conclusion thereof resteth now in their hands, either to keep us as friends, or to render us hostile. To this present nothing hath been laid down nor yet proclaimed against them, but the whole power hath been to us transferred, which is what the Pope and the Cardinals should desire, if they are not minded to despise our friendship.

It will be your part, as often as there is any mention of this Statute, with the most effectual words you can, again and again to inculk and set forth with how much goodwill and solicitude we have studied that, although importunately and daily our subjects beset us with complaints and prayers, contending by all means that instantly and without delay this Statute for the abrogation of Annates be promulgated, nevertheless their efforts should be diverted; that indeed they should submit everything to our arbitre and judgement, and that whatsoever is enacted shall be so hidden and concealed from all, that no foreign Prince shall be able to take occasion from it to decree a like edict for the abolition of Annates in his own kingdom. In which thing, that the Pope himself and the Cardinals may recognize the greatness of our affection towards them, you must exert yourselves with all zeal and prudence. If, however, it shall not be given to you to obtain this from them, and they are pleased to misconstrue our amiability and friendship, you must put them in mind what inconveniences and hurt to the Roman Curia and to their own dignity are like to ensue thereof, if we, for their ingratitude, openly acquaint the world with what is now secret, and confirm it by our authority, whence that other Princes and realms may draw example is not unlike. . . .

In May, 1532, an even more significant step was taken. The Commons were busy pressing their grievances against the clergy, and when convocation appealed to the King for help to resist the proposed encroachments upon their power Henry made his bargain, which resulted in nothing less than the famous 'Submission of the Clergy'. Put briefly, on May 10 Convocation was told, firstly, that there was to be no more ecclesiastical legislation made unless it received the royal assent; secondly, that the existing body of ecclesiastical law was to be revised by a committee chosen by the King, half of whom were to be laymen; and that finally, the laws thus approved were to be submitted to the King for his assent. By May 15 these terms had been accepted by the clergy of England. It was the first triumphant assertion of Supreme Headship.

The end of the story can now be quickly told. In January, 1533, Henry secretly married Anne Boleyn, knowing her to be pregnant of the child that he intended to be the legitimate heir of England. For the Pope, therefore, he must substitute another ecclesiastical authority that must be the highest authority recognizable for Englishmen. Cranmer, now Archbishop-Elect of Canterbury, was the man, but before he could be consecrated he must have his bulls from the Pope. Henry, still on good terms with Clement, asked that these might be hurried through, suggesting that if he were thus obliged by the Pope he might go on withholding the royal consent to the Act of Annates. In consequence the bulls were granted in February. In the meantime, at home, Parliament was persuaded to pass the Act of Appeals, forbidding appeals to Rome, and thereby making the Court of the Archbishop of Canterbury the final court for the hearing of ecclesiastical causes in England. The only appeal from the Archbishop's court was to the King in Chancery.

The next move is described by Henry himself in the following letter.

VI. To Cranmer

[*April* 12, 1533.]

Most Reverend Father, &c., we greet you well. Doing you to understand that the 12th day of this month of April we received letters from you, dated at Lambeth the 11th day of the said month, in which letters ye write that forasmuch as our great cause of matrimony (which hath long depended in question), is divulgated (as it is thought) through out all Christentye, and it is commoned of the mouths of no small number of our people, and that many of them fear not to say and report that thereof is likelihood hereafter to ensue great inconveniences, dangers and perils to this realm, and much uncertainty to our succession, whereby our said people is seen to be not a little offended: whereupon ye, whom God and we have ordained Archbishop of Canterbury, and primate of all this our realm of England, to whose office it hath been, and is, appertaining by the sufferance of us and our progenitors, as ye write yourself both justly and truly, to order, judge, and determine mere spiritual causes within this our realm; having due consideration to the said inconveniences, dangers, perils, and uncertainty, if the said cause of matrimony should be suffered still to continue in question, undecided; and, also, reducing to your remembrance the great blame that hath been arrected to the clergy of this our realm, and specially to the heads and presidents of the same, because they have not hitherto studied and travailed for remedies to exclude and put out of doubt such uncertainty, inconveniences, perils, and dangers; be moved in your conscience, by reason of the premises, to endeavour yourself, as far as ye may, by reason of your said office of Primacy, to set some direction and end in the said cause of matrimony, according to the pleasure of Almighty God; and thereupon ye, duly recognizing that it becometh you not, being our subject, to enterprise any part of your said office in so weighty and great a cause pertaining to us, being your prince and sovereign, without our licence obtained so to do; and, therefore, in your most humble wise, ye supply unto us in your said letters, to grant unto you our licence to procede to the examination and final determination of the said cause, in exoneration of your conscience towards God and for the satisfying of your bounden duty towards us, our realm, succession, and posterity, in advoiding of the said inconveniences. And finally, in the end of your said letters, ye beseech us to pardon your boldness and rude writing in that behalf, and to take the same in good sense and part as ye do mean, calling God to your record that only for the zeal that ye have to the premises, ye have written your said letters, and for none other intent, cause or purpose.

My Lord, where ye write in the last part of your said letters, whereunto we make you first answer, that ye be moved only by the zeal that ye have to justice, and for the exoneration of your conscience against God, to write as ye do unto us, we cannot, of reason, be discontented therewith, but condignly praise you therein. And for that we perceive that ye have such a good mind and fervent zeal to do justice, according to your office, for the quieting of our realm, and for the excluding of such dangers and perils as be in your said letters mentionate, and also for putting our succession and posterity out of question, doubt, and uncertainty; we cannot but much commend and laud your good and virtuous intended purpose in that behalf. In consideration whereof, albeit we, being your King and Sovereign, do recognize no superior in earth, but only God, and not being subject to the laws of any other earthly creature; yet because ye be, under us, by God's calling and ours, the most principal minister of our spiritual jurisdiction within this our realm, who we think assuredly is so in the fear of God, and love towards the observance of his laws (to the which laws we, as a Christian King, have always heretofore, and shall ever most obediently submit ourself), will not therefore refuse (our pre-eminent power and authority to us, and our successors, in this behalf, nevertheless saved) your humble request, offer, and towardness; that is, to mean to make an end, according to the will and pleasure of Almighty God, in our said great cause of matrimony; which hath so long depended undetermined, to our great and grievous unquietness and burden of conscience. Wherefore we, inclining to your humble petition, by these our letters, sealed with our seal and signed with our Sign Manual, do licence you to proceed in the said cause, and to the examination and final determination of the same; not doubting but ye will have God and the justice of the said cause only before your eyes, and not to regard any earthly or worldly affection therein. For assuredly, the thing that we most covet in this world is so to proceed, in all our acts and doings, as may be most acceptable to the pleasure of Almighty God, our Creator, and to the wealth and honour of us, our succession, and posterity, and the surety of our realm and subjects within the same.

Early in April Katharine was informed that Henry had married 'the other lady' more than two months before.[1] Cranmer was consecrated on March 30, and on May 10 he opened his court at Dunstable. On the 23rd he gave his sentence:[2] Henry and Katharine had never been lawfully married. On the 28th he declared that the King and Anne Boleyn were lawfully married, and on June 1 he crowned Anne. The summons to her coronation, it will be noticed, is dated April 28.

[1] Chapuys to the Emperor. *L.P.* VI, 351. April 16, 1533.
[2] *L.P.* VI, 528, etc. *S.P.* I, 396.

VII. To the Lady Cobham

By the King

HENRY R. [1533.]

Right dear and well beloved, we greet you well. And forasmuch as we be determined upon the feast of Pentecost next coming to keep and do to be celebrate at Westminster, with all due circumstances of honour, the coronation of our dearest wife the lady Anne our Queen, as to her estate and dignity doth appertain, and have appointed you among other, at the same time to give your attendance on horse-back, in such place as to your degree appertaineth, We therefore desire and pray you, to put yourself in such a-readiness as ye may be personally at our manor of Greenwich the Friday next before the said feast, then and there to give your attendance upon our said Queen, from thence to our Tower of London the same day, and on the next day to ride from the same our Tower through our City of London unto our manor of Westminster; and the next day, Whit-sunday, to go unto our Monastery there, to the said coronation; providing for yourself and your women some fair white or white gray palfreys or geldings, such as ye shall think most fit to serve for that purpose. And as concerning the apparel of your own palfrey, ye shall be furnished thereof by the Master of the Horses with our said dearest wife the Queen, at any your repair or sending hither for the same in every behalf, saving for your bit and your bosses; trusting that for the liveries and ordering of your said women, as well in their apparel as in their horses, ye will in such wise provide for them as unto your honour and that solemnity appertaineth; and your own robes and liveries shall be delivered, at anytime when ye shall come or send for the same, by the keeper of our great wardrobe; not failing hereof as ye intend to do us pleasure. Given, under signet, at our manor of Greenwich, the 28th day of April.

On July 9 Henry gave his assent to the Act of Annates. On Sunday, September 7, 1533, Anne's daughter Elizabeth was born at Greenwich. The Pope drew up excommunications, and thundered anathemas: Charles V investigated the whole position very carefully, and decided that it would be admirable if

James of Scotland would depose his uncle, but that the Pope must be urged not to lay England under an interdict, as that would upset the trade of the Emperor's Flemish and Spanish subjects. Nothing of this appeared to disturb Henry. He assured Chapuys that 'God and his conscience were on very good terms',[1] and in all his actions 'fortified himself by the consent of Parliament'.[2] Moreover, though Francis might disapprove as a Catholic, as a monarch he was in no hurry to rush into enmity against England.

The Pope, therefore, finding himself totally unable to rely on any secular power in Europe to bring the offending Henry to book, delayed publication of his sentence. Henry, however, delayed not at all. In Parliament fresh Acts confirmed with greater precision and some amplification the anti-papal measures of 1532. On March 30, 1534, Parliament settled the succession by Act on Henry's heirs by Anne Boleyn, and in June 'the abolishing of the usurped power of the Pope' was proclaimed.

VIII. The King's Proclamation for the Abolishing of the Usurped Power of the Pope

Yet once again by the King to the Sheriffs

[*June* 9, 1534/5.]

Trusty and well beloved, we greet you well. And whereas not only upon good, just, and virtuous grounds and respects, edified upon the laws of God and holy Scripture by due consultation, deliberate advisement and consent, as well of all other our nobles and commons temporal assembled in our high court of Parliament, and by authority of the same, we have by good and wholesome laws and statutes made for the purpose, extirped, abolished, separated and secluded out of this our realm the abuses of the Bishop of Rome, his authority and jurisdiction of long time usurped as well upon us and our realm as upon all other kings and princes and their realms, like as they themselves have confessed and affirmed: but also forasmuch as our said nobles and commons, both spiritual and

[1] *L.P.* VI, 351. [2] *L.P.* VI, 720.

temporal, assembled in our said court of Parliament have upon like good, lawful, and virtuous grounds, and for the public weal of this our realm, by one whole assent granted, annexed, knit, and united to the crown imperial of the same, the title, dignity, and style of Supreme Head in earth immediately under God of the Church of England, as we be, and undoubtedly have hitherto been, which title and style both the bishops and clergy of this our realm have not only in convocation assembled consented, recognized and approved lawfully and justly to appertain unto us, but also by word, oath, profession, and writing under their signs and seals have confessed, ratified, corroborated, and confirmed the same; utterly renouncing all other oaths and obedience to any other foreign potentate and all foreign jurisdictions and powers, as well of the said Bishop of Rome, as of all other, whatsoever they be, as by their said professions and writings corroborated with the subscription of their names and appension of their seals more plainly appeareth. We let you wit, that calling unto our remembrance the power, charge, and commission given unto us of Almighty God, and upon a vehement love and affection toward our loving and faithful subjects, perceiving right well what great rest, quietness, and tranquillity of conscience, and manifold other commodities might insurge and arise unto them, if that the said bishops and others of the clergy of this our realm should set forth, declare, and preach unto them the true and sincere word of God, and without all manner colour, dissimulation and hypocrisy manifest and publish the great and innumerable enormities and abuses which the said Bishop of Rome, as well in the title and style, as also in authority and jurisdiction, of long time unlawfully and unjustly hath usurped upon us and our progenitors and all other christian princes, have therefore addressed our letters unto the bishop of the diocese, straightly charging and commanding him in the same, that not only he in his own proper person shall declare, teach and preach unto the people forthwith upon the receipt of our said letters unto him directed, every Sunday and other high feast through the year, the true, mere, and sincere word of God, and that the said same title, style, and jurisdiction of Supreme Head appertaineth only unto our crown and dignity royal: likewise as the said bishop, and all other the bishops of our realm have by oath affirmed, and confirmed by subscription of their names and setting to their seals; but also give warning, monition and charge to all manner abbots, priors, deans, archdeacons, provosts, parsons, vicars, curates, and all other ecclesiastical persons within his said diocese, as well to preach, teach, publish and declare in all manner churches our foresaid just title, style and jurisdiction, every Sunday and high feast through the year; and furthermore to monish and give commandment to all manner schoolmasters within his said diocese to instruct and teach the same unto the children committed unto them, as also to cause all manner prayers, orisons, rubrics, canons in mass-books and all other books used in the churches, wherein the said bishop of Rome is named, or his presumptuous and proud pomp and authority preferred, utterly to be abolished, eradicate and razed out, and his name and memory to be never more (except to his contumely and reproach) remembered; but perpetually suppressed and obscured; and finally to desist and leave out all such articles as be in the general sentence, which is usually accustomed to be read four times in the year, and do tend to the glory and advancement of the Bishop of Rome, his name, title, and jurisdiction. . . .

Given under our signet at our palace of Westminster the 9th day of June.[1]

Finally, in November, the Act of Supremacy was passed, in which Parliament affirmed that the King and his heirs are to be taken, accepted and reputed

> the only Supreme Head in earth of the Church of England called Anglicana Ecclesia, and shall have and enjoy annexed and united to the Imperial Crown of this realm as well the title and style thereof as all the honours, dignities, preeminences, jurisdictions, privileges, authorities, immunities, profits, and commodities, belonging and appertaining thereto.[2]

The title was incorporated in the royal style in January, 1535, and Henry's victory was complete. The authority of Rome had

[1] For note on text see App. I, Notes. [2] *Statutes of the Realm.*

been successfully repudiated. He had proved that the Pope could not, and the Emperor would not take effective measures against him. The Tudor will to power had triumphed, and Henry was, as he said, Pope and Emperor in England.

Two unhappy women still resisted it, however—Katharine of Aragon and her daughter Mary. The account of the ill-treatment meted out to them both by Henry makes bad reading in the letters sent by Chapuys to the Emperor. Comment and protest had no effect. That conscience which was on such very good terms with God justified Henry to himself probably in much the same way that he justifies his behaviour in the following extract.

IX. To His Ambassador with the Emperor

[*Sept.*, 1534.]

. . . Ye shall understand that, as touching the bruit in the Emperor's court ayenst the misentreatie of the Lady Katherine, Princess Dowager, and our daughter, the Lady Mary, which we do specially note in your said letters, surely considering and taking the case as it standeth, that every man, without respect of any earthly thing, is bound to regard the laws of God, and to fear and dread Him specially in so great a matter, whereupon dependeth not only the salvation of the parts spiritually, but also the weal of our realm, and, consequently, of all Christendom, the justness of the cause, and our due, sincere, and deliberate proceeding in the same, by so long time approved and discussed, as may well appear to all the world, as we doubt not but ye can well declare and show. It is not a little to our marvel that, touching the fact, either the Emperor, or any of his wise council, learned, or other discreet person would in anything think of us, touching our proceeding therein, but that which is godly, honourable and reasonable, agreeing both to the laws of God and our most bounden duty towards the observance of the same. And, as touching that which is spoken there, that the said Lady Katherine should not be honourably and well entreated, as to such a personage appertaineth; to that, both unto the Emperor and his council, or to any other that will so affirm, ye may truly allege that such report and bruit is untrue, affirming that in all things belonging to the said Lady Katherine, both in the honourable establishing of her house with her officers and servants, and in the allotting and appointing unto her of lands, tenements, possessions, and all other things condign for such an estate, it is done in every thing to the best that can be devised; and the like also of our daughter, the Lady Mary, whom we do order and entertain as we think most expedient, and also as to us seemeth pertinent, for we think it not meet that any person should prescribe unto us how we should order our own daughter, we being her natural father; which things our pleasure is that ye boldly and assuredly shall declare at any time, as well to the said Emperor as to any that shall minister to you any occasion so to do. . . .

And albeit the said Lady Katherine hath very disobediently behaved herself towards us, as well in contemning and setting at nought our laws and estatutes, as many other ways, yet for the conservation of our honour, ye may assure the said Emperor and all men, that we have, nevertheless, as much devised for her honourable entrenement, in all points as was beseeming for her estate; insomuch as we have at many and sundry times sent unto her not only our right trusty and right well-beloved cousin and councillor, the dukes of Norfolk and Suffolk, with other our nobles and councillors, but also the most Reverend Father in God, the Archbishop of York, the Reverend Fathers in God, the Bishops of Durham and Chester, and other spiritual persons, right well learned, and also being men of great virtue, to intimate and declare unto her, as well the justness of our cause, and all the determinations thereupon affirmed by the most famous universities and clerks of Christendom, with the whole conclusions and circumstances of the same, as also to declare unto her our laws and ordinances, made for the establishment, weal, honour, and surety of us, our realm, succession and posterity, in most loving fashion, and by all the honourable and gentle means that could be; persuading, moving, and exhorting her to conform herself to the following and obedience of the same accordingly, showing and declaring to her the dangers and great inconveniences that might ensue and happen to her, if she should offend, or in anywise resist and withstand the same; offering further unto her such honourable dowry, lands, tenements, and possessions, being already to her allotted, as were condign for her estate, with any other reasonable entertainment that she should and might lawfully require, which (nevertheless notwithstanding), she hath in most ungoodly, obstinate, and inobedient wise, wilfully resisted, set at nought, and contemned our said laws and ordinances, so as if we should or would attempt or minister unto her any rigour or extremity, she were undoubtedly within the extreme danger of our said laws.

Before and after all which said intimations and declarations, or the most of them, by our said councillors intimated and declared to the said Lady Katherine, as is aforesaid; the same offers were made, opened and declared unto the Emperor's ambassador here resident in our realm, who, if he would, could have certified the said Emperor, his master, the verity and truth, how honourably the said Lady Katherine was by us in all things entreated, as is aforesaid; and again, in acquittal of the same, how contemptuously, uncharitably and disobediently, she hath used and showed herself towards us and our laws. So as, if the said ambassador, according to his duty, and for the conservation and continuance of the peace, zeal, amity and love betwixt us and his said master the Emperor, had certified the premises according to the mere verity and truth, we think there could have no such bruit been there untruly noised, surmised and spread in those parts as now by your letters we do perceive there is, without any good, reasonable or just cause in the world.

Wherefore, first, and afore any manner of credence had been given thereunto by the Emperor, we would have thought he would have advertised us of the same, and so to have known our answer and declaration, whereby all such feigned, supposable and evil opinions might have been razed and abolished from those minds that might give light credence; as in like and semblable wise for the entire love, amity and friendship that is and hath been between the said Emperor and us, we would have used ourself towards him afore we would have given credence or been contented to have heard seriously any like matters or tales that should have touched him so near; as ye may exhort him not to give ear to any such feigned bruits without perfect knowledge of the truth, as it is the office of one friend to do to another. Declaring furthermore unto the said Emperor and other, as ye shall have occasion, and as ye right well can after your accustomed wisdom and dexterity, that considering not only our first marriage contracted with the said Lady Katharine to have been by the most famous clerks of Christendom proved, adjudged, and determined very incestuous and unlawful, and directly against the laws of Almighty God (wherewith no man can dispense) but also perpending the danger that thereof might have ensued hereafter to us, our realm and succession; we could no less do, (unless we should seem to contemn the word and laws of Christ), than utterly renounce and forsake the said incestuous and unlawful matrimony, which being so found, justly proved and determined as is aforesaid, we have now God's word and laws standing with us, with no little advice and deliberation, and in clearing and discharging of our conscience, lawfully ensued and accomplished. Trusting that not only the Emperor, but all other good people sincerely revolving and animadverting our lawful and just proceedings, with also the sincerity and justness of our cause, which the Bishop of Rome himself confessed to be just and lawful, and that by him we therein had sustained no little injury; insomuch that he promised our good brother the French King that, if we would send a proxy, he would, at his meeting with our said good brother at Marseilles, give sentence in our principal cause with us and on our part, which we, being a king, and (knowing ourself not bound so to do by the laws of God), utterly refused, so as because we would not thereby condescend nor agree to the usurped jurisdiction and authority of him that is and ever hath been the only enemy of kings, ne would, in derogation of ours and all other princes' powers, consent to support and condescend to his long said usurped jurisdiction and authority which so much hath heretofore blemished and defaced the privileges given by God to all princes and kings. He therefore unjustly and maliciously hath pronounced sentence against us, notwithstanding our appeal to the general council lawfully made before. Whereby you may perceive he did the same rather for malice and the maintenance of his own usurped power, authority, and too much mundanity, than for any respect that he had to the mere truth and verity. . . .

At last, on January 8, 1536, Katharine of Aragon died at Kimbolton, and Henry summoned 'a good many ladies of honour and others' to attend as mourners at her interment at Peterborough. She is described in the letters as 'the right noble and excellent Princess, our dearest sister, the Lady Katharine, widow and dowager of the right excellent Prince, our dearest and natural brother, Prince Arthur, of noble and famous memory deceased.'[1] It is reported that Henry, on hearing of her death, exclaimed, 'God be praised, we are free from all suspicion of war.'[2] And within four months Anne Boleyn, condemned on charges of incest and adultery, perished on the scaffold.

The following extract represents the greater part of a letter written by Henry to the Pope in or after 1530. It is used here to conclude the story of 'the King's great matter', because it is written in English, instead of the usual Latin of Henry's communications with Clement, and because it is, in itself, an outstanding specimen of his eloquence, and expresses with proper dignity and vigour his feelings with regard to the treatment he had received from Rome.

x. To Clement VII

[?1530.]

. . . [3]But to speak plainly to your holiness; forasmuch as we have suffered many injuries, which with great difficulty we do sustain and digest; albeit that among all things passed by your holiness some cannot be laid, alleged nor objected against your holiness, yet in many of them some default appeareth to be in you, which I would to God we could so diminish as it might appear no default; but it cannot be hid, which is so manifest, and though we would say nothing, the thing itself speaketh.

But as to that that is affirmed in your letters, both of God's law, and man's, otherwise than is necessary and truth, let that be ascribed to the temerity and ignorance of your counsellors, and

[1] Stowe's Collections: Harl. MS. 540, f. 52b. A similar letter, addressed to Lady Bedingfield, has been printed by Halliwell, *Letters of the Kings of England*, p. 352.

[2] L.P. X, 141.

[3] Beginning at f. 168v

your holiness to be without all default, save only for that ye do not admit more discreet and learned men to be your counsellors, and stop the mouths of them which liberally would speak the truth. This truly is your default, and verily a great fault, worthy to be alienate and abhorred of Christ's vicar, in that ye have dealt so variably, yea rather so inconstantly and deceivably. Be ye not angry with my words, and let be lawful for me to speak the truth without displeasure. If your holiness shall be displeased with what we do rehearse, impute no default in us, but in your own deeds; which deeds have so molested and troubled us wrongfully, that we speak now unwillingly and as enforced thereunto.

Never was there any prince so handled by a pope as your holiness hath entreated us. First, when our cause was proponed to your holiness, when it was explicate and declared afore the same; when certain doubts in it were resolved by your counsellors, and all things discussed, it was required that answer might be made thereunto by the order of law. There was offered a commission, with a promise also that the same commission should not be revoked; and whatsoever sentence should be given, should straight without delay be confirmed. The judges were sent unto us, the promise was delivered unto us, subscribed with your holiness' hand; which avouched to confirm the sentence, and not to revocate the commission, nor to grant any thing else that might let the same; and finally to bring us in a greater hope, a certain commission decretal, defining the cause, was delivered to the judges' hands. If your holiness did grant us all these things justly, ye did injustly revoke them: and if by good and truth the same was granted, they were not made frustrate and adnihilate without fraud; so as if there were no deceit nor fraud in the revocation, then how wrongfully and subtilly have been done those things that hath been done! Whether will your holiness say, that ye might do those things that ye have done, or that ye might not do them? If ye will say that ye might do them, where then is the faith which it becometh a friend, yea, and much more a pope to have, those things not being performed which lawfully were promised? And if ye will say that ye might not do them, have we not then very just cause to mistrust those medicines and remedies with which, in your letters, ye go about to heal our conscience, especially in that we may perceive and see those remedies to be prepared for us, not to relieve the sickness and disease of our mind, but for other means, pleasures, and worldly respects? And as it should seem profitable, that we should ever continue in hope or despair, so always the remedy is attempered; so that we being always a-healing, and never healed, should be sick still.

And this truly was the chief cause why we did consult and take the advice of every learned man, being free, without all affection, that the truth (which now with our labour and study we seem partly to have attained) by their judgements more manifestly divulged, we might more at large perceive; whose judgements and opinions it is easy to see how much they differ from that that those few men of yours do show unto you, and by those your letters is signified. Those few men of yours do affirm the prohibition of our marriage to be induct only by the law positive, as your holiness hath also written in your letters; but all others say that prohibition to be inducte both by the law of God and nature: those men of yours do suggest, that now may be dispensed for avoiding of slander; the others utterly do contend that by no mean it is lawful to dispense with that that God and nature hath forbidden.

We do separate from our cause the authority of the See Apostolic, which we do perceive to be destitute of that learning whereby it should be directed; and because your holiness doth ever profess your ignorance, and is wont to speak of other men's mouths, we do confer the saying of those with the sayings of them that be of the contrary opinion; for to confer the reasons it were too long. But now the universities of Cambridge, Oxford, in our realm; Paris, Orleans, Bituricen,[1] Andegaven,[2] in France; and Bononia[3] in Italy, by one consent; and also divers other of the most famous and learned men, being free from all affection, and only moved in respect of verity, partly in Italy, and partly in France, do affirm the marriage of the brother with the brother's wife, to be contrary both to the law of God and nature; and also do pronounce that no dispensation can be lawful nor available to any Christian man in that behalf. But others think the contrary,

[1] i.e. Bourges. [2] Angers. [3] Bologna.

by whose counsels your holiness hath done that that sithence ye have confessed ye could not do, in promising to us as we have above rehearsed, and giving that commission to the Cardinal Campeggio to be showed unto us; and after, if it so should seem profitable to burn it, as afterwards it was done indeed as we have perceived. Furthermore, those which so do moderate the power of your holiness, that they do affirm, that the same cannot take away the appellation which is used by man's law, and yet is available to divine matters every where without distinction. No princes heretofore have more highly esteemed nor honoured the See Apostolic than we have, wherefore we be the more sorry to be provoked to this contention, which to our usage and nature is most alienate and abhorred. Those things so cruel we write very heavily, and more glad would have been to have been silent if we might, and would have left your authority untouched with a good will; and constrained to seek the verity, we fell, against our will, into this contention; but the sincerity of the truth prohibited us to keep silence, and what should we do in so great and many perplexities? For truly if we should obey to the letters of your holiness, in that they do affirm that we know to be otherwise, we should offend God and conscience, and we should be a great slander to them that do the contrary, which be a great number, as we have before rehearsed. Also, if we should dissent from those things which your holiness doth pronounce, we would account it not lawful, if there were not a cause to defend the fact, as we now do, being compelled by necessity, lest we should seem to contemn the authority of the See Apostolic. Therefore your holiness ought to take it in good part, though we do somewhat at large and more liberally speak in this cause, which so doth oppress us, specially forasmuch as we pretend none atrocity, nor use no rhetoric in the exaggerating and increasing the indignity of the matter; but if we speak of any thing that toucheth the quick, it proceedeth of the mere verity, which we cannot nor ought not to hide in this cause, for it toucheth not worldly things but divine, not frail but eternal; in which things no feigned, false, nor painted reasons, but only the truth, shall obtain and take place. And God is the truth to whom are we bound to obey rather than to men; and nevertheless we cannot but obey unto men also, as we were wont to do, unless there be an express cause why we should not; which by those our letters we now do to your holiness: and we do it with charity, not intending to spread it abroad, nor yet further to impugn your authority, unless ye do compel us. . . .

On the origin of the divorce opinion differs. It is obvious that we cannot know the whole truth, and it is probable that it began in a more fortuitous manner than the results suggest. It may possibly have been proposed by Wolsey as a solution of the succession problem; but that it was the necessity of an heir which was fundamental, and which supplied the driving power, I am convinced. Henry had the whole weight of the political thought of the day behind him, in his incapacity to conceive of the idea of a woman ruler. Moreover, to a man of Henry's dominating temperament, a son was an essential expression of his personality, and the lack thereof a continual thwarting of his deepest instincts. When to these impulses we add the motive power supplied by a passionate attraction to an individual, and also the weight carried by the religious sanction to a man with Henry's theological bent, there is no difficulty in understanding his methods and his amazing persistence. Wolsey's vital mistake was made when, for the sake of his own power, he decided that the divorce must come through that power and from its source. At the beginning he threw all his influence into the scale of the necessity of the Papal sanction, and convinced an even more tenacious and determined nature than his own. Had he risked following the Pope's advice, and given Henry his divorce on his own legatine authority, he would have thrown upon Clement the onus of playing for time with the Emperor. As it was, the temporizing victimized Henry instead of Charles, cost Wolsey his power, and separated England from the Roman Catholic faith. 'Would to God,' wrote Sanga to Campeggio,

> the Cardinal had allowed the matter to take its course; because if the King had come to a decision without the Pope's authority, whether wrongly or rightly, it would have been without blame or prejudice to his Holiness.

That the most amazing expedients were considered by Rome is evident from the rest of the letter.

> With regard to the dispensation for marrying the son to the daughter of the King, if on the succession being thus established the King will reject his first thought of the divorce, the Pope will be much more inclined to grant it.[1]

What cannot be over-emphasized, however, is the fact that the divorce was always something more than a political problem. The validity of the original dispensation of Julius II was definitely open to question. It hinged upon an obscure point in canon law, and left room for honest doubt and honest disagreement. To miss this point is to get the whole thing out of focus, and to judge from the modern angle something that can only be understood if the sixteenth century attitude of mind is accepted. To the Pope and his advisers, to Henry and his, to the bishops and universities and all who were asked for their opinions, canon law in the fifteen-thirties was as important, as real and as difficult as Covenant 'sanctions' in the nineteen-thirties. That the upshot of the whole matter was determined by purely political considerations must not blind us to the religious and moral problems which fortified, upheld and embittered all those who were vitally concerned. A large part of Henry's power derived from the fact that he never suffered from the divided mind, or the conflict of heart and head. Conscience and desire may have been nearly conterminous, but we argue with little comprehension either of Henry or his age if we say that *because* he desired Anne Boleyn *therefore* his conscience first received 'tenderness, Scruple and prick'. He was the father of a son; and he would have been peculiarly free from what we may, if we like, call the 'superstition' of his day if he had not seen in the death of four heirs and other children by Katharine the fulfilment of the judgement of Leviticus (xx. 21) that declared 'if a man shall take his brother's wife . . . they shall be childless'. Unless we can work our way back to what people really *felt* at the time about the dispensation and the divorce we cut ourselves off from any real

[1] Quoted from *L.P.* IV, 5072. 'The son' was the King's bastard, the Duke of Richmond: 'the daughter' was Mary!

comprehension. To put it all down to a blind passion for a woman is to misunderstand all that is most fundamental in Henry's nature, to lose sight of what it was that Tudor settled rule meant to sixteenth century England, and to ignore Henry's understanding thereof.

That the divorce was the turning point in Henry's career as a monarch must, however, be apparent. The seven years' struggle with the papacy had called for all his strength and cunning, all the control, energy and foresight that the son of Henry VII, the pupil of Wolsey, could show himself master of in his maturity. 'If the lion knew his strength,' More once said of Henry, 'hard it were to rule him.' For good and ill, he learnt it in those seven years, and he learnt, finally, where to look for the source of real power—not abroad, but at home.

PART III

'THE IMPERIAL THEME'

'. . . by divers sundry old authentic histories and chronicles it is manifestly declared and expressed that this Realm of England is an Empire . . . governed by one Supreme Head and King, having the Dignity and Royal Estate of the Imperial Crown of the same.'

ACT OF APPEALS: 24 HEN. VIII, C. 12

'Where the word of a King is, there is power; and who shall say unto him, What doest thou?'—ECCLESIASTES VIII. 4.

'Quia solum Deus haeredem facit.'

BRACTON: F. 62B, CAP. 29. ON ACQUIRING THE DOMINION OF THINGS

CHAPTER I

THE PILGRIMAGE OF GRACE

(*September, 1536—February, 1537*)

'This is no fashion for subjects.'
HENRY VIII

THE Pilgrimage of Grace was the most considerable domestic crisis of Henry's reign. It lasted for six months; but once it was over, home policy gave him little further trouble for his remaining ten years. Although an armed rising, the Pilgrimage of Grace was not strictly speaking a rebellion. The insurgents cried 'God save the King' as heartily as the army that was sent to subdue them, and the oath they swore was to be true to 'God, the king, the commons and the Holy Church'. It was the one great spontaneous outburst of feeling in which the country voiced its natural conservatism, its affection for the old order that was rapidly vanishing, and its inevitable and steadily accumulating hatred for Cromwell's policy. It was never, at any moment, directed against the King himself, nor against any of the established institutions of the realm.

The visitation of the monasteries, which had begun in July, 1535, had yielded by March, 1536, all the evidence that Cromwell required. Their 'great and abominable' enormities, and the 'manifest sin, vicious, carnal, and abominable living' of the monks, were laid before the reformation parliament; and before its own dissolution in April it passed the bill for the dissolution of the lesser monasteries. The commissioners set to work with a will, and in no parts of England did they wreak more havoc than in Yorkshire, where no less than fifty-three religious houses were destroyed, and in Lincolnshire where they suppressed thirty-seven.

In both these districts, as well as in the other more backward and remote parts like Devon and Cornwall, the dissolution was viewed with the deepest hostility. And at the same time the general feeling of disaffection was aggravated by yet another group of government commissioners, engaged in levying on all incomes of more than £20 the second instalment of the two-and-a-half per cent subsidy which had been granted in 1534. All kinds of rumours added to the suspicion and irritation: word flew round that licences would have to be bought by those who ate wheaten bread, capons and pigs: that weddings, christenings and burials were to be taxed; that all church jewels and plate were to be confiscated, and also all unmarked cattle.

Matters came to a head on October 1, when the dissolution commissioner arrived at Louth. Under the leadership of a shoemaker named Melton a crowd became a mob, and by October 3 the mob had become a body of insurgents with a programme. They burnt the assessment books, refused to pay the subsidy, and sent one of the commissioners to the King with their petition, which was, in sum, a detailed criticism of the government policy. It voiced the general hatred of Cromwell and other upstart members of the Council, asking that they and the new bishops should all be removed. It protested against the levying of the subsidy, and asked that in future the King should not demand money from his subjects, except for the defence of the kingdom in time of war. It also asked for the restoration of the suppressed monasteries.

In a surprisingly short time the whole of the county of Lincoln was up. Monks and priests, clerks, artisans, peasants and yeomen all rallied to the movement, sweeping in with them large numbers of the local gentry. By October 6 about forty thousand insurgents had gathered at Lincoln, under the banner of the five wounds of Christ. Henry, meanwhile, had commissioned two armies, one to be led by the Duke of Suffolk, the other to operate under his own direction. By the tenth, Suffolk had reached Stamford, but his army was a mere handful of less than a thousand men, and he had neither guns nor money. Had the rebels moved at once they might have swept southwards, carrying all before them. As it was, they waited at Lincoln for the King's reply to their petition, which was brought by Lancaster herald on the eleventh.

1. Answer to the Petitions of the Traitors and Rebels in Lincolnshire

[*Oct.* 10, 1536.]

First, we begin and make answer to the fourth and sixth articles, because upon them dependeth much of the rest. Concerning choosing of counsellors, I never have read, heard, nor known that prince's counsellors and prelates should be appointed by rude and ignorant common people; nor that they were persons meet, or of ability, to discern and chose meet and sufficient counsellors for a prince. How presumptuous then are ye, the rude commons of one shire, and that one of the most brute and beastly of the whole realm, and of least experience, to find fault with your Prince for the electing of his counsellors and prelates; and to take upon you, contrary to God's law and man's law, to rule your Prince, whom ye are bound by all laws to obey and serve, with both your lives, lands and goods, and for no worldly cause to withstand: the contrary whereof you, like traitors and rebels, have attempted, and not like true subjects, as ye name yourselves.

As to the suppression of religious houses and monasteries, we will that ye, and all our subjects, should well know that this is granted us by all the nobles, spiritual and temporal, of this our realm, and by all the Commons of the same, by Act of Parliament; and not set forth by any counsellor or counsellors, upon their mere will and fantasy, as ye full falsely would persuade our realm to believe. And where ye allege that the service of God is much thereby diminished, the truth thereof is contrary; for there be no houses suppressed where God was well served, but where most vice, mischief, and abomination of living was used: and that doth well appear by their own confessions, subscribed with their own hands, in the time of our visitations. And yet were suffered a great many of them, more than we by the Act needed, to stand; wherein, if they amend not their living, we fear we have more to answer for, than the suppression of all the rest. And as for their hospitality, for the relief of poor people, we wonder ye be not ashamed to affirm that they have been a great relief to our people, when a great many, or the most part, hath not past four or five religious persons in them, and divers but one, which spent the substance of the goods of their house in nourishing of vice, and abominable living. Now, what unkindness and unnaturality may we impute to you, and all our subjects that be of that mind, that had liefer such an unthrifty sort of vicious persons should enjoy such possessions, profits, and emoluments, as grow of the said houses, to the maintenance of their unthrifty life, than we your natural Prince, Sovereign Lord, and King, which doth and hath spent more in your defences, of his own, than six times they be worth!

As touching the Act of Uses,[1] we marvel what madness is in your brain, or upon what ground ye would take authority upon you, to cause us to break those laws and statutes which, by all the nobles, knights, and gentlemen of this realm, whom the same chiefly toucheth, hath been granted and assented to; seeing in no manner of thing it toucheth you, the base commons of our realm! Also the grounds of those Uses were false, and never admitted by any law, but usurped upon the Prince, contrary to all equity and justice, as it hath been openly both disputed and declared, by all the well learned men of England in Westminster Hall; whereby ye may well perceive how mad and unreasonable your demands be, both in that and the rest, and how unmeet it is for us, and dishonourable, to grant or assent unto, and less meet and decent for you, in such rebellious sort, to demand the same of your Prince.

As touching the fifteenth, which ye demand of us to be released, think ye that we be so faint hearted, that perforce ye of one shire (were ye a great many moe) could compel us with your insurrections, and such rebellious demeanour, to remit the same? Or think ye that any man will or may take you to be true subjects, that first maketh a show of a loving grant, and then, perforce, would compel your Sovereign Lord and King to release the same; the time of payment whereof is not yet come?

[1] Henry had tried to extract this Statute from the Reformation Parliament on various occasions, but it was rejected every time until the last session in 1536. Its aim was to protect the feudal rights of the King in the property of deceased persons. Although a man could not leave his land by will, he could and did enfeoff it, or put it in trust, for the use of those to whom he wished to leave it.

Yea, and seeing the same will not countervail the tenth penny of the charges, which we do, and daily must, sustain, for your tuition and safeguard? Make ye sure, by your occasions of this your ingratitudes, unnaturalness, and unkindness to us now administered, ye give us cause, which hath always been as much dedicate to your wealths as ever was King, not so much to set our study for the setting forward of the same, seeing how unkindly and untruly ye deal now with us, without any cause or occasion. And doubt ye not, though ye have no grace nor naturalness in you, to consider your duties of allegiance to your King and Sovereign; the rest of our realm, we doubt not, hath: and we and they shall so look on this cause, that we trust shall be to your confusion, if, according to our former letters, ye submit not yourselves.

As touching the First Fruits, we let you wit, it is a thing granted us by Act of Parliament also, for the supportation of part of the great and excessive charges which we support and bear for the maintenance of your wealths and others our subjects. And we have known, also, that ye, our commons, have much complained, in times past, that the most of the goods, lands, and possessions of the realm were in the spiritual men's hands; and yet now, bearing us in hand that ye be as loving subjects to us as may be, ye can not find in your hearts that your Prince and Sovereign Lord should have any part thereof (and yet it is nothing prejudicial unto you, our commons), but do rebel and unlawfully rise against your Prince, contrary to your duty of allegiance and God's commandment. Wherefore, Sirs, remember your follies and traitorous demeanours, and shame not your native country of England, nor offend no more so grievously your undoubted King and natural Prince, which always hath showed himself most loving unto you; and remember your duty of allegiance, and that ye are bound to obey us, your King, both by God's commandment and law of nature. Wherefore we charge you, eftsoons, upon the forsaid bonds and pains, that ye withdraw yourselves to your own houses, every man; and no more to assemble, contrary to our laws and your allegiances; and to cause the provokers of you to this mischief to be delivered to our Lieutenants' hands, or ours, and you yourselves to submit you to such condigne punishment, as we and our nobles shall think you worthy. For doubt ye not else, that we, and our nobles, can nor will suffer this injury at your hand, unrevenged, if ye give not place to us of Sovereignty, and show yourselves as bounden and obedient subjects, and no more to intermeddle yourselves from henceforth with the weighty affairs of the realm; the direction whereof only appertaineth to us your King, and such noble men and counsellors as he list to elect and chose to have the ordering of the same. And thus we pray unto Almighty God to give you grace to do your duties, and to use yourselves towards us like true and faithful subjects, so as we may have cause to order you thereafter; and rather obediently to consent amongst you to deliver into the hands of our Lieutenant 100 persons, to be ordered according to their demerits at our will and pleasure, than by your obstinacy and wilfulness to put yourselves, your lives and wives, children, lands, goods and chattles, besides the indignation of God, in the utter adventure of total destruction, and utter ruin by force and violence of the sword.

It was a vigorous and characteristic document, in Henry's grand manner. And as the rebels brooded over it the royal forces grew into a formidable army. The rebels hesitated, and were lost. As Froude says, 'There was no forethought, no efficient leader—sixty thousand men had drifted to Lincoln, and had halted there in noisy uncertainty till their way to London was interrupted'. By the thirteenth the commons had begun to disperse, and the gentry were undertaking to prevent further outbreaks. Then came the King's vengeance. The gentry were to be spared if they would police the country: and the commons were to be pardoned if they surrendered their leaders to the royal justice. Lincoln, Louth and Horncastle were singled out, to be terrorized as examples, and in these towns forty-six of the rebel leaders were hanged.

Before the Lincolnshire rising had collapsed, however, trouble of a much more serious nature had broken out in Yorkshire. News of their neighbours' revolt had spread quickly to the northern county, where the resentment at the changes was just as deeply felt. By October 14 nearly the whole of Yorkshire was up in defence of the old order, and more particularly in defence of the monasteries. The oath administered to all who joined this ' pilgrimage of grace for the commonwealth ', bound them to ' the maintenance of God's faith and Church militant, preservation of the king's person, and purifying the nobility of all villein's blood and evil counsellors, to the restitution of Christ's Church, and the suppression of heretics' opinions '.

The Yorkshire rising was not only on a much larger scale, but was rendered more formidable than that of Lincolnshire by the fact that it acquired at the outset a real leader. Swept into the movement partly by chance, Robert Aske, Yorkshire landowner and London lawyer, possessed qualities both of the good soldier and of the shrewd man of affairs; and by October 19 he had already achieved an important strategic triumph, having gained for the side of the rebels the venerable Lord Darcy, the one hope of the royal party in the north. With Darcy went the rest of the nobility and gentry who had taken refuge with him in Pomfret Castle, but were persuaded by Aske's mingling of eloquence and intimidation to throw in their lot with the commons, with whose complaints most of them genuinely sympathized. York, Pomfret and Hull were quickly in Aske's hands, and by the twenty-fourth he had a force of some thirty-five thousand men ready to oppose the King's forces who were occupying Doncaster.

The two letters from Henry that follow introduce us to the royal commanders. Suffolk, having dealt with the Lincolnshire trouble, was ready to go north. The Earl of Shrewsbury, who had raised the Derbyshire levies as soon as the first outbreak began, was encamped at Nottingham, awaiting orders. The Marquis of Exeter, Henry's own cousin, and the Earls of Rutland and Huntingdon, were all in the field, and in Doncaster was the Duke of Norfolk, son of the victor of Flodden.

11. To the Duke of Suffolk and Others

[*Oct.* 24, 1536.]

Right trusty and right entirely beloved Cousin, right trusty and well beloved, and trusty and right well beloved, We greet you well. And have received your letters of the 22nd of this present, written at 12 of the clock at night, containing your discreet and substantial proceedings in the conducing of the charge there committed unto you, to our desired end and purpose, with the two schedules of the names; the one of such persons as be newly sworn, the other of such notable traitors as have been presented unto you by the township of Horncastle, and other places thereabouts: For your diligent endeavours wherein, we give unto you our right hearty thanks; trusting you will, with such dexterity, travail for the speedy finishing of the same, as the harness and weapons may be also shortly brought in to you; which, next the ordering of the passages, for your good direction, also, wherein we do right heartly thank you, is a special point, and a thing the finishing whereof we have much to heart. You shall also understand, that this present Tuesday, in the morning, we have received letters, as well from our Cousin of Shrewsbury, as others from our Cousin of Norfolk; the first, declaring our said Cousin of Shrewsbury, with his forces, to lie within one mile of our town of Doncaster, and to have already sent 1100 of his men, with six pieces of ordnance, to Doncaster and Rasshington Bridge, to keep the passages there; so that the rebels shall enter no further, but to their pains: the second, written from our said Cousin of Norfolk, declaring himself to abide at Newark, and that his forces could not come unto him until this present Tuesday; and that our Cousin of Exeter could not, with his forces, be at Newark till to-morrow. Whereupon, remembering as well that Doncaster is 30 miles from Newark, which, with the bands of our said Cousin of Norfolk, cannot be passed in any short time; as that, in case it should fortune our said Cousin of Shrewsbury, either being pressed thereunto by the rebels, or else thinking himself to have some great advantage, to give the onset of them, and in such an adventure to have the worse (which God defend); it should be very necessary for us, in such case, to see the passages in those parts so kept that the said rebels might be constrained to remain on the other side of the water; and so finally, of necessity, for want of victuals and such success as they would desire, to disparkle,[1] and retire themselves again to their houses: we have thought convenient to signify unto you, that our mind and pleasure is, in case you shall receive advertisement from our said Cousin of Norfolk, upon any such chance, which God defend, that it should be necessary for us, for the sure stopping of the passages, to keep the rebels on that side Trent, to have your aid and assistance, you shall then leave SUCH ONE RULER AS YOU SHALL THINK MEET, with such number of men as your wisdom shall think ALSO CONVENIENT, to remain at Lincoln, AND THEREABOUTS; and yourself, BEING THEN JOINED IN COMMISSION WITH THE SAID DUKE, with the rest of your forces, shall, for the purpose specified, repair unto SUCH PLACES, AS BETWEEN YOU SHALL BE THOUGHT MEET, and so join together for the accomplishment of our desire, in the sure keeping of the said passages, AS MAY REDOUND TO THE SURE KEEPING OF THE SAME, AND OUR HONOUR ALSO.[2] And to the intent you shall have special commission authorizing you thus to do, we have herewith sent a commission, under our Great Seal, wherein we have joined you and our said Cousin of Norfolk togethers, as our Lieutenants to serve us, if such perverse chance should happen, as we trust in God there shall not, as is before mentioned.

III. To the Duke of Norfolk

[*Windsor, Oct.* 27, 1536.]

Right trusty and right entirely beloved Cousin, we greet you well. And have received your letters, written unto us from Welbeck, on Wednesday last past, at midnight. . . . We have thought convenient for our answer to your said letters now sent from Welbeck, to signify unto you that like as we cannot,

[1] Disperse.

[2] The passages printed in CAPITALS in this and subsequent letters are insertions or alterations in Henry's own writing.

being here absent from you, prescribe unto you so certain an order for your proceedings, but that you shall, percase, having the things treated of before you, and in the experience in your eye, perceive necessary cause of alteration; so we desire and pray you, specially, and above all things, never to give stroke, if these our letters may come in time to your hands, as we doubt not but they shall, unless you shall, with due advertisement, think yourself to have great and notable advantage for the same : but rather, in case you shall think the rebels over-strong for you, or if you shall judge any of the company of our said Cousin of Shrewsbury to be evil-willing, froward, if you shall think requisite, to retire yourself to the passages of Nottingham and Newark, and by good means to persuade our said Cousin of Shrewsbury to do the semblable; and there according to your device strongly to fortify the same, till, with our Army Royal, which we do put in areadiness, we shall repair unto you; and so, with God's help, be able to bear down the traitors before us; having ever more regard for the defence of us and of your natural country, than to any dishonour that might be spoken of such retirement; which, in the end, shall prove a great deal more honourable, than with a little hasty forwardness to jeopardy both our honour and your lives. For we assure you, we would neither adventure you, our Cousin of Norfolk, our Cousin of Shrewsbury, nor our other Cousins there with you, or our good and true subjects with the same, in such perilous sort, as there should be but a likelihood of wilful casting of any of you specially away, for all the land and dominion that we have on that side Trent. And therefore eftsoons we require you, now you be there together, as we think, to weigh things in such wise, and with such circumspection of all parts, that you may preserve yourselves and our people, without adventuring any further than manhood and courage, directed by wisdom, would require; and then shall you preserve ever our honour, and do good service to your own natural country. Now concerning your promises to be made to the rebels for the stay of them till your forces shall be come, and joined with the others; albeit we certainly know that you will pretermit none occasion wherein by policy or otherwise you may damage our enemies, yet we doubt not again but in all your proceedings you will have such a temperance, as our honour, specially, shall remain untouched, and yours rather increased, than by the certain grant of that you cannot certainly promise appear in the mouths of the worst men any thing defaced. And therefore we remit all other things to your good discretions, and shall beseech the giver of victories to send to you, in every condition, as good success as we would wish to ourself, if we were there with you; whereof we have no manner of doubt; our hope being reposed in His goodness, that never failed them, at length, that assuredly trust in Him.

Finally, whereas you desire us, in case any mischance should happen unto you, to be good Lord unto your children; surely, good Cousin, albeit we trust certainly in God that no such thing shall fortune; yet we would you should perfectly know, that if God should, by the end of the course of nature in you, take you out of this transitory life before us, we should not fail so to remember your children, being your lively images, to remember and in such wise to look of them with our Princely favour, for your assured truth and service, as others by their example should not be discouraged to follow your steps in that behalf. . . .

One brief extract, however, voices perhaps more clearly than the longer letters Henry's absolute determination to carry through the work of the Dissolution at whatever cost. Writing to the Earl of Derby on October 28, 1536, he instructs him that if he finds the monks of Sawley have returned to their Abbey, after being dispossessed,

> you shall then, without further delay, cause the said Abbot and certain of the chief of the monks to be hanged upon long pieces of timber, or otherwise, out of the steeple; and the rest to be put to execution in such sundry places as you shall think meet for the example of others.

As a piece of imaginative terrorism it is hard to beat. And this was the mind that the people of the North hoped to influence without resorting to desperate measures and bloodshed—the mind that while occupied with the quelling of an armed rebellion kept such a grip of accessory detail that it could pause for a moment to excogitate this particular visual horror and calculate its moral effect!

Once again, as in Lincolnshire, the fundamental loyalty of the rebels proved their ultimate undoing. Norfolk, in Doncaster, had barely eight thousand men to oppose to Aske's thirty-five thousand, and so offered to treat with his opponents. Aske, unwilling to force a pitched battle, conferred with him at Doncaster Bridge. The grievances of the insurgents were drawn up, and it was agreed that a truce should be maintained until the King's answer to their demands should be received. Norfolk himself, and the Earl of Shrewsbury, escorted Sir Ralph Ellerker and Robert Bowes, the pilgrims' spokesmen, to Henry at Windsor. And so the rebels' one chance was thrown away, for the sake of an as yet obscurely-realized national feeling and a deep loyalty to the Tudor monarchy—the two emotions destined to destroy England's adherence to the Catholic faith, at work already even in the hearts of those who were taking up arms in its defence.

Henry's reply to the northern rebels was even more masterly than his answer to the Lincolnshire petition. He took their five articles one by one, riddled them with the skill of a prosecuting counsel, and effectively demonstrated yet once again his own mastery of controversy and statecraft. It was drawn up ' with his own hand ', and he ' made no creature privy thereunto until it was finished '.

IV. To the Rebels in Yorkshire[1]

[*Nov.* 2, 1536.]

First, as touching the maintenance of the Faith; the terms be so general that hard they be to be answered; but if they mean the Faith of Christ, to which all Christian men be most obliged, we declare and protest ourself to be he that always do and have minded to die and live in the purity of the same; and that no man can or dare set his foot by ours in proving of the contrary;

[1] It is suggested in Dodds's *Pilgrimage of Grace* that this letter was never sent.

marvelling not a little that ignorant people will go about or take upon them to instruct us, (which something have been noted to be learned) what the right Faith should be, or that they would be so ingrate and unnatural to us, their most rightful King, without any our desert, upon false reports and surmises to suspect us of the same, and give rather credence to forged light tales than to the approved truth by us these twenty-eight years used, and by our deeds approved.

To the second, which toucheth the maintenance of the Church, and liberties of the same; this is so general a proposition that, without distinctions, no man, with truth, can answer it, neither by God's laws nor by the laws of the realm. For first, the Church which they mean must be known; secondly, whether they be lawful or unlawful liberties which they require: and this known, I doubt not but that they shall be answered according to God's law, equity and justice. But yet for all their generality, this I dare assever, that (meaning what Church they list) we have done nothing in their prejudice that may not be abidden by, both by God's law and man's; and in our own Church, whereof we be the Supreme Head here in Earth, we have not done so much prejudice as many of our predecessors have done upon much less grounds. Wherefore, since it is a thing which nothing pertaineth to any of you, our commons, nor that you bear any thing therein, I cannot but reckon a great unkindness and unnaturalness, in that ye had liever a churl or two should enjoy those profits of their monasteries, in supportation of vicious and abominable life, than I, your Prince, for supportation of mine extreme charges done for your defence.

The third toucheth three things; the laws, the common wealth, the directors of the laws under us. Touching the laws, we expressly dare testify, that (blind men deeming no colours, nor yet being judges) it shall be duly proved that there were never, in any of our predecessors' days, so many wholesome, commodious and beneficial acts made for the common wealth; and yet I mean it since their time, that would fain have thank without desert. For Our Lord forbid (seeing we have been these twenty-eight years your King) that both we and our Council should have lost so much time as not to know now, better than when we came first to our reign, what were the common wealth, and what were not. And though owtherquedaunce of some, may chance, will not let them to knowledge it so, yet I trust and doubt not but the most part of our loving subjects (specially those which be not seduced by false reports) do both think it, accept it, and find it so. Now, touching the common wealth; what King hath kept you all, his subjects, so long in wealth and peace; so long without taking or doing wrong, one to the other; so indifferently minister justice to all, both high and low; so defended you all from outward enemies; so fortified the frontiers of this realm, to his no little, and in a manner, inestimable charges? and all for your wealths and sureties. What King hath given among you mo general or freer pardons? What King hath been loather to punish his subjects, or showed more mercy amongst them? These things being so true, as no true man can deny them, it is an unnatural and unkind demeanour of you, our subjects, to believe or deem the contrary of it, by whose report so ever it should be. As touching the beginning of our reign, where ye say so many noble men were Counsellors; who were then Counsellors I well remember, and yet of the Temporalty I note none but two worthy calling noble; the one Treasurer of England, the other High Steward of our House; others as the Lord Marney, and Darcy, but scant well born gentlemen; and yet of no great lands till they were promoted by us, and so made Knights and Lords; the rest were lawyers and priests, save two Bishops, which were Canterbury and Winchester. If these, then, be the great number of noble men that ye speak of, and that ye seemed then to be content withal; why then, now, be ye not much better content with us; which have now so many nobles indeed, both of birth and condition? For first of the Temporality; in our Privy Council we have the Duke of Norfolk, the Duke of Suffolk, the Marquess of Exeter, the Lord Steward (when he may come), the Earl of Oxford, the Earl of Sussex, the Lord Sandes our Chamberlain, the Lord Admiral, Treasurer of our House, Sir William Paulet, Comptroller of our House: and of the Spirituality; the Bishop of Hereford, the Bishop of Chichester and the Bishop of Winchester. Now how far be ye abused, to reckon that then there were mo noble men in our Privy Council than now? But yet, though I now do declare the truth, to pull you from the blindness that you were led in, yet, we ensure you, we would ye knew that it appertaineth nothing to any of our subjects to appoint us our Council, ne we will take it so at your hands. Wherefore, henceforth, remember better the duties of subjects to your King and Sovereign Lord, and meddle no more of those, nor such like things, as ye have nothing to do in.

To the fourth; where ye, the commons, do name certain of our Council to be subverters both of God's law and the laws of this realm; we do take and repute them as just and true executors, both of God's laws and ours, as far as their commissions under us do extend. And if any of our subjects can duly prove the contrary, we shall proceed against them, and all other offenders therein, according to justice, as to our estate and dignity royal doth appertain. And in case it be but a false and untrue report (as we verily think it is), then it were as meet, and standeth as well with justice, that they should have the self-same punishment which wrongfully hath objected this to them, that they should have had if they deserved it. And one thing amongst others maketh me think that this slander should be untrue; because it proceedeth from that place which is both so far distant from where they inhabit, and also from those people which never heard them preach, nor yet knoweth any part of their conversation. Wherefore we exhort you, our commons, to be no more so light of credit, neither of ill things spoken of your King and Sovereign, nor yet of any of his Prelates and Counsellors; but to think that your King, having so long reigned over you, hath as good discretion to elect and chose his Counsellors as those (who so ever they be) that hath put this in your heads.

Here, in this final point, which ye, our Commons of Yorkshire, do desire, and also in the matter of the whole, we verily think that the rest of our whole commons (whereof ye be in manner but an handful) will greatly disdain, and not bear it, that ye take upon you to set order both to them and us, your both Sovereign; and that (though ye be rebels) ye would make them as bearers and partakers of your mischief; willing them to take pardon for insurrections, which verily I think and doubt not they never minded; but, like true subjects, to the contrary, hath both with heart and deed been ready at our call, to defend both us and themselves.

And now, for our part; as to your demands, we let you wit that pardon of such things as ye demand lieth only in the will and pleasure of the Prince; but it seemeth, by your lewd proclamations and safe-conducts, that there be amongst you which take upon them both the King's and Councillors' parts, which neither yet by us, nor by consent of the realm, hath been admitted to any such room. What arrogancy, then, is in those wretches, (being also of none experience) to presume to raise you, our subjects, without commission or authority, yea, and against us, under a cloaked colour of your wealth, and in our name, and, as the success will declare, (we being no more merciful than ye yet hitherto do deserve) to your utter confusions? Wherefore we let you wit, ye, our subjects of Yorkshire, that were it not that our princely heart cannot reckon this your shameful insurrection and unnatural rebellion to be done of malice or rancour, but rather by a lightness given in a manner by a naughty nature to a commonalty, and a wondrous sudden surreption of gentlemen; we must needs have executed another manner of punishment, than (ye humbly knowledging your fault and submitting your selves to our mercy) we intend to do. And to the intent that ye shall all know that our princely heart rather embraceth (of his own disposition) pity and compassion of his offending subjects, than will to be revenged of their naughty deeds; we are contented, if we may see and perceive in you all a sorrowfulness for your offences, and will henceforth to do no more so, nor to believe so lewd and naughty tales or reports of your most kind and loving Prince and his Council, to grant unto you all our Letters Patents of pardon for this rebellion; so that ye will deliver unto us ten such of the ringleaders and provokers of you to this rebellion as we shall assign to you and appoint. Now, note the benignity of your Prince. Now note how easily ye may have pardon, both gentlemen and other, if ye list. Now note how effusion of blood may be eschewed. Now note what this little while of your rebellion hath hindered yourselves and country. Now learn, by a little lack, to eschew a worse. Now learn, by this small warning, to keep you true men. Thus I, as your head, pray for you, my members, that God may light you with His grace to knowledge, and declare yourselves our true subjects henceforth, and to give more credence to these our benign persuasions, than to the perverse instigations of malicious disposed persons.

This reply was discussed by the rebels at a conference at York on November 21, at which it was agreed that the Archbishop of York should gather his clergy together to put forward with precision and detail the religious demands made by the pilgrims. They intended, in fact, to treat with Henry, who expressed his indignation forcibly in the following letter.

He begins by marvelling at the 'ingratitude and unkindness administered unto us in this Insurrection, specially by those persons that should show themselves to be of nobility and worship'. He then proceeds:

v. To Ellerker and Bowes

[*Nov.* 27, 1536.]

. . . Secondly, it is no little marvel unto us that seeing the commons be now down, and peradventure not even so willing to rise again as some make pretence and report, the nobles and you the gentlemen have subscribed such a letter as you have now sent to our said cousin of Norfolk; by the which it appeareth they make themselves a party with the commons, which is clean contrary to the report of you Sir Ralph Ellerker and Robert Bowes, who declared them to have been taken against their wills, which did then chiefly move us to take the more pity and compassion of them. And now the intent of your pilgrimage, with the devotion of the pilgrims, may well appear. For who can reckon that foundation good which is contrary to God's commandment, or the executors to be good men, which, contrary to their allegiance, presume with force to order their prince? For God commandeth them to obey their prince, whatsoever he be, yea, though he should not direct them justly, and their oath of allegiance, which passeth all oaths, and is the foundation without the keeping of which all other oaths be but naught and vain, bindeth them to the same. Wherefore who can think that you, persevering in this madness you be now in, which daily by your letters and doings ye declare yet more and more, should not be ashamed to call yourselves humble subjects, when your deeds be so far contrarious. For who would think that true subjects, though they were offenders, would not come to any part of our realm that we should allot under our safe-conduct? And who can believe that they should be true subjects, though they declare it in words, that will not repair to the place appointed by their prince and sovereign lord, having his safe-conduct? The Scots, when they were most enemies, would do so much and more, for they did sometime resort upon our said cousin of Norfolk's word into his camp. How much less, then, ought subjects to indent with their prince and sovereign either of the place or the coming in arms and forcible array. This is no fashion for subjects, but rather after the fashion of war between prince and prince, which maketh us to marvel that they would thus blind us with fair words, calling as their natural and most dread sovereign lord under God, with desire of our mercy and pity, when nevertheless the effect of your said letters in sundry points (as in desiring hostages, a place indifferent, and abstinence of war for fourteen days after the meeting) showeth the contrary. What madness is entered into their heads, that they cannot remember that a small continuance of this mischief among them shall very shortly destroy themselves, and utterly devast those parts which they do inhabit under us? Can they think they shall be able to work any other effect in the end by this their rebellion against us their prince and sovereign lord, than to convey themselves to their own destruction? It is surely much to our regret to see this folly, ingratitude and unkindness in them towards us; but we would be more sorry to see them persevere in such sort in their folly, that we should be enforced on all sides to extend our princely power to their repression, and so to destroy the members of our own politic body. And yet you may assure them that, rather than they should thus put us, their head and king, and all the rest of our good subjects to these daily pains and travail, we shall devise to cut them off, as corrupt members, in such time as their malices shall, we trust certainly in God, redound to themselves.

Thirdly we think it no little shame to all you that note yourselves and have been taken of the nobility to suffer such a villain as Aske is, having neither wit nor experience, to subscribe to the letter sent to our said cousin of Norfolk before you all, as though he were your ruler and guide. Where is your nobility become? And it were not extinct, you could not suffer such a villain to be amongst you, or to be privy to any of your affairs, which was never esteemed in any of our courts nor in any other place within our whole realm, but for a common pedlar in the law. And surely we and all our nobles here take your hands greatly touched by the same, and think verily it is only his filed tongue and flattery, with false surmises, that hath thus deceived you, and brought him in this unfitting and ungoodly estimation among you.

Finally, our pleasure is, you shall advertise them that we be as much inclined to show our clemency and mercy unto them as ever was prince to his subjects in such a case, so as we may first perceive in them an aptness and disposition to seek and receive the same, which every reasonable man must needs grant to be meet and convenient. And that unless they will permit our subjects to have free recourse unto us leave the interception of our letters to our said subjects and of theirs to us, withdraw their men from our towns and castles which perforce they do now keep, contrary to the duties of good subjects, restore the ship that was sent to Evers, and no further to molest the said Evers, and like true subjects submit themselves unto us, confirming the same submission with their deeds and proceedings, we intend not that my Lord of Norfolk shall commune any further with them, but to stay him till we may know by your answer to these, to be sent to our said cousin of Norfolk, whether we shall repute them as good and true subjects or as our traitors and rebels. . . .

At the beginning of December the leaders met at Pomfret and defined their grievances and demands. No longer could the King complain of their vagueness and general terms. The heresies and heretical works of Luther, Wyclif, Huss and others were to be destroyed. The supremacy of the Church touching 'cura animarum' was to be reserved to Rome as before. The Princess Mary was to be declared legitimate. The suppressed abbeys were to have their lands, houses and goods restored. So the recital went on, for twenty-four heads, the eighth requiring the condign punishment of Cromwell and Rich as 'subverters of the good laws of the realm and maintainers and inventors of heretics'. A Parliament at Nottingham or York, 'and that shortly' was also required. Such were a few of the articles that Aske took to Doncaster and presented to Norfolk on December 5: and that Norfolk was well prepared for their demands is evident from the following extract from one of Henry's letters, dated by the *Letters and Papers*, December 2.

VI. To Norfolk

. . . And first, we marvel much that you do all write unto us in such extreme and desperate sort, as though the world should be in manner turned uppe soo down, unless we would, in certain points, condescend to the petitions of the rebels; that is to say, specially, for a free general pardon and a Parliament; having not yet spoken with them; ne any other grounds or foundation to maintain your opinions and desires for our agreement therunto; as it appeareth unto us both by your said letters and by the relation of our said servant, but only such general bruits as be conveyed unto you by your espials: whereunto as we cannot deny but you must adhibit some credit, so we think your wisdom should again have considered that all devices and idle words, set forth and spoken by light and seditious persons, take not, even by and bye, that effect that they would desire. But admitting that the rebels be, indeed, as cancredly disposed and in as good areadiness as you write, and as is reported; we marvel greatly that neither you, our Cousin of Shrewsbury, have been so diligent in the viewing, storing, and fortifying of the fords of the River of Don as our former letters, long sithens addressed unto you for that purpose, did require; ne that you, our Cousin of Norfolk, and our Admiral, have no more earnestly, sithens your arrival in those parts, devised upon the same; both knowing that we had the doing thereof much to heart, and writing from Sir Robert a Lee's house that, considering the time of meeting was protracted, you would, in the mean season, travail therein to our satisfaction. And yet we do a great deal more marvel that in case you have certain knowledge that the rebels have levied such forces as is reported, neither you, our Cousin of Shrewsbury, nor any of the rest of you that be our Counsellors there, have raised other forces, in all events to withstand, or, at the least, to stay them; considering that we gave long sithens, also, special commandement for that purpose. For if, by your negligences therein, the rebels should march forward, and suddenly do any exploit upon our good subjects on this side Don, we should have just cause to think ourself evil served, and our commandments less regarded than appertained.

But imputing these matters to negligence, and so leaving all contention thereof, upon the perfect and assured trust and confidence we have in you, with the certain hope we have conceived that with diligence and good endeavour to serve us you will again repair and redub[1] the same; forasmuch as by your said letters and the said credence it appeareth not only unto us that the day of your meeting shall be on Tuesday next coming, but also that of likelihood the rebels will then show themselves very stiff and wilful touching the two points before specified, of the free pardon and the Parliament; considering how much our honour should be touched in such sort, as it were by a constraint, to grant them their desire therein, or to permit you in any wise to common with them, unless they will either first cause such forces as they have levied eftsoons to retire to their houses and dwelling places, or else, at the least, for the sureties of your persons, which we esteem as our own, to permit you to levy such forces again, before the meeting, as shall countervail the same: we have determined that you shall proceed with the said rebels in manner and form ensuing.

First, you shall signify by your letters unto them that being we advertised that they have made, of new, a great assembly and levied a great force, that is to say the number in all of

[1] Put right. Obs., but very frequent in sixteenth century official documents.

20,000 men, as it is reported, we cannot a little marvel at their exceeding ingratitude and most indiscreet proceeding in that behalf. . . . And that we have given you, therefore, strait commandment, that unless they will again cause their said forces to retire, and so meet with you, out of arms, in a peaceable sort: in which case we shall be content that, as our Heralds shall view the country on their side, for the more perfect surety of your persons, so shall their messengers, again, view the country on this side, to the intent they may be out of all suspicion and jealousy of danger; you should not be hasty to proceed to the meeting, or enter any communication with them, till you may, for your sureties, levy like forces, for your parties, as they have already done for theirs. Which, as we think it should be expedient for you to do, so, nevertheless, we remit that point to your discretion; trusting you will not indeed meet with them but in such sort as shall be for your perfect sureties.

And if so be that the heads and captains of the rebels shall, upon this declaration, which we desire you with all dexterity to set forth unto them, condescend and agree, as well to dissolve again their forces and garrisons, as to meet with you in a peaceable sort and out of arms; then our pleasure is, you shall keep the day of meeting appointed, or such other day as shall be agreed upon between you and them. And at your coming together, you shall first engrieve their attemptates sithens the appointment taken at Doncaster; dilating as well therein their new assembly made at this time, the taking of Ralph Evers and Edward Waters, with our ship, munitions, and money, and the sending of Robert Bowes to take our Cousin of Cumberland; as all other their innovations mentioned in our former instructions given to you, our Cousin of Norfolk, and our Admiral, at your departure from us. And thereupon, moving them first by all the good means you can devise to repair and redub all their attemptates, you shall then declare unto them, how that, of our most inestimable clemency and goodness, we have not only made answer to such petitions as they have exhibited unto us, but also granted their suit and desire for their pardon, in such a liberal and free sort as they may have good cause, both to receive it most humbly, and to devise, by their lowly submission and fidelity, to be showed hereafter towards us, to show themselves so true and faithful subjects, as, with their present repentance for this offence, and their good continuance after, they may repair and redub that which hath been, in this part, transgressed and offended; which pardon you shall, by all the ways and means to you possible, induce them humbly to desire, and so to receive, in such form, as in you former instructions is prescribed. And if they shall, nevertheless, refuse to accept the said pardon, unless it were general and without exception, and either make desire for a Parliament, or for the granting of any other articles, which percase in speciality they shall express unto you; you shall thereunto make answer that your commission extendeth not to the granting of any of those things; nevertheless, such is your love and zeal to those parties, and such is your desire to do that thing that might avoid that extremity of mischief from them which they seek by this their folly, that in case they will frankly signify unto you what they would have, what they do desire, and what they have resolved upon, you will adventure to take an abstinence; and not only advertise us thereof, but also join with them as humble suitors and petitioners unto us, if their requests, petitions, and desires shall be such as subjects may, in any case, offer to their Prince and Sovereign Lord, and as the same may again grant unto them with his honour. And if they shall, upon this general overture, declare unto you that they desire only the said free pardon and Parliament, you shall promise them, as is aforesaid, to be suitors with them; so as they will set their hands to the articles thereof, and, with the same, promise no further to molest us with other particular or public matters, ne to administer unto us any further occasions that might provoke our indignation against them, but to use themselves in all things like good and faithful subjects. And having once concluded upon the same and received their writing thereof, you shall take an abstinence for 6 or 7 days, as though you should send hither unto us, specially, for that purpose; and when that time shall be expired, at the day to be prefixed, declare unto them that with great suit you have obtained their petitions; and so present unto them the general pardon, which at this time we send unto you by our servant, Sir John Russell, whom we have specially commanded not to deliver them out of his hands to any person, until such time as they shall determine to receive the same, in such sort as we have prescribed; having first advised them to apply themselves to receive it with such humility as shall appertain to subjects, not only in the receiving of the oath, but also into the withdrawing of all their violent demeanours, and the peaceable yielding of themselves to their labours: and semblably you shall grant them a Parliament, to begin at such place as we shall appoint for the same.

Now, if they shall to the two points before specified, whereof one (that is, for the Parliament) is not comprised in their articles, but named only for the surety of their pardon, add any other special articles; because we purpose as well, in such case, to have some time to weigh them well, as, the case so requiring, to put ourself in further preparation and areadiness; we will, that perceiving they will in no wise be brought to condescend only upon the pardon and Parliament, in manner and form aforesaid, you shall then declare that it shall be meet that we shall call our nobles together and advise us thereof: and thereupon, considering the same cannot be done in a short time, ye shall then take an abstinence for 20 days, or longer, as your wisdoms shall think meet; and with all possible diligence not only advertise us of their petitions, but of your advice touching the same. And thereupon we shall also, in that case, send unto you our resolution with convenient diligence. Using, nevertheless, in the communication thereof, all the dexterity and good means you can possible to induce them to consider the innumerable and infinite mischiefs that may ensue of the extremity of this matter; and so to advise them, like humble subjects to make their suit, and to desire those things that may be obtained by suit and petition, and not such as the Prince's honour will neither permit him to grant nor any honest man to ask of him. And if they will in no wise ne by any means be persuaded to stay only upon the said pardon and Parliament, but add thereunto other articles, so that you shall thereupon take the said respite for 20 days; our pleasure then is, that you shall not only with all possible diligence, in the closest and secretest manner you can, write unto our Cousin of Derby suddenly to put himself, with all the forces of Cheshire and Lancashire, in arms; and likewise to our Cousin of Suffolk, that he may put himself in like areadiness, with the force of Lincolnshire; but that you, our Cousins of Norfolk, Shrewsbury, and others of our Council there, shall immediately levy all the forces ye be able to make in those parts; putting yourselves in order with the same to keep the passages of Don, which we will you shall then travail to cleanse and fortify, in such sort as the rebels may be stayed, till we may here put ourself in some areadiness to advance towards them. . . .

Post scripta. We have received your sundry letters, the one written at Newark, the other at Nottingham. Touching your device contained in those written from Newark, for the taking of a new day if you shall not agree with the rebels, and the preparation thereupon of 5 or 600 horses, and 200 or 300 footmen; you shall understand, we do not mislike the taking of a further day; for that is conformable to such advertisement as you shall now receive from us upon the credence of Sir John Russell and the letters sent by the same. Concerning the horses and men to be shipped in Norfolk, we do neither yet condescend to the device, nor yet disapprove it; for the success thereof may be good, albeit we trust it shall not come to such extremity. We would you should, in the mean season, advertise us where you think meetest to have those horses levied; and thereupon we shall advertise you of our further mind in that behalf. Now to your letters written at Nottingham; whereas you think it meet, considering the fury and areadiness of the rebels, that we should send unto you some degrees, so that they might, at the least, be stayed till we might again put our forces in such order as should be convenient, supposing it should be meet for us for that purpose; and for that also that you have no man there that can enter in the number of the days to be inserted in the safe-conduct, but the same should appear done of two hands, which might administer cause of argument, to send unto you sundry safe conducts for sundry times. To the first, for the degrees, you may perceive by these our letters that we have therein waded as far as we may possibly with our honour; conveying the end of your communication to a delay, though you should certainly condescend upon the two points of the pardon and the Parliament; and if you shall not agree, then to a longer delay. For the better conducing also whereof, we have herewith sent unto you one safe conduct one for 16 days; and we shall send you two more with all convenient diligence, the one for 20 days, the other for 40 days; to the intent you may put forth such and as many of the same as your wisdoms shall think meet and convenient, and as may serve best to the advancement of our purpose; referring the order thereof to your discretions accordingly. Finally, forasmuch as by the said letters written at Nottingham, it appeareth the River of Don is much fallen, and the rebels very mad and furious; we doubt not but having now all the means to stay them that can be devised, you will take such courage unto you and use such diligence and circumspection, specially for the fortification of the fords, that whatsoever the end of the meeting shall be, you will provide both for the preservation of our honour, and for your own sureties, in as prudent and substantial sort as the time and case will possibly permit and suffer. Albeit it is much to our marvel to receive so many desperate letters from you, and in the same no remedies. We might think that either things be not so well looked on as they might be, when you can look but only to the one side; or else that you be so perplexed with the bruits of the one party that ye do omit to write the good of the other; and yet we could be as well content to bestow some time in the reading of an honest remedy as of so many extreme and desperate mischiefs. And if so be that any man shall find any occasion of argument upon any quality touching the free pardon, you shall upon your honours promise that the same shall, both generally and severally, to them all be maintained good; and that they shall, at all times, have it again, in as vailable sort, out of our Chancery, in due form, as any of them can devise the same.

That it was Henry's own determination, vigour and resource, rather than the spirit of his generals in the field, which brought about the downfall of the rebels, is evident in several of the letters, and not least in the one that follows.

VII. To Fitzwilliam and Russell

[*Dec.* 8, 1536.]

. . . We cannot a little marvel at the contents of the same, being written in such a desperate sort as though it were neither possible to finish that matter with the accomplishment of any part of that thing which we do most desire, that is with the resignation of some persons to be punishment [*sic*] for the example of others, ne to appease the fury of the commons unless we should condescend to the standing of such abbeys as in those parts be to be suppressed, by virtue of the act of parliament passed for that purpose.

For first, touching the inclination of the commons, almost all men that have either been in those parts or have any practises that way, do signify unto us that the people be rather repentant and sorry for that they have already done, than anything disposed to make any new commotion. We have talked here with one Steward, a gentleman of Scotland, which repaired unto us lately with letters from the Queen of Scots our sister and from the regent in Scotland, and he showed us plainly that he perceived no great stirring in all his passage, and yet he travelled in the most used and common ways, only he gathered that the people were weary of their folly and would be glad with a merciful remission thereof to use themselves as to their duties of allegiance appertaineth. There came out of those parts, lately, also a servant of Master Coffin's which affirmeth the very same thing: another of the Lord Privy Seal's which telleth the very same tale. And likewise Master Franklin declareth that the commons were at his coming quietly in their houses and no man abroad, but such as were with the gentlemen or belong unto them, which he sayeth also he declared unto you.

There hath been also divers men of reputation dwelling in Kendal and those quarters here sithens your departure, which do all agree in one saying, touching the repentance of the people, and you alone write unto us all extremities, without remembrance of such remedies or likelihood of remedies as you have or be likely to attain for the counterpoising of the same; as though we should be drawn by means to agree to all things that can be devised, though the same were never so much against our honour.

The least that we can conceive and gather of this manner of proceeding is that there [is] none of you all so diligent to advise us of both parts, of the good with the evil, as reason would you should be, and as we do at your hands look for. For either must we impute it to negligence, or else must we think we be not so well handled by some of them that we specially trust, as their duties towards us would require; which part we cannot impress in our breast, except the success of things should thereunto enforce us.

And to ascertain you plainly of our mind in that point touching the Abbeys, we shall never consent to their desires therein by any such mean, but adhere to our right therein to the uttermost, being as greatly entitled thereunto as to the Imperial crown of this our realm; and resolved with the force of the one to maintain and defend the other, as a member so united and knit thereunto, that whilst it shall please God we shall enjoy the one, we purpose not with any violence to depart with one part of the other.

Wherefore we desire and pray you in that matter and the other of resignation heretofore recommended unto you, to consider our honour, and to bend all your wits as well to advise other to do the semblable, as to frame such an end there as may be quadrant with the same. . . . It is not possible for a patient to have his disease cured that will not give credit to his physician ne receive any medicines but such as contrary to his physician's mind who knoweth the cause of the disease, and the very remedies thereof, he will receive without knowledge either of the cause of his malady, or of the operation of this medicine himself liketh.[1] Ne it shall be possible to reduce those rebels to a perfect obedience, unless they may first cast away all their wilfulness and obstinacy, knowledge their offences, and so submit themselves to the order and discretion of the laws, without such conditions as shall be plainly repugnant to the same. And

[1] Was Henry perhaps unconsciously remembering and improving upon Cardinal Simonetta's description of the methods employed by the King and Wolsey when trying to extract a decretal commission from the Pope? 'The sick man on consulting a physician does not himself prescribe the medicine.'

rather than we will permit their malices to enforce us to such extremity we shall, we doubt not in God, so provide for their repression that those shall first repent it that be the greatest fautors, maintainers and abettors of them in their mischief, and therewithal cut away all those corrupt members that with wholesome medicines will not be recovered and brought to perfect health. . . .

Aske had nearly forty thousand armed men at his back, and Norfolk, unable to meet him in the field, took refuge in diplomacy. He promised the free pardon under the King's seal, also the Parliament that they demanded, on the authority of the above letter (No. VI). Getting their substantial demands the rebels imagined they had had everything conceded. The northern parliament was to meet in the summer. The pardon was proclaimed, and the pilgrimage dispersed.

Henry was shrewd enough to know that dispersal was not enough. Nor had he any intention of keeping the pledge given by Norfolk. To submit in any way to rebel demands was to 'distain' his honour. He realized, however, that Aske must be persuaded of the integrity of his purpose. Aske was summoned to court under a safe-conduct. Henry gave him a personal interview, and renewed and amplified his promises. Aske went back to Yorkshire, convinced that the King would keep his word; but he went back to a people who had not listened to the royal eloquence and who were still deeply distrustful of Henry's intentions. And he went back to a movement which he could no longer control. Early in January parties of rebels attempted to take Hull and Scarborough. Aske, Lord Darcy and others were largely instrumental in suppressing these outbreaks; but their good faith and loyalty counted for nothing as against the opportunity with which the rebels themselves had now provided the King. They had broken their pledges: the royal pardon could be recalled; and the rebel leaders must be punished. Darcy and Aske were committed to the Tower, tried and condemned: the former was beheaded on Tower Hill on June 20: Aske was hanged in chains at York. Abbots and friars, nobles and gentry suffered like fates.

In February there was a rising in Cumberland and Westmorland. It was dealt with immediately, and martial law was proclaimed by the Duke of Norfolk throughout the north. The following extracts from a letter of Henry's written on February 22 show clearly enough the ruthless measures taken to ensure that there should be no more such outbreaks. It also suggests that here, perhaps even more than in Yorkshire, the dispossessed monks were to a very large extent responsible for stirring up the people.

VIII. To the Duke of Norfolk

[*Feb.* 22, 1537.]

Right trusty and right entirely beloved Cousin, We greet you well. Letting you wit that we have as well received your letters of the 16th of this month, declaring the new assembly made in Westmorland, with your prudent determination for the repression of the same, as your other letters of the 17th of the same instant, sent unto us by our trusty and well-beloved servant, Sir Ralph Evers, Knight, declaring the valiant and faithful heart and courage of our trusty and well-beloved servant, Sir Christopher Dacres, Knight, and his most thankful and acceptable service done unto us, in the overthrow of the traitors and rebels of the said assembly, which also made an assault upon our city of Carlisle; with the good service done also unto us, in the chase of the same, by Thomas Clifford; and semblably the perfect arreadiness, great forwardness, and hearty good wills of all the nobles, gentlemen, and honest men of our county of York, and of all other quarters in those parts, to have served us in your company for the repression of the same rebels (if they had tarried togethers till you might have come to them); with your determination for the punishment of that attemptate in such sort as all others shall have cause to beware by the example thereof. For answer whereunto, you shall understand that in your earnest setting forward for the repression of the said traitors, and the semblable following of the same, both with your own speedy preparations and by your earnest and hearty letters written to our said servant, Sir Christopher Dacres, you have done unto us such thankful and acceptable service as we shall never put in oblivion; but in such wise remember the same towards you as you shall have good cause to rejoice of your doing in that behalf. And surely it is much to our contentation to hear and understand by the relation and advertisement of sundry of our servants and good subjects of those parties, both how earnestly you do advance the truth, and declare on the other part the great usurpation of the Bishops of Rome in this realm; and also how discreetly, plainly, and truly you paint and set forth those persons that call themselves religious in the colours of their hypocrisy; that the ignorant people may perceive how they have been abused in them, and the rather leave the superstitions in to the which they have of long time trained them; and we doubt not, but the further you shall wade in the investigation of their behaviours, the more ye shall detest the great number of them; and the less esteem the punishment of such as you shall find, in will or deed, culpable in things that may touch us, or the common quiet of our realm. . . .

. . . We do right well approve and allow your proceedings in the displaying of our Banner. And forasmuch as the same is now spread and displayed, by reason whereof, till the same shall be closed again, the course of our laws must give place to the ordinances and estatutes martial; our pleasure is, that before you shall close up our said banner again, you shall, in any wise, cause such dreadful execution to be done upon a good number of the inhabitants of every town, village, and hamlet, that have offended in this rebellion, as well by the hanging of them up on trees as by the quartering of them and the setting of their heads and quarters in every town, great and small, and in all such other places, as they may be a fearful spectacle to all other hereafter that would practise any like matter: which we require you to do, without pity or respect, according to our former letters; remembering that it shall be much better that these traitors should perish in their wilful, unkind, and traitorous follies, than that so slender punishment should be done upon them as the dread thereof should not be a warning to others: whereof shall ensue the preservation of a great multitude; which, if the terror of this execution should not lie in the eye of their remembrance, might percase upon light rumours, tales, and suggestions of evil persons, fall into the pit of like mischief. And when you shall have done such execution as is before specified, then we be content that, upon your discretion, ye shall close up our said banner; both for the advancement of ordinary justice between party and party, and for the due punishment of other malefactors according to the order of our laws: for which purpose we have also herewith sent unto you the commissions for Westmorland and Cumberland, to be put in execution and experience when you shall see cause and think meet.

Fourth, our pleasure is that you shall with diligence send up in perfect surety unto us the traitors, Bigod, the Friar of Gainsborough, Leach, if he may be taken, the Vicar of Penrith, and Towneley, late Chancellor to the Bishop of Carlisle, who hath been a great promoter and procurer of all these rebellions, and one Doctor Pickering, a Canon of Bridlington, or as many of them, immediately, as you have or can get, and the rest after, as they may be apprehended.

Sixth, we desire and pray you to have good respect to the conservation of the lands and goods of all such as shall be now attainted; that we may have them in safety, to be given, if we shall be so disposed, to such persons as have truly served us; for we be informed that there were among them divers freeholders and rich men, whose lands and goods, well looked unto, will reward other well that with their truths have deserved the same; not doubting but you have already put such order for this point as shall appertain.

Finally, forasmuch as all these troubles have ensued by the solicitation and traitorous conspiracies of the monks and canons of those parts; we desire and pray you, at your repair to Sawley, Hexham, Newminster, Lanercost,[1] Saint Agatha, and all such other places as have made any manner of resistance, or in any wise conspired, or kept their houses with any force, sithens the appointment at Doncaster, you shall, without pity or circumstance, now that our banner is displayed, cause all the monks and canons, that be in any wise faulty, to be tied up, without further

[1] MS. Leonarde cost.

delay or ceremony, to the terrible example of others; wherein we think you shall do unto us high service.

Within six months of its outbreak, therefore, the only serious domestic trouble of the reign was ended. Norfolk remained in the north till September, 1537, to settle the country, and administer justice. But the promised northern parliament was never held, nor did the King visit the disaffected counties. The destruction of the monasteries proceeded apace: and Cromwell remained in power. In the letter which follows, the King explains to Norfolk his reasons for not going north.

IX. To the Duke of Norfolk

Right trusty and right entirely beloved Cousin, We greet you well. And have as well received your letters of the second of this month, as seen your sundry letters addressed to our trusty and right well-beloved Councillor, the Lord Privy Seal, the continues[1] whereof do well declare both your discreet proceeding in all our affairs there, and your joyful and loyal heart expressed upon the news of the quickening of our most dear and most entirely beloved wife, the Queen; for the which, as we do give unto you our most hearty thanks, so ye may be well assured that we shall retain the premises in such wise in our good remembrance, as both for your estimation in our heart, and otherwise, the same shall redound much to your comfort.

And whereas your desire is to know our pleasure, how we would be received, and what numbers of men should repair from all parts of that country to attend upon us; upon the arrival of your letters containing that request for the knowledge of our pleasure in that behalf, calling to our remembrance the present state of the things, and with our Council debating the same, we have, for sundry skylles,[2] thought it more convenient to protract and defer our journey into those parts till another year, than to perform it according to our former determination.

The first ground and cause that moveth us, and in manner enforceth, to break our appointment therein, is, for that the

[1] Contents. [2] Reasons.

Emperor, having lately sent hither a nobleman to make certain overtures unto us touching matters of high consequence, the good conclusion whereof should be for the public weal and benefit of all Christendom, hath also determined, as his ambassador hath related unto us, to send hither with convenient speed, for the more certain, perfect, and special entreaty of such matters as be now generally proponed, two other personages of great honour; at whose arrival it shall be very expedient and necessary that we should be in these parts, as well for their more honourable entertainment, which shall be requisite to be of the best sort, both for our honour and the honour of this our Realm, as for the better furtherance and speedy conclusion of such matters as have been already proponed and shall be then thoroughly entreated between us.

A second cause is, for that being our said most dear and most entirely beloved wife, the Queen, now quick with child, for the which we give most humble thanks to Almighty God, albeit she is, in every condition, of that loving inclination, and reverend conformity, that she can in all things well content, satisfy, and quiet herself with that thing which we shall think expedient and determine; yet considering that, being a woman, upon some sudden and displeasant rumours and bruits that might by foolish or light persons be blown abroad in our absence, being specially so far from her, she might take to her stomach such impressions as might engender no little danger or displeasure to that wherewith she is now pregnant, which God forbid; it hath been thought to us and our Council very necessary that for avoiding of all perils that might that way ensue, we should not extend our progress this year so far from her; but direct the same to such place as should not pass 60 miles or thereabouts from her, when we should be at the furthest; specially she being, as it is thought, further gone by a month or more than she thought herself at the perfect quickening. Which counsel, therefore, remembering what dependeth upon the prosperity of that matter, we think not amiss to follow, both for our own quiet and for the common wealth of our whole realm; being the thing of that quality as every good Englishman will think himself to have a part in the same.

A third cause that moveth us somewhat to continue our demore in these parts for this year, and not to proceed in our intended journey, is, for that the Emperor and the French King be now both in armies, and have, on either part, great numbers of men of war upon the frontiers of our Marches of Calais. And albeit that we have furnished our town of Calais and castle of Guisnes, with all other places of force on that side in such sort, as, God being our good Lord, as we trust He is, and will be, against all such as would attempt any thing against us, we doubt not but our things there be in such strength and force, with the furniture of all things convenient for their surety and defence against all men that would attempt any thing against them: yet knowing the nature of men of war, which be desirous both of spoil and glory, and considering that our being in the remote parts of our realm might give them some courage to make some enterprise, upon hope to do some exploit before we could, being so far off, send any succour in to those parts; which (though none other hurt should ensue of it) might both trouble our good servants and subjects there, whom we tender, as we do all the rest of our subjects, as the members of our body, and put us to great charges, and our subjects here in great disquiet, in preparations to be made against them, they being ever at advantage to slip away when they should perceive any force to be in a readiness against them; which danger of inconvenience, though there is no great likelihood of the same, specially for that we be in league and amity with both Princes, will be certainly avoided by our continuance here in these parts, being so near unto them as they cannot almost look towards any such thing, but we be in a perfect areadiness to empeache their purpose in the same, to their displeasure that would attempt any such matter: yet we have thought good to join this also as a piece of a cause requiring our demore hereabouts, and the rather to determine and resolve to defer our journey till another year, as is before specified.

A fourth cause is, that we consider that sithens the beginning of our Reign we have not visited those North parts of our Realm; and if we should keep our purposed journey, being the year so far spent, and the country so devasted,[1] which made us, of neces-

[1] Devastated.

sity, to stay so long, neither should we tarry any convenient time in any place, ne pass our City of York; by reason whereof, neither should our people of those North parts have any fruition of our presence, ne we should have any time to peruse our frontiers, or to see our towns joining upon the same; which also made us, upon the other grounds before specified, to stay the more willingly; being minded, God willing, and no great occasions ensuing to the let and empeachement of our purpose therein, the next year not only to visit our said City of York, but also Hull, Carlisle, Newcastle, Durham, Berwick, with all the most part of the notable towns in those parts.

Upon which grounds, having, as is aforesaid, resolved to put off our progress thither for this year, and calling to our remembrance your prudent considerations, signified unto us by Maunsell, when ye desired to know our resolute mind touching our intended journey into those parts, both for a pardon to be else granted, to put the people out of fear, and for the stay of such provisions as they minded to make for the better furniture of our train, in case they should not know but we should repair thither; like as ye shall understand that we have certainly determined with all convenient speed and celerity to send down a personage of honour, with our said pardon, according to your advice and counsel, who shall with diligence resort thither to you with the same: so, as well to the intent the people may enter some hope, as that they may, in time, stay in their said preparations, our pleasure is, that, upon the receipt hereof, ye shall, in York, and also in all such good towns there, as whereunto without your great incommodity or disease ye may travel, not only declare and signify by your own mouth the causes before specified of our not repair thither for this year, causing others of our Council with you to do the same in the meaner towns about the country; but also that you and the rest having, by your appointment, like charge, shall therewith intimate and expressly declare unto them that we have resolved with diligence to send down a personage of honour and of our Privy Council with a general pardon for all their former offences, which shall to your hands deliver it, and at length signify our clemency unto them. Like as we desire and pray you somewhat to extend the same at the publication of these matters; expressing that we, having no manner of doubt but they will from henceforth remain our true, faithful, and loyal subjects, have resolved clearly to put all their unkindness towards us out of our heart, and have them in all things hereafter no less dear than they should have been if they had never offended; as our said Councillor at his repair shall further declare unto them.

Now touching your suit for your return; albeit your wisdom and circumspection is such as we think we shall hardly devise to be so well served there as we might be assured to be by your continuance in those parts, yet minding to grant your desire, for your better quiet, satisfaction, and the recovery of your health, which we do more tender and regard than we can almost express; we do purpose shortly to revoke you, and to establish a standing Council there, for the conservation of those countries in quiet, and the administration of common justice: which being once set in a frame, we shall incontinently call you unto us, according to your own desire; trusting that in the mean season, the time now being very short, ye will no less gladly take pain there to serve us than ye have already done, to our honour and perfect contentation, and to the great increase of your own honour and estimation with us; requiring you to advertise us by your next letters of your advice touching the said council, and what persons you think meet for the same; and also, after what disposition and of what inclination you find the country there.

Finally you shall understand that upon the arrival here of Thomas Strangways, we do not only perceive that he hath been a most arrant traitor towards us, but that he doth both manifestly continue in his treasons; expressing plainly in his words the same, labouring to excuse wholly the Lord Darcy and Constable, and that with such an advancement of the favour of the country towards them, as though our subjects there do much repine at their punishments; saying also, plainly, that they be more meet to rule there than you be, and much better beloved than you be amongst the people of those parts. Wherefore, considering that this matter of the insurrection hath been attempted there, and thinking that as well for the example, as to see who would groan at their execution, it should be meet to have them executed at Doncaster, and thereabouts, minding, upon their sufferance, to knit up this tragedy, we think it should not be amiss that we should send the said Darcy, Constable, and Aske down for that purpose; requiring you with diligence to advertise us of your opinion in that behalf. And if you shall think this our device good, then we require you to put yourself in such order, as, at their coming down, they may be executed in such sort as shall be prescribed; though there should be any naughty hearts that would grudge or maligne at the same.

Thus have we declared unto you the causes that have specially moved us to stay in our intended journey for this year; which we require you to set forth as is before expressed, with our determination upon the same for the sending down of our pardon. Nevertheless, to be frank with you, which we desire you in any wise to keep to yourself, being an humour fallen into our legs, and our physicians therefore advising us in no wise to take so far a journey in the heat of the year, whereby the same might put us to further trouble and displeasure; it hath been thought more expedient that we should, upon that respect only, though the grounds before specified had not concurred with it, now change our determination, than that we should be too precise in that which to us and our whole Realm might after minister some cause of repentance. But this we write to you alone, as is aforesaid, and require yourself to retain it accordingly.

It is significant of the real strength of Henry's position that the only attempt at interference made by Catholic Europe was entirely abortive. Both Charles and Francis were far too busy with their own war to have anything but sympathy to spare for the insurgents. Then, in February, 1537, when it was all over except the executions, the Pope dispatched Reginald Pole, now Cardinal, as legate *a latere*, to encourage the Catholics. Anything more hopelessly belated and stupidly calculated, either as a practical measure or as a gesture, can hardly be imagined. When Pole's mission was known Henry at once wrote to the English agents abroad to prevent him from reaching England. The following was addressed to Hutton, at Brussels.

x. To Hutton

[*April* 15, 1537.]

Trusty and well-beloved, We greet you well. And forasmuch as by letters addressed unto us from our Orators with the French King, it appeareth that our traitor Pole is now arrived at Paris, and that it is uncertain whither he will from thence direct his journey, our pleasure is, that immediately upon the sight hereof, whether the Bishop of Winchester have therein written to you or not, and whether the said Pole do still remain at Paris or be removed from thence to any other place, you shall deliver unto the Regent our letters for the stay of his entry into the Emperor's dominions, and in all things proceed, touching that matter, according to your former instructions. And if the Regent or any of the Council shall say that they cannot accomplish the contents thereof, for that they shall allege him to be entered already, you shall nevertheless affirm and stick fast in this point, that you have certain advertisement it is not so, but that he remaineth still in the French King's countries; pressing them temperately, as much as you may, to observe their treaties with us in that part. And if so be that you shall perceive that he should indeed be secretly arrived in the country, so that they shall be able to justify his entry into the Emperor's dominions before the delivery of our letters of requisition for the stay thereof, you shall then press them to give him monition to avoid within the time limited by the treaties aforesaid, and during his abode there neither to admit him to her presence, ne to suffer unto him to have any other entertainment than beseemeth the traitor and rebel of their friend and ally, and as by the said treaties may be maintained. And furthermore our pleasure is that, in case the said Pole be either entered already into Flanders, or shall, notwithstanding our letters, be received or suffered to resort thither, you shall in any wise cause good, secret and substantial espial to be made upon him from place to place where he shall be, what entertainment he shall have, who shall resort unto him, and, as nigh as you can possibly attain, what he purposeth to compass in those parts; advertising us thereof from time to time, as you shall have any matter worthy the same; the charges of which espial we shall see eftsoons repaid unto you accordingly.

Henry's protests were effective. The Regent would not allow Pole to enter the Netherlands, and Francis refused to let him remain in France; with the result that he was escorted into neutral territory, and had to return ignominiously to Italy, having accomplished nothing. It showed conclusively enough that in spite of their outward adherence to the Papacy neither Charles nor Francis was prepared to offend the heretic Henry for the sake of Paul III and the true religion. It was a signal defeat for the Pope, and a further proof, for Henry, of the fundamental religious insincerity of France and the Empire, devoted each to the pursuit of its own policy and interests. Though in no sense a spectacular triumph, the failure of Pole must have made it quite clear to Henry and his Council, that upon whatever pretext Charles and Francis might in the future combine against him, England had no need to fear any enterprise vitally animated by fanatic crusading zeal. If any such attack could ever have succeeded it would have been during this domestic rebellion, when it might perhaps have found in the Catholic insurgents the traitor within the gates.

Norfolk was recalled to London in September, but the council which had assisted him was left behind to work as a properly constituted 'Council of the North', in pursuance of a plan suggested by Cromwell in 1535. It was a salaried, working Council, with governmental responsibility. Tunstall, Bishop of Durham, was its president, and four knights and seven gentlemen were appointed to do the work. If Norfolk had nourished dreams of becoming the great man of the north he was promptly disillusioned. 'Surely,' wrote Henry in May, 1537, 'we will not be bound of a necessity to be served there with lords, but we will be served with such men, what degree soever they be of, as we shall appoint to the same.' It is another and a significant example of the Tudor policy, which used the nobility and at the same time refused them power, making its own men for its own purposes, who could be broken or dispensed with, if and when necessary.

Henry had no further trouble in the north. Order was effectively restored and preserved. And on October 12, 1537, his triumph was crowned by the birth of Jane Seymour's son, Edward—the legitimate heir and Tudor prince, symbol and guarantee of the security of the power which Henry had now so effectively established within his own kingdom.

CHAPTER II

AN EXERCISE IN DIPLOMACY (1537-1539)

'A little judicious meddling.'
JAMES GAIRDNER

It was perhaps fortunate for Henry that his domestic rebels chose the end of 1536 for their ineffectual revolt. Had they waited till the end of the next year it would have synchronized with a truce between France and the Empire, which might have made feasible some intervention upon their behalf by Charles—nominally, if not in practice, the supporter of orthodoxy, and of Princess Mary's legitimacy. Even as it was, the truce of November, 1537, brought Henry back at once into the diplomatic arena. It was to his advantage to foment rivalry and discord, to keep his powerful neighbours busy with their own troubles. As soon as there was any rumour of a truce, therefore, he took up his favourite and accustomed rôle of mediator. It was very necessary that England should play a part in the councils of Europe: if treaties were to be made, she must be included in them, and secure something for herself. Moreover, if Henry was to face the prospect of peace abroad, he wanted to be very sure that it would not be a peace which would join Francis and Charles with the Papacy, in league against himself, the arch-heretic.

England's chief marketable asset was nothing less than Henry's own royal hand. Jane Seymour's death in October had left the King again a widower, and as soon as the truce was announced he began marriage negotiations with France and Spain. Besides himself he had also his three children to dispose of—his newly-born son and heir, Edward, and Mary and Elizabeth. In France his transparent manœuvres were treated for what they were worth. First he made proposals for the hand of Mary of Guise, when he knew perfectly well that Francis had promised her to James V of Scotland. Had Francis been tempted, Henry might have struck a shrewd blow at the ancient friendship between France and Scotland: but Francis was not tempted, and Mary married James; and Henry was driven back on the suggestion that some of the ladies of the French court might be sent to Calais for his inspection. To this the French retorted that their ladies were not to be trotted out like hackneys!

More interest attaches to his negotiations with the Emperor. For one thing, they were conceived in a more serious spirit; for another, a voluminous and characteristic correspondence survives, which enables them to be followed in detail. Thirdly, the English ambassador at Madrid was no less a person than the soldier-poet, Sir Thomas Wyatt, and it is to him that, with one exception, all the letters which follow are addressed. The entire correspondence has been printed in full in G. F. Nott's edition of the poetical works of Wyatt and Surrey.[1] Here only a few letters and some extracts can be given to indicate the nature and contents of the whole group.

The first gives Wyatt his instructions. He is to propose peace as if the idea was Henry's, to propose Henry as the proper mediator, and is ' to fish out how the Emperor is disposed '.

1. To Sir Thomas Wyatt
By the King

Henry R. [1537.]

Trusty and well-beloved we greet you well; letting you to wit, that whereas heretofore considering the great extremity that was like to ensue between the Emperor and the French King by the continuance of their wars, both to the disquiet and enfeeblishing of the whole state of Christendom, and to the great danger and peril of both their persons, realms, dominions and subjects: upon the entire love, zeal, and desire which we bear to either prince, and have to the common quiet and tranquillity of Christendom, we did address our letters, as well to the said Emperor as to the French King, advising them, like a perfect friend to both parties, to desist from the following of their quarrels by such extreme and dangerous means, and to suffer the same to be finished and compounded between them by some

[1] This text is not as reliable as it might be, but its mistakes are not as a rule of much importance.

friendly and amicable mediation: which our gentle motion and overture in that behalf neither part showed himself at that time much inclinable to follow, being both parties then in areadiness for the wars, and every of them thinking percase to achieve things which have not sithence succeeded according to their expectations; but the same notwithstanding, proceeded to their determined enterprises to the great trouble and charge of both parties, with the like annoyance of their subjects and the danger and peril of all Christendom.

Forasmuch as having ever in our mind the great good of peace, and joining therwithal the perfect and entire love and amity which we bear to both Princes, we think none opportunity is to be passed over which might serve either to the conducing of a quiet in Christendom, or to the avoiding from our so great friends and allies the dangerous extremities and uncertainties of the wars, the time of the year now enforcing both parties to fall to an abstinence for a season, we have resolved eftsoons to accomplish the office of a good Prince, and a most assured friend; that is to say, in this mean time when they shall be constrained to forbear to put in ure the extremity of arms, to travail to conduce and frame some good peace and final end between them. Wherefore our pleasure is that upon the receipt hereof ye shall require access to the Emperor's presence, and after our most hearty commendations to the same, ye shall declare our intent and purpose unto him in the premises, and that for the respects expressed we can be content and will be right glad to take upon us the office of a mediator between him and the French King, for the maynyng[1] of such a peace and a perfect amity, if they can be contented to accept this our gentle and friendly overture in this behalf, which ye may say we desire to know for his part how he shall embrace, and whether he can be contented to commit all his quarrels between them to our determination and arbitrament, supposing that the French King will do the semblable, to whom ye shall say ye doubt not but we have made motion to like purpose.

And if he shall hereunto answer that he hath already committed the maynyng of that matter to some other person, or that

[1] Managing, conducting of an affair, from *mayne*, obs.

he will not now leave the advantage which percase he shall allege he hath of his adversary; to the first part ye shall say, that ye marvel much, that seeing we have once so friendly offered to travail between him and the French King therein, he should choose any man before us to have the doing of it. Ye may of yourself say that he could not in Christendom have chosen an arbiter of such honour as we be, ne one to whom he hath more cause to show all gratuity and kindness that he could imagine, than to us. And ye shall say, that being in that place there that ye be, it is much to your discomfort to see that we should find so little friendship and tokens of love at his hands, for whom we have done so much, that ye think, under his pardon to speak frankly to him, he should omit none occasion wherein he might seem to have our great love and affection heretofore declared unto him, in remembrance, and that when ye were appointed to come thither, though ye knew that he had been so moved by affection to his parentage that he had not in our most just proceedings touching our matter of marriage showed that correspondence of love that our merits towards him had deserved, yet ye thought and verily trusted that the cause of his affection therein being removed, he would now by all means have travailed so to revive and quicken the amity that hath been between him and us as ye should have had a pleasant office; the doing whereof, in your opinion, should be much to his honour, and all things well considered, nothing to his disadvantage, if he would justly weigh whether we or the Bishop of Rome may stand him in better stead.

And if he shall answer that he will not grow to any peace, nor leave the advantage as is aforesaid that percase he shall allege that he hath at this present, ye shall thereunto lay before his eyes the manifold mischiefs and inconveniences of the war, with the uncertainty of the victory; and thereupon of yourself dissuade him from extremity therein, and advise him rather to temper his affections, having so honourable an overture made unto him for the mediation of the peace as this is, than to dwell in that which may bring forth in the end repentance: requiring you to set forth this matter with all your wisdom and dexterity, and in the same so to observe the answers of the Emperor, and of his councillors, as we may thereby perceive the inclination of the Emperor towards us: for next the maynyng of a peace, which we chiefly desire as a thing not only beneficial to our friends but necessary for Christendom, we be much desirous to know whether he do indeed favour and love us as he pretendeth; or in words only set a colour of affection forth for some other his purposes. And if he shall speak any thing unto you of his overture, made for the marriage of our daughter Mary, and to marvel that the same hath had no further furtherance, ye shall thereunto of yourself answer that there is no fault to be arrected unto us for that matter; for that Monsr. de Mendoza brought not with him any commission for that purpose; whereof, as we did not marvel when it appeared how slenderly he was dispatched towards us, so we have marvelled yet more to see that the default thereof hath not been sithens supplied. Ye may say unto him that we proceed in our things plainly and frankly, and when we perceive not the like in them with whom we would have any entreaty we think their doing with us to be rather a practice than a matter earnestly intended; eftsoons desiring you both to travail earnestly to fish out how the Emperor is disposed, and to advertise us of your conference with him, and your opinion upon the same with all possible diligence. And if ye shall find the said Emperor inclinable to our motion herein, ye shall say unto him, that in case the other party will do the like, it shall be meet in your opinion that every of them shall send unto us, upon a full conclusion in it, certain persons instructed to declare their rights and titles, to the intent we know the grounds of the same: whereupon ye may say ye doubt not but we would proceed in such upright and friendly fashion as we trust he shall be therewith contented; and to the intent he shall give the better ear unto you, we have herewith sent unto him a letter of credence for that purpose, which we desire and pray you to deliver unto him accordingly.

Given under our signet at our manor of Hampton Court, the 10th day of October, the 29th year of our reign.

In January, 1538, the idea of a marriage between Henry and the Duchess of Milan was mooted. The Duchess was the

Emperor's niece.[1] She had been married to the Duke of Milan, and was now a young widow of sixteen. Wyatt was to suggest the match ' as it proceeded of your own head '. If anything came of it, the proposal would be welcome to all, as it would confirm the alliance between England and the Emperor. The Duchess herself, when sounded by Henry's ambassador at Brussels, had averred, ' As for mine inclination, what should I say? You know I am at the Emperor's commandment.'

II. To Sir Thomas Wyatt

By the King

HENRY R. [1538.]

Trusty and right well beloved, we greet you well, letting you wit, that sithens the dispatch of our last post unto you, by whom we signified our mind and purpose upon the relation of our trusty and well beloved servant Sir John Dudley knight made unto us at his return out of those parts,[2] we have with more deliberation revolved and digested the right hearty, gentle, and friendly behaviour of our good brother the Emperor in the entertainment of the said Sir John Dudley, and in such discourse as you twain had with the same, and with his Council touching such points as whereof we wrote in our last letters unto you, for the which we desire and pray you, as occasion shall serve, earnestly to thank our said good brother, assuring him that he shall find us of semblable sort again towards him, and specially you shall desire him on our behalf to perform his promise touching the joining of us in this league between him and France as a principal contrahent; and likewise of his promise touching their Council; but in any wise you shall so solicit that matter of the comprehension forsomuch as may concern the observation of all leagues, pacts and treaties between him, us and France as it be in no wise pretermitted. And forasmuch as we have conceived that he doth bear unto us a most hearty and sincere affection, we

[1] Daughter of his sister, Isabella, who had married Christian II of Denmark.

[2] He had been sent to the Emperor to announce the birth of Prince Edward.

have not only much suppressed all remembrance of such old things as have interrupted of late days our amity, but also the same hath revived in us such a love again towards him, that we should be right glad to embrace an occasion to express and declare the same. Whereupon, devising with ourself, it came to our remembrance, that being now the purposed marriage between the Duchess of Milan, and the son of the Duke of Cleve and Juliers stayed, it might percase come to pass that we might honour the said Duchess by marriage, her virtue, qualities and behaviour being reported to be such as is worthy to be much advanced. And to the intent there might be an occasion thereof ministered unto us, we have thought good to signify unto you that our pleasure is, that commoning as opportunity shall serve you, either with the Emperor himself, or Monsieur de Grandvelle,[1] or Mons. Covos, you shall not only of yourself seem to commend and rejoice in our good affection towards the Emperor, but also you shall likewise, as it proceeded of your own head, wish that we might join in marriage on that side, and so advise them to set forth some overture of the said Duchess of Milan for that purpose, to the intent we may have that occasion thereby ministered that may give us commodity to enter further into communication of the same: which matters we desire and pray you to handle with no less dexterity than diligence, that we may with speed hear from you what is to be looked for touching the same. Given under our Signet, at our palace of Westminster, the 22nd of January, and the 29 year of our Reign.

The proposal was well received by the Emperor, who suggested in his reply that Henry's daughter Mary might bestow her hand on Don Louis, the heir of Portugal. Not to be outdone, Henry replied with offers of his infant son and the four-year-old Elizabeth. Negotiations were begun, and Holbein painted a portrait of the Duchess of Milan,[2] to show what a charming and distinguished-looking young lady she was—' very

[1] Nicolas Perrenot de Granvella, Chancellor of the Empire.

[2] But not, apparently, the delightful full-length one of her now in the National Gallery.

tall, of competent beauty, soft of speech and gentle of countenance '. The following extracts from two of Henry's letters show the 'progress' that was made in January and February, 1538. Even more noticeable than his eagerness for the matrimonial alliances is Henry's anxiety to make sure that whatever happens the Papacy shall not be allowed to interfere. How could the Pope, he asks indignantly, be a proper and indifferent arbitrator, when he has such large territorial interests in Italy?

III. To Sir Thomas Wyatt

[*Westminster, Feb.* 15, 1538.]

. . . But in case of the committing of this matter to our judgement, they may not give any authority therein to the Bishop of Rome, whom we refuse, not so much for that he is our manifest and notorious enemy, as for that in case he should have anything to do in it we could hope for none other effect than hath ensued of like things handled by his predecessors in like cases, whose practices have been ever to make themselves means to knit up the amities of Princes, not for any zeal they bare to the good of peace, but for that they had ever thereby an occasion to encroach upon them, and to confirm and establish their own glory. As now, for example, how shall he be an indifferent arbitrer in any matter that should touch the Duchy of Milan which pretendeth an interest to Parma, Placenza, and to the county of Novarcia, being a great part of the same. And besides that, whensoever there hath been quiet in Christendom, whereby Princes living in rest might have taken some occasions to have seen their abuses, it hath been their most certain and common practice, either directly or indirectly, to set forth one bug or other, whereby they have brought the estate of the same, or at the least some of them, into trouble and business. And undoubtedly if he might now get into his hands the mediation of this peace, it should rather bring forth a greater war, if he might set it forward, than that Christian peace and quiet that is to be desired. . . .

And finally, to declare to our good brother that we be most desirous to help the establishment of an unity and quiet in

Christendom, ye shall say unto him, that being ourself at liberty from marriage, and having a Prince our son and two daughters, we can be content to make connection and alliance with us all, to be bestowed on either part as upon just consideration shall be thought for the purpose most expedient. And forasmuch as the same hath no great obstacle but the Duchy of Milan, seeing our good brother the Emperor hath already offered it with a restraint of a little time for the conclusion of a certain end, he could be content to refer the moderation of that matter unto us, as he shall be assured that we shall weigh all parts with a most just weight of indifferency, and so bestow it with his consent also as shall be most to his honour and to the benefit of Christendom, so the same shall give us good esperance to conduce all other things to a perfect conclusion. And for a further demonstration of our most perfect desire to enter a fruitful travail in this behalf, in case our good brother will condescend to our purpose herein, we shall in other his desires concerning the Turk impart as liberally with him in any expedition to be made to that purpose as he himself can reasonably desire of us; and as the world shall say we do as much desire the suppression of that common enemy as he doth, having a just consideration what we may depart withal, without too great injury to our policy here at home. And if our good brother shall reply to the overtures of marriage, and show himself desirous to know in speciality how the same should be appointed, ye may in that case of your self desire him to declare unto you how he would himself wish the same to be ordered; assuring him that ye know from sundry of our Council here that they cannot be denied after any reasonable sort that the same may be demanded. And if he shall any thing reply to the young and tender age of our son, ye may thereto answer that we will be bound that at the years of the consent he shall marry that person, if God send them life together, to whom he should in this conclusion be promised. All which things we desire and pray you to set forth with your accustomed dexterity, and even so desire our good brother in his answers to the same to use like frankness of stomach as we do use towards [him], which we trust should the sooner work things to some good frame.

IV. TO SIR THOMAS WYATT

[*Westminster, Feb.* 22, 1538.]

. . . Second, where our commissioners desired of the same ambassadors, that in case the Emperor should purpose to go through with these things with us, he will neither grow to any further conclusion with the French King till these our treaties shall be finished with the same, ne after take any end with the same, but with our express consent and knowledge. . . . Wherefore seeing he hath already granted, when there was no great likelihood of any such renouvellance of amity to ensue between us, that he would take no peace but we should be in the same a principal contrahent and also that he would agree unto nothing in any Council that might be prejudicial to us, or to our realm, our pleasure is, that taking your occasion to remember those his promises unto him, ye shall of yourself, by way of friendly advice, for your own discharge, lest full credit should not be given to your rude and bare writing, as earnestly labour that for a demonstration and assurance of his hearty good will towards us in that same he will withsave[1] by his familiar letters, signed with [his] own hand to be sent unto us to express and signify that he would observe these promises made unto us, which in case ye can by any good means induce him to, write unto us in form desired.

Ye shall, before the dispatch, travail that ye may see the minute of his letters to the intent that they may be couched plainly, with the same words that the promises by him and his Council made: which matter ye shall solicit with such wisdom, dexterity, and discreet attemperance as to it may be attained, without instillation of any opinion that it should be desired for any mistrust of the Emperor's faith, but as a thing by you devised upon a good zeal for your own discharge, and for a furtherance of the rest of the purposes in treaty between us, knowing that the same shall much conduce to the framing of things to that end which shall redound to both our honours, with the great good of our realms, dominions and subjects, and consequently of whole Christendom.

[1] Obs. for vouchsafe.

Third, as concerning the overture of the Duchess of Milan, they showed themselves very desirous that the same might take effect: and likewise in the overture of marriage between our daughter Mary, and the Infant Don Louis of Portugal: and after some disputation, showed themselves also contented to take her in the state and terms that we will give her: that is to say, to succeed only in case of default of all other lawful issue male or female already, or to be, born of any other lawful venture; and likewise they were content to take for her dote in such marriage a hundred thousand crowns, which in case the Emperor should give investiture of the Duchy of Milan, should be a great help for his Grace's establishment. And whereas in the discourse of the matter, touching the Duchess of Milan, our said commissioners made overture that the Regent of Flanders, with the said Duchess of Milan [and] Don Louis, might all at convenient time and leisure come to Calais, there to meet with us for the more speedy conclusion of all things now moved between us and the said Emperor: and in case at our arrival together every part should so like, and favour should be to every of their satisfactions, the same ambassadors have promised earnestly to solicit the accomplishment also of that overture, and seemed not to doubt but that part thereof, touching the Regent and the Duchess, should be granted and take effect very shortly; albeit they did put some difficulty, lest Don Louis, being further off, could not so soon conveniently repair thither as the other might, being at hand.

Further, they seemed with most hearty good will desirous to embrace the overtures, touching the Prince to one of the Emperor's daughters, and of our daughter Elizabeth to one of the King of Romans' sons, or to one of the sons of Savoy, and to take her in such estate also as we may by our laws give her, in so much that as they made a most humble suit that they might see the Prince, which at time convenient we have granted they shall do accordingly.

Now ye see by this how far we have here proceeded, and in what terms we rest at this present, if our good brother the Emperor shall now show himself earnestly to desire this amity, we be of that inclination for our part that we doubt not but everything shall succeed between us without any great stay or difficulty. Nevertheless ye shall, on our behalf, desire and most heartily pray him, that seeing we have here been so frank and open with his orators in these conferences, he will again show such frankness both to you there, and to his ambassadors here, by his letters and instructions to be sent with their commission as they may, without long tract, condescend to such honourable and reasonable conditions in all things as may be embraced; in which case ye may say ye doubt not but he shall both for contribution against the Turk, as after such reasonable rate as it may be borne, and in all other things to be done on our part, find us so conformable as he shall have no just cause to put any lack in that behalf. . . .

So far the business of mediation between Francis and Charles appeared to promise well for Henry. But in March Francis got wind of these amiable projects and took fright. A close alliance between England and the Emperor was the very last thing he wanted; so the Bishop of Tarbes was dispatched to London to offer Henry the position of sole mediator, and to insinuate doubts of the Emperor's good faith. To the Bishop Henry replied that he placed the most complete reliance upon the Emperor's honour: but to Sir Thomas Wyatt Cromwell wrote in a different key: 'Mr. Wyatt, now handle this matter in such earnest sort with the Emperor, as the King (who by your fair word hath conceived as certain to find assured friendship therein) be not deceived. The Frenchmen affirm so constantly and boldly that nothing spoken by the Emperor, either touching the principal contrahent, the Council, or further alliance, hath in the same any manner of good faith, but such fraud and deceit that [although] the King had gathered a certain confidence in the Emperor's honour and trust, upon your letters and the relation of Mr. Dudley, I assure you, on my faith, it would make any man to respect his proceeding.'

In April the Spanish commissioners arrived in London, apparently to settle the details of the various marriages. To the intense disgust of Henry and his Council it was then discovered that they had not been empowered to conclude anything at all. Hence a letter of indignant protest, from which the following is a substantial extract. After the ambassadors had been asked to show their commission, 'the said ambassadors, wanting such power, were forced to confess that they had no manner of commission to commune of those matters'. They gave 'gay words', but were obviously only anxious 'to continue us in suspense'.

v. To Sir Thomas Wyatt

(f. 27) [*April* 5, 1538.]

. . . First, when they proponed two overtures of marriage, the one between us and the Duchess of Milan, the other between our daughter the Lady Mary, and Don Louis the Infant of Portugal; for the matter of our marriage we demanded, how, and with what dote they would offer her unto us; whereunto they first answered that they would give her the sum of 100,000 crowns in money and 15,000 crowns of yearly rent.

Then it was demanded why they should not give her with all her rights in Milan, due by the force of her marriage there, but limit unto her only 15,000 crowns: and here it was alleged, what dishonour it should be to us by our part to put her from her right and duty[1] whatsoever it were.

They granted then that she should have dower there, and required for that to know how the issue between us and her should be provided for. It was answered, that albeit we have a Prince which we trust in God shall live and reign after us, yet we be not without provision of ordinary Dukedoms within our realm for our younger sons, as York, Gloucester, Somerset, and other, so as that issue could not be without certain living to furnish them in their degree, which have been always by all our progenitors applied to those uses, the least whereof is worth 16,000 ducats, or thereabouts by estimation.

Then was it demanded what assurance should be made for the payment of that dowry; and also how the money should be paid.

To the money they answered generally that there should be good assurance put in for it.

[1] i.e. the portion due to her.

But as to the dowry they said it should be paid of the revenues of the Duchy: but to the assurance they could say nothing.

Well! it was further demanded by us, what assurance we should have, in case the Duchy should hereafter come to any other hands; as to the French King's hands or some other stranger's: and whether the Emperor could be content to receive that dowry himself and to lay[1] us so much as it should amount unto, to be levied in his Low Parties, giving bond of some towns there for the same.

They would neither answer to this point for assurance, ne yet to the overture for the assignment of payment of the dowry to be made in the Low Parties, but said plainly they had no commission to speak further of those matters.

Then came we to the point of her inheritance for Denmark which Covos and Granvelle told you, as appeareth by your letters in express terms, that the Emperor would cause Duke Frederick County Palatine to resign wholly unto us for the interest that he hath in the same by his wife, being the elder sister to the said Duchess: and asked of them, whether the Emperor would promise to compass that matter according to their saying, and also whether he would aid us in the recovery thereof, as the said Covos and Grandvelle said unto you that he would.

To this they answered with a flat denial that any such words had been spoken, saying that they doubted not but you took them amiss. Marry! they came to the point that she should have her part of her father's patrimony; and that the Emperor should travail with Duke Frederick to resign his interest in Denmark and those parties, upon a reasonable recompense at the Emperor's arbitre: and as for aid, they would express no certainty: but said the Emperor would aid us, in like sort as we should aid him again in another like case. We asked what her part of her father's patrimony is, besides the kingdom, and how it should be levied: and what recompense they would demand for Frederick?

To the point of her Father's patrimony, they could neither answer what it was, ne tell how it might be levied and assured.

[1] Pledge.

And as touching Duke Frederick's recompense, they would not speak of it, but would have it referred absolutely to the Emperor's arbitre to give him what he would, and where he would assign it, so as by that part it might have been at his liberty to have laid him in the midst of our realm of England, which doth well declare, by the iniquity of it, that they meant not to proceed with us as they pretended; seeing that all the rest that she hath is already due unto her, and that the Emperor shall show neither to her nor to us any other gratuity for her preferment but only in the bringing to her of the whole title in Denmark, and the helping to the recovery of the same.

We asked them further, what burthen Duke Frederick would bear towards the recovery of Denmark, in case he should have a portion after the same: they would make thereunto no manner of answer.

For the traduction of the Duchess they granted it should be at the Emperor's charge, and for a reciproque demanded of us that we should transport our daughter Mary into Portugal, the long time and distance whereof hath none equality.

Then, albeit we had, as you may perceive in these matters before touched received no manner of direct or reasonable answer whereupon any man might reasonably and honourably join in any certainty, yet we proceeded to the matter of our daughter the Lady Mary and offered, first, with her 100,000 crowns, according to their demand at the first breaking of their matter, and to put her in condition to inherit in our realm, if it should please God to call us hence not leaving behind us any other issue male or female of any lawful marriage; requiring to know what dower they would again give unto her for the same, and what inheritance should descend to the issue of her and Don Louis.

To this they answered now, notwithstanding their first demand, that they found the dote[1] too little, and therefore would require us to be therein more large: when we stack nevertheless upon it, thinking that large enough for our daughter, when they

[1] The dote (*dot*) or dowry was the marriage portion given with the bride by her father: the sum settled on her by the husband was the jointure or dower.

promised nothing to us, being a King in possession, but that whereunto the party is already entitled, and instanced their answer to the whole question.

They said first, that for a 100,000 crowns in dote, they would give her a dower of 5,000 crowns by year, which is the 20th part, and that she should have the fourth part of his goods.

It was demanded by us what they would promise that fourth part of goods should amount unto: whereunto they said they could make no answer.

Then was it told them that their offer of the 20th part seemed rather a mock than any thing else; for we said we could bestow her here in our own realm to more than 1,000l. or 2,000 marks by year for a quarter of the money, where this whole sum of 100,000 crowns would purchase as much land as they offered in dowry for term of life; alleging that the dote and the dower must agree and concur by all laws, civil and others, as by a common usage in all realms in an equality of proportion; and that commonly where the dote is but 20,000 crowns, the dower is 5,000, which is the fourth part, and surely in this part we took it not a little to heart, that they should seem to set so little by our daughter as to offer her so exile and tenuous a living that she might rather think herself married to misery, than advanced according to her estate and degree, having both such a sum of money in dote, and such a possibility depending over her. But forasmuch as they seemed to think the dote too little, to the intent our good will to have joined with them might the better appear, we told them that if the Emperor would prefer him to Milan whereof once they made half an overture, or to any other convenient honour, or assure unto him and her and their posterity, as much yearly rent as the late Duke of Richmond our only bastard son had of our gift within this our realm, and appoint her thereof a convenient dowry, we would augment the dote, and give her proportion after the rate that was given with our sister Mary the late Queen of France.

They answered plainly that they could neither speak of any such preferment to be given unto him, ne yet could they tell us what inheritance he hath already, ne yet what inheritance should descend to their children; but still they stack firmly that they would not exceed their proportion of the 20th part; so that for 200,000 crowns, if we should have come so far, they would have offered 10,000 crowns in dowry, which we think all the world will judge too far under the foot, and must think such manner of proceeding strange; and yet would have us to have given as large a dowry as ever was given in this realm to any Queen.

It was further by us demanded of them, what aid the Emperor would give us for the recovery of our pensions in France, in case the French King should upon this agreement allege the treaty of the perpetual peace broken, and so deny the payment of the said pensions.

They made answer they had no commission to entreat of any such matter.

It was by us asked of them, whether they could not be content to conclude the marriage with us; wherein, percase, we might rest much in the Emperor's honour, and leave the other till a further consultation with the Emperor.

They refused it; and said they would not meddle in the one without the other.

It was of us asked of them, because they have before-time spoken much of a renovation of amities, whether they would treat any thing in that part.

They refused that also, unless they might first conclude the marriage as they would; neither having commission nor yet coming to any manner of reason or certainty in the points of the same.

Now if our good brother the Emperor do but half so much esteem our amity as he hath in words pretended, he may see that we have used more frankness towards him than we suppose any Prince would in such a case have used to another: and that his orators here have on the other part proceeded more coldly, and much more perversely, than was in any part answerable to their good words, many times before uttered.

Wherefore you shall on our behalf desire our good brother, in case he do mind any such amity with us, not only to consider our demands, and to make such reasonable answers to them as we may with our honour embrace the same, but also to send hither sufficient commission for the conclusion of such things as shall be agreed upon between us, in which case he shall find as friendly a conformity in us, to all things reasonable and honourable, as he hath pretended an earnest zeal towards the same. In which case of his conformity to come to reason and to send such commission, it shall be most convenient, considering the distance between us and Spain, that he send absolute power to the Lady Regent to resolve and conclude in all things that may touch those purposes, or the renovation or increase of our amities, or any of them; unless he will wholly trust these men in that behalf, giving them sufficient commission and power also, which they have ever lacked, to conclude in the same; or else we cannot think he meaneth uprightly, as one good friend should to another: for it were time for us to know whereunto to trust, and not thus to delay the wealth of our realm in hearkening always and not concluding.

It is an interesting document, admirably concise, temperately worded, entirely to the point, and characteristically 'foreign office' in its tone. It provides also a good example of a typical royal marriage bargaining in the sixteenth century. The following extract from another letter of slightly later date amplifies one or two of its points in an interesting manner.

VI. To Sir Thomas Wyatt

(fol. 70.) [*June*, 1537.]

. . . The first is, the condition of aid that is joined to the overture of the Duchy, extending as well to all wars offensives, as to defence; which hath in it no manner of egality, considering the present state of both princes, with the compass and limits of either their dominions, and scite with the standing of the same. For the King's Majesty is in peace with all men, the Emperor is already in war; many of his dominions join so upon France and firm land with other Princes, or be so inhabited by men that after a sort claim a large title, that he is very like to have continual war either with his open enemies, or with some of them whom he calleth his subjects, so that if the King's Majesty should enter into such a party with him, the said Emperor might keep his Grace in a continual war at his own will and pleasure, which with friendship cannot (without a much further and greater consideration and respect than for such alliance) be desired. Wherefore the said Sir Thomas Wyatt shall require the said Emperor with his wisdom to weigh and consider this point; and then he shall perceive the King's Majesty cannot without too great an inconvenience agree to the same.

The second is, the condition for the marriage for the King's Highness own person, wherein his Majesty findeth also great causes of some longer delay before it could grow to any certain end and conclusion; not only for that his Grace, prudently considering how that marriage is a bargain of such nature as must endure for the whole life of man, and a thing whereof the pleasure and quiet, or the displeasure and torment of the man's mind doth much depend, thinketh it to be much necessary both for himself and the party with whom it shall please God to join him in marriage, that the one might see the other before the time they should be so affianced, as they might not without dishonour or further inconvenience break off; which point his Highness hath largely set forth heretofore, and likewise at this last conference to the said Emperor's ambassadors; but also, because there appeareth both a great charge, and no less difficulty in obtaining of her inheritance in Denmark, which at the first setting forth of the overture of that marriage was alleged as a special mean to cause his Majesty to look towards her: for, by the treaty of her marriage with the late Duke of Milan, she renounced, and was bound to renounce, all her right and title of Denmark, with all the parties of the same to her elder sister, wife to Duke Frederick Count Palatine; so as the whole interesse there remaining by that pact in the said Duke Frederick's wife, if the King's Majesty should mind any title thereto, he must in that case agree to the whole with the said Duke Frederick: and when he should have agreed with him for it, yet it would not be obtained without great aid, charge, adventure, and difficulty, which, before any conclusion should be taken, ought to be well weighed and considered, and will require a time of good deliberation, specially considering, that if his Grace should enter into any war for the recovery thereof, being the matters of all other Princes before componed, he might also be noted a new beginner of the wars in Christendom, which should redound to his dishonour; which enforceth his Majesty with a longer time so to consult thereupon as might bring forth a more certain and perfect conclusion, than the demeure here of the said Sir Thomas Wyatt, returning in such diligence by the Emperor's desire, will permit and suffer; so that unless his Grace would send his commission so rawly forth; and to such raw men for such a purpose as no Prince of wisdom and experience would, his Majesty could not at this present time satisfy the Emperor in that behalf. . . .

In the meantime Charles and Francis had been quietly getting on with their own affairs. Paul III was offered, and accepted, the position of sole mediator; and in June, at Nice, both sovereigns met the Pope—though not each other—and agreed to a ten years' truce, which they confirmed a month later in a personal meeting at Aigues Mortes, in Provence. Charles reiterated his professions of friendship towards Henry, but it was obvious that the first round had concluded with England left out in the cold, and France and the Empire pledged to peace.

The second round began in the autumn. The Emperor had persuaded Wyatt, who had in turn done his best to persuade Henry, that he was still anxious to complete the matrimonial negotiations which had collapsed in the spring. Henry, urged by his Council to remarry and beget another heir, was only too ready to believe that Charles was in earnest, as it is possible he may have been.

This time the negotiations were handed over by Charles to his sister Maria, Regent of the Netherlands, and Sir Philip Hoby was dispatched to join Wyatt, with the following letter containing their instructions. It is a notable letter, in spite of its diplomatic nothings, its curtsyings, its verbosity, and its concern with things that never happened. It stands out amongst all Henry's letters as about the best piece of evidence available to show us not only the exact relation between his own mind and hand, but also the extent of his responsibility for the composition and wording of his diplomatic correspondence.

After the fall of Wolsey, when Henry became his own foreign minister, his more important or difficult letters were, I believe, drafted in discussion or according to instructions, and then written out in a form suitable for emendation and alteration—that is to say, on pages with wide margins and with a space of about three-quarters of an inch, an inch, or even more between each line. There are various original drafts of this kind still in existence, but the one under discussion is the most illuminating of them all. The original draft of these instructions given to Hoby and Wyatt is to be found in one of the Cotton MSS., Vespasian C. VII (fol. 71 ff.). Two pages have been added to it by Henry in his own handwriting (fols. 74 and 76), and with them should be grouped another page at present bound up in another of the Cotton MSS., Vitellius B. XXI (fol. 60; modern pagination, fol. 64).[1] We have, therefore, in the first place, three pages which show us Henry at work on his own rough draft, where we can see for ourselves how few deletions, second thoughts and re-phrasings he required.[2] We have, secondly, the original draft of the whole, with a large number of cancellations and additions in Henry's hand; and we have, thirdly, in Harleian MS. 282 (fol. 73 ff.), the fair copy made from these drafts, and signed by the King, and dispatched.[3] Finally, if evidence of Henry's

[1] Although the water-mark only appears on the two Vespasian pages there can be no doubt that the Vitellius page is written on the same paper. Further, this paper does not correspond to the paper used either for the Vespasian draft, the Harleian fair copy, or the Vitellius fair copy, although the same water-mark appears in all three. The chain-lines in the paper of the three pages written by Henry are quite unusually and unmistakably close together—somewhat irregular in their spacing, but at most never more than ¾ inch apart.

[2] Though we have no reason to suppose that the various letters in Henry's own hand which survive are his own fair copies, at the same time there is no evidence to prove that they are not. Hence the value of these three pages, which suggest very plainly that he wrote not only with ease, and with real mastery of the elaborate Tudor sentence, but also with force, concentration and a clear perception of what he intended to say.

[3] There is also in existence another fair copy of this letter in Vitellius B. XXI, fol. 170 ff. It is not signed by Henry. It corresponds almost exactly to Harleian 282, fol. 73 ff., and is apparently written in the same hand. It was, presumably, the fair copy kept for reference. The cataloguing of these various items in *L.P.* XIII. ii. 622 is descriptive rather

complete responsibility for his foreign policy is required, the letter itself informs us that Hoby took with him not only these instructions, but also 'the King's letters of his own handwriting'—presumably further and perhaps secret instructions which were to be read and then destroyed.

An extraordinarily interesting sidelight on Henry's methods—and also on his character—is to be found in a note from Ralph Sadler to Cromwell, written in January, 1536. Speaking of the instructions given to Lord William Howard for his Scottish embassy, Sadler writes, 'The King's Highness first appointed me to come to him at mass time to read the same unto his Grace, at which time when I came he said he would take a time of more leisure, commanding me to tarry until the evening, when he said he should have best leisure, because he would maturely advise and peruse the said instructions'. Then, after a complaint that he expects, in consequence, to be kept in attendance until late, he adds, 'as ye know his Grace is always loath to sign, and I think deferred the reading of the instructions at mass time because he was not willing to sign'.[1] The instructions to Howard survive (see *Scottish Policy*, pp. 282-3), but they bear no signs of the way in which Henry's mature advising and perusing made themselves felt. In the letter to Wyatt, however, we can see for ourselves exactly the kind of thing that happened at one of those evening interviews that Sadler was anticipating. Moreover, in the light of Sadler's note, and of the large number of letters subscribed 'at midnight' we may quite reasonably assume that it was Henry's custom to do much of his best work, and to make his final decisions, in those midnight hours when certain temperaments find their powers at their highest pitch (see also p. 73).[2]

To return, however, to the actual letter under discussion. The text that follows is that of the final letter in Harleian 282, signed at the head by Henry. The passages which correspond to the three pages drafted by Henry in his own hand are indicated

than critical; and is liable to mislead the student who cannot examine the originals.

[1] P.R.O. S.P.I., §101, pp. 57-8.

[2] It is extremely interesting to realize that Elizabeth was not the only Tudor who found it difficult to sign, finally and irrevocably.

by a black rule in the left-hand margin. The changes between his draft and the final version are very slight—a word here and there, and the substitution of the formal 'his Highness' or 'his Grace' for the personal 'I'.[1] To appreciate the care and methods and results of his alterations in the original draft, however, reference has to be made to the document itself, which has been so pulled-about, rearranged and emended that no idea of the work he put into it can really be gathered except by studying it as a whole. The facsimile reproduced in the frontispiece to this book is one of the most interesting pages.

VII. INSTRUCTIONS TO SIR THOMAS WYATT, KT., AND PHILIP HOBY, ONE OF HIS GRACE'S PRIVY CHAMBER

HENRY R. [*Oct.* 16, 1538.]

Whereas his Majesty hath appointed his trusty servant Philip Hoby, one of the grooms of his Grace's Privy Chamber, to resort in post with all convenient diligence to Sir Thomas Wyatt, Knight, his Grace's Ambassador in the Emperor's Court, the said Hoby taking with him these instructions with the King's letters of his own hand-writing, and such other things as be prepared for his dispatch, shall with celerity take his journey and speedy resort thither; first of all to the said Wyatt, and deliver unto him such letters as he hath addressed unto him, and these present instructions, which they shall peruse and make themselves ripe and perfect in the whole tenor of the same, and therewith cause the arrival of the said Hoby to be signified unto the Emperor, with requisition of access to deliver such the King's letters as they have unto him; and time appointed for the declaration of their charge, the which being assigned unto them, they shall both together resort to the Emperor's presence, and jointly together with most hearty and affectuous commendations deliver his Grace's letters, declaring therewith his Highness's good health and prosperity, with vehement desire to hear the like of the said Emperor, which shall be much to his joy and consolation.

And so coming to the declaration of their credence they

[1] Changes from first and second to third person are not noted.

shall on his Highness' behalf REQUIRE OF THE EMPEROR THAT BOTH HE SHALL TAKE THE OVERTURES IN GOOD PART, PROCEEDING OF SO FRIENDLY AN HEART; AND ALSO PROMISE IN THE WORD OF A PRINCE, THAT HE SHALL NOT DISCLOSE THEM TO NONE BUT TO SUCH OF HIS SECRET COUNCIL AS SHALL BE SWORN TO THE SECRECY OF THE SAME. Which promise obtained, they shall first express that his Highness hearing that the Emperor upon a godly purpose to prosecute his enterprise against the TURK,[1] enemies of our Christian faith, doth intend, for the ampliation and magnification of Christ's glory, the next year to set upon them in his own person with a great army. Although his Grace thinketh THAT THE EMPEROR of his high wisdom and discretion will afore his departure not only consider all things to be considered for the establishment and assurance of his estate and prosperity,[2] OR THAT HE WILL PUT HIS OWN PERSON IN ANY SUCH DANGER, specially in a matter of such difficulty and so high an enterprise, FROM the which nevertheless his Grace (THOUGH HE WOULD BE SORRY THAT THE EMPEROR SHOULD EXPONE HIS OWN PERSON TO ANY SUCH JEOPARDY) WILL NOT ATTEMPT TO DIVERT HIS afFIXED PURPOSE BEING CHRIST'S cause, at whose calling we be all, and of whose hand and providence we do all depend; YET HE THOUGHT IT THE PART OF A VERY FRIEND NOW TO PUT HIM IN REMEMBRANCE so to dispose all things BEFORE HIS DEPARTURE as the Prince of Spain his son, which is but young yet, may, whatsoever chance, FORTUNE escape the dangers that might sundry ways HAPPEN TO HIM, UNLESS THEY WERE WISELY FORESEEN AND PROVIDED FOR THEREAFTER.

His Grace FURTHER of very friendship and pure amity TAKETH GREATER BOLDNESS THUS TO DO, thinking that a friend seeth sometimes in his friend's causes, WHEN THEY CONSIST IN DIVERSITY OF MATTERS, more, PERADVENTURE, THAN HE TO WHOM THE matter toucheth NEAR; FOR HE THINKETH THE EM-

[1] Originally *Mahometans* [2] *Posterity*

PEROR'S COURAGE SO GREAT, AND SO FULLY BENT UPON his[1] HIGH ENTERPRISE, THAT HIS MIND BEING OCCUPIED WITH INFINITE THINGS APPERTAINING THERETO, MIGHT PERADVENTURE PRETERMIT THIS, WHICH TO HIS GRACE'S JUDGEMENT IS MOST NECESSARY, AND THEREFORE HATH THOUGHT IT convenient[2] TO open unto HIS MAJESTY HIS FRIENDLY OPINION and advice, how in all casualties his Highness judgeth that the Emperor's estates and posterity may be so established as, whatsoever shall chance, they may continue, stand, and prosper, whosoever would attempt the contrary; WHEREOF HIS GRACE[3] WOULD BE MOST JOYOUS; AND FOR THAT INTENT DOTH NOW OPEN PLAINLY HIS MIND.

HIS HIGHNESS FIRST THINKETH AND FEARETH THAT UNLESS IT BE BETTER PROVIDED FOR THAN HE KNOWETH OF YET, OR BY ANY OUTWARD INTELLIGENCE CAN PERCEIVE (THOUGH MOST PART OF CHRISTENDOM IN AFFAIRS DOTH PRACTISE WITH HIM) THAT the Emperor's SON AND PRINCE OF SPAIN IS SLENDERLY YET FURNISHED OF TRUSTY FRIENDS; FOR HE HEARETH OF NONE THAT IS JOINED WITH HIM WHICH MAY IN HIS MINORITY STAND HIM IN FRIENDLY STEAD, WHICH TRULY HE LAMENTETH.

SECONDLY, his Highness doubteth not but the Emperor considereth very well, THAT IF IT SHOULD PLEASE GOD TO CALL HIM TO HIS MERCY IN THIS HIS INTENDED ENTERPRISE, OR BY ANY OTHER MEANs, THAT THE IMPERIAL DIGNITY IS ELECTIVE, AND NOT LIKE TO DESCEND TO HIS HEIRS BY SUCCESSION, FOR[4] THAT THE ALMAINS WILL BE LOATH TO HAVE THE SPANISH NATION TO BE THEIR SUPERIOR.

THIRDLY, THAT MILAN TAKETH INVESTITURE OF THE EMPIRE, AND THAT IN SOME CASES IT IS CONFISCABLE,[5] AS WE UNDERSTAND HIS CHIEF

[1] THIS [2] NECESSARY [3] ~~HIGHNESS~~ [4] FOR ~~AND~~ THAT [5] ~~CONFISKD TO~~

A line drawn through a word indicates a deletion made by Henry.

CLAIM IS NOW, or[1] ELSE THE FRENCHMEN's CLAIM BY INHERITANCE SHOULD SERVE THEM; WHEREFORE UPON THESE FOUNDATIONS IS NO SURE BUILDING FOR HIS SON'S SURETY,[2] FRIENDSHIP, OR AID.

FOURTHLY, THE Emperor may WELL CONSIDER THAT in case of disfortune in that enterprise what disquiet and sedition by some evil-disposed persons might rise and be spread in Spain, Queen Joan his mother being yet alive, of whose right and title the Crown of Spain dependeth, AND HIS SON BEING OF SMALL AGE, THE PEOPLE always BEING much dedicate to novelties, SPECIALLY WHERE THEY LIKE; AS BY EXAMPLE IN OUR TIME it hath been seen[3] BY THE SAID EMPEROR'S FATHER KING PHILIP, WHOM IF THE KING[4] HAD NOT AIDED BY COLOUR OF MAMBORNSHIP,* THE KING FERDINAND OF ARAGON HAD KEPT HIM FROM HIS RIGHTFUL POSSESSION,[5] AND YET FOR ALL THAT FOUND SUCH MEANS (AS IT WAS SAID) THAT HE SOON AFTER DIED.

FIFTHLY, it is considered, that albeit the Emperor shall leave his son a great Prince, lord of sundry great realms and ample dominions, yet a great incommodity there is, that they do not lie together, but far asunder one from another; Naples and Sicily far from Spain; Flanders and other his Low Countries in another part far asunder from them both, and so other dominions dispersed and separate one from another.

SIXTHLY, it is to be weighed, that his Uncle the King of Romans, of whom he should have the chief help, succour and comfort, is far distant, and his countries standing very unhandsomely, to give present aid and speedy assistance if need were. Whereupon the King's Highness not doubting but the Emperor BOTH CAN AND WILL better ponder and weigh THESE things with HIS WISE COUNCIL, BEING ADMONISHED BY HIS TRUSTY FRIEND OF THE SAME, before the EMBRACING OF any so high and difficile enterprise,

[1] FOR [2] SURETY ~~OR AID~~ [3] WE SAW [4] ~~WE~~ THE KING OUR MASTER
[5] POSSESSION ~~AND YOU ALSO~~

* Relationship on the mother's side.

REMITTETH THE DISCREET ORDERING AND PULLING AWAY OF THESE DOUBTS TO HIS AND THEIR HIGH WISDOM, TRUSTING THAT THE EMPEROR AND HIS COUNCIL WILL TAKE HIS FRANK KINDNESS IN GOOD PART: WHEREOF[1] his Grace desireth, and would be glad to be advertised with diligence.

FURTHERMORE, IF the Emperor BE DESIROUS TO KNOW HIS Grace's OPINION HOW TO REMEDY THESE,[2] his pleasure is, that the said Sir Thomas Wyatt and Hoby shall declare the same WHEREBY the Emperor MAY WELL PERCEIVE WHAT HEARTY AND UNFEIGNED GOOD WILL his Highness BEARETH unto him.

Corresponding to Vitell. B. XXI, f. 64.

FIRST TOUCHING⋌[3] TO ESTABLISH HIS SON AND SUCCESSION WITH ⋌ ASSURED FRIENDSHIP, his Grace thinketh THAT THE EMP[EROR OUGHT], WITHOUT AFFECTION, UPON APPARENT REASONS AND LIKELIHOODS SO TO [CHOOSE THEM], AS ALL MEN OF WIT⋌ AND KNOWLEDGE⋌ COULD NOT DISAPPROVE THEM, AND SPECIALLY [ABOVE ALL] THINGS TO REGARD THAT THEY SHOULD BE SUCH AS BOTH BE OF ABILITY, [AND] NOT PRETENDING TITLES TO ANY such DOMINIONS as[4] HE INTENDE[TH] TO LEAVE TO HIS SON. BESIDES THAT, CONSIDERING HIS DOMINIONS BE DISPERS[ED], TO MAKE FRIENDS IN DIVERS PARTS, BY WHOSE MEANS the Prince HIS SON SHALL THE BETTER DEFEND ⋌ HIS RIGHT ⋌. AS BY EXAMPLE; TO LEAVE THE DUCHY OF MILAN TO DON LOUIS Infant of Portugal, WHO IS NIGH OF KIN TO HIS FORESAID SON, WHICH BINDETH HIM BY NATURE TO BE ASSURED TO HIM; AND HIS GRACE THINKETH, (AND SOMEWHAT THEREIN KNOWETH) THAT THE POTENTATES OF ITALY HAD LIEFER, (IF THEY DURST BE A-KNOWEN OF IT) TO HAVE ONE AMONGST THEM THERE, THAN THAT THE

[1] WHEREOF TO BE ADVERTISED WITH DILIGENCE HE HATH COMMANDED US

[2] THESE, HE HATH COMMANDED US ALSO TO DECLARE HIS MIND ALSO

[3] Passages enclosed in caret marks are insertions made by Henry in his own draft.

[4] WHICH

EMPEROR SHOULD DETAIN IT STILL IN HIS OWN CUSTODY;[1] ⋌ FOR AS LONG AS HE DETAINeth IT[2] ⋌ THEY ARE ALWAYS IN FEAR THAT HE PRETENDETH THE MONARCHY OF ALL ITALY, WHICH ABOVE ALL THINGS THEY DETEST AND FEAR; WHEREFORE HIS GRACE'S OPINION IS, THAT THE GIVING OF IT TO DON LOUIS SHALL INDEED BE AS GOOD TO THE EMPEROR, AND AS MUCH FOR HIS SURETY AND HIS SUCCESSION, AS THOUGH HE KEPT IT TO HIMSELF. FOR IF IT PLEASE HIM HE MAY HAVE IT AS MUCH AT HIS COMMANDMENT,[3] FURNISHED WITH HIS SOLDIERS, AS IT IS NOW, OR ELSE IT WERE PITY OF HIS LIFE, BEING BRED UP AT THE EMPEROR'S HAND AS HE HATH BEEN, AND IS YET, HAVING LITTLE OR NOTHING ELSE BUT WHAT HE SHALL HAVE OF HIM.

FURTHER, HIS GRACE THINKETH, THAT IF IT WOULD PLEASE THE EMPEROR TO WIN[4] ALLIANCES AND FRIENDSHIP, PUTTING (UPON SOME GOOD LIKELIHOODS) CONFIDENCE IN SOME OF THE POTENTATES OF ITALY, AS IN THE DUKE OF FERRARA, MANTUA, OR FLORENCE, AND SO WITH AMITY,[5] KINDNESS ⋌ AND ALLIANCE ⋌ TO ALLURE THEM, THAT IT SHOULD MAKE TO HIM AND HIS A PERFECT ASSURANCE OF ALL THEIR DOMINIONS ON THAT PART OF ITALY,[6] AND SO BETWEEN the said DON LOUIS AND THEM HE AND HIS SHOULD EVER B[E ASSURED] OF THOSE PARTS, FOR THESE PRETEND NO TITLE TO ANY OF [HIS DOMINIONS, AND SHALL EVER HOPE] BY HIS ASSISTANCE TO ENJOY THEIR [OWN, THE EMPEROR AND HIS SUCCESSION BEING MUTUALLY] BOUND WITH ⋌ THEM AND ⋌

[1] ~~CUSTODY; AND THAT NO OTHER DEVICE HEREAFTER FOLLOWING~~ deleted by Henry.

[2] ~~IN HIS OWN CUSTODY~~ deleted.

[3] COMMANDMENT, AND TO BE FURNISHED

[4] WIN BY

[5] AMITY ~~AND~~

[6] ITALY ~~THEY BEING BOUND ALSO TO DEFEND HIS~~ inserted and deleted.

THEIRS [FOR THE DEFENCE OF EACH OTHER'S DOMINIONS].

Corresponding to Vesp. C. VII, f. 74.

AS CONCERNING SPAIN WITHIN ITSELF, the said Sir Thomas Wyatt ⁁MAY SAY⁁ that IF the King's Highness WERE[1] AS WELL ACQUAINTED AS His Grace hath BEEN IN TIMES PAST, his Majesty COULD AND WOULD GIVE SOME COUNSEL IN THAT BEHALF: BUT SURELY his Highness hath HAD NO PRACTICE IN THOSE AFFAIRS THESE MANY YEARS, WHEREFORE his Grace remitteth WHOLLY THAT[2] TO HIS MAJESTY AND HIS DISCREET COUNCIL, WHICH CAN A THOUSAND TIMES BETTER DETERMINE THAT THAN his Highness; YET his Grace will NOT, WHEN OCCASION SHALL serve,[3] PRETERMIT THE OFFICE OF A PERFECT FRIEND IN SHOWING his ADVICE, THOUGH IT BE BUT slender.[4] AS BEFORE he hath DONE AND IN OTHER THINGS HEREAFTER FOLLOWING intendeth TO DO, TRUSTING THAT THE EMPEROR WILL TAKE IT AS PROCEEDING OF the[5] SINCERE HEART of[6] AN OLD ASSURED FRIEND. BUT AS FOR ⁁OUTWARD⁁ FRIENDSHIP BOTH of[7] SPAIN AND FLANDERS, his Grace trusteth (IF THE EMPEROR TAKEth IT SO) THAT his Highness AND his[8] POOR ISLAND MAY AND WOULD STAND HIM IN AS GOOD STEAD AS ANY OUTWARD PRINCE OR REALM IN CHRISTENDOM; AND IF IT WILL PLEASE HIM AS SINCERELY on[9] ⁁HIS⁁ PART TO GO FORTH WITH THESE AMITIES AND ALLIANCES ALREADY[10] BEGUN, AND NOW YET IN COMMUNICATION, AS his Majesty OF his SIDE SHALL, it is not to be doubted BUT IT SHALL BE[11] A PERDURABLE KNOT[12] between their Majesties and posterities, AND A PERFECT UNION AND SURETY FOR BOTH their REALMS AND DOMINIONS; whereof the King for his part SHALL GREATLY REJOICE, TRUSTING THE EMPEROR WILL DO THE SAME. AND FOR THAT PURPOSE the said Sir Thomas Wyat and Hoby SHALL MOST HEARTILY REQUIRE[13] HIS MAJESTY

[1] ~~HAD BEEN~~ [2] THAT WHOLLY [3] GIVE [4] FOOLISH [5] A [6] AND [7] FOR [8] THIS [9] OF [10] ALREADY BETWEEN US [11] BE ~~FOR~~ [12] KNOT TO ALL OUR BLOOD [13] REQUIRE OF

THAT, FOR aVOIDING OF DELAYS, WHICH BE ALWAYS SUSPICIOUS, HE WILL EITHER SEND TO MY LADY REGENT HIS SISTER, FULL AND UNRESTRAINED POWER BRIEFLY TO[1] DELEGATE MINISTERS TO COMMUNE AND CONCLUDE THE SAME UPON REASONABLE CONDITIONS, OR ELSE WITH DILIGENCE TO SEND GRANDVELLE OR[2] COVOS inTO FLANDERS, fully instructed of[3] THE BOTTOM OF his STOMACH, FOR PERFORMING OF THIS INDISSOLUBLE KNOT BETWEEN their Majesties and posterities,[4] TO THE PERFORMING WHEREOF they MAY ASSURE HIM[5] on the King's BEHALF THAT THERE SHALL NEITHER LACK GOOD WILL NOR SPEEDY EXPEDITION, so that his Grace find THE SEMBLABLE correspondence in the Emperor; AND THAT IT SHALL NOT STAND BY his Highness FOR LACK OF CONDESCENDING TO A REASONABLE AID FOR MILAN, SO THAT, AS REASON WOULD, his Grace MAY HAVE A REASONABLE RECIPROQUE FOR IT.

FURTHERMORE, they MAY DECLARE UNTO THE EMPEROR, IF IN COMMUNICATION ANY SLACKNESS BE LAID unTO his Grace, THAT IT WERE NO MARVEL THOUGH his Highness DID DELAY; FOR his Grace was BUT STRANGELY HANDLED BY HIS AGENTS, WITH UNJUST AND UNREASONABLE[6] DEMANDS, AND UNLIKE TO PROCEED OUT OF A WILLING HEART TO CONCLUDE; and BESIDES THAT, WHO WOULD BE GLAD TO PUT HIS FOOT IN THE BRIAR AND TAKE THE WHOLE BURTHEN ON HIS NECK, THESE WEIGHTY CAUSES[7] AFORE REHEARSED, NOT BEING OTHERWISE THAN his Grace knoweth PROVIDED FOR.

Corresponding to Vesp. C. VII, f. 76.

ALSO, THIS NEW RECONCILED AMITY OF OLD ENEMIES NOW ⋏ ENTIRE FRIENDS[8] ⋏ BLEW SO STRANGE A BLAST IN his Grace's EARS, SO FAR FROM THE SURETY OF THE EMPEROR'S SUCCESSION, THAT IT HAD BEEN ENOUGH ALONE TO[9] discourage His High-

[1] TO ~~CONCLUDE WITH AND~~ [2] ~~AND~~ [3] WITH [4] BETWEEN US AND OURS [5] ~~THEM~~ OF [6] ~~UNLAWFUL~~ [7] CAUSES ~~NOT BE~~ [8] ~~FRIENDS~~ [9] DESESPERATE US

ness FROM JOINING THERE; CONSIDERING THAT BESIDES THE TITLE OF MILAN, THERE BE SO MANY OTHER TITLES DEPENDING STILL ⋌ BETWEEN THEM, ⋌ AS NAPLES, the SOVEREIGNTY OF FLANDERS, GENOA AND PIEDMONT, WITH NICE ALSO. THESE THINGS WELL CONSIDERED, his Grace reporteth himself BOTH TO THE EMPEROR AND HIS COUNCIL, WHETHER he hath NOT HAD CAUSE BOTH ⋌ TO[1] ⋌ SLACK AND OCCASION FOR TO THINK, THAT HE AND HIS ⋌ AGENTS[2] ⋌ DID BUT DISSEMBLE WITH his Majesty FOR WINNING OF TIME, WHICH WAYS BEING FAR FROM A SINCERE FRIEND'S DEMEANOUR, his Highness HEARTILY requireth ⋌ HIM[3] ⋌ TO cause his Commissioners NO[4] longer to use with his Majesty, BUT SINCERELY HENCEFORTH TO PROCEED, AS UNDOUBTEDLY the King for his part will do, OMITTING ALL BY PAST QUARRELS, AND ENDEAVOURING their Majesties ON BOTH PARTS TO RECOMPENSE THEM WITH PERFECT LOVE AND KINDNESS.

In the meantime, however, in October, 1538, an event took place in England which changed the whole situation—the destruction and the desecration of the relics of St. Thomas of Canterbury. To Catholic feeling abroad this was the final outrage, and in December Paul III decided, at last, that the moment had come to publish his Bull of Deposition against Henry.[5] France and Scotland were urged to refrain from all commerce with England, and Reginald Pole was sent to Toledo to urge Charles to invade England and reclaim it for the Catholic faith. In January it became plain, even to Henry's hopeful envoys, that a marriage with the Duchess of Milan was out of the question; and it looked for the moment as if the Pope might at last have succeeded in uniting the Empire, France and Scotland against heretical England.

[1] ⋌ TO ⋌ BE [2] ~~COUNCIL~~ [3] ~~THEM~~ [4] MORE PUT IN USE WITH US

[5] Though even now, when he discovered how little likelihood there was of either Charles or Francis putting it into execution, he refrained from actually issuing it.

In the letters that follow Henry protests first against the growing coldness and delay in the negotiations, then against the reception by the Emperor of Cardinal Pole. He also wrote personally in French to Charles, his good brother and 'perpetual ally', to reinforce his ambassador's request.

VIII. To Wriothesley, Vaughan and Carne[1]

By the King

[*Dec.* 23, 1538.]

Trusty and well-beloved, we greet you well. Advertising you, that after long expectation to hear of your proceedings and other occurrences there, whereof we be much desirous more often to be advertised, at the last arrived here the 20th of this month our courier Francisco, who brought unto us your letters dated from Brussels the 16th of this present, whereby we perceive right amply your discourses had with the Queen Dowager our sister, and with her Council there appointed to confer with you, upon the contents of our last letters sent unto you. And like as we like well and take in good part the discourses and remonstrations made unto them for your behalf, so we cannot a little marvel of the very frosty coldness and slack remissness they show now, in very deed far from the correspondence of the sincerity we looked to have had, as well upon the Emperor's promises and offers largely made unto us, and also upon the good and fair words ye had of them at the beginning of your conferences, and at your arrival there. We cannot but think it very strange that whereas ye desired of our said sister, the Queen Regent, having no power by her commission to substitute any Commissioners under her, a bill signed with her hand, promising upon her honour to observe, conclude and ratify all that should be concluded between you and them, or to have it by copy under her Secretary's hand, she will, and her Council also, so much stick at a thing, which is but a trifle unto them, but to us a thing of good moment and importance. For albeit we call not their honour and the observation of their word in question, yet prudent dealing requireth that in such

[1] His ambassadors at Brussels.

case it should be so provided, that, whatsoever chance, ye be not driven to that the answer of imprudent persons, '*non putabam*'. Princes of circumspection, intending sincerely and in all points to observe for their part their promises and treaties, (as we do for our behalf) cannot but like, as they do mean well, to foresee and provide that, in case of instability, there be left inconsiderately no starting hole for such as they treat with to digress from that sincerity of proceedings that is so meant. As we have the more cause to do, specially seeing that, after such vehement heat of promises and offers, we find in them such cold and slack proceedings. We see the meagreness of the power; we see by their own confession the slender instruction they have in all points to be treated; we perceive they allege upon things already agreed here, that their ambassadors passed the bonds of their commission, and that they make as much strangeness at the declaration of their offer made to conclude a straighter amity as though there had never been any such thing offered, but to refer unto you the opening of all together, as though we should sue for it, as they never had offered or heard of any such thing; and at the least they refuse to proceed to the other overture of marriage, minding not to conclude unless upon both together.

This their strange and marvellous coldness should utterly discourage us further to treat with them, were it not that we be of such constant mind as we be loath to have entered so far conferences and no resolution to follow thereupon, and that we will leave no good office to entertain and increase the old and ancient amity that hath been ever between us and them, our progenitors and theirs. As we caused our good zeal and affection therein lately to be showed unto the Emperor by Sir Thomas Wyatt, Knight, our ambassador with him, and by our servant Philip Hoby, whom we sent thither for that purpose, with such instructions as we doubt not but our Council hath made you, Thomas Wriothesley, participant of, and ye your colleagues. Whereunto, as we understand by the report of our said servant Hoby, who returned thence about the 17th of this present, the Emperor made answer[1] that he took our advertisements and gentle kindness, as well concerning the conservation of his own

[1] This is the answer to No. VII.

person in his intended enterprise against the Turks and Machometistes, as also the surety and establishment of his son and posterity, in a very thankful part; and that the same were much according to the confidence he had ever put in our friendship, and so with long discourse declared his resolution and provision made for the same, to be reported unto us: the discourse whereof is long and nothing toucheth your charge. But as touching Milan to be given to the Infant of Portugal, Don Ludovic, according to his offer, the said Emperor answered, that the time was not now to resolve in that, what he would do; but to dispose it, in despair of the Frenchmen, he thought it utterly to be eschewed, saying that they themselves be content, he reserving it in his own hands, to remain with the hope, and so he could not at this present dispose Milan to the said Infant of Portugal. Requiring that we should proceed upon the other marriage, and let the same remain till more commodity; or that if we liked not the alliance of the Infant of Portugal, in terms as it was communed of before the naming of Milan, whatsoever party we could devise more convenient for our daughter the Lady Mary, the said Emperor would employ himself therein, as honesty and reason should require; like as we think the said Emperor hath already, or will shortly, advertise the Queen Regent his sister thereof: and also that he is contented she shall proceed to treat upon the marriage of the Duchess of Milan, for the assurance of whose dowry, he affirmed, the said Regent hath sufficient commission and instruction, but that he will no further charge his Low Countries.

For your more ample instruction wherein, ye shall understand that on the 28th of the last month we dispatched one of our couriers, called Nicholas, to the said Mr. Wyatt, with our letters concerning those matters and other; whereof (being our said servant Hoby departed from the Emperor's court, and far on his way hitherward before the arrival of our said courier to the Emperor's court) we cannot as yet have none answer. By the same we willed our Ambassador, amongst sundry other things and considerations, to declare unto the Emperor, that seeing his untowardness to give Milan to the said Infant Don

Ludovic, and for the great zeal we have to the common peace of Christendom, and that we should be loath that the giving of Milan should stir dissension or war, we intended no further to instant or press him thereof, but evermore continuing our good mind and affection to join with him, his said untowardness and coldness notwithstanding, we would be contented, upon honourable and reasonable conditions, to enter with him in alliance for the marriage of our own person with the Duchess of Milan, with the straighter amity between us to be concluded, so that the said Emperor would be content, amongst other things, to provide that the said Duchess may have her dote paid, and her dowry well assigned upon some good place, so that certain his towns of the Low Countries would be bound for the payment thereof, or else that he should make with sufficient surety of bankers for the true payment of the same, with the considerations in our last letters declared unto you amply. And we would our said Ambassador to declare unto the Emperor likewise the points of the straighter amity, which we would be contented to enter with him; such as in our said letters to you be specially declared. Upon the declaration whereof we look shortly to have advertisement and answer of his resolute mind, and that also he shall send more particular instructions to the Queen Regent, both upon the straighter amity, and the alliance of our marriage, and (as we think, and reason would) a more ample and express commission of power. Of which advertisement, and of our pleasure thereupon, we shall give unto you diligent and speedy knowledge, incontinent upon the receipt thereof, for your better instruction. These points to be kept secret unto you, and no further uttered there than hereafter shall be touched.

In the mean time we will that at your next opportunity after the receipt of these presents, ye shall obtain your access unto the Queen Regent, and after our hearty commendations, to declare unto her that, seeing the cold answer ye had received at the beginning, both of the Deputies appointed to confer with you and of her also upon your exposition of the three points, which we desire to be agreed for the marriage of our daughter the Lady Mary with the Infant of Portugal, by the which answer they proceeded as they had known nothing of the offer made of Milan, and as though they had had no advertisement of the other two points agreed here by Messires Chapuys and Don Diego;[1] which thing enforced us, (thinking that she had no ample instructions of those matters) to dispatch our servant Philip Hoby to the Emperor, conjointly with our trusty and right well-beloved Councillor, Sir Thomas Wyatt, Knight, our Ambassador, to expound unto him how strange we found the said Regent was no better instructed by him, that she might have given other answer that ye had received. Whereunto he answered that the said Regent was fully instructed of his whole mind, and had sufficient power to confer, treat and conclude with you, as well for the straighter amity, as for the one alliance as the other. . . .

At this point the letter repeats almost word for word what has just been said in the two paragraphs immediately preceding the above. Henry then continues:

. . . Wherefore ye shall require the said Regent, that having full instruction, as the Emperor hath answered she hath already, leaving and setting aside that coldness heretofore used with you; which although we think it strange and far from the expectation we have conceived of her sincerity towards us, yet nevertheless passing over the expostulation thereof, she will plainly and frankly, as she tendereth the good increase of our alliance and amity, utter and expound unto you without any longer delay or timing, proceed to the resolution and conclusion of the said alliance with the Duchess, and the straighter amity; appointing unto you certain brief and short time, within the which ye may have a resolute knowledge of their minds, and proceed to a conclusion. And in case she be not disposed to use speed therein, nor inclined to any conclusion within some short time, ye shall not only declare unto her, that seeing the Emperor hath affirmed that she is fully instructed and hath sufficient power to treat, as well upon the straighter amity as upon both alliances and either of them, we shall have good

[1] The resident and special ambassadors of the Emperor to England.

cause to think that she is not so well inclined and affectionate to show correspondence to our sincere amity, as she hath evermore in words affirmed unto you, and born in her countenance she was, but rather all the world that shall know the same shall reckon her a hinderer and letter of this noble amity and alliance, so much honourable and commodious to the common wealth of all our and their realms and dominions, and generally of the whole Christendom; which should be a great spot to her good estimation: but also ye shall require, that of her honour, and for the amity between us, she will well advise herself, and plainly declare the bottom of her mind herein unto you.

For ye may say unto her we be daily instanted by our nobles and Council to use short expedition in the determination of our marriage, for to get more increase of issue to the assurance of our succession, and that upon their often admonitions of age coming fast on, and that the time slippeth and flyeth marvellously away, we be minded utterly to be within short space at a full resolution, one way or other, and no longer to lose time, as we have done this whole year, and above; which is of all losses the most irrecuperable, for it can never be redeemed with no manner price nor prayer; and that we being a Prince of courage, and of such prudence as can discern and esteem the doings as they be, unless we shall see other towardness of better speed on that part, ye mistrust, that upon the diffidence of sincerity and plainness of their proceedings, we should withdraw, by their slackness, the great zeal we have to join with them, and through their negligence seek that alliance with other that we could not, with honest and reasonable conditions, obtain sincerely of them, although we have merited to have the same, and better: which ye may say, as of yourselves, should be much to your discomforts, bearing so good will and affection towards them, and the accomplishment of those matters whereof ye have had the charge and commission to treat, and little to their honour and commodity.

The which thing ye shall desire the said Regent to weigh and consider, and so thereupon sincerely to proceed with such frankness, as the correspondence of your faithful amity towards them, and the good disposition and desire she affirmeth the Emperor and she hath to the continuance and increase of the perfect and ancient amity which hath long endured between us and our progenitors, and them and theirs, doth of most reason require. And in case she will signify unto you (as we think she will not), that she is not disposed to use other frankness, then ye shall declare the regret ye have to perceive such strange proceeding of her part, supposing rather the same to proceed of evil councillors, being more inclined to their private and particular affections than to the good and wealth of both Princes and their dominions, than of her own self or the Emperor. Requiring you to give you then leave to return hither to us, rather than to keep you there any longer to lose more time. But in case (as it is the more like) she shall affirm herself, as she hath heretofore said, ready and most affectionate to conclude those alliances with us, and so appoint other meetings with such as she shall appoint to the same, to treat for her with you, ye shall desire that they will use both frankness and speed, and protest before a notary, that forasmuch as her power beareth no authority of substitution, and that she refuseth to deliver unto you the writing desired, that, upon her honour, she shall observe all that they treat and conclude with you; ye therefore, although ye have our commission, do intend to have like liberty as they would have, and that we shall be none otherwise obliged to observe your conclusions than they will be to observe theirs, as reason requireth that the liberty be like to either party. And so with that protestation, as commoning at large with them, ye shall proceed to entreat upon the said alliance and straighter amity, according to the instructions heretofore given unto you, and as upon further knowledge of our pleasure in that behalf, keeping this our expectation to have knowledge thence secret unto you, and as though we thought none otherwise, but that she hath already full instruction of the Emperor's mind upon the same matters.

And in the end, if ye shall perceive that they will condescend to no conclusion, and that ye should return without any resolution of those alliances and amities; then, under colour of taking of your leave of the chief and principal gentlemen, as Monsr. de Bures, Monsr. de Berghes, and such as by familiarity ye know to be of estimation in the Court, ye shall lament to them, as of yourselves, that ye have found there, for their behalf, such coldness and slackness, that ye, for their indisposition to join with us, could nothing conclude, but have lost much time in vain, declaring the good will and inclination we have towards them and those parties, and that we have omitted no good office, for our part, for the continuance of the same, but were desirous before any other to join with them; requiring them to be bear you witness, that nothing may be arrected to our fault, neither concerning the straighter amity and alliance, nor concerning our good affection towards them and their dominions; wherefore they ought not to think strange if we shall otherwise provide for ourself, and join with other, when we find no conformity nor towardness with them.

Likewise ye taking also your leave of the Duchess shall declare unto her the good mind and affection we bear unto her, and how earnestly we have been minded to honour her by our marriage, if on their behalf we had found reasonable conditions and conformity; but finding the contrary, she shall not marvel if we join with other: lamenting your evil chance to have been commissioners and ambassadors in a matter of such honour, and that after long delays you could get none effect nor success therein; with such good words as ye can otherwise devise, whereby they may not only print in their heart our loving and gentle proceedings, and think that we have omitted no part of a Prince that favoureth them, but also conceive a grudge, or at the least less favour, to them that have been letters of such honourable and commodious alliances.

Given under our signet, at our palace of Westminster, the 23rd of December, the 30th year of our Reign.

IX. To Sir Thomas Wyatt

By the King

Henry R. [*Jan.* 19, 1539.]

Trusty and right well-beloved, we greet you well. And as well by your letters sent unto us in cipher by Tarbes post, as also more expressly by your other letters, dated the second of this present month, and brought by our courier Nicholas, we perceive on that side daily more and more delays, remissness, and such cold proceeding, after their vehemence showed outward in appearance that as, after so hot a summer, we saw never so cold a winter. Whereby it appeareth, like as ye have right prudently objected unto them, that they seek friends for their need, and that, thinking themselves escaped their hands, they do but little regard their friends; which is not the true rule to knit a steadfast and certain knot of amity. They do far unlike to the good turns we have showed unto them, not at our need but at theirs. But as for that we let pass, and intend not to reproach it unto them; but rather, in the meantime, to content ourself with the honest virtue of our benefits showed for perfect love and amity; seeing that, between so sundry qualities of him and his two councillors (the mixtion whereof in the end is but a cold frost) we can have no certain answer, but be referred to two uncertain contingents; the one is declared unto yourself by the Emperor, to Duke Frederick's advice at his coming into Spain unto the Emperor's court; the other contingent, long to come is, as appeareth by the effect of the Emperor's letters lately sent unto the Lady Regent by way of instruction, (as the chancellor of her court hath declared unto our ambassadors there) that concerning the alliance between us and the Duchess, the said Frederick should, at his return into Flanders from Spain, bring shortly resolution. Whereupon, what they will do we cannot well guess; but the same nevertheless, for to show ourself firm, constant, and steadfast in a good affection, once thoroughly printed in our heart, we will once essay whether they shall change their disposition.

And therefore, forasmuch as one party is in Flanders, and our ambassadors have been there by the space of sixteen weeks, or thereabouts, and the Emperor said of his mere mind that he would send instructions, ample and sufficient, unto the Lady Regent of Flanders, and the purpose opened there although to a small purpose as yet, ye shall require the emperor for the same. And also because we intend not to treat upon one matter in two places, nor so far distantly from us, it may like him therefore, according to his offer and very promise, to send full instructions as he hath oftentimes affirmed and affirmed again to have done, when in deed the said lady denieth to have received any such thing; but is ready (as constrained of necessity) to send upon any point purposed, in post to that court. And yet, when any such returned unto her, the answer is such, that she must as yet tarry for another; and that the said Emperor in a matter of such importance unto us as the matter of our marriage, wherein for the effect of succession, time and age be of marvellous high importance; and whereby the nobles and estates of this realm do much press us (as it were of urgent necessity) that we would no longer defer to be at a point with some one or other, they care not greatly where, so that we may have increase of issue. Whereupon ye shall eftsoons require him, as he will show himself zealoter of our ancient fraternal amity, that he will, without further protract and dilation of time, observe and fulfil his whole promise in sending these instructions; and that, in case he should not intend to join with us, that then, as it appeareth to honesty, honour, and the word of a prince according to our amities, he will plainly and frankly declare unto us his mind with a flat refusal and nay; rather than, so knitting one delay to the tail of another, to keep us longer in balance and suspense, and at last give us occasion to say that, whereas upon alliance offered unto us, we have sought increase of amity, after long and constant continuance, we have found for conclusion so cold proceeding, as to be ever so unkindly delayed, or else to have a flat nay. Which the Emperor's discretion may well think and foresee to be a thing much contrary and unlike to his imperial estate, and to the high degree wherein he is collocate, and to the correspondence of the very amity that we looked to find in him.

And in case in any conference there shall be any motion made unto you, concerning assistance to the recovery of Gueldres, ye shall give no ear thereto; but answer that ye have no instruction of us in that matter, and allege that it were too much to be desired of, or moved unto us, and that ye referred the same to the conferences to be had in Flanders; for we intend not to treat in two places, nor so far from us, as is before said.

As touching Camerin,[1] upon occasion whereof ye much harp

[1] i.e. the Duchy of Camerino, to which the young Duke of Urbino laid claim through his marriage, and which the Pope was trying at this juncture to add to the Papal States.

we have and should take opportunity to do things, ye shall understand that we have and do know our right occasion and take your advertisement therein in good and thankful part; signifying unto you that, (by the advice of our Council in the same and other things) we shall not neglect nor pass over any opportune occasion, finding good towardness in the parties, and forwardness in the matter. Wherefore ye shall declare unto his secretary there that, upon your advertisement, ye perceive such good inclination in us towards that family, and that we know so well the Bishop of Rome's ambition and cruelty, where he may obtain the upper hand upon the princes of Christendom, whose powers he ever practiseth to usurpate, and that, seeing our good disposition, ye can think none otherwise; but be assured that if the Duke, his master, shall require us as appertaineth, and show the justice of his cause, we shall not fail to have regard to the honour of God, the support of princes, and such respect to the amity and affection we bear and have borne to that family, as they shall have cause to be contented. Therefore, adhorting ye him to write unto his master, the Duke, thereupon, and to use all celerity convenient, ye shall advise him, as of your self, that he shall also counsel to the said Duke, that he shall use of all possible diligence in sending a man unto us; trusting assuredly that he is like, for the reasons before mentioned, to have good answer, and find subvention and support at our hand, if he shall duly require and show his right unto us.

As for those barking preachers, their slanderously defaming us in so celebre a place, which rather ought to be called false prophets and sheep-cloaked wolves, we pray you to continue your instant requisition to the Emperor and his Council, with your objections to their unreasonable answers, as ye have done hitherto, much to our contentment and thankful acceptation; alleging unto him that ye much marvel they proceed none otherwise to stay such false and untrue slanders against us being a king; seen that, of late, at Rouen, where a Grey Friar likewise slandered us, he was constrained to recant, and in plain pulpit to withdraw his words, and to declare that he had belied us and our nation; and that therefore he cried God, us, and our nation, mercy; and that done, yet he was reserved in prison to further punishment.[1]

As for your return hither in March next, we have deferred it until April; by all the which month, another shall arrive in your stead; requiring you to take it in so good and patient part, as at your return we may have for the same, amongst your other good merits, occasion to thank you heartily, and look upon the same hereafter. Not failing from time to time (as ye have of good custom used) diligently to advertise us of all your proceedings, occurrents, and doings there, as well concerning our own matters as others; as of Italy, of the Emperor's voyage, and of French practices with him, and of all other things worthy knowledge.

This day is arrived unto us some advertisements from Rome, wherein it was mentioned, that it is commonly spoken at Rome that the ambassador of England, being in Spain, hath made large promises unto the Duke of Urbino's secretary. We cannot think but that, like as they meant by you, so they have, for some purpose, bruited and set forth this rumour abroad for their advantage; and that, although you have put him in some comfort, yet ye have not been so large to offer anything unto them, without our advice and pleasure. We trust your fidelity and discretion better than so. Yet, nevertheless, we have thought thereupon to warn you, that ye shall beware to speak so largely unto them; but with good sobriety and temperature, as we have before written. For, like as doubtless we would be glad to help the truth and right of princes, specially against the enemy of princes, the Bishop of Rome; so should we be loath to incur the name and renome of a setter-forth, cherisher, and maintainer of dissension and war in Christendom, where indeed we love peace, union, and amity; except only that we fear no such suspicions, where we be compelled against the enemies of God and ours, and the adversaries-general of princes.

Given under our signet, at our palace of Westminster, the 19th day of January, the XXXth year of our reign.

[1] Henry had insisted, and Francis had, ostensibly at least, complied.

x. To Sir Thomas Wyatt
By the King

Henry R. [*Westminster, Feb.* 13, 1539.]

Trusty and right well-beloved, we greet you well . . . Upon the receipt hereof ye shall resort unto the Emperor, and like as ye have done already of yourself, so shall ye now in our name not only declare unto him that we have been credibly informed that our rebel and traitor Pole is coming towards him, as sent Legate to the Bishop of Rome, but also that forasmuch as the said Pole is by the laws of our realm found manifestly to be our rebel and cankered traitor against our crown royal and the Majesty of the same, ye shall in our name require him, that in case the said Pole be not as yet arrived within this his realm and dominions, that then he shall not only forbid unto him the entry and access unto the same, but also command his officers and subjects in no wise to admit and suffer him to be or remain there, but to expel him out thereof if he shall be entered therein. And in case the said Pole shall be arrived already to the Emperor's court, then ye shall require the Emperor in that case that he will not only forbear all manner conference and communication with him, and in no wise to give ear unto his words, nor honourably recueil nor entertain him, but rather to despise him and contemn him like a rank traitor; and according to the treaties and alliances between us confirmed at Cambrai, (the copy whereof, as much as concerneth this point, ye shall receive herewith for your better instruction) to show unto him no manner of favour nor support, but command him out like a rebel traitor unto us his ancient ally and friend, and cause him incontinent to depart out of all his dominions, and in no wise to come, abide, or return into the same or any place thereof. And in case the Emperor shall answer unto you that the said Pole is sent thither rather for our good and common quiet in Christendom, than to perform any thing against us, then shall you answer thereto, that the said Pole having once traitorously thus persisted against us, (who not only made his house and whole family of nought, and enhanced them to so high degree, nobility and honour as they have been, as long as they were true and fidele unto us, but also, amongst other, specially favoured and gave honest exhibition out of our own coffers to the said Pole, and maintained him to the study), hath proved himself so lewd and extremely ingrate, that no Prince, knowing his temerity and offences against us his Sovereign Lord and Prince, should esteem him worthy to be spoken with, nor to give him any credence nor audience.

And in case the said Pole shall have had audience of the Emperor before the receipt thereof, then ye shall say that, under his correction, it had been more consonant to ancient amity and alliance between him and us, to have set the said Pole aside, and not to have given him audience, and to have advertised us by his letters of the same, before he had perceived upon what points his commission was, and so to have proceeded upon our answer thereunto, thereafter. Who would believe that out of so cankered and malicious a stomach, and proud mind and heart as he is of, there could come out or proceed any goodness or sincerity, specially being sent from such a place as he is. His words, as such deceitful traitors be commonly hypocrites may be, might fortune, fair and pleasant; but howsoever the head thereof be coloured, the tail thereof is always black and full of poison; and so shall find them any man that will give them ear.

And if the Emperor shall answer unto you that Pole cometh unto him as a public and not as a private person, and that *de jure gentium*,[1] ambassadors have and ought to have special privilege to be admitted and in no wise thus rejected as we required, then shall you persist in the words of the Treaty, which be general; and to his reason *de jure gentium* and other that he could make to you, ye shall reply and answer, yea and confute the same, by such reasons and allegations as upon the said Pole's arrival into France and the Low Countries were made to the French King and the Lady Regent, the summary whereof for your better information ye shall also receive herewith. In your conferences hereupon with the Emperor, ye shall ever inculcate the ingratitude of the Poles, the benignity we ever used towards them, who by the counsel of the Cardinal, his brother Montague and the Marquis of Exeter, with their adherents, had conspired not only divers seditions within this our realm but also imagined the way

[1] By the law of nations.

to destroy us and our dearest son the Prince, with the Lady Mary and the Lady Elizabeth our daughters, for to take upon them the whole rule, whereunto the said Marquis had fixed his mind and sought his opportune occasion these ten years, and practised to have conduced that mischief to his intent, (had not God favoured us, and we been ware in all things of such practices, and taken heed thereunto.)

All these things have been disclosed by Sir Geoffrey Pole, Montague's own brother, and openly proved before their faces, and by the law convicted thereof; yea, and the mischief, after their execution, declared by sundry their letters found, and by the same known that Sir Nicholas Carew was one of the chief and principal of that faction. Ye shall obsecrate the Emperor that he will remember the ancient amity between us, and have in memory his solemn oath and sacrament to observe the Treaties of Cambrai, and how oaths and promises of Princes ought to be observed; and require him to consider the effect thereof, and to ponder how odious and detestable traitors ought to be unto Princes; how they ought not to be suffered in any good company, but banished out of the same, declaring unto him what fruit doth commonly succeed of conferences, and communication of traitors; whereupon of late there is a pretty book printed in our realm, which ye shall receive herewith.

We be about to provide some meet person to reside there in your stead, trusting so to speed him that he may be there with you by March, or half April, at the which time we shall willingly will you to take your leave thence, and so to return hither to do unto us such other service as ye shall be meet for, that shall be less to your charge and with our good favour.

By the treaties it seemeth we should have written herewith to the Emperor concerning the said Pole, the which nevertheless for cause (albeit the letters were already conceived) we have stayed for this time. We send you herewith the copy thereof, requiring you to peruse it and to send your advice thereupon; and afterward, if we shall see cause, we will send them unto you. In the mean season, if the Emperor shall object unto you that we should have written our letters unto him, ye shall answer it is not requisite, and that we trust so much upon the amity and alliance between us, that having received heretofore letters of credence unto you, he shall be contented for this time to allow the same as part of your credence, and give no less faith unto your declaration and requisition than if he had received our letters thereupon. Ye may add thereunto, if ye see cause, that the fault we wrote not, to your judgement, is to be imputed to the negligence of the Secretary, who gave us no warning thereof. . . .

xi. To Charles V

[*Feb.* 13, 1539.]

Right high, right excellent and mighty Prince, our very dear and well-beloved brother, cousin, and perpetual ally, in the most effectual and hearty manner we recommend us unto you. Having of late been credibly informed that Cardinal Pole hath set out to journey towards you, the cause of which, is, as we understand, for no good, but to sow discord and dissension where is amity and concord: moreover his disposition, as we have proved, is so cankered that from it can no good thing proceed; but weeping crocodile tears he will, if it be possible, pour forth the venom of his serpent nature.

Not only, therefore, do we desire to advertise you by these presents that he is to us very ingrate, rebel and traitor; and that since he has received the cardinal's hat, and before that, he, with divers other traitors, being of his kindred, hath conspired the destruction of our person, of Prince Edward our son, and of the Lady Mary and the Lady Elizabeth our daughters; of the which, by the laws of our kingdom, he has been indicted and found guilty: but also, by these our letters, to pray and require you, as he is undoubtedly our rank rebel and traitor, that you will neither do nor show him any favour, support nor comfort, as a person malicious to all Princes, according as the ancient friendship and alliances between us, and the treaties of peace require, that you will refuse him access to you, and send him forth and expel him from your dominions, and otherwise treat him as our traitor, according to the treaties and as you would that we in like case should do for you.

We have charged our trusty and well-beloved councillor Sir

Thomas Wyatt, our ambassador resident with you, to signify and declare to you the above, praying and requiring you thus to do, and if you should so require of him, to declare to you his unthankfulness, and the conspiracy that he with his accomplices hath practised against our said person and offspring. . . .

He finishes with a polite reiteration of his demands, and the usual courtesies.

Pole was a papal envoy, and as such, Charles replied, he was bound to receive him. More menacing still, on February 21, all English ships in Flemish ports were put under arrest, and Mendoza the Spanish ambassador was recalled. Everywhere the talk was of a great fleet that was gathering at Antwerp. Wriothesley wrote from Brussels to Cromwell, 'It is in every man's mouth that we shall have war'. Castillon, the French ambassador, was recalled. Wriothesley could get no satisfaction when he protested against the arrest of English ships. The Emperor, he was told, needed sailors for his fleet: once it had sailed the ships would be free. Guns and ammunitions accumulated at Antwerp. 'An innumerable sum of money' was levied from the clergy for a holy war against England. Wriothesley reported all the rumours: 'I have also heard that the French King, the Bishop of Rome, and the King of Scots should be as it were in league to invade us this summer: and how the Emperor will send to their aid certain Spaniards which shall arrive in Scotland.' But it is significant that he adds, 'which purpose I take for no gospel', and that in March, while making all reasonable preparations for defence, Henry was still keeping up the proper diplomatic relations with Charles, and protesting through his ambassador at the detention of the English merchant ships in Flanders.

XII. To Sir Thomas Wyatt

By the King

HENRY R. [*Westminster, March* 10, 1539.]

Trusty and right well-beloved, we greet you well; and declare unto you that we do take and accept agreeably the great diligence, dexterity and activity, which ye have used to bring the affairs of our traitor Pole to that he might depart miscontented from thence; and to have such plain conference with the Emperor, Covos and Granvelle his Counsellors, as ye have had, and in attaining the true knowledge of things, as appeareth ye have done by the tenor of your letters of the 23 of this last month; for the same we thank you full heartily and will remember your good service accordingly, willing you, as soon as ye can, upon the receipt hereof, to get your access and audience of the Emperor. At the first entry whereof, with our right affectuous commendations, thanking him for the good purpose he is in to keep and observe the treaties and alliances between us entirely, and in every point as a Prince of honour regarding his oath and promise, and to show all friendship and amity; ye shall show unto him that we do very thankfully accept of him the refuse he hath made unto the traitor Pole, to assent and condescend unto the inique censures and requisitions of the Bishop of Rome lately pronounced unjustly against us and our subjects; and that the miscontentment of our said rebel Pole at his departure is much to our contentment as whereby we may have a demonstration that the Emperor hath fulfilled indeed the same that his friendly words unto you did report; which (as ye shall declare plainly unto him) be far discrepant from the doing of his officers and subjects in the Low Countries, where of late we have found a marvellous strangeness, our ambassadors and merchants also. For upon Ash Wednesday, by a general proclamation made at Antwerp and elsewhere in the Emperor's name, all our ships with the goods therein (as they were ready to return from the mart) have been arrested, and for colour, as we understand, ships of other nations have been arrested withall. Sithens for any suit that our ambassadors could do, as yet our ships with all the merchandises be detained there, under the pretence that the Emperor lacketh mariners for his navy to go against the Turk, as the saying is. There was joined thereto such sudden strangeness showed unto our ambassadors, as whereas the day afore they were much made of; the next day or second, beyond man's expectation, skant in the Regent's Court any man would speak or make any countenance towards them, nor direct them to show where they should attend upon the Regent, at whose hands they found marvellous strange countenance and skantiness of words, and, to comprehend in few words, they were never so well entertained as they have at the beginning been indeed. But sithens Lent began, as for a penance, their entertainment hath been marvellous strange; yea, and stranger than we will rehearse: strangeness, in having audience with long delays both at the Queen's hands and other her chief Counsellors: strangeness, in answers and fashion. Also, our ambassadors have been sithens that constrained to pay the excise there, which no ambassador of England paid in any man's remembrance. They be the first that ever paid it. The taske thereof is 18d. on every barrel of beer, above the price of the brewer. They have showed it and complained to the Queen, but nevertheless they must pay it, or lack drink.

Besides this, through all the said Low Countries incontinently rose a bruit among all manner of men, which was published through the High Almayne and other parts, that the Emperor and the French King, and other Princes of Christendom, at their exhortation, and by the Bishop of Rome's provocation and procurement, should forthwith have war against us: and that the Emperor's navy was only addressed for that purpose, to invade us suddenly and afore any full preparation.

The conjectures written to us from Almayne, Spain, and other parts were, that (known it was everywhere) the Emperor hath broken his intended journey against the infidels, and that therefore that navy must be for another purpose. Not against the Lutherans, for the ships will not serve there: nor also for the custody of Guelders, being the contention before the Princes Electors. Then concluded they, that it was against Denmark, or against us; but for as much as his treaties with Denmark doth last yet for a year and a half, the conclusion remained, that it was meant against us, as a common confederacy to disquiet us and our subjects.

It seemeth to us by all report, there was never a bruit and rumour so suddenly spread, so constantly affirmed, and so spitefully uttered in all the peoples' mouths, in the most vehemency whereof Monsieur Chapuys, the Emperor's ambassador, without any ostentation of letters, but only, (as he said) the Queen's commandment, required in the mean time, (when the most fire and fervour of the same bruit was), leave and licence to depart; and instanced us, and our Council very much. We showed unto him the said bruits and rumours, and that if he should depart at that time the suspicion and bruit should increase; and that he was the Emperor's ambassador and not the Queen's, by such letters of commission as he brought unto us at his coming hither; and that the custom was never between Princes to revoke their ambassadors resident without letters, and unless they should send some other in his stead to supply his room after him; and that we thought not meet for the Emperor's service, nor for the expedition of our common affairs, that he should depart hence and no man succeed in his stead. And yet, nevertheless, that we knowing it should be the Emperor's pleasure signified unto us that he should depart, not only we would not detain him, but gave him kindly leave, and liberally rewarded him as appertained.

These rumours and bruits of war against us, the arrestment of our ships, the strangeness showed to our ministers there, that navy and army in a readiness for the Emperor, the requisition of the said Chapuys to depart, ran abroad this our realm and almost everywhere. Whereupon our merchants complained sore unto us, and in such wise, that for their indemnity we have been constrained to arrest the ships of the Emperor's countries, as well of Flanders as of Spain. For assuredly in Spain our subjects be marvellously in sundry parts of the sea coasts evil entreated, arrested, and put to great trouble, molestation, and losses, through the means of certain slanderous preachers subornate thereto by the Bishop of Rome and his adherents, and suffered by the said Emperor, (but not as we think in any wise by his commandment or consent.) Wherefore, after declaration of those things, ye shall require him to show you his mind thereupon plainly and roundly, and that like as we have found the same proceedings in his Low Countries and in his coasts of Spain, very strange unto us, so he ought not to marvel that we have made the same arrest upon his ships,[1] but consider how much more he would have done if he had been in our case; assuring him, that upon the delivery of our ships, all his shall, without any loss or damage, be likewise

[1] By proclamation, on March 1, 1539.

delivered. We do not write unto you the rumours half so spiteful, and the entertainment half so strange as it hath been. I think never such a thing was heard of, and specially after treaty of marriage, such a banquet, without any manner cause given unto them.

We have well noted, seen, and perused the answer given unto you in writing, concerning the treaty of straighter amity, and the alliance with the Duchess of Milan, that they will not proceed thereto without the Bishop of Rome's dispensation, &c. Ye shall show unto the Emperor that he may well perceive that we and the Bishop of Rome be at such terms, that there is on neither part such motion to be made. And that therefore, we look no longer to treat thereupon. We had been glad to increase our amity and alliance with him that way, and should be yet, were it not that age cometh on apace upon us, and that we be daily instanced and importunately called on by all our nobles not to defer our marriage so long, and that the loss of time in that behalf is irreparable; requiring us, that for more assurance of our succession we shall protract the time no longer. Wherefore ye shall require him, sithens we cannot go thorough with him, that he shall not think strange if we shall otherwise provide for us, and seek elsewhere, as we intend to do, that alliance that we could not have with him: and that he may be assured that the amity and alliance for our part shall be no less observed and kept, than the tenor of our treaties doth purport, and that he shall ever find in us correspondence of the old and ancient amity.

We purpose, according to our Letters sent heretofore unto you, to send shortly thither our trusty and well-beloved servant Richard Tate, to succeed there in your place and stead; and according to your desire, give unto you our favourable leave to return hither. In the mean time we pray you to be as ye have always, vigilant and diligent in seeking knowledge of the dispositions and minds there, as far as ye can; and also of all other occurrents to advertise us with celerity, wherein we shall take your doings in thankful part. . . .

It is difficult to be sure how far Henry was bluffing when he wrote, on March 10, of Pole's mission as if it had failed, although it is a fact that his reception had been both cold and discouraging. To all appearances, however, Henry was pretty sure of his ground. England was actively in a state of defence: the fortresses on the Border and along the south coast were strengthened: ships were ready in the Thames: and the English ambassadors had not been recalled from Spain or Flanders. In spite of all the rumours and threats Henry was keeping his powder dry at home and diplomatically keeping his temper abroad. Nominally he was threatened with just that combination of foreign forces he had always striven to prevent: apparently the danger of invasion was imminent: yet no one seemed unduly scared, and though the great fleet at Antwerp was due to sail any day, still the English ambassadors were not recalled. Why?

To understand Henry's diplomacy it is necessary to go back to Letter x, and to read again what he has to say about 'the ingratitude of the Poles'. It is here that we shall find the grounds of his confidence in the spring of 1539, in the point of cohesion between his domestic and foreign policies.

The story of the Pole family, and its terrible downfall, is so well known that only a brief recapitulation should be necessary. Through their mother, Margaret Pole, Countess of Salisbury, Reginald Pole and his brother Henry, Lord Montague, were of royal Plantagenet descent, their grandfather being George, Duke of Clarence, brother of King Edward IV. With his cousin, Henry Courtenay, Marquis of Exeter, a grandson of Edward IV, Montague stood near the succession, if Henry's issue should fail. Moreover, he was the son-in-law of George Neville, Lord Abergavenny, himself the son-in-law of the Duke of Buckingham who had been executed in 1521, nominally on suspicion of treason, actually for his nearness to the throne. Montagues, Courtenays and Nevilles, in fact, came as near to constituting a party with rival claims to the throne as was possible in the England of Henry VIII. In Cornwall and Devon the power and prestige of the Courtenay family was enormous, and whatever doubt there may be as to the actual disaffection of these noblemen, there is no doubt whatever that France and Spain and their ambassadors regarded this family group and its possible pretenders as the enemy within the gates upon whom would largely depend the successful issue of any foreign invasion of England. That Henry was equally alive to this danger hardly needs stating.

To Henry, Reginald Pole was a traitor, and the love of their early years had converted to the bitterest hatred. Pole was working abroad against the King: the European situation looked doubtful: the conduct of the Marquis of Exeter had been for some time under suspicion: Pole's mother and brother had been in correspondence with him during his exile. The combination of circumstances gave Henry his excuse and his opportunity. Sir Geoffrey Pole, a younger brother, was arrested at the end of August, 1538, and after some two months in the Tower was reduced to a state in which he was ready to say or swear anything that was required of him. He implicated his brother Lord Montague, the Marquis of Exeter, Sir Edward Neville and various others by his evidence, and early in November these three were committed to the Tower.

The case against them was grounded largely on the fact that they had corresponded with Cardinal Pole, and on the allegation that they were traitors who had ' machinated ' the King's death. Technically, they were condemned for treason: actually, because the King believed that the very existence of the now-hated Pole family was a menace to the throne. They were executed on December 9, 1538. Geoffrey Pole, as king's evidence, was pardoned, but the Countess of Salisbury was imprisoned in the Tower, until an abortive rising under one of the Nevilles in Yorkshire sealed her fate, and led to her execution in May, 1541. To Spain Wyatt passed on the ' explanation ' given in Letter x. France was informed that the Marquis of Exeter had plotted to destroy the prince, and to usurp the kingdom by marrying his own son to the Princess Mary.

Henry's vengeance had been swift and terrible, but it is difficult to believe that its synchronization with the threat of danger from abroad was a matter of chance. While the Cardinal was busy revising and printing his attack on the King—his *Liber de Unitate*—while the Pope was preparing to launch his Bull of Deposition, and was urging the Emperor to invade England, Henry quickly and ruthlessly destroyed at one blow the family of his eloquent enemy and the sole remaining focus of possible domestic treason. Charles V was an astute judge of a situation, and knew something of England and Englishmen. The information so politely conveyed in the letter of February 13 was probably understood as Henry meant it to be. In the event of an invasion England would present a united and determined front to the enemy: there would be no 'malice domestic', no faction, to welcome the invader. Charles, however conscientiously he might listen to Pole, found his coming most inopportune: he was anxious to undertake a campaign against the Turk; and affairs were not going too well in Germany, where the Lutheran princes made continual trouble. Henry went on showing the diplomatic amiability of the strong man who knows his position is sound: and by the middle of April, 1539, the mighty fleet that had gathered at Antwerp was dispersed: and the invasion alarm was over. The letter recalling Wyatt and dispatching his successor was dated Greenwich, April 12, 1539. On the 28th, Edmund Harvel, acting in Venice as Henry's agent in the matter of the Duke of Urbino and the Pope's usurpation of Camerino, wrote to Cromwell, 'the babblings against England are everywhere ceased'.

As a diplomatic episode this particular example of Henry's 'judicious meddling' is typical of a great deal of his foreign policy.[1] To Henry and his advisers the whole affair must have seemed considerably more important and less abortive than it looks to us now. If we feel that nothing was achieved by it, to Henry everything was achieved, in that for eighteen months of Anglo-European tension the *status quo* was successfully maintained. It proved to Henry that Charles and Francis at peace were actually no more dangerous—though doubtless less profitable—than Charles and Francis at war. It was a practical demonstration of two things of which England could not, beforehand, be theoretically sure—namely, of the impotence of the Papacy and of England's real security.

Of equal importance in any study of the development of

[1] For a similarly voluminous and apparently useless group of letters see the French correspondence of 1535-6 to be followed in Addit. MS. 25114. Amongst these letters Calig. E. II, f. 208 gives a good but dull example of Henry's handling of a draft.

Henry's character is this story of the fate of the Pole family. As he grew older his purpose grew more implacable. With the birth of his son, the fate of the Poles was sealed. The successor lived: his succession must be ensured. If Henry had been ruthless about Katharine of Aragon and his daughter Mary ten years before, he was ten times more ruthless now. It is not without significance that just after the executions of Montague and Courtenay, the French ambassador Castillon writes in January, 1539, begging to be recalled, because he 'has to do with the most dangerous and cruel man in the world'.[1] The cruelty and ruthlessness of this later period of Henry's reign reveal a hardening of character, a degeneration of the finer qualities of his mind, and the development of that giant tyranny which has led H.A.L. Fisher to speak of 'these grim unlovely years'. If the first unmistakable sign of it was the execution of Sir Thomas More and Bishop Fisher in 1534, its unequivocal and consummate expression was found in the calculated and deliberate destruction of the Poles. Principles and individuals alike were to go down before the one dominating concept of strong rule, and absolute sovereignty—the Tudor *imperium*.

[1] *L.P.* XIV, 144.

CHAPTER III

THE RELIGIOUS SETTLEMENT

'The only Supreme Head in earth of the Church of England, called Anglicana Ecclesia.'—ACT OF SUPREMACY: 1534.

IN the chapters on the divorce and the Pilgrimage of Grace we have seen something of the way in which the breach with Rome was accomplished, and have also seen Henry's chief measure of religious reform. His attack on ecclesiastical wealth and corruption reached its most destructive climax in the dissolution of the monasteries. The abolition of papal authority was completed by the Act of Supremacy, by which, and by the submission of the Clergy, supreme control in all matters ecclesiastical passed to the State. By 1536 Henry had concentrated in himself not only the complete control of state policy, but also the spiritual and temporal power of the church in England. He was, as he boasted, Pope and Emperor, within his own dominions.

It is not necessary to labour the point that the 'reformation' carried out by Henry was political and not theological, both in origin and scope. His measures of reform attacked both the privileges and the property of the Church, but not its doctrine. To the end of his days Henry remained the 'Defender of the Faith'. Time and again he asserted his unwavering adherence to the Catholic faith, as witness, for example, the two brief extracts that follow.

The first is taken from his instructions to Gardiner, Bishop of Winchester, who in 1535 was sent as ambassador to Francis I, to negotiate an alliance between England and France.

> . . . whatsoever false reports and untrue surmises should be by any man made unto him to slander the truth, the King's Highness nevertheless is in all his doings as becometh a Christian prince to be, confessing Christ and his true doctrine, abhorring, detesting, punishing and pursuing all heresy, without any other innovation, the mo such as the necessity of the truth hath required, declaring unto him how all such cere-

> monies and orders in the Church and religion of Christ as may by any temperance be suffered, be in the realm of England untouched and immoved. . . .[1]

The second, which emphasizes Henry's abhorrence of heresy, is taken from the manifesto which, in 1538, he addressed to the Emperor and all Christian princes.

> As we have abrogated all old Popish traditions in this our realm, which either did help his tyranny or increase his pride, so, if the Grace of God forsake us not, we will well foresee that no new naughty traditions be made with our consent to bind us or our realm.[2]

Equally to the point is the evidence of his daughter Mary—not only a devout Catholic, like her father, but also a fundamentally religious woman. During the reign of Edward VI, when repeated efforts were made to bring her to conform to the newly-established order of service, she protested that rather than agree ' to use any other service than was used at the death of the late King her father she would lay her head on a block and suffer death '. She used and would use ' the accustomed Mass, which the King, your father and mine, with all his predecessors evermore used; wherein also I have been brought up from my youth '.

Henry VIII, in fact, while responsible for what we loosely describe as ' The Reformation ' in England, neither accepted nor tolerated the thought and doctrine of the Reformers. Their opinions were heresy. They might welcome many of his measures as triumphs for their party, especially when in September, 1538, it was ordained that an English Bible ' of the largest volume ' should be set up in every church, and that the Pater Noster, the Creed and the Ten Commandments were to be publicly recited in English. But beyond the rejection of papal authority, the demand for reform of the clergy, a dislike of superstition, and a desire to have an English Bible, King and

[1] Addit. MS. 25114, f. 96.
[2] *An Epistle . . . written to the Emperor's Majesty.* Berthelot. 1538.

reformers had nothing in common. And the country, as a whole, was as conservative as its King.

The Act of Supremacy (see p. 125) was followed up by the administration to all the King's subjects of the Oath to the Succession, the preamble to which meant that clergy and laity alike had to accept Henry's divorce under pain of misprision of treason. For their refusal to swear to this Sir Thomas More and Bishop Fisher were attainted in 1534, and on their further refusal to acknowledge Henry's supremacy they were condemned under the Act of Treasons. This Act, as from February, 1535, rendered any one who denied the royal supremacy liable to the death penalty, and both suffered on the scaffold in 1535.

It was an Act of deliberate terrorism, of the most doubtful legality, and only the deliberate assertion of Henry's will made it possible. In a circular letter, issued to the Justices of the Peace in June, 1535, they were commanded to declare at their sessions

> the treasons traitorously committed against us and our laws by the late bishop of Rochester and Sir Thomas More, knight, who thereby and by divers secret practices of their malicious minds against us, intended to seminate, engender, and breed amongst our people and subjects a most mischievous and seditious opinion, not only to their own confusion, but also of divers others, who lately have condignly suffered execution according to their demerits. And in such wise delating the same with persuasions to the same our people, as they may be the better riped, established, and satisfied in the truth; and consequently that all our faithful and true subjects may thereby detest and abhor in their hearts and deeds the most recreant and traitorous abuses of the said malicious malefactors as they be most worthy; and finding any default, negligence, or dissimulation in any manner of person or persons, not doing his duty in this part, ye immediately do advertise our council of the default, manner and fashion of the same. (*Cleo. E. VI, f. 218.*)

In 1536 Henry endeavoured to control diversity of religious opinion by issuing Ten Articles defining the faith of the Church of England. The King's own statement is that he was 'constrained to put his own pen to the book, and conceive certain articles which were agreed upon by Convocation'.[1] The first five deal with points of faith, including the sacraments of baptism, penance and the altar. The remaining five deal with rites and ceremonies; and it is here that the influence of Cranmer and the reformers makes itself most felt. The three extracts which follow show how closely Henry adhered to Catholic doctrine, while at the same time encouraging needed practical reforms and checking superstition.

1. The Ten Articles

. . . we being of late, to our great regret, credibly advertised of such diversity in opinions as have grown and sprungen in this our realm, as well concerning certain articles necessary to our salvation, as also touching certain honest and commendable ceremonies, rites and usages in our said Church, for an honest policy and decent order heretofore of long time used and accustomed; minding to have that unity and agreement established through our said Church concerning the premises; and being very desirous to eschew not only the dangers of souls, but also the outward inquietness which by occasion of the said diversity in opinions (if remedy had not been provided) might perchance have ensued: have not only in our own person at many times taken great pain, study, labour and travail, but also have caused our bishops and other the most discreet and best learned men of our clergy of this our whole realm to be assembled in our Convocation, for the full debatement and quiet determination of the same; where after long and mature deliberation and disputations had, of and upon the premises, finally they have concluded and agreed upon the said matters. . . .

(f. 68) *The Sacrament of the Altar*

Fourthly, as touching the sacrament of the altar, we will that all bishops and preachers shall instruct and teach our people committed by us unto their spiritual charge, that they ought and

[1] *L.P.* XI, 1110.

must constantly believe that under the form and figure of bread and wine, which we there presently do see and perceive by outward senses, is verily, substantially, and really contained and comprehended the very self-same body and blood of our Saviour Jesus Christ, which was born of the Virgin Mary, and suffered upon the cross for our redemption, and that under the same form and figure of bread and wine, the very self-same body and blood of Christ is corporally, really, and in the very substance exhibited, distributed and received of all them which receive the said sacrament; and that therefore the said sacrament is to be used with all due reverence and honour. And that every man ought first to prove and examine himself, and religiously to try and search his own conscience, before he shall receive the same; according to the saying of St. Paul, *Quisquis ederit panem hunc aut biberit de poculo Domini indigne, reus erit corporis et sanguinis Domini; probet autem seipsum homo, et sic de pane illo edat et de poculo bibat; nam qui edit aut bibit indigne, judicium sibi ipsi manducat et bibit, non diiudicans corpus Domini.*

(f. 69v) *Of Images*

As touching images, truth it is that the same have been used in the Old Testament, and also for the great abuses of them sometime destroyed and put down; and in the New Testament they have been also allowed, as good authors do declare. Wherefore we will that all bishops and preachers shall instruct and teach our people, committed by us to their spiritual charge, how they ought and may use them. And first, that there may be attributed unto them, that they be representers of virtue and good example, and that they also be by occasion the kindlers and stirrers of men's minds, and make men oft to remember and lament their sins and offences, especially the images of Christ and our Lady: and that therefore it is meet that they should stand in the churches, and none otherwise to be esteemed: and to the intent the rude people should not from henceforth take such superstition, as in time past it is thought that the same hath used to do; we will that our bishops and preachers diligently shall teach them, and according to this doctrine reform their abuses, for else there might fortune idolatry to ensue, which God forbid. And as for the censing of them, and kneeling and offering unto them, with other like worshippings, although the same hath entered by devotion, and fallen to custom; yet the people ought to be diligently taught, that they in no wise do it, nor think it meet to be done to the same images, but only to be done to God, and in his honour, although it be done before the images, whether it be of Christ, of the cross, or of our Lady, or of any other saint besides.

(f. 71v) *Of Purgatory*

Forasmuch as due order of charity requireth, and the book of Maccabees, and divers ancient doctors plainly shewen, that it is a very good and charitable deed to pray for souls departed, and forasmuch also, as such usage hath continued in the church so many years, even from the beginning, we will that all bishops and preachers shall instruct and teach our people, committed by us unto their spiritual charge, that no man ought to be grieved with the continuance of the same, and that it standeth with the very due order of charity, a Christian man to pray for souls departed, and to commit them in our prayers to God's mercy, and also to cause other to pray for them in masses and exequies, and to give alms to other to pray for them, whereby they may be relieved and holpen of some part of their pain. But forasmuch as the place where they be, the name thereof, and kind of pains there, also be to us uncertain by scripture; therefore this, with all other things, we remit to God Almighty, unto whose mercy it is meet and convenient for us to commend them, trusting that God accepteth our prayers for them, referring the rest wholly to God, to whom is knownen their estate and condition; wherefore it is much necessary that such abuses be clearly put away, which under the name of purgatory hath been advanced, as to make men believe that through the Bishop of Rome his pardons, souls might clearly be delivered out of purgatory, and all the pains of it, or that masses said at *Scala Coeli* or otherwhere in any place, or before any image, might likewise deliver them from all their pain, and send them straight to heaven, and other like abuses.

The following are a few extracts from the article dealing with the sacrament of penance, (f. 66v)

. . . Item, that this sacrament of perfect penance . . . consisteth of three parts, that is to say, contrition, confession, with the amendment of the former life, and a new obedient reconciliation unto the laws and will of God, that is to say, exterior acts in works of charity according as they be commanded of God. . . .

. . . the said contrition consisteth in two special parts, which must always be conjoined together and cannot be dissevered: that is to say, the penitent and contrite man must first knowledge the filthiness and abomination of his own sin . . . he must also conceive not only great sorrow and inward shame that he hath so grievously offended God, but also great fear of God's displeasure towards him, considering he hath no works or merits of his own which he may worthily lay before God as sufficient satisfaction for his sins; which done . . . must needs succeed and be conjoined the second part, viz. a certain faith, trust and confidence of the mercy and goodness of God, whereby the penitent must conceive certain hope and faith that God will forgive him his sins, and repute him justified and of the number of his elect children, not for the worthiness of any merit or work done by the penitent, but for the only merits of the blood and passion of our Saviour Jesus Christ.

Item, that this certain faith and hope is gotten and also confirmed, and made more strong by the applying of Christ's words, and promises of his grace and favour contained in his gospel, and the sacraments instituted by him in the New Testament; and therefore to attain this certain faith, the second part of penance is necessary, that is to say, confession to a priest, if it may be had; for the absolution given by the priest was institute of Christ to apply the promises of God's grace and favour to the penitent.

Wherefore as touching confession, we will, that all bishops and preachers shall instruct and teach our people committed by us to their spiritual charge, that they ought and must certainly believe that the words of absolution pronounced by the priest be spoken by the authority given to him by Christ in the gospel.

In the two paragraphs that follow, the penitent is told that he must accept the church's absolution as if it were 'the very words and voice of God himself', and that auricular confession is to be nowise contemned, but taken as 'very expedient and necessary'.

As touching the third part of penance . . . although Christ and his death be the sufficient oblation, sacrifice, satisfaction and recompense, for the which God the Father forgiveth and remitteth to all sinners not only their sin, but also eternal pain due for the same; yet all men truly penitent, contrite and confessed, must needs also bring forth the fruits of penance, that is to say, prayer, fasting, almsdeeds, and must make restitution or satisfaction in will and deed to their neighbour in such things as they have done them wrong or injury in, and also must do all other good works of mercy and charity, and express their obedient will in the executing and fulfilling of God's commandment outwardly, when time, power and occasion shall be ministered unto them, or else they shall never be saved. . . .

Item, that by penance and such good works of the same, we shall not only obtain everlasting life, but also we shall deserve remission or mitigation of these present pains and afflictions in this world. . . .

The end of the third decade of the reign marks the climax of Henry's assertion of his supreme headship. The rising tide of heretical and sectarian opinion had to be stemmed, and the following proclamations, issued in November, 1538, and April, 1539, show how carefully Henry himself worked over every document he issued for the regulation of religion. It must always be remembered that religious heresy, more especially Anabaptist or Wyclifite heresy, was practically political heresy—a definite source of danger to such a kingship as Henry sought to establish. It threatened his conception of sovereignty in much the same way that Bolshevism or Communism to-day threatens the monarchical system.

11. THE KING'S PROCLAMATION FOR BRINGING IN SEDITIOUS BOOKS

[*Nov.* 16, 1538.]

The King's most royal majesty being informed that sundry contentions and sinister opinions HATH BY WRONG TEACHING AND NAUGHTY PRINTED BOOKS INCREASED AND[1] grown within this his realm of England and other his dominions amongst his loving subjects of the same CONTRARY TO THE[2] true faith, reverence and due observation of such sacraments and sacramentals and laudable rites, ceremonies, as heretofore have been used and accustomed within the Church of England, whereof his Highness immediately under God is justly and lawfully Sovereign, chief and supreme head in earth immediately under Christ. ESTEEMING ALSO THAT[3] by occasion of sundry printed books in English tongue as be brought from outward parts, and by such like books as have been printed within this his realm, set forth with privilege, containing annotations and additions in the margins, prologues, and calendars, imagined and invented by the makers, devisers and printers of the same books, as by sundry strange persons called Anabaptists AND SACRAMENTARIES which be lately comen into this realm where some of them remain privily unknown; and by SOME other his Highness' subjects, using some superstitious speeches and rash words of erroneous matters, and fantastical opinions BOTH in their preachings and familiar COMMUNICATIONS[4] whereby diverse and many of his SIMPLE loving subjects have been induced and encouraged arrogantly and superstitiously to argue and dispute in open places, taverns and alehouses NOT ONLY UPON BAPTISM BUT ALSO UPON[5] the holy and blessed sacrament of the Altar, AND FARTHER also to break, contempne and despise of their own private wills and appetites, other holy sacraments, laudable rites and ceremonies heretofore used and accustomed in this his

[1] Henry deletes this and the following phrases: are lately sprung and
[2] for and concerning the
[3] and that such strife sinister opinions and contentions is risen, sprungen and increased as well
[4] opinions
[5] upon

grace's realm and church of England not only to the great slander of sundry the King's true, simple and unlearned subjects and other, but also to the reproach and vituperation of this said whole realm and church, to his Grace's high discontentation and displeasure, with danger of increase of the said enormitics and abuses, unless his highness should speedily redress the same.

There follow instructions for the examination and licensing of such books by the Privy Council. The remainder of the proclamation is then concerned with the measures to be taken against the Anabaptists, with the Sacrament of the Altar, ceremonies, and the marriage of priests.

Item, forasmuch as diverse and sundry strangers of the sect and false opinion of the Anabaptists AND SACRAMENTARIES been lately comen into this realm, where they lurk secretly in diverse corners and places, minding craftily and subtly to provoke and stir the King's loving subjects to their errors and opinions, whereof part of them by the great travail and diligence of the King's Highness and his counsel be apprehended and taken. The King's most royal Majesty declareth and notifieth to all his loving subjects that his Highness, like a godly and catholic prince, abhorreth and detesteth the same sects and their wicked and abominable errors and opinions, and intendeth to proceed against such of them as be all ready apprehended according to their merits and the laws of his realm, to the intent his subjects shall take example by their punishments and not adhere to their false and detestable opinions, but utterly forsake and relinquish the same; which his Highness straightly commandeth them SO to do upon pain of like punishment; AND ALSO THAT WHERESOEVER ANY SUCH BE KNOWN THEY SHALL BE DETECTED AND WITH AS CONVENIENT DILIGENCE AS MAY BE INFORM HIS MAJESTY OR SOME OF HIS COUNCIL TO THE INTENT THEY MAY BE PUNISHED ACCORDING TO THEIR DESERTS, AND THE MAINTAINERS, ABETTORS OR PRINTERS OF THE SAME OPINIONS WITH ANY OTHER OBJECTIONS OF ALL BOOKS OUT OF WHICH ANY SUCH

LEWD OPINIONS MIGHT BE GATHERED. And over this his Majesty straightly chargeth and commandeth all other strangers of the same Anabaptists AND SACRAMENTARIES, erroneous sects not being apprehended OR KNOWN, that they WITHIN VIII OR X DAYS after this present proclamation, with all celerity shall depart out of this realm and all other his dominions, upon pain of loss of their lives and forfeiture of all their goods without any favour, remission or indulgence to be administered to any of the offenders against the tenor of this present Article.

Item, forasmuch as the most blessed and holy sacrament of the Altar is the very body and blood of our Lord Jesus Christ, our only Saviour and Redeemer, and so hath and ought to be taken and believed by the whole congregation of Christian men, upon the peril of damnation, truly and without any sinister arguments or sophistical opinions grounded without faith upon fantastical reasons. His Highness, therefore, minding earnestly to conserve his people in the true and just faith of the said holy and blessed sacrament, and that they shall not be seduced or beguiled by fantastical reasons and arguments, straightly chargeth and commandeth all and singular his loving subjects and other residents within this his realm and all other his dominions, that they nor any of them from henceforth shall reason, dispute or argue upon the said holy and blessed sacrament, nor of the mysteries thereof, upon pain of loss of their lives and forfeiture of their goods, without any favour or pardon to be showed by his Majesty to any offending in this behalf. Except and reserved to learned men in holy scripture, instructed and taught in the Universities, their liberty and privilege in their schools and places accustomed concerning the same, and otherwise in communication without slander of any man for the only confirmation and declaration of the truth thereof.

Item forasmuch as diverse and sundry persons have presumed and do arrogantly attempt of their sensual appetites and froward rash wills to contempne, break and violate diverse and many laudable ceremonies and rites heretofore used and accustomed in the Church of England, and yet not abrogated by the King's Highness authority, whereby daily riseth much difference, strife and contention amongst diverse and sundry his loving subjects; as for and concerning the ceremonies of holy bread, holy water, procession, kneeling and creeping ON GOOD FRIDAY TO the cross and Easter day, setting up of lights before the Corpus Christi, bearing of Candles upon the day of the purification of our Lady, ceremonies used at the purification of women delivered of child, and offering of their crysomes, keeping of the four offering days, payment of tithes according to the old customs of the realm, and all other such like LAUDABLE ceremonies heretofore used in the church of England which as yet be not abolished nor taken away by the King's Highness: His Majesty, for avoiding such contentions and the occasions of the same amongst his loving subjects, doth straightly charge and command all and singular his subjects and other residents within this his realm, that they and every of them shall observe and keep all and singular the ceremonies before specified, and all other such like ceremonies heretofore used and accustomed in this realm and not abrogated nor abolished by his Highness nor by his laws or authority royal; so as they shall use and observe the same without superstition and esteem then for good and laudable ceremonies, tokens and signs, to put us in remembrance of things of high perfection and none otherwise, and not to repose any trust of salvation in them but take them for good instructions until such time as his Majesty do change or abrogate any of them, as his Highness upon REASONABLE considerations and respects,[1] if it shall hereafter seem to his most excellent wisdom so to be convenient and expedient for the quietness of his people and the advancement of his common wealth, BOTH MAY AND INTENDETH TO DO.

Finally, his Majesty understanding that a few number of this his realm being priests, as well religious as other, have taken wives and married themselves contrary TO THE WHOLESOME MONITIONS OF SAINT PAUL *AD THIMOTHEUM, AD TITUM* AND *AD CORINTHEOS*, BOTH FIRST AND SECOND, AND CONTRARY ALSO TO THE OPINIONS OF MANY OF THE OLD FATHERS AND EXPOSITERS OF SCRIPTURE, NOT ESTEEMING ALSO THE avow and

[1] *may lawfully do* deleted by Henry.

promise of chastity which they made at the receiving of their holy orders, HIS HIGHNESS in no wise minding that the generality of the clergy of this his realm should with the example of such a few number of light persons proceed to marriage without a common consent of His Highness and the realm, doth therefore straightly charge and command as well all and singular of the said priests as have attempted marriages, as all such as will hereafter presumptuously procede in the same, that they ne any of them shall minister any sacrament or other ministry mystical, ne have any office, dignity, cure, privilege, profit or commodity heretofore accustomed and belonging to the clergy of this realm, but shall utterly after such marriages be expelled and deprived from the same, and be had and reputed as lay persons to all purposes and intents, and that such as shall after this proclamation, contrary to this commandment, of their presumptuous mind take wives and be married, shall run in his Grace's indignation and suffer further punishment and imprisonment at his Grace's will and pleasure.[1]

III. The King's Proclamation for Uniformity in Religion

[*April*, 1539.]

The King's most royal majesty hath been informed that great murmurs, malice and malignity is risen and sprung amongst divers and sundry of his subjects by diversities of opinions, some of them minding craftily by their preachings and teachings to restore into this realm the old devotion to the usurped power of the Bishop of Rome, the hypocrite religion, superstitious pilgrimages, idolatry, and other evil and naughty ceremonies and dreams, justly and lawfully abolished and taken away by authority of God's word, and to allure the people again to the same. And some other taking and gathering divers holy Scriptures to contrary senses and understanding, do so wrest and interpret, and so untruly allege the same to subvert and overturn as well the sacraments of holy church, as the power and authority of princes and magistrates, and in effect generally all laws and common justice, and the good and laudable ordinances and ceremonies necessary and convenient to be used and continued in this realm,

[1] For note on text see App. I, Notes.

which were ordained for the increase and edifying of virtue and good Christian living. Some of them also using the Scripture, permitted to them by the king's goodness in the English tongue, MUCH CONTRARY TO HIS HIGHNESS' EXPECTATION: FOR HIS MAJESTY'S INTENT AND HOPE WAS, THAT THEY THAT WOULD READ THE SCRIPTURE, WOULD WITH MEEKNESS AND WILL TO ACCOMPLISH THE EFFECT OF IT READ IT, AND NOT TO MAINTAIN ERRONEOUS OPINIONS AND PREACH, NOR FOR TO USE THE READING OR PREACHING OF IT IN UNDUE TIMES AND PLACES, AND AFTER[1] such fashions and sorts, as it is not convenient to be suffered. And thus each of them dispute so arrogantly against each other of their opinions, as well in churches, ale-houses, taverns, and other places and congregations, that there is begun and sprung among themselves slander and railing each at other, as well by words as writing: one party of them calling the other papist, the other party calling the other heretic; whereby is like to follow DISSENSION and tumult, NOT ONLY TO THEIR OWN CONFUSIONS THAT TEACH AND USE THE SAME, BUT ALSO TO THE DISTURBANCE AND LIKELIHOOD OF DESTRUCTION OF ALL THE REST OF THE KING'S TRUE AND WELL BELOVED SUBJECTS, if his Majesty, like a godly and catholic prince, of his excellent goodness, by his princely power and authority given him by God, should not politicly in the beginning provide for the same. For remedy whereof, his most royal Majesty by his most excellent wisdom knowing and considering his kingly office and charge touching the premises, and daily painfully studying and devising with a most noble and earnest heart to reduce his people committed by God to his care, to unity of opinion, and to increase love and charity among themselves, and constantly to conserve them in the same, intendeth, (God willing,) by advice of his prelates and clergy, and other of his Council, to proceed to a full ORDER and resolution to extinct all such diversities of opinions by GOOD AND JUST laws to be made for the same by authority of his parliament; and yet nevertheless now in the beginning of his

[1] This is another spaced draft, and this whole passage is an insertion.

parliament, of his most excellent and virtuous goodness, mindeth by A proclamation set forth BY HIS HIGHNESS, WITH the advice of his Council, ACCORDING TO AN AUTHORITY OF PARLIAMENT ALREADY TO HIS HIGHNESS' SUCCESSORS AND COUNCIL GRANTED, to extirp and take away some occasions, AS HEREAFTER FOLLOWETH, which have moved and bred division among sundry of his subjects: and therefore by authority of this his present parliament, straightly chargeth and commandeth, that no person or persons shall from henceforth slanderously and maliciously name or call any other papist, nor heretic, unless the person or persons so using themselves can and do lawfully and justly prove the same to be true, upon pain of .[1]

And over this his Majesty straightly chargeth and commandeth, that no person, except such as be curates or graduates in any of the universities of Oxford or Cambridge, or such as be or shall be admitted to preach by the king's licence, or by his vicegerent, or by any bishop of the realm, shall teach or preach the Bible or New Testament, nor expound the mysteries thereof to any other: nor that any person or persons shall openly read the Bible or New Testament, in the English tongue in any churches or chapels, OR ELSEWHERE, with any loud or high voices, AND SPECIALLY during the time of divine service, or of celebrating and saying of masses, but virtuously and devoutly to hear their divine services and masses, and use that time in reading or praying with peace and silence, as good Christian men ought to do, FOR HIS OWN ERUDITION, upon the like pains as is afore rehearsed. NOTWITHSTANDING his highness is pleased and contented, that such as can AND WILL read in the English tongue, shall and may quietly and reverently read the Bible and New Testament by themselves SECRETLY, at all times and places convenient, for their own instruction and edification, to increase thereby godliness and virtuous living; WITH THIS ADMONISHMENT NEVERTHELESS, THAT IF THEY SHALL HAP TO FIND any doubt of any text or sentence in the reading thereof, to beware and take heed of their own presumptuous and arrogant expositions of the letter, but

[1] A space of nearly four inches is left in the MS. at this point.

TO resort humbly to such as be learned in holy Scripture for their instructions in that behalf.

Finally, his highness signifieth to all and singular his loving and obedient subjects, that his majesty was nor is compelled by God's word to set forth the Scripture in English to his lay subjects, but of his own LIBERALITY and goodness was and is pleased that his said loving subjects should have and read the same in convenient places and times, to the only intent to bring them from their old ignorance and blindness to virtuous living and godliness, to God's glory and honour, and not to make and take occasion of dissension or tumult by reason of the same: wherefore his Majesty chargeth and commandeth all his said subjects to use the holy Scripture in English according to his godly purpose and gracious intent, as they would avoid his most high displeasure and indignation, besides the pains above remembered.

The culminating point of the ecclesiastical legislation of the reign was reached in the Act of Six Articles, known to the Reformers as 'the whip with six strings'. The Parliament which met early in 1539 appointed a committee of two archbishops, six bishops, and Cromwell as vice-gerent, to examine the state of religious belief. The Duke of Norfolk, one of Cromwell's chief enemies, precipitated matters by putting before the house six articles, which dealt with the main points of difference between Catholic and Protestant. He proposed that these points should be debated, and a penal statute then framed accordingly, to secure the religious conformity and uniformity that Henry so greatly desired. Cranmer and Latimer led the cause of the Reformers, with Gardiner, Bishop of Winchester, and Tunstall, Bishop of Durham, as two of the chief defenders of the old faith. Henry himself argued against the Reformers in the House of Lords, and according to Cranmer secured the passage of the measure thus determined on, and known as the 'Act for abolishing Diversity of Opinion'.[1] That he was intensely concerned about the precise wording, and was himself responsible for much of it, is evident from the following extract dealing with the six articles of belief.

[1] cf. his own statement, p. 252 and p. 256.

IV. THE KING'S DRAFT OF AN ACT OF THE SIX ARTICLES

Whereas the King's most excellent Majesty IS BY GOD'S LAW supreme head immediately under HIM of THIS WHOLE church AND CONGREGATION of England, intending the conservation of the same church AND CONGREGATION in a true, sincere, and uniform doctrine of Christ's religion, hath in his own person laboured, travailed, AND DISPUTED with the prelates and clergy of this his Grace's realm, IN HIS COURT OF PARLIAMENT, to hear, know, and understand what might be said, alleged, and brought forth out of the Scriptures, ANCIENT AUTHORS, AND HOLY WRITERS, concerning the truth of these articles following; that is to say,

1. Whether in the most blessed sacrament of the altar remaineth, after the consecration, the substance of bread and wine, or no?

2. Secondly, whether it be necessary BY GOD'S LAW, that all men should be communicate in both kinds, or no?

3. Thirdly, Whether priests, THAT IS TO SAY, MEN DEDICATE TO GOD BY the order of priesthood, may by the law of God marry AFTER, or no?[1]

4. Fourthly, Whether vows of chastity OR WIDOWHOOD MADE TO GOD ADVISEDLY by men or women, be by the law of God to be observed or no?

Fifthly, Whether private masses STAND WITH THE LAW OF GOD, AND BE TO BE USED AND CONTINUED IN OUR CHURCH AND CONGREGATION, AS THINGS, WHEREBY GOOD CHRISTIAN PEOPLE MAY AND DO RECEIVE BOTH GODLY CONSOLATIONS AND GOODLY BENEFITS, OR NO?[2]

Sixthly, Whether auricular confession is necessary to be

[1] Henry originally inserts WILLINGLY TAKING ON THEM, and then deletes it, as he also does with BY WHICH THEY DEDICATE THEMSELVES FIRST TO CHRIST.

[2] In making his insertion Henry originally wrote BE TO BE ADMITTED IN THE CHURCH, AS GODLY AND GOODLY CONSOLATIONS AND FRUIT TO CHRISTIAN FOLK AND AGREEABLE TO THE LAW OF GOD OR NO?

retained and continued, used and frequented in the church, or no?

Forasmuch as after a mature discussion it hath pleased almighty God so to assist the King's said Majesty in the searching and finding out the truth, as the same, after all arguments had and made for both parties, hath been by (IN MANNER) an uniform consent of all and singular THE SPIRITUAL AND TEMPORAL ESTATES OF THE REALM, LED (AS SEEMETH) by one spirit of truth, agreed and condescended unto, with special request made to the King's said Majesty, that the said agreement might be by act of parliament testified and established, with such pains and punishments, as good men rejoicing in it, the evil might also for fear abstain and forbear to interrupt and impeach this notable unity and concord, much to the honour of God, and setting forth of his truth, and perpetual renown and fame of the King's said Majesty, the surety and quietness of this realm, with the increase of Christian charity, most requisite and necessary.

Be it therefore enacted by authority of this present parliament, that all and singular the King's subjects, spiritual and temporal, shall LOVINGLY receive, accept, allow, and approve, AND in their words and deeds uphold and maintain these truths and verities in the said articles agreed and concluded BY THE KING'S HIGHNESS, AND HIS COURTS OF PARLIAMENT, as followeth:

First, that in the most blessed sacrament of the altar,[1] by the strength and efficacy of Christ's mighty word, THAT BEING SPOKEN, is present really the natural body and blood of our Saviour Jesus Christ, CONCEIVED OF THE VIRGIN MARY, under form of bread and wine; and that after the consecration there remaineth NONE OTHER SUBSTANCE, BUT THE SUBSTANCE OF HIS FORESAID NATURAL BODY.[2]

Secondly, that communion in both kinds is not necessary AD SALUTEM BY THE LAW OF GOD; AND THAT IT IS TO BE BELIEVED AND NOT DOUBTED OF, BUT

[1] Henry inserts, and then deletes *after the consecration*

[2] Henry substitutes this for the original's *neither the substance of bread nor of wine.*

THAT IN THE FLESH, UNDER FORM OF BREAD, IS THE VERY BLOOD; AND IN THE BLOOD UNDER FORM OF WINE, IS THE VERY FLESH, AS WELL APART, AS THOUGH THEY WERE BOTH TOGETHER.

THIRDLY, THAT priests, after the order of priesthood received, AS AFORE, may not marry by the law of God.

Fourthly, that vows of chastity OR WIDOWHOOD made by men or women, MADE TO GOD ADVISEDLY, be to be observed by the law of God; AND THAT IT EXEMPTETH THEM FROM OTHER LIBERTIES OF CHRISTIAN PEOPLE, WHICH WITHOUT THAT THEY MIGHT ENJOY.

FIFTHLY, THAT IT IS MEET AND NECESSARY THAT PRIVATE MASSES BE CONTINUED AND ADMITTED IN THIS OUR ENGLISH CHURCH AND CONGREGATION, AS WHEREBY GOOD CHRISTIAN PEOPLE (ORDERING THEMSELVES ACCORDINGLY) DO RECEIVE BOTH GODLY AND GOODLY CONSOLATIONS AND BENEFITS, AND IT IS AGREEABLE ALSO TO GOD'S LAW. AND

SIXTHLY, THAT auricular confession is necessarily to be retained and continued, used and frequented in the church of God. . . .

For the penalties inflicted for disobedience in thought or deed we have to turn from Henry's draft to the Act itself. This provided that any one who by word or writing should teach or hold any opinion contrary to the first article was to be condemned as a heretic, and burnt, forfeiting his goods and lands. Any who denied the other five, and priests who married after taking their vows, were to be adjudged felons, condemned to forfeit all their goods for a first conviction, and to die if convicted a second time.

Incidentally, when considering the Act of Six Articles it is as well to remember two things: the first, that after a year the severity with which it was put into execution was considerably relaxed: the second, that Professor A.F.Pollard is able to describe it as 'rather a popular measure', and to say in his life of Cranmer that 'The Catholic bishops would have been powerless to carry the Act, and Henry VIII would not have helped, unless the mass of the laity had been on the same side'. 'Toleration,' he adds, 'was shocking to the minds of the most enlightened.'

That Henry himself scrutinized with minute care the wording and the intention of every single article of religious legislation carried in these years is amply demonstrated by a large number of documents, and more particularly by those collected together in the Cotton volume known as Cleopatra E. V, from which the above draft has been taken. Amongst other items this volume contains a lengthy exposition of the meaning of the twelve articles of the Creed, most of which have been annotated by Henry in his own hand, some very fully. Characteristically, when the exposition of 'I believe in God the Father Almighty' begins with 'For the plain understanding of this article . . .', Henry immediately inserts 'Ye must understand that we intend to declare every material word of the same'. Equally, it is noticeable that on the eighth ('I believe in the Holy Catholic Church') he has more alterations and comments to make than anywhere else.

On the questions of doctrine which were discussed by the bishops he has made many comments. Their statements on the subject of confirmation he criticizes: 'This answer is not direct'.[1] When they write that 'Making of Bishops hath two parts, Appointment and Ordering', Henry demands 'Where is this distinction found?' When they give the former to 'Christian princes and rulers', but keep for themselves ordination 'wherein grace is conferred', Henry writes 'Now since you confess that the Apostles did occupate the one part, which now you confess belongeth to princes, how can you prove that ordering is only committed to you bishops?'[2]

On two drafts of an act concerning the degrees of consanguinity that are to be held prohibited in matrimony he has commented freely in execrable handwriting,[3] and a Latin defence of auricular confession he has annotated in Latin. He has also expressed some of his opinions on purgatory, in the note which follows.

[1] f. 39v. [2] f. 42. [3] ff. 112 and 115.

v. *Ubicunque lignam cecederit ibi erit*

This text is itself, (speaking but of a stick), doth not deny purgatory, nor the example of a dead stick can well, without great forcing, be attribute to a soul repentant, not yet having his full judgement. And if you will turn it to a lively stick, then it seemeth me that it will make much against your purpose: for a lively stick may chance with falling to grow—though not suddenly—and so come to perfection of his fruit; so may the soul of man, (by this example,) departing hence to purgatory in right faith, grow there towards his perfection, abiding the day of Judgement.

Beati quorum Ihesus

How do you descant on this psalm, and also on Saint Augustine, when you would make folk believe that this was meant against purgatory, when the very text declareth nothing but the beatitude and happiness of them that hath their sins hid and forgiven. Herein do you show your carnal wit which in preaching you disprise so much.

Another question that was very fully debated was the necessity for auricular confession. It roused Henry to express himself at length in three large holograph pages. This and the three autograph pages already described in Part III, Chapter II, are the two longest documents in his own handwriting which we possess. On this one point Henry stood with Cranmer and the Reformers —that auricular confession was not enjoined by the Scriptures. Tunstall, Bishop of Durham, pursued the argument in writing after the debate was finished, whereupon Henry dealt with him in the following letter.

VI. TO TUNSTALL

[*c. March*, 1539.]

Since methought, (my Lord of Durham[1]), that both the bishops of York, Winchester,[2] and yours reasons and texts were so fully answered this other day in our house,[3] as to my seeming

[1] Tunstall. [2] Lee and Gardiner. [3] i.e. in Parliament.

and supposal the most of the house was satisfied; I marvel not a little why eft-soons you have sent to me this now your writing, being in a manner few other texts or reasons than there were declared both by the bishop of Canterbury and me, to make smally or nothing to your intended purpose. But either I esteem that you do it to prove my simple judgement alone, which indeed doth not much use, (though not the wisest) to call in aid the judgements of other learned men, and so, by mine ignorant answer, seem to win the field; or else that you be too much blinded in your own fancy and judgement, to think that a truth, which by learning you have not yet proved, nor, I fear me, cannot, by scripture, nor any other direct and provable ground; though I know mine unsufficiency in learning, if the matter were indifferent, and that the balance stood equal, since I take the verity of the cause rather to favourize the part I take than yours, it giveth me therefore great boldness, not presuming in learning, but in justness of the cause, seeing by writing you have provoked me to it, to make answer to your arguments. Therefore I beginning now to reply to your first allegation, shall essay to prove, if I can, that your own author, in place by you alleged, maketh plain against your opinion; for, as you allege him, St. Chrysostom saith, *quod sufficit solus pudor pro pœna,* then *auricularis confessio* is not by commandment necessary; for it were, this word *solus* is by your author ill set; therefore your author in this place furthereth you but little. To your *fallax* argument, I deny your consequent, founded only upon small reason, which is the ground of your *fallax* argument: which reason I need not to take away, for your alleged author doth show too plainly, in his 5. Homily, tomo 5. that you gather a wrong sense upon his words, for he saith, with much more touching this matter, these few words, *non hominibus peccata tua detegere cogo*; then his other text afore rehearsed, is not to be understood as you would wring it. Further, methinketh I need not (God thank you) too greatly study for authors to conclude your wrong taking of texts, for those yourself allege serveth me well to purpose: for all your labour is to prove that auricular confession were by God commanded, and both your authorities of Bede and Pole, showeth nothing but that they did confess their sins, and yet do not they affirm that it was by commandment; wherefore they make for mine argument and not for yours.

Your other texts of John 21. and Matthew 18. were so thoroughly answered this other day, and so manifestly declared not to appertain to our grounded argument, that I marvel you be not ashamed eft-soons to put them in writing, and to found your argument now so fondly on them; for what fonder argument can be made to prove thereby a necessity of confession, than to say, If you confess not, I cannot forgive? Would a thief which committeth felony, think himself obliged by the[1] law to disclose his felony, if the[1] law say no more, but if thou confess not I cannot forgive thee? or would he trust the sooner therefore to be forgiven? This is matter so apparent, that none can but perceive except he will not see. As touching Origen's places by you alleged; as the first, *in Leviticum*, showeth that we be as much bound *lavare stratum lacrymis*, as *dicere sacerdoti*, which no man, I think, will affirm that we be bound to do; and yet he affirmeth not that any of them is commanded: the text also whereby he would approve his so saying, doth not yet speak *quod pronunciabo injusticiam meam sacerdoti,* but *Domino*: the other of James seemeth better to make for extreme unction, than for confession; for when was ever the use, that folk coming only to confession, were wont to be anointed with oil; therefore these make nothing to your argument. As touching Origen in Psal. 37. he saith not *quod obligamur dicere sacerdoti*, but *si confiteantur;* and seemeth rather to persuade men that they should not *parvi pendere confessionem*, (as all good folk would) than that they were obliged to confess them to a priest. Though Ciprian, *de Lapsis*, doth praise them which doth confess their faults to priests, yet doth he confess that we be not bound to do so; for he saith in the highest of his praise these words, *How much be they then higher in faith, and better in fear of God, which though they be not bound by any deed of sacrifice, or book, yet be they content sorrowfully to confess them to the priest.* Since he knowledgeth no bond in us by neither fact of sacrifice or libel, why allege you (though he praise auricular confession) that we should be bound by God's law thereto? This is no proof there-

[1] Henry originally wrote *my*.

of, neither by reason nor [y]et by scripture, or any good authority. And whereas he saith further, *confiteantur singuli, quaeso vos fratres, delictum suum*; this doth not argue a precept; nor yet the saying of Esay, cap. 43. *secundum Septuaginta*; nor Solomon in the *Proverbiorum* 18. For these texts speak rather of knowledging our offence to God in our heart, than of auricular confession; after David the prophet's saying and teaching, when he said, *Tibi soli peccavi*, that was not to a priest. By the text also which you allege, beginning, *circa personas vero ministrorum*, etc. you do openly confess that the church hath not accepted auricular confession to be by God's commandment; or else by your saying and allegation, they have long erred; for you confess that the church hath divers times changed, both to whom confession shall be made, and times when; and that also they have changed divers ways for divers regions. If it were by God's commandment they might not do this: wherefore, my lord, since I hear none other allegations, I pray you blame not me though I be not of your opinion; and of the both, I think that I have more cause to think you obstinate, than you me, seeing your authors and allegations make so little to your purpose. And thus fare you well.

Whether we call it a God-complex or megalomania, it is quite obvious, by the end of the third decade of the reign, that Henry's growing sense of his own self-importance and omnipotence had come completely to dominate both his character and his policy. Whatever it might mean to his predecessors or successors, to Henry the Supreme Headship of the Church was not a formula but a function, co-equal with his temporal jurisdiction; and the merging of the two in his own person meant to him the realization of real—or imperial—sovereignty.

It is perhaps arguable whether we are to take literally the story that Henry VIII, as second son, had originally been destined by his economically-minded father for the Archbishopric of Canterbury, but there can be no doubt whatever of his keen and consistent interest in theological questions all his life. In the thirty-year-old author of the *Assertio Septem Sacramentorum* and extirpator of Lutheran heresy, as in the man of fifty who sought to abolish 'diversity of opinion', there is to be found the same upholder of orthodoxy. Typical, as always, of the people he ruled, it was on national, political and personal grounds that, all unwittingly, he laid the foundations upon which the triumph of the Reformed Faith in England was eventually to be built. And there is great appropriateness in the fact that, under this most English of monarchs, that independence of the Papacy, which for centuries English rulers and statesmen had felt to be essential for a true sovereignty, should have been, at last, triumphantly asserted.

CHAPTER IV

SCOTTISH POLICY

'Alas, poor country!'
SHAKESPEARE

'Woe to thee, O land, when thy king is a child.'
ECCLESIASTES X. 16

FOR sustained interest and dramatic quality the story of Henry's Scottish policy, if followed in detail, can hardly be rivalled by any other aspect of the reign, except the Divorce. It is not merely a record of diplomacy and well-kept tempers, though these play their part: it is a violent, vivid story—shot through with passionate impulse, streaking cruelties and hatreds—where intrigue goes armed not with silken phrases and well-leashed indignation but with sword and dagger for the thrust in the back. Its vigorous assertive personalities attack our senses with a fiercer impact: there is in them and in their deeds a wild and sinister quality which makes an episode such as that narrated in Chapter II appear to belong to another world—modern, civilized, complaisant, passionless. And though Henry's letters by themselves cannot give the full quality and colour of the story, nevertheless enough comes through to make the material stand out in vivid contrast to the elegant chess-playing of some of his foreign diplomacy.

The story of Scotland during Henry's reign begins and ends in death and disaster for her kings—with Flodden Field in 1513 and Solway Moss in 1542. Once again the political ineptitude of the Stuarts presents itself in striking contrast to the sheer sense of the Tudors, which is illustrated at nearly every stage by Henry's intelligent, and forbearing yet ultimately ruthless policy. From first to last he kept always in view the necessity of union between the two countries. The initial step had been taken by Henry VII, when he married his daughter Margaret to James IV: and in spite of the enduring tradition of hostility, aggravated by the tradition of Border warfare, and by the traditional Franco-Scottish friendship, Henry VIII never relinquished the aim.

Flodden, for all the glamour that attaches to its tragic, chivalrous and futile story, was the usual thrust in the back that English kings had learnt to expect from their neighbours if they made war on France. On the whole, Henry's ' reprisals ' show a calculated temperance, being confined to the customary devastation of the Border by Dacre, the Warden of the English Marches. In the meantime his sister Margaret had become Regent for her infant son James V, with the Earls of Angus, Arran and Huntly, and James Beton, Archbishop of Glasgow, as councillors. Henry doubtless hoped to bring the Scots round to an alliance with England, partly by a show of strength, and partly by reason of his relationship to the Queen and her son. Unfortunately for any such plans, however, that most unreliable and erratic of all the Tudors, the Regent Margaret, took a second husband, without any thought of the consequences. As if totally unaware that clan and family jealousies, hatreds and loyalties were the backbone of Scottish life and character, and the determining factor in Scottish politics, she married Archibald Douglas,[1] Earl of Angus and head of the great Douglas family. The placing in authority of one of themselves as the Regent's husband was more than the Scots lords would stomach. By 1515 Margaret had been deposed and a new Regent appointed.

The new Regent was the Duke of Albany, who was in every way a danger to Henry's plans. He was the late king's cousin, and next heir to the throne, after Margaret's two sons. Brought up in France, regarding it as his own country and owning large French estates, he was entirely in favour of the old alliance, and the maintaining thereby of Scotland's independence of England. The country received him enthusiastically on his return, and appointed him guardian of the princes. The result can be gathered from the following extract from a letter in which Henry protests to Francis that it was an unfriendly act to allow Albany's return, and one that will redound to his scandal and reproach.

1. To Francis I

[*Aug.* 20, 1515.]

. . . Secondly, we have of late been credibly ascertained that our cousin, the Duke of Albany, whom you have sent into

[1] Grandson of the famous Archibald ' Bell-the-Cat '.

Scotland, will not only take upon himself the government of the kingdom and reject from it the Queen, our good sister, contrary to the testament and last wishes of the king her late husband, who had willed that she should have the ordering and rule of the said realm, and of our nephews her children; but demandeth also to have the keeping of these children in his own hands.

And because our said good sister will not by any means consent thereunto, she has been forced by him, for the security of herself and of our said nephews, to take refuge within the strong hold called Stirling, to which the said Duke has laid siege, to cut them off, and to prevent victual being brought in, thinking by these means to starve them out and so have them: and then to do with them as he will, and afterwards to make himself king, which is a proceeding utterly to be reprobated; and we for our part, as well you know, are constrained by the inclination of nature not to suffer such enormities nor oppressions to be used against our said good sister and these our nephews, her children. And as you know by virtue of your good and sufficient prudence, it being understood that you have sent him there to the said country, howsoever much we believe right firmly that this has been done of a good inclination, always if such a thing should chance—which God forbid—it would redound greatly to your dishonour, and vile reproach and common rumour will overwhelm you and report that this has been with your will, knowledge and agreement, howsoever we may be convinced to the contrary.

Wherefore, most affectuously we pray you, as much for the avoidance of the said dishonourable reproach and evil imaginings, which would be showered upon you, and other inconveniences like to ensue therefrom, as also to dispel all scruples which at the least might be engendered of this and arise between yourself and us, to write with all possible diligence to the said Duke, expressly commanding him to cease from such hurts and enterprises against this our said good sister, and her said children, our nephews; and also that he shall permit, suffer and allow to this our good sister to enjoy and use, plainly and peaceably, that which the king, her said late husband, had ordered and appointed unto her in his said testament, as appertaineth to right, reason and good conscience.

Albany forced Margaret to surrender herself and her children, after which she and Angus fled to England. It was in England, in consequence, that their daughter Margaret Douglas was born —she who was to become Countess of Lennox and mother of Henry Darnley, the father of James VI and I.

To deal with the family feuds and the rapacity of the nobles and clergy of Scotland would have required a Henry VIII in his maturity. Had it not been for Henry's consistently-followed policy, however, Albany might have made a better show than he did. Alarmed by Albany's initial success in getting rid of any powerful interests opposed to his French policy Henry determined to get rid of Albany. Disaffected Scots were encouraged by English pay, and feuds and intrigues were nourished, more particularly by the Warden, Lord Dacre. Better still, from England's point of view, friendly relations between England and France enabled Henry to have Albany detained in France, where he had gone on a six months visit that eventually lasted for four years. The unfriendly dealing of France strained relations with the Scots, and gave the Earl of Angus, now definitely allied to the English interest, his chance to make a bid for power. Albany returned again in 1521, partly at the request of Margaret, who was by then scheming to get rid of her second husband. Francis, on the point of war with Henry, found it convenient to allow Albany's return, in order to put Henry in much the same position he had been in at the time of Flodden. Hence the following protest from Henry.

11. To the Duke of Albany

[*Dec.* 10, 1522.]

We have received your letters by your secretary, containing credence not only touching your arrival in that realm, but also the mind that ye be of, as well to do service to the king our nephew there, as to the continuance of peace betwixt both realms; desiring the further prorogation of the truce which shall expire at Candlemas next ensuing; to the intent ambassadors may be sent to us for treating and concluding of and upon a final peace betwixt us and our entirely beloved brother and nephew the king of Scots.

And, first, as touching your coming into Scotland, considering that the same is contrary to the pactions, oath, and promises of our right dear brother, confederate, and ally, the French king, who hath expressly declared to our ambassador resident in his court, that ye be thither comen without his knowledge, consent, or good will; remembering also the manifold dangers that may ensue to the person of our said brother and nephew, ye pretending to be next in succession to the crown there, having also the custody of his person (at your deputation and governance of his whole realm) with the dishonourable and damnable abusing of our sister, inciting and stirring her to be divorced from her lawful husband (for what corrupt intent God knoweth); we cannot be contented with your said arrival, ne yet take your being there in good part, but will and shall, by all the ways and means that we can devise or imagine, with the help, aid, and assistance of our confederates, do all that we can for your removing thence, in eschewing the inconveniences before specified.

And surely, if ye regarded and tendered your own honour, and the evil bruits that be divulged and spread, by your thither coming, through all Christian regions, ye would avoid all occasions whereby any suspicion might arise to the peril of the said king our nephew, by your being in that realm: which cannot be purged by any colour during your abode there. Wherefore we, for the surety of our said nephew, and considerations before specified, mind not to take any peace or abstinence of war at your hand, as long as ye continue there, like as this bearer, Clarencieux, our officer at arms, shall more at length declare unto you and other the nobles and states of Scotland.

Henry's accusations were nonsense, but that he was absolutely determined to force the Scots to throw over Albany is very evident in this and in the letter from which the extracts on pp. 268-9 are taken.

At the end of 1522 Albany sailed for France, and Henry at

once tried to pursue a policy of conciliation and union. He offered the hand of his daughter Mary to the young James V, but in the struggle that ensued between the as-yet barely existent new young English interest and the old-established French faction the latter won. In 1523, therefore, the Earl of Surrey[1] wasted the Border and burnt Jedburgh, for which he received the following letter of thanks.

III. To Surrey

[*Oct.* 5, 1523.]

. . . We have this day received and read, as well your letters directed to our self, dated at our town of Berwick the 27th day of September last passed, as also your letters directed unto the Most Reverend Father &c. my Lord Legate; By the continue whereof we perceive, as well the goodly valiant exploit of our army under your wise and politic conduct accomplished at Jedburgh, with the arrazing and destruction of the same, as also the winning of the castle of Ferneherst, the devasting and wasting of the country about: which your honourable service, done unto us in your so highly well achieved enterprise, greatly redounding to the loss, confusion, rebuke and shame of our enemies, with the profit, surety, honour and good renown of us and our realm, is to us especial pleasure and contentation; for which we give unto you and all other our Lords, gentlemen and good subjects there, for their labour, pain, travail, and faithful devoir under you, our right hearty thanks, and very joyous be we of your and their safe and prosperous return. And as for the loss misfortuned among my Lord Dacre's horses,[2] albeit that for the tender favour we bear him we be right sorry that any harm should in any wise come to him; yet considering that the same grew but by mere chance, whereof our enemies can claim none honour, we reckon your commendable exploit nothing blemished thereby: which chance also might well have happened

[1] Son of the victor of Flodden, and afterwards third Duke of Norfolk; uncle of Anne Boleyn and of Katharine Howard, and father of the poet Surrey.

[2] Some eight hundred of them were stampeded by the Scots and lost.

though they had been in the camp, not without greater commotion and more sudden affray. And, sith also the adventures of the war seldom pass without some mishap, we be well content and right glad that it is rather fallen upon the horses than upon the men; of whose return so whole, with so few of our well beloved subjects lost, we right heartily thank God, your and their valiant acquital, with your good and prudent conduct. And we desire you to give on our behalf our right especial thanks to the Lord Dacre for his valiant, faithful, diligent and painful service, as well at Jedburgh as at Ferneherst. . . .

Moreover, where it is your conjecture and opinion, that the Duke will suddenly gather up thirty thousand men of the countries next adjoining to our Borders, and with them so reared, and with the Frenchmen, make an invasion into our land for two or three days, and thereupon suddenly depart, and that he were likely thus to do before the Saturday next after the said date of your letters; albeit this thing was by you right wisely doubted and forecast, yet we verily think that ye have by this time found it otherwise. For we cannot suppose either that he can well come with his company, sea-beaten, from Dunbritain[1] so far off, so soon, nor with so great celerity raise so much people, and march on so fast, nor will himself come in person to that invasion that should hold so few days. But for the doubt of all sudden invasions, whereof is not unlikely diverse at sundry times to be made, our advice and counsel is, that our subjects the Borderers, as much as they conveniently can, should convey farther up from the Borders all such things as by sudden incursions might be bereft them or destroyed. And if ye shall perceive great gathering toward, and assembling of much people, and mighty puissance reared, we wot it well we shall not need to admonish you to strength your self with substantial number according, out of the shires within your commission. And else we doubt it not we shall need as little to put you in remembrance to spare our charges, to the good husbanding whereof ye have, and have had, in all your doings, a right vigilant eye. . . .

[1] i.e. Dumbarton.

In September, Albany returned to Scotland with a French force, and advanced to meet Surrey. In spite of the fact that national feeling had rallied the Scots to his banner, Albany, after an initial skirmish, turned tail and fled. What the Scots lords regarded as his cowardice and incapacity finally wrecked his chances, though they themselves were largely responsible for his enforced flight, having refused to support the French troops in their assault on Wark. In 1524, he left Scotland for ever, driven out largely by Henry's determination, which is well shown in the following extract. Though written by Wolsey it is undoubtedly a direct communication of the King's will. It was written in answer to letters from Surrey, which, 'being the King's Highness here at my poor house, I have showed and declared unto His Grace: who, after good and perfect debating thereof, by the deliberate advice of his Council, hath willed me to advertise you his mind and pleasure . . . in manner following'.

> First, it is considered and remembered by His Highness and his Council, that in all writings and intimations made unto the Scots in this time of the wars, it hath been plainly declared and showed unto them, for a final and resolute answer, that the King's Grace, who maketh war unto that country not for any displeasure of the young King, but to compel those which favour the Duke and the French faction, suspect unto the life of the said young King, to abandon the same, would never grant unto them any truce or peace, unless the said Duke were first expelled and removed from the governance of the said young King's person and realm. Which thing, by your answer now lately made unto the Queen of Scots' former letters, was again largely confirmed; by means whereof, as it is thought, the said Duke, who, having up his said army, supposed with a visage to have had his truce at his pleasure, was clearly disappointed of his purpose; and, contrary to his hope, thinking, the truce once attained, to have returned with glory, was g[ ] to recule and fly with shame. Wherefore, if the King's Highness should now, contrary to the former plain

answers made, consent unto a truce with Scotland, the said Duke remaining in the same as Governor, it might be thought that either His Grace were fatigate and wearied by the Scots, or else not able longer to continue the wars in justifying his firm resolution and answer often times made to them as is aforesaid.

Finally, after adducing other reasons for Henry's refusal, Wolsey concludes:

Fourthly, what commodity might be given unto the said Duke, a truce so attained, to convey with him in to France the young King, or to do some other notable act sounding to his danger and destruction, and to the King's dishonour; and semblably, what hinderance may ensue unto him, lacking the truce, he being in universal hatred and indignation of the people of Scotland, is facile and easy to be considered. Wherefore, the premises with many other things concerning the same well pondered and remembered, the King's resolution and determination in nowise is, that by this means or fashion any truce or abstinence of war shall be granted or taken with Scotland, ne that it shall be thought, either by them or any other, that the King's Highness would be glad or inclinable to send his Lieutenant, or any other noble men or Commissioners, to meet by way of a diet to be kept in any place within his realm or without, for treaty to be made with the said Scots. But, in case they, expelling the Duke of Albany from the said governance, shall fortune, in the name of the said King, being once established in his authority royal, and the Queen, with consent of the Lords of Scotland, to send unto the King's Highness an honourable ambassiate, or at the least some good personage, to require or desire truce, peace or abstinence of war; His Grace, finding once his young nephew out of danger and peril of the said Duke, and the Scots inclined and disposed to live in good rest, tranquillity and love with England, shall make unto them such benign and gracious answer as shall be for their weal, and as they shall have cause to be contented therewith. Which final resolution His Highness will ye intimate and notify by your letters to the Queen of Scots accordingly.

(*Nov*. 26, 1523.)[1]

With Albany finally out of the way, Henry again opened negotiations for the betrothal of James and Mary, and though nothing came of his proposals it becomes evident from now on that at least the first step in his policy had at last been attained. Though the French faction might continue stronger, it was now opposed in the councils of Scotland by a small party, definitely favourable to the idea of an English alliance, and aware of the benefits to be gained from it. Writing to Francis, in 1523, Albany had mentioned the increasing influence wielded by England in Scots affairs. The first Earl of Arran, next heir after Albany to the throne, allied himself with Margaret in a pro-English policy. James V, aged twelve, assumed power as king, and the government was henceforth carried on in his name. That the project had been both urged and aided by Henry is obvious from the following letters. With no regent to intervene, he hoped, no doubt, eventually to prevail in his nephew's counsels. He must certainly have reckoned that he was more likely to succeed with a boy of twelve than with any of the Scots lords or even his 'dearest sister'.

The following extracts from the letters he wrote to Margaret and to James are extremely interesting and serve to show his methods.

IV. To James V

[*July* 21, 1524.]

Dearest nephew, in our most hearty and affectuous manner we recommend us unto you: letting you wit that by letters lately received from our dearest and best beloved sister the Queen your mother, we to our great comfort and gladness do understand that ye, like a virtuous, wise and discreet young prince, have substantially considered and regarded the effect of our former letters to you addressed: wherein, for the tender love which we bear,

[1] Calig. B. II, f. 12.

and always have born unto your person, life, estate, and surety, we exhorted, advised and counselled you, in avoiding the extreme danger which ye be in by reason of the suspect governance of the Duke of Albany, to take upon you the rule and order of yourself, and that your realm, by the advice of the discreet lords and nobles of the same. And that ye now do perceive whereof hath proceeded the war, trouble and damage, which the same realm in this your minority hath sustained, and is like to do, as long as the said Duke shall continue in that governance: for the which your good respect and well understanding of our said letters, proceeding of the fresh wit and great towardness of wisdom which is reported to be in you, we do give unto you not only singular laud and praise, but also our most hearty and cordial thanks: assuring you that one of the principal things which we tender in earth is the surety and preservation of your person, being so nighly conjoined unto us in proximity of blood, and the increase of your honour with your erection to your estate and dignity royal.

Wherefore, dearest nephew, since almighty God hath provided for you so great, so perfect and so faithful a friend, to assist, maintain and defend you herein as we be, and that it cannot, ne God willing shall lie in the power of any prince, king or other to annoy or impeach you in this honourable purpose, we taking your part, as we will not fail to do to the uttermost; we eftsoons exhort and most tenderly and entirely require you, that regarding the commodity of the time present and the danger which your said life shall stand in if the Duke of Albany before your said erection should return into Scotland with strength and power had of the French king, ye will, all persuasions and motions which may be made to the contrary set apart, underlayedly and without any tract of time, if it be not done already, assume and take upon you your said estate, rule and governance. . . .

Any one who advises contrary, he continues, is no true subject, but a mortal enemy, and should be treated as such.

In his letter to Margaret he begins in the same strain about

Albany, and describes him as 'servant unto the French king' If he returns to Scotland, then he,

v. To Queen Margaret

[*July* 21, 1524.]

with the help and advice of the French king, to whom nothing is in greater abomination than the proximity of blood being between us and our said dearest nephew, will by all ways to him possible study and compass the total extermination and destruction of the same our nephew, and to assure himself unto the crown of that realm, as we have as well by letters intercepted as by divers other credible ways be advertised that he intendeth to do. . . . And for our part, like as hitherto to our no small travail, charges and expenses, we have earnestly and effectually put our hands, by making war to those that have adhered to the Duke of Albany, for the preservation of our said nephew, which if we had not done the same our nephew should not have failed to have been in extreme danger. . . .

Howbeit, dearest sister, this matter being of so great weight, moment and importance, and whereupon dependeth the life of our said nephew, and percase of you also, is not for any persuasions to be deferred for four or five days, ne for one day or hour, but incontinently and without delay or tract of time in avoiding manifold dangers and inconveniences, is to be amplected, embraced, and the conduct thereof undelayedly taken and used, all sinister compasses, delays and colourable persuasions that may be made to the contrary notwithstanding. . . .

We have in great diligence depeched our entirely well beloved cousin and counsellor the Duke of Norfolk unto our Borders foreanent that realm, as our lieutenant, not only to give unto you and our said dearest nephew his best counsel and advice for performance of the premises, but also if need be and upon your requisition to raise up our power for the repressing of all such as would intend to impeach the same, which assistance ye shall not lack, both of men and money, as need shall require.[1] . . .

Over this, dearest sister, as touching the mean and way for

[1] He actually sent two hundred men as a bodyguard for the young king.

conducing of good peace between the two realms we assure you that we never were ne yet be minded that any other living person shall have the honour and doing thereof, but ye, who like a most tender mother, for the weal and surety of your son, and the benefit of that realm, have always most diligently laboured and procured the same, ne it is any matter to be attempted by a personage but of such great and high estate as ye be of, being sister to us, and mother to our said dearest nephew. . . .

After this delicate approach, he comes to the real point. Angus shall not have any credit for the peace.

We have expressly ordained and determined all to be done by your hands and conduct, ascertaining you that concerning the repair into that realm of our said cousin of Angus, or his further proceeding, we have taken and shall take such ways that he remaining on the Borders shall enterprise or intermeddle no further than ye shall will or command, and be contented withal.

(*July* 21?, 1524.)

The English ascendancy, however, was lost as quickly as it had been gained, this time largely through the instrumentality of Queen Margaret. As she had not yet obtained her divorce from Angus she was technically 'living in sin' with Henry Stewart, Lord Methuen, and was consequently determined to prevent Angus from returning to Scotland. When she realized that her brother, in spite of his promises, meant to allow Angus to return she threw in her lot with the French faction. 'I will not labour no more to the pleasure of the king my brother,' she wrote, 'but look the best way I may for myself.' She released the Chancellor, Beton, whom she had previously imprisoned, and sent his nephew David, afterwards Cardinal Beton, to the court of France. It was a set-back for Henry, who at this juncture left Wolsey and Norfolk[1] to tell his sister exactly what he thought of her. Again the words may be Wolsey's, but the tone is Henry's.

[1] Thomas Howard, Earl of Surrey, succeeded his father as Duke of Norfolk in May, 1524.

(Wolsey to Norfolk)[1]

[*Nov.* 5, 1524.]

. . . For verily, when the King's Highness heard and understood by your said letters how the Queen of Scots hath ordered herself at this time, first in stopping and countermanding the ambassadors of Scotland, making communications unto the King's Grace of their not coming, with other things, if the Earl of Angus were suffered to enter Scotland; secondly, in putting the late Chancellor to liberty, whom she hath in all her writings reported to be the most enemy in all Scotland to herself and to the young King's erection, and greatest friend and favourer of the Duke of Albany and the French faction; and thirdly, having knowledge that the Bishop of Dunkeld[2] was minded to discover certain great matters touching the surety of the King's person, that she would so long and with such slack and remiss demeanour pass it over; and finally give answer that he should not utter any thing thereof till such time as she might perceive what answer were made unto her unreasonable desires, which implieth in itself that she not only little cared or esteemed what danger the King's most royal person were in, but also percase conceiving a malicious and rancorous displeasure towards His Highness, because His Grace would not fulfil and satisfy to her arrogant and dishonourable requests, rather consented in her heart and mind unto such danger, than studied to eschew the same: this manner of doing, with other her insolent behaviours, sounding openly to her extreme reproach, and the blemishing of the royal house and blood whereof she is descended, causeth the King's Highness to think that she is not only the most ingrate and unkind sister that ever was, to whom His Grace neither in her tender youth ne since hath given any such cause; but also that she, digressing from all good qualities and virtues, doth in manner alter, vary, and decline from the loving affections and direct operations and course of nature towards herself, her blood, and the house that she is come of; showing thereby that she is to be accounted rather like an unnatural or transformed person than like a noble Princess, or a woman of wisdom, regard, honour or

[1] Calig. B. II, f. 8v.

[2] The poet Gavin Douglas.

kindness; whereby she so continuing should give His Highness occasion utterly to refuse, abandon and forsake her for his sister, and to repute her as one which more desireth the destruction of His Grace, than by her good help and means to put remedy or help to any danger imminent to the same. And assured may ye be that there hath been no matter which in my life I have perceived His Grace to take more unkindly, or that more hath moved his royal and princely courage to think extreme high ingratitude and unnatural dealing in any person, than this most strange answer given to the said Appleby, and the continual delay which the said Queen hath used in opening and disclosing a matter, sounding, as it is said, so much to the danger of the King's life and person. So that, to satisfy unto her own malice, it seemeth she not only would lean herself and train her son and his realm to enmity with the King's Highness, relinquishing His Grace, and adhering to the faction of France, to her own utter undoing and the destruction of her said son; but also she could be contented to conceal and not suffer to be discovered that thing which she might think should sound to the danger of her own brother's life, and consequently do that in her is rather to destroy her brother, her son, and herself for revenging of her own rancour and malice, than to follow any wholesome, loving and honourable counsel, exhortation or persuasion given her by her best friends, sounding to the pleasure of God, the weal, surety and exaltation of her said son, and her own singular benefit, profit and comfort. And whether this manner of proceeding be to be reputed by any good and gracious Prince or other man as a thing unnatural or not, and what inconveniences be like to ensue of such demeanour, if she thus continue, whereby many one shall hereafter have cause to be sorry that ever she was born; I pray God she may have grace to consider. . . .

By 1525 something of a compromise between the English and French interests was reached, both being represented in the Council of Eight which was appointed to govern the country. Moreover, the alliance between England and France made pro-French feeling in Scotland no longer synonymous with hostility towards England. Again Henry proposed union by means of the betrothal of James and Mary, but again he was defeated by the French faction, as dominated by Beton, now Archbishop of St. Andrews. The Scots would agree to no treaty of perpetual peace unless the betrothal was first an accomplished fact. A three years' pact, however, was arranged, during which time Scotland, left more or less to itself, pursued its own faction fights, which in 1528 culminated in the escape of the King from the hands of the Douglases, and the exile of Angus, still the chief friend to English interests. England and France being still at peace, however, a five years' peace was concluded between James and Henry in the same year. Angus took refuge in England, and James was at last master in his own kingdom.

After the fall of Wolsey it is noticeable that there are more letters available written by Henry direct to his nephew. James, moreover, was growing up, and although in 1525 Henry's agent Magnus wrote to Wolsey that 'as yet the said young king cannot by himself read an English letter', it is probable that by 1530 he was slightly more capable of dealing with his own correspondence. During the divorce years Henry seems to have been too much occupied with his own affairs to pursue any particularly vigorous line of policy in connection with Scotland. But the spirit of antagonism died hard, and there was constant raiding and quarrelling on the Border. Henry wrote various protests to his nephew, with little or no effect; and as the five years' truce went on, James, instead of being gradually drawn towards the idea of union with England, became more committed to friendship with France. In his endeavours to keep peace and good order within his kingdom his somewhat arbitrary methods of dealing with his nobles had, by 1532, alienated most of them, and left him almost entirely in the hands of the clergy for support and counsel. Moreover, Henry's quarrel with Rome struck no sympathetic chord in James, who was genuinely devoted to the Catholic faith. Border warfare again broke out in the autumn of 1533: and during the year two large detachments of fighting men from the Isles went to Ireland to lend support to Henry's rebels. Nevertheless, when a peace was finally negotiated in 1534 Henry again made friendly overtures, the gist of which can be gathered from the following instructions given to Lord William Howard,[1] who was sent to Edinburgh to take James the Order of the Garter.

VI. INSTRUCTIONS TO LORD WILLIAM HOWARD[1]

[*Oct.* 1534.]

First, at his arrival at the Court of the King's said dearest brother and nephew the King of Scots, after most hearty recommendations unto him made on the King's behalf in the most loving and hearty manner that he can devise, with also like thanks for his noble and gentle present of falcons lately sent to the King's said Highness, which His Majesty most thankfully taketh and esteemeth with no less delight and pleasure in the same than the gentle and kind remembrance of his said dearest brother and nephew in that behalf requireth; he shall deliver to the said King of Scots the King's letters, declaring unto him the great joy, desire and gladness that the King's Highness hath to hear of his prosperity and welfare, which he coveteth as much to hear as of any other his friend or ally, not only for the nighness and proximity of blood that they been of, but also for the great amity concluded by the league lately made and passed betwixt them both, which undoubtedly shall be to the great honour of both Princes, and the great commodity, wealth and profit of both their realms and subjects.

Item, the said Lord William shall further, taking his best opportunity, in the King's Highness name, after the goodliest wise he can, salute the Queen of Scots the King of Scots mother,[2] sister to the King's said Highness, showing not only unto her how glad and desirous His Majesty is to hear of her prosperous health and welfare, but also giving unto her most loving and hearty thanks, as well for her natural love, good zeal, mind, and affection, always tended and born towards the King's said Highness, his realm and subjects, as for her good propice mind and

[1] Eldest son of the second Duke of Norfolk by his second wife; created Baron Howard of Effingham by Mary I for helping to quell Wyatt's rebellion.

[2] This is yet another specimen of the inch-spaced drafts. It has been revised, altered and rewritten throughout, though not in Henry's hand. The elaboration of the message to the Queen-Mother is all inserted, probably at Henry's dictation or command.

will at all times showed towards the setting-forth, preservation and continuance of that that should or might redound to the weal of peace, unity and love betwixt the King's said Highness and her loving son the King of Scots, both their realms and subjects; in which good, virtuous and loving mind and will, His Highness nothing doubteth she will still persist and continue, which undoubtedly shall redound to her great honour, the weal and surety both of the King's said Highness and her son, their said realms and subjects.

Item, after the delivery of the King's said Highness' letters, or before, as he conveniently shall have opportunity, he shall practise with the Lord Treasurer by some ways and means to get the measure of the King of Scots' person; and the said measure attained, he shall forthwith, with all speed and diligence, cause such garments to be made for him, of such stuff as he shall have with him for that purpose, in the best fashion that can be devised, by such a tailor and broiderer as he shall carry with him for that intent; which garment, speedily finished and made, he shall thereof, with such horses as he shall have to him assigned for that purpose, make present unto the said King of Scots: setting the same forth after such sort and fashion for the advancement and praise thereof as may be to the honour of the King's Majesty, and the more estimation of the present.

Item, after the delivery of the said present, he shall further declare unto the said King of Scots that nothing may better please the King's Highness than to remember that he is comen to his lawful age, and of the activity and nobleness that is reported to be in him; by reason whereof His Majesty is greatly desirous, and nothing more coveteth, than to see his person, and especially to have conference and communication with him, in matters that shall undoubtedly redound to both their honours and glory, and the weal of their realms and subjects: upon which overture to be made thereof to the said king of Scots, in such sort and manner as is afore premised, and none otherwise, the said Lord William shall more amply open, set forth and declare that matter to the Bishop of Aberdeen, Treasurer of Scotland, in manner and form as hereafter followeth.

First, the said Lord William shall in the King's name salute the said Bishop in right loving and hearty wise; and then, taking good opportunity, shall declare unto him that, forasmuch as an interview is like very shortly to ensue betwixt the King's Majesty and his good brother and perpetual ally the French King, at which meeting and interview the King's said Highness, of the especial zeal and desire that he hath to see his said good nephew, would be right joyous and glad to have him present. His Highness therefore, considering both what honour and surety may ensue thereof to his said good nephew, and also having a special confidence and trust in the said Bishop, that he will not only, according to his duty like a faithful and discreet Counsellor, put to his uttermost devoirs, good will, advise, policy, and counsel for the setting forth and accomplishing of that, that shall seem to stand [most with the] honour and surety of his Realm, [ ][1] Bishop so to use his industry and good will towards the furtherance of this interview and meeting, as the King his said master may be the rather animated and conduced thereunto: which if it shall take effect, considering the great puissance, fame and renown of those three Princes, when they shall assemble all three togethers in peace, amity and concord, shall not only by their mutual conferences and lively communications one to another, demonstrating a true visage of perfect love and amity, knit such an indissoluble knot of love and affection amongst them as shall be to the great honour, weal and comfort of them, their realms and subjects, for ever after: but also in such wise augment and increase their force, strength and power as shall give occasion as well to all Princes, being their friends and confederates, to love and rejoice with them, as to all other Princes, being their enemies, utterly to dread and fear them. For the which considerations, and to the intent that at the said meeting such things may be determined, as shall be for the wealth of those three Princes, their realms and subjects, the King's said Highness (as it becometh all good Princes to do) devising how to nourish and entertain love, peace and unity betwixt Prince and Prince, and to show the especial zeal that he beareth towards his said good nephew, only coveteth and desireth to have his said good nephew present at the said meeting and

[1] The MS. is torn at this point.

interview. Which matter the said Lord William shall earnestly propone and set forth to the said Bishop, and further shall say unto the said Bishop that, in case the said King of Scots can be contented to conform and prepare himself to be at the said interview, it shall be great commodity and pleasure to the King's Highness to have his said good nephew, whom he so much loveth and esteemeth, first to enter into this his realm, where he may both lovingly embrace, salute and welcome him, and also gratify him with such pleasures and commodities as be within his said realm, and so to pass thorough the same, with such company as shall like him, towards Calais, for the accomplishment of the said interview. And herein the said Lord William shall somewhat press the said Bishop so to use his industry, and in such wise to counsel the said King his master, as may best conduce to the attaining of the King's Highness desire in that behalf. And after all those overtures made, in case the said King of Scots, or the said Bishop on his behalf, shall say that the said King of Scots is not of hability nor yet well furnished for the said interview, then the said Lord William, on the King's Highness' behalf, shall further say, that being none other urgent matter or consideration why the said King of Scots should refuse this interview, so it may please him first to enter this the King's Highness realm, and so to pass thorough the same as is aforesaid, His Highness will not only take great pleasure and rejoice thereof, but also so ordain and provide for the furniture of the same meeting, as shall be both for their honours, and with small charges, specially for his said good brother and nephew.

[And where] as the King's Majesty hath lately been informed that divers of the subjects of his said good brother and nephew have given aid and succour to Thomas Fitzgaret,[1] and other the King's rebels in Ireland, which the King's said Highness (having a special trust that his said good brother and nephew will nothing do contrary to the league concluded betwixt them) supposeth to proceed rather of the obstinacy, malice and wilfulness of his said good nephew's subjects than by any part of his

[1] i.e. Thomas Fitzgerald, tenth Earl of Kildare, known as 'Silken Thomas', who had rebelled against Henry in June, 1534, and was finally executed at Tyburn in 1537.

mind, will or consent; His Majesty therefore not only desireth his said good nephew to cause his said subjects to be retired, and in such wise to be governed from henceforth as they do nothing that shall sound to the breach of the said league, but also specially trusteth that his said good brother and nephew will rather study for the conservation and continuance of the love and amity, which is already so firmly knit betwixt them as the same for ever seemeth indissoluble, than in any wise suffer anything to be done or attempted whereby the said league and treaty, or any the pacts therein contained, might be dissolved, blemished, or interrupted in any manner of wise, likewise and in semblable manner as His Majesty doth and daily will do.

And farther, forasmuch as the King's Highness, minding by some noble means to declare his integrity of heart and entire zeal towards his said nephew, is content to ordain, constitute and make him one of the Honourable Order of the Garter, the rather for that the Emperor, the French King, and the King of Romans, have already accepted and taken that Order, which should be very honourable to his said good nephew to be joined with such noble Princes in the same Order, the said Lord William thereof shall advertise and make privy the said Bishop of Aberdeen, declaring unto him the same considerations, to the intent that he may the better set forth the same to the King his master. And upon knowledge of his pleasure and advertisement thereof unto the King's Majesty, His Highness will be content to prepare and send all thing propice and meet therefore accordingly.

Finally, the said Lord William, taking his best opportunity and occasion, shall on the King's Highness behalf further declare and say to his said good brother and nephew, that where the King's said Highness hath before this sundry times written unto his said good brother and nephew for the restitution and reconciliation of the Earl of Angus, and Sir George Douglas his brother to the grace and favour of his said dearest nephew, without receiving again his desired answer, which (the King's said Highness cannot otherwise think) hath been suspended and deferred by the suit of some of them that procured his exile and banishment; yet the King's said Highness, considering that not only the ancestors of the said Earl of Angus have been of noble continuance within the realm of Scotland, and have ever done good service there to their Prince and Sovereign Lord, but also that this man hath ever in heart been as true and loyal unto his Sovereign Lord the King's said good brother and nephew, as any of his house hath been aforetime : and also certainly knowing the faithful hearts of the said Earl and his brother to have been ever in such sort preserved towards their said natural Sovereign and liege Lord, and their doings indeed, in case the same had been indifferently weighed, not such as hath deserved the punishment, which by the mean of their back friends and by their sinister information they have sustained, cannot forget eftsoons to recommend unto his said dearest brother and nephew the restitution and reconciliation of the said Earl and his brother to his grace and favour, as whereby they may again, at this the King's Highness' special request and contemplation, and for his sake enjoying the same, have their estate, degree and possessions within the said realm of Scotland. And therein the said Lord William shall not only very effectually, in the King's Highness name and behalf, move and desire his said good nephew for his sake to receive them to grace and favour, which without desert, to their extreme sorrow, hath long suffered exile and banishment, but also shall make privy thereunto the said Bishop of Aberdeen, requiring him on the King's behalf semblably to further and set forth the same, as the desired end thereof may the more facilly be obtained and take effect.

The interview that Henry was so anxious to secure was again urged by Howard when, in February, 1536, he was sent on another mission to James, with Barlow, Bishop-elect of St. Asaph, as his coadjutor. In dealing with James himself, trying to persuade him to agree to the interview, and sounding him as to his views on Henry's religious policy, they were commanded (f. 61^{v}) ' dulcely to inculce into the said King of Scots' head the argument of the instructions heretofore given to the said Elect of St. Asaph . . . foreseeing ever that they do not in any wise by communication of those matters irritate the said King, or bring the same into such disputation, question or argument as should be displeasant unto him, whereby he might, by counsel of his bishops, and such as favour not his Grace's most godly and honourable proceedings, be induced to stay rather in the conclusion of this interview.' In dealing with his Grace's sister, however, (f. 64^{v})

VII

[1536.]

they shall travail . . . to beat into her head the great honour, joy and comfort that shall ensue unto her by this interview, in the persuasion of which thing they shall not omit, as of themselves, likewise to advise her to be vigilant that the King her son savour no contrary persuasion which might be set forth by some of his prelacy, which percase, blinded with their own worldly glory and ambition, do not so much favour the truth as their profession doth and would require of them; with whom also they must proceed so temperately as they provoke her not to any displeasure, ne in any wise give her occasion to judge that the King's Highness so much for any respect desireth this interview, as for the satisfaction of the great and inward zeal and desire which his Grace hath to see her and his dearest nephew her son the King of Scots. And finally, they shall set forth all other points contained in their other instructions, specially persuading the interview to be had as far within England as they can. . . . And forasmuch as the said Lord William Howard is not so furnished to treat in such matters as touch our religion and the contents of the said former instructions as the said Elect of St. Asaph both for his learning, knowledge and experience is, like as the King's Majesty will that the said Elect shall not only in their journey communicate the effect of the said instructions unto him, but also make him a certain abbreviation shortly containing certain authorities of Scripture meet to be spoken for the furtherance of that purpose, so his pleasure is that the said Lord William Howard shall rather in the setting forth of his Grace's proceedings and the persuasion of the King of Scots to embrace the semblable, inculce and harp on the string of honour and profit. . . .

James was apparently anxious to meet his uncle, but in spite of all Lord William's eloquent 'harping' nothing came of the proposal. Beton was in every way as shrewd a diplomat as Henry, and must have noted with grim amusement the sinister touch of ' the interview to be had *as far within England* as they can '—that is, supposing Lord William to have conveyed the proposition as naïvely as it is couched in his master's instructions. It was not the first time Henry had tried to lure the wily old Archbishop over the Border;[1] and whether or not James had any real inclination to the meeting—as Henry apparently believed—Beton, with all the ecclesiastical strength and wealth of Scotland behind him, did his utmost to prevent it, partly, no doubt, because Henry was trying to persuade the young king to follow England's example and break with Rome. Whether Henry's force of character and personal magnetism could have prevailed with James it is impossible to say; but obviously Beton feared it. In consequence, no meeting took place in 1536: instead, James paid a lengthy visit to France, and on January 1, 1537, married Madeleine, the daughter of Francis I. It was a decisive move, and Henry must have recognized it as such. That indeed every one recognized it is revealed in a very interesting letter from the Bishop of Faenza, who, as papal nuncio at Paris, interviewed James in November, 1536. He mentions first the domination exercised by the Betons: the nephew, David Beton, was with the young king throughout the interview, and acted as his interpreter. Faenza describes him as ' one of his *prelati* who conducts everything and is a man of good wit '. He finds James ' utterly opposed ' to the methods of England: the young king has assured him that he ' will always act, with the assistance of France, to bring England to reason '. Faenza sees Scotland as ' the true bridle of England ', and considers that ' if Scotland keeps him (i.e. Henry) in apprehension it will make him keep his money to himself and not give it to the Emperor '. Finally he reports that he has told James that the Pope had always relied on Francis and James to make trouble for England, and as the disturbances in the north have ceased he has begged the King of Scots ' to try and stir up others for the service of God and his own interest '.[2]

[1] cf. *S.P.* IV, p. 343, etc.
[2] Quoted from *L.P.* XI, 1173.

The marriage with France was in itself a plain enough declaration. James made it even more pointed by omitting to observe the customary formality of announcing it to England. Henry ignored the discourtesy, and sent his nephew the proper letter of congratulation.

VIII. To James V

[*Dec.* 22, 1536.]

RIGHT EXCELLENT, RIGHT HIGH AND MIGHTY PRINCE, OUR DEAREST BROTHER AND NEPHEW, We commend us unto you in our most hearty and effectual manner; letting you wit that having certain knowledge from those parts of your determination and conclusion for marriage with the daughter of our dearest brother and perpetual ally the French king—our office, our proximity of blood, and our friendship towards you have moved us to congratulate with you in the same, and to desire almighty God to send you that issue and fruit thereof that may be to your satisfaction, and to the weal, utility and comfort of your realm.

And forasmuch, dearest nephew, as we have made sundry requests heretofore unto you for the restitution of our right trusty and right well beloved cousin, the Earl of Angus, and his family, to your grace and favour, which as we have not grounded so much upon any one thing as upon the respect of their loyalty towards you, with the great love and honour they have and bear to your person; so the iniquity of the time hath not yet permitted our earnest and friendly desires therein to take that place that we wished unto them, considering how much their restitution and reconciliation to your grace and favour should tend to your honour and surety, both for that they be and have been ever true and faithful towards you, and obtaining this grace may do unto you at all times right good stead and service. And for that they have suffered a long exile without the perpetration of any so heinous an offence worthy the same, as might not with honour be remitted, trusting that the instance of our good brother the French king, who will, we doubt not, earnestly join with us in this our most earnest desire, with the grace of the time, will work that effect in this matter that may be to our satisfaction, we could not forget eftsoons and again to recommend unto you the restitution of the said Earl and his family to your grace and favour aforesaid, and to his estate and honour within your realm.

Most heartily, therefore, requiring you, dearest nephew, now to condescend to this our most instant and often repeated desire, and to vouchsafe to signify your conformity therein by your letters, wherein you shall not only administer to us such pleasure as we must both most thankfully accept and requite, as occasion may thereunto serve us, but to yourself also, and your realm, do such good as we doubt not but you shall have good cause hereafter to thank us for the notion of it.

Right excellent . . . nephew, we beseech our Lord have you in his tuition. Given under our signet at our palace of Westminster, the 22nd day of December, the 28th year of our reign.

Your loving brother and uncle,

HENRY REX.

It is interesting to note in this and a preceding letter (No. VI), the pertinacity with which Henry still tries to persuade James to allow the Earl of Angus to return to Scotland. The relationship between Henry and Angus is established clearly enough by the following letter, which helps to explain James's persistent refusal of the request. Apart from this, however, the request was bound to be refused: James never forgot nor forgave the way in which Angus and his brother had tyrannized over his boyhood, and regarded them both as his inveterate enemies. Such was the hatred with which he pursued the family that in 1537 Lady Glamis, sister of Angus, was burnt, and the Master of Forbes, his brother-in-law, was executed, on the grounds that they had plotted against the King's life.

IX. To Angus

[*Aug.* 25, 1532.]

Henry the Eighth by the grace of God King of England and of France, Defender of the Faith, and Lord of Ireland, greeting. Whereas our right trusty and right well beloved cousin, Archibald Earl of Angus, hath, by his writing subscribed with his hand, dated the 25th day of August the 24th year of our reign, promised us by his oath, and in the word of a gentleman, that in case we should move actual war to the King of Scotland, he to his possible power, with such his servants, adherents and friends as he can by any means procure, shall truly and faithfully serve us in the same; with other conditions, as in the said writing is contained. To the intent the said Earl should not in that case despair of our goodness, but be encouraged to do us service with the better good will, we have thought good to make promise to the said Earl in writing, and do promise unto him by these presents, that in case war doth ensue between us and the said King of Scots, and in the same war the said Earl of Angus do use himself according to the purport of the said writing, truly and faithfully serving us, as in the same writing is contained, and over that at the commencement and beginning of the said war, the said Earl do make unto us oath of allegiance, and recognize us as Supreme Lord of Scotland, and as his Prince and Sovereign: we then, the said Earl doing the premises, shall be reputed and taken as bound, and by these presents bind ourself, to pay yearly unto the said Earl the sum of one thousand pounds sterling, and the same yearly payment of one thousand pounds sterling to continue unto the said Earl and endure until we have by our said war reduced the said Earl into possession of his lands in Scotland, either at our hand by conquest, or at the hand of the King of Scots by our means; and further promise unto the said Earl that, he serving us in the said wars if the same chance, we shall take no appointment of peace with the said King, without comprehension, restitution of lands, and reconciliation of the said Earl. And for witness of the promises we have signed these presents with our own hand after our accustomed manner, the said 25th day of August, the 24th year of our reign.

On the early death of his first wife James confirmed the French alliance by marrying, in 1538, Mary of Lorraine, daughter of the Duke of Guise and widow of the Duc de Longueville.

The next year David Beton, who had succeeded his uncle as Archbishop of St. Andrews, was created a Cardinal by Paul III. From thenceforth the Cardinal and the Queen, both passionately devoted to the Catholic faith, were to be successively the arbiters of Scotland's policy, were to do their utmost to preserve the ancient friendship with France, and to foment hostility towards England, linking together, in a common cause, fidelity to Rome and Scotland's national independence.

Year by year, however, Henry persevered in his endeavour to establish friendly relations. In 1540 he made another overture, dangling various baits.

x. INSTRUCTIONS . . . TO RALPH SADLER,[1] ONE OF THE GENTLEMEN OF HIS GRACE'S PRIVY CHAMBER, WHOM HIS MAJESTY SENDETH AT THIS TIME INTO SCOTLAND, FOR THE PURPOSES ENSUING

. . . The second thing whereof his highness thought meet to advertise his good nephew, is, that by some it is bruited that he should gather into his hands numbers of sheep, and such other vile and mean things in respect of his estate, being the livings of the poor men, therewith to advance his revenue. Of the whilk thing the said Ralph shall say unto him, that the King's Majesty hath somewhat advised himself; and considering how, that though the things may be profitable, yet as the kind of profit cannot stand well with the honour of his estate; so it might be a mean in time to cause his subjects to mutter and mutiny, and to conceive that their livings should be by the great personages there taken from them, when they may therein be born by the like precedent and example of their prince and sovereign; whereof might ensue some inconveniences. Wherefore his majesty would wish and desire, that his good nephew, seeing the untruth and beastly living of those monks, and such other of that kind, as occupy a great part of his realm to the

[1] Sadler or Sadleir was first patronized by Cromwell, and became a gentleman of the Privy Chamber in 1536. On his return to England after this mission he became one of the King's two principal Secretaries of State. He served the state in various capacities until 1587. His last task was to reconcile James VI to the idea of the execution of his mother, Mary Queen of Scots.

maintenance of their voluptie, and the continual decay of his estate and honour, would rather apply himself by good and politic means to increase his revenue, by taking of some such of their houses and possessions in his hands, as might best be spared, and such of the rest as be most notable, to alter, as his Majesty hath done here, and convert into better uses; whereby he should well see, that one house so altered should tend more to the honour of God, and to the good order of his realm, than a number of them now doth: and with the same he might easily establish his estate in such wise as he should be able to live like a king, and yet meddle not with sheep, and those mean things, which be matter whereupon to occupy the meanest of his people. And if he will hereafter, in this point, work any thing to his commodity, giving us knowledge of his mind therein, we shall not only give unto him our best advice and counsel, but also therein to aid and help him, to bring his good determination to a perfect end and conclusion. But, if ever he will do any thing this way, he must keep it very close and secret; for, if any of his clergy may smell it, they will not fail, either by suggesting him to the wars, or by procuring some other prince or potentate to make war upon him, or by provoking of inward rebellion and treason, or by one false and untrue mean or other, to keep him in business and extreme need, or else utterly to destroy him. And therefore he must in this case (if ever in his life he intend to take any just advantage of that kind) keep it close in his own heart, making very few, and these tried and trusty, of his counsel (for eschewing of the danger, which else thereby might come to his person), to be foreseen therewith, lest if they should savour it, he live not (as the King's Majesty trusteth he shall) till he have an hoary head.

A third thing that his Majesty having upon this his most fervent love and zeal to his nephew the said king of Scots, revolved in his remembrance, is the general state and proceeding of Christendom, which his highness, being a king, hath well observed these thirty years and more, and doth by the same perceive and perfectly see, what difference there is between the honest and politic keeping, using, and living within a man's own limits, with the just consideration of his own quiet and commodity, and the following and satisfying of other men's fantasies, to their advantages and his damage; of which conclusion the king of Scots is not ignorant, knowing what displeasure happened to his father, making himself another man's instrument, to annoy his own friend and ally in his absence. Wherefore being this amity between his Majesty and the said king of Scots so like to increase and grow, as well by the mutual affection on both parties, as by the proximity of blood in the same, which can by no mean be taken away in such sort, but nature will have her instinct and operation, where too much ingratitude shall not utterly corrupt the same: His Highness having his promise of silence, and the friendly hearing and containing of his friendly advices, cannot but plainly open his heart and stomach unto him, trusting that he will no less thankfully accept his good affection therein, than deeply ponder his said good advices and counsels proceeding from the same, and to descend with him frankly to the utterance of his grace's said affection: his Majesty doth wish and desire, and even most heatily require him to weigh and ponder, what prince or potentate in Christendom may stand him in best stead, and at whose hand he may receive greatest comfort, quiet, and benefit. To speak of the Emperor, or the French King, which be nearest to us, what can he look for at either, or at both their hands, but fair words and entertainment for a time, as their instrument with his own danger to serve their purposes? Again, what stay can he think to have, or that either of them would or could stand him in, if at either of their contemplations he should bring himself to be in need of friendship and help, by attempting any thing at their desires? Now let him turn over the leaf, and consider what commodity he may attain by the favour of the King's Majesty, if he continue thus loving towards him, and show himself from time to time desirous further by his deeds to express the same. First, by the continuance of his amity with his Highness, he shall be sure to live in rest and quiet, without danger of trouble or business. Again, he can reasonably desire nothing of his Majesty to his pleasure, honour, and commodity, but he may easily obtain it. Thirdly, his Majesty would have him consider, and put in his mind, that he is his Grace's nephew, and thereby must have such place in his Highness's estimation, (dealing like a nephew towards him,) as if God should call out of this life my lord the Prince's grace, (which his mercy forbid,) and that his Highness should leave none other child of the queen that now is, or any other lawful wife which he might have hereafter; his Majesty is, by the consent of the whole realm, put in such trust for the provision of his successor, as he might of any sort or nation, without exception, at his pleasure name and appoint the same, being thereby in his free-will and power, whether he would in that case name any of his two daughters, his said nephew, or any other that for his quality, activity, and kindness to the realm, should be thought expedient. And though his Majesty may and shall, by God's grace, have some better store of issue, yet his Highness being now well stricken in years, he would not have his good nephew to forget, what nature might and peradventure would work in that case, being himself of so good a disposition towards him as he is: and so that his Majesty may perceive, on his part again, such evident arguments of sincere love and amity, as ought to be for due correspondence; showing such kindness unto his Majesty, and also to his people, as should move them to increase and augment their affection towards him, which, by reason of the ancient enmity heretofore, can hardly be pulled out of their stomachs unless a perfect and open declaration be by him and his showed now daily from henceforth to the contrary; which if it be effectually executed, his Majesty doubteth not, but verily trusteth, that those old faults shall be neglected and put in oblivion. And this is one point, which only for a perfect declaration of his most entire love and affection, his Majesty hath thought meet to open unto himself, to be by him wisely perpended, and throughly digested, and not to be opened to any other of his council, till some effect thereof may ensue. To the help and sooner setting forth whereof, his Majesty thinketh such a meeting, as in a manner was almost at a point between them, should greatly help and further. And willeth the said King of Scots to think that these things be opened unto him, only for the perfect love and affection which he beareth unto him; and not because his Grace thinketh either the French King, or the Emperor, will move him to any such attempt, as should utterly banish him for ever out of the favour of his Majesty and the realm, thinking assuredly they will never do it; but that he may by this both the better take heed to it, if they or any of them should so move him, and also know the affection of his Majesty better than ever he did, and thereupon so deal and make answer unto his Majesty as shall be most meet for his own honour, quiet, commodity, and benefit.

In the declaration of which things, the said Ralph Sadler shall most diligently note and observe his countenance, gesture, and fashion, with the very words of his answers as near as he can, and the manner of the speaking of the same; that at his return he may the better express the same to the King's Majesty, using in his declaration of those secret things a good temperance, and pithily inculking the King's Majesty's affection towards him, with the points of his advice which do touch his honour and profit, as before is declared. And if the said King of Scots shall chance, by any occasion, to speak of the King's Majesty's fortifications, the said Ralph Sadler shall recount unto him how the same be not only done in those parts, but much more in sundry other parts of the realm, in such sort as England was never the third part so strong, all things considered, as it is at this present. . . .[1]

Again in 1541 it looked for a time as if at last the often-planned meeting between Henry and his nephew might really happen. Henry was on progress in Yorkshire: James agreed to meet him; and Henry was so far convinced of his good faith as to arrange for the necessary safe-conducts.

XI. TO THE LORD CHANCELLOR (AUDELEY)

[*Aug.* 29, 1541.]

Right trusty and well beloved, we greet you well. Letting you wit, that sithens our repair towards these parts, there hath been made an overture unto us by one of the King of Scot's most secret Councillors, sent unto us for that purpose, for a meeting to be had between us, before our return in to those parts.

[1] This extract represents about half of the whole letter.

Whereunto we have made such an answer, as it is not unlike but the same may take effect. Wherefore, considering that in case the same should succeed, it is like that he will not only desire our safe conduct for himself, but also that he will send before some of his noble men and councillors to conclude upon the same, and all other things meet to be remembered in so weighty a matter, for whom he will percase also desire conduct; we have thought meet to have it, in all events, in such areadiness, as there ensue no lack or protraction, by reason of the default of the same. Wherefore our pleasure and commandment is, that, by warrant hereof, you shall cause a large and ample safe-conduct to be made and sealed with our Great Seal for the said King himself; leaving therein void spaces for the time of his abode, for the number of his train, and for his horses; and likewise that you shall make and seal with [our] Great Seal three other safe conducts for his Councillors, leaving spaces for their names, their time of abode, their horses and servants, and the same to send to us with all possible diligence. And forasmuch as this matter is yet uncertain, our pleasure is, that you shall in no wise disclose it to any of our Council there, ne that you make any mo privy to the writing and sealing of them, than very necessity shall require; the same to be first sworn that they shall disclose it to no living creature, as they will answer to God, and to us, at their uttermost peril.

Henry had the gift of persuading men of riper years and stronger character than his nephew, as witness his success with Robert Aske;[1] and it is tempting to wonder how far this interview with James might have changed the course of events, if it could have been achieved. Once again, however, Beton and the clergy intervened, and James went back on his promise. In October, Margaret Tudor died—the breaking of a link, even if it had been but a slight one at best. France, on the verge of war with England, requested that there should be no meeting between James and his uncle. James, like his father on the eve of Flodden, threw in his lot with the kingdom's ancient ally, and

[1] cf. p. 167.

refused to meet his uncle without the consent of Francis. The following extract voices Henry's righteous indignation at such treatment from his own nephew.[1]

XII. To the Scottish Ambassadors

[*Feb.* 6, 1542.]

. . . To the iiijth article, wherein our said nephew showeth that he will yet make further labour to the French king for his consent to such a meeting, and if he cannot obtain that, he will, if it please us, labour at the least for a meeting between us, the French king, and him, and there to treat a perpetual league betwixt us three: and also offereth, if it so like us, to take labours in the causes and controversies between us and the said French king, not doubting but in things honest and reasonable, the same king will use his counsel; desiring us finally to continue in hearty love towards him till such a meeting may be had, with assurance that he will in that time do the semblable: we answer touching his further labour for any such meeting between him and us, THAT IN SO DOING WE WOULD BE LOATH TO PUT HIM TO SO GREAT PAINS, SEEING HE CANNOT WITHOUT LEAVE OF OTHERS DO IT; FOR SURELY WHEN WE MADE ANSWER TO BELLENDEN OF OUR TOWARDNESS CONCERNING THE MEETING, WE THOUGHT VERILY THAT HE NEITHER NEEDED NOR WOULD HAVE ASKED ADVICE OF ANY OTHER PRINCE TO HAVE MET WITH SUCH AN UNCLE AS SINCE HIS TENDER AGE HATH SHOWED HIMSELF SO CAREFUL OVER HIM AS FEW IN CHRISTENDOM HATH SHOWED THE LIKE. AND AS TOUCHING THE MEETING BETWEEN US THREE, I HEAR NOTHING OF IT FROM OUR GOOD BROTHER OF FRANCE, WITHOUT WHOM WE PERCEIVE YOU WILL DO NOTHING; FROM WHOM IF ANY THING COME TO US IN THAT BEHALF WE DOUBT NOT TO MAKE

[1] Though it is also to be noted that in the final draft of the letter, as actually sent, the expression is briefer and more moderate, if less distinctive and vigorous. See *S.P.* V, p. 201.

HIM SUCH ANSWER AS SHALL BE TO HIS CONTENTATION AND AS DOTH APPERTAIN TO SUCH STRAIGHT AMITY AS IS BETWEEN US.

The tone of the addition in Henry's own hand[1] is eloquent of his irritation. Having made friendly advances, at intervals, for more than thirty years, he was growing exasperated at his lack of success. As in the case of his divorce, he was convinced that what he wanted was the right and proper thing; and the year 1542 marks the end of his patience. He even went so far as to be willing to agree to a plan to have James kidnapped. His Privy Council, quite properly, were shocked at the notion, and nothing came of it. But in the summer hostilities broke out once again on the Border. Sir Robert Bowes, Warden of the Middle Marches, made a raid into Teviotdale in pursuit of a party of Scots raiders. At Haddon-rigg he fell into an ambush and was taken prisoner. Henry took up the gage, and declared war, giving the following reasons.

XIII. A Declaration containing the just causes and considerations of this present war with the Scots: wherein also appeareth the true and right title that the King's Most Royal Majesty hath to his sovereignty of Scotland

Being now enforced to the war, which we have always hitherto so much abhorred and fled, by our neighbour and nephew the King of Scots, one who above all other for our manifold benefits towards him hath most just cause to love us, to honour us, and to rejoice in our quietness: We have thought good to notify unto the world his doings and behaviour in the provocation of this war, and likewise the means and ways by us used to eschew and avoid it, and the just and true occasions whereby we be now provoked to prosecute the same, and by utterance and divulging of that matter to disburden some part of our inward displeasure and grief; and the circumstances known, to lament openly with the world the infidelity of this

[1] The whole letter has corrections and additions by Henry.

time, in which things of such enormity do burst out and appear.

The King of Scots, our nephew and neighbour, whom we in his youth and tender age preserved and maintained from the great danger of other, and by our authority and power conduced him safely to the real possession of his estate, he now compelleth and forceth us, for preservation of our honour and right, to use our puissance and power against him. The like unkindness hath been heretofore showed by other in semblable cases against God's law, man's laws, and all humanity: but the oftener it chanceth, the more it is to be abhorred, and yet in the persons of princes, for the rarity of them, can so happen but seldom, as it hath now come to pass.

It hath been very rarely and seldom seen before that a King of Scots hath had in marriage a daughter of England: we can not, ne will not reprehend the king our father's act therein, but lament and be sorry it took no better effect. The king our father in that matter minded love, amity, and perpetual friendship between the posterity of both, which how soon it failed, the death of the King of Scots, as a due punishment of God for his unjust invasion into this our realm, is and shall be a perpetual testimony to their reproach for ever, and yet in that present time could not the unkindness of the father extinguish in us the natural love of our nephew his son, being then in the miserable age of tender youth: but we then forgetting the displeasure that should have worthily provoked us to invade that realm, nourished and brought up our nephew to achieve his father's possession and government, wherein he now so unkindly useth and behaveth him towards us, as he compelleth us to take armour and war against him.

It is specially to be noted upon what grounds and by what means we be compelled to this war, wherein among other is our chief grief and displeasure, that under a colour of fair speech and flattering words we be indeed so injured, contemned and despised, as we ought not with sufferance to pretermit and pass over. Words, writings, letters, messages, ambassiates, excuses, allegations could not more pleasantly, more gently, ne more reverently be devised and sent, than hath been made on the King of Scots behalf unto us; and ever we trusted the tree would bring forth good fruit, that was of the one part of so good a stock, and continually in appearance put forth so fair buds: and therefore would hardly believe or give ear to other, that ever alleged the deeds of the contrary, being nevertheless the same deeds so manifest, as we must needs have regarded them, had we not been so loath to think evil of our nephew, whom we had so many ways bound to be of the best sort towards us. And therefore having a message sent unto us the year past from our said nephew, and a promise made for the repairing of the said King of Scots unto us to York, and after great preparation on our part made therefore, the same meeting was not only disappointed, but also at our being at York, in the lieu thereof, an invasion made by our said nephew his subjects into our realm, declaring an evident contempt and despite of us: We were yet glad to impute the default of the meeting to the advice of his Council, and the invasion to the lewdness of his subjects: and according thereunto gave as benign and gentle audience to such ambassadors, as repaired hither at Christmas afterward, as if no such causes of displeasure had occurred, specially considering the good words, sweet words, pleasant words, eftsoons proponed by the said ambassadors, not only to excuse that was past, but also to persuade kindness and perfect amity to ensue. And albeit the King of Scots having contrary to the article of the league of amity, received and entertained such rebels as were of the chief and principal in stirring the insurrection in the north against us with refusal before time, upon request made to restore the same: yet nevertheless upon offer made the said ambassadors, to send commission to the Borders, to determine the debates of the confines in the same, with so great a pretence of amity and so fair words, as could be in speech desired: we were content for the time to forbear to press them over extremely in the matter of rebels. Albeit we never remitted the same, but desirous to make trial of our said nephew in some correspondence of deeds, condescended to the sending of commissioners to the Borders, which to our great charge we did, and the King of Scots our said nephew the semblable. Where after great travail made by our commissioners, this fruit ensued, that being for our part challenged a piece of our ground, plainly usurped by the Scots, and of no great value, being also for the same showed such evidence, as more substantial, more authentic, more plain and evident, can not be brought forth for any part of ground within our realm. The same was nevertheless by them denied, refused, and the evidence only for this cause rejected, that it was made (as they alleged) by Englishmen. And yet it was so ancient, as it could not be counterfeit now, and the value of the ground so little, and of so small weight, as no man would have attempted to falsify for such a matter. And yet this denial being in this wise made unto our commissioners, they nevertheless by our commandment departed as friends fro the commissioners of Scotland, taking order as hath been accustomed for good rule upon the Borders in the mean time.

After which their recess, the Lord Maxwell, Warden of the West Marches of Scotland, made proclamation for good rule, but yet added therewith, the borderers of Scotland should withdraw their goods from the borderers of England: and incontinently after, the Scottish men borderers, the fourth of July, entered into our realm suddenly, and spoiled our subjects, contrary to our leagues, even after such extremity as it had been in time of open war. Whereat we much marvelled, and were compelled therefore to furnish our Border with a garrison for defence of the same. Whereupon the King of Scots sent unto us James Leyrmouth, Master of his Household, with letters devised in the most pleasant manner, offering redress and reformation of all attemptates. And yet nevertheless at the entry of the said Leyrmouth into England, a great number of Scots, then not looked for, made a foray into our borders, to the great annoyance of our subjects, and to their extreme detriment, wherewith and with that unseemly dissimulation, we were not a little moved, as reason would we should. And yet did we not finally so extremely persecute and continue our said displeasure, but that we gave benign audience to the said Leyrmouth, and suffered our self to be somewhat altered by his words and fair promises, tending to the persuasion that we ever desired, to find the King of Scots such a nephew unto us, as our proximity of blood, with our gratuity unto him did require.

In the mean time of these fair words, the deeds of the borders were as extreme as might be, and our subjects spoiled:

and in a road made by Sir Robert Bowes for a revenge thereof, the same Sir Robert Bowes with many other taken prisoners, and yet detained in Scotland, without putting them to fine and ransom, as hath be ever accustomed. And being at the same time a surceance made on both sides at the suit of the said Leyrmouth for a season: the Scots ceased not to make sundry invasion into our realm in such wise, as we were compelled to forget fair words and only to consider the King of Scots' deeds, which appeared unto us of that sort, as they ought not for our duty in defence of our subjects, ne could not in respect of our honour, be passed over unreformed: and therefore put in a readiness our army, as a due mean whereby we might attain such a peace, as for the safeguard of our subjects we be bound to procure.

After which preparation made, and knowledge had thereof, the King of Scots ceased not to use his accustomed mean of fair words, which in our natural inclination wrought eftsoons their accustomed effect, evermore desirous to find in the King of Scots such a regard and respect to be declared in deeds as the correspondence of natural love in the nephew to such an uncle, as we have showed ourself towards him doth require. Wherefore upon new request and suit made unto us we determined to stay our army at York, appointing the Duke of Norfolk our Lieutenant, the Lord Privy Seal, the Bishop of Durham, and the Master of our Horses, there to common, treat and conclude with the Ambassadors of Scotland for an amity and peace upon such conditions as by reason and equity were indifferent, whereby the war might be eschewed, being by sundry invasion of the Scots then open and manifest.

In this communication between our and their commissioners, after divers degrees of commissions showed by the Scots, and finally one that was by our commissioners allowed, matters were proponed for conclusion of amity, nothing difficile or hard on our part, but so agreeable to reason, as the commissioners of Scotland said, they doubted not, but if it might be brought to pass, that if the King of Scots our nephew might have a meeting with us, all matters should easily be componed and determined. . . .

The communication of meeting was so handled by alteration of commission and instructions on their behalf as it appeareth a plain device only excogitate for a delay, which hath given us light whereupon more certainly to judge the King of Scots inward affection towards us, whose deeds and words well weighed and considered doth us plainly to understand how he hath continually laboured to abuse us with sweet and pleasant words, and to satisfy the appetites of other at home and abroad with his unkind and displeasant deeds. In his words he professeth an insoluble amity, he allegeth kindred, he knowledgeth benefits, only the fault is that he speaketh another language to all the world in deeds, and thereby so toucheth us in honour and denegation of justice, as we be enforced and compelled to use the sword, which God hath put in our hand as an extreme remedy, whereby to obtain both quietness for our subjects, and also that is due unto us by right, pacts, and leagues.

We have patiently suffered many delusions, and notably the last year when we made preparation at York for his repair to us: but should we suffer our people and subjects to be so oft spoiled without remedy? This is done by the Scots whatsoever their words be. Should we suffer our rebels to be detained contrary to the leagues without remedy? This is also done by them whatsoever their words be. Should be suffer our land to be usurped contrary to our most plain evidence, only upon a will, pride, and arrogance of the other party? This is done by them whatsoever their words be. And all these be over presumptuously done against us, and give such signification of their arrogance, as it is necessary for us to oppress it in the beginning, lest they should gather further courage to the greater displeasure of us and our posterity hereafter. And yet in the intreating of this matter, if we had not evidently perceived the lack of such affection as proximity of blood should require, we would much rather have remitted these injuries in respect of proximity of blood to our nephew, than we did heretofore the invasion of his father. But considering we be so surely ascertained of the lack thereof, and that our blood is there frozen with the cold air of Scotland, there was never prince more violently compelled to war than we be, by the unkind dealing, unjust behaviour, unprincely demeanour of him that yet in nature is our nephew, and in his acts and deeds declareth himself not to be moved therewith, ne to have such earnest regard to the observation to his pacts and leagues, ne such respect to the entertainment of the administration of justice, as natural equity bindeth, and conservation of amity doth require: which we much lament and be sorry for, and use now our force and puissance against him, not for revengence of our private displeasure (being so often deluded as we have been) but for recovery of our right, the preservation of our subjects from injuries, and the observation of such leagues as have passed between us, firmly trusting that Almighty God, under whom we reign, will assist and aid our just proceedings herein to the furtherance and advancement of the right, which we doubt not shall ever prevail against wrong, falsehood, deceit and dissimulation.

Hitherto it appeareth how this present war hath not proceeded of any demand of our right of superiority, which the King of Scots have always knowledged by homage and fealty to our progenitors even from the beginning:[1] but this war hath been provoked and occasioned upon present matter of displeasure, present injury, present wrong ministered by the nephew to the uncle most unnaturally, and supported contrary to the deserts of our benefits most unkindly. If we had minded the possession of Scotland, and by the motion of war to attain the same, there was never king of this realm had more opportunity in the minority of our nephew. Ne in any other realm a prince that hath more just title, more evident title, more certain title, to any realm that he can claim, than we have to Scotland, not devised by pretence of marriage, not imagined by covenant, or contrived by invention of argument, but lineally descended from the beginning of that estate established by our progenitors, and recognized successively of the kings of Scotland by deeds, words, acts and writings continually almost without interruption, or at the least intermission, till the reign of our progenitor Henry VI, in whose time the Scots abused the civil war of this realm, to their licence and boldness, in omitting of their duty: which for

[1] For the original nature of the English over-lordship of Scotland see Freeman, *Norman Conquest*, I, Chapter 3.

the proximity of blood between us, we have been slack to require of them, being also of ourself inclined to peace, as we have ever been always glad, rather without prejudice to omit to demand our right, if it might conserve peace, than by demanding thereof to be seen to move war, specially against our neighbour, against our nephew, against him whom we have preserved from danger, and in such a time as it were expedient for all Christendom to be unite in peace, whereby to be the more able to resist the common enemy the Turk.

But for whatsoever considerations we have omitted to speak hitherto of the matter, it is nevertheless true that the kings of Scots have always knowledged the kings of England superior lords of the realm of Scotland, and have done homage and fealty for the same.

This appeareth first by history, written by such as for confirmation of the truth in memory, have truly noted and signified the same. Secondly it appeareth by instruments of homage made by the kings of Scots, and divers notable personages of Scotland, at divers and sundry times sealed with their seals, and remaining in our treasury. Thirdly it appeareth by registers and records judicially and authentically made, yet preserved for confirmation of the same. So as the matter of title being most plain, is furnished also with all manner of evidences for declaration thereof. . . .

Law and reason serveth, that the passing over of time not commodious to the purpose, is not allegeable in prescription for the loss of any right. And the minority of the King of Scots hath endured xxi years of our reign, which being an impediment on their part, the whole prescription of the Scots, if the matter were prescriptible, is thus deduced evidently to xiii year, which xiii year without excuse we have ceased and forborne to demand our duty, like as the Scots have likewise ceased to offer and tend the same. For which cause nevertheless we do not enter this war, ne minded to demand any such matter, now being rather desirous to rejoice and take comfort in the friendship of our nephew, as our neighbour, than to move matter unto him of displeasure, whereby to alienate such natural inclination of love, as he should have toward us. But such be the works of God, superior over all, to suffer occasions to be ministered, whereby due superiority may be known, demanded and required, to the intent that according thereunto all things governed in due order here, we may to his pleasure pass over this life to his honour and glory: which he grant us to do, in such rest, peace and tranquillity as shall be meet and convenient for us.

Henry's temper had got the better of him. It was impolitic to the last degree for England to revive her old claim to suzerainty, if she wanted to procure an amicable union with Scotland. But the Henry of the forties was not the Henry of the twenties or the thirties. Always ready to be ruthless, if necessary, his real strength of character had been undermined by the almost limitless power which had gradually become vested in the crown; and the ruthlessness and anger which had once been his good servants were becoming bad masters. From the date of Haddon-Rig anger against the Scots for thirty years of thwarting of his wise designs and desires dominates the spirit of his dealings with them. It undoes to a great extent all the good that had been done by his more conciliatory policy, and introduces into his schemes, proposals and methods, a note of hard bargaining and of vindictiveness that were to make him in his last years the very scourge of Scotland.

Norfolk crossed the Border in October, 1542, on a punitive expedition, and laid waste the district round Tweed. He then retired to Berwick, and James planned a retaliatory raid into England. On November 24 he marched his army to the Border, hoping to take the English by surprise. But Sir Thomas Wharton, Warden of the Western Marches, was ready for them, and with a force about a sixth the size of the Scots met them and drove them back. As the Scots retreated they found the tide flowing up the Solway: many were drowned either in the sea or the Esk; and the main body, trapped in the Solway Moss with their horses, were either drowned in the bog or taken prisoner. It was a shameful and devastating defeat, and it was James's last futile gesture of defiance. The news of the disaster broke him. On December 8 Mary of Lorraine bore him a daughter. The story goes that the dying king turned his face to the wall, murmuring, 'The deil go with it. It will end as it begun. It came wi' a lass, and it will pass wi' a lass.' Within a week he was dead, and the infant Mary Stuart was Queen of Scotland.

The last letter received by James V from Henry is typical enough of the whole of their relationship—a protest from England in the matter of an outrage for which probably James himself neither was nor would have been responsible, but which was the logical outcome of the mistaken and antagonistic policy he had always pursued. Somerset Herald, returning from Edinburgh to London, had been murdered near Dunbar by two Englishmen, fugitives from the northern rebellion. Under examination one of them alleged that though not explicitly commissioned they had done the deed on the understanding that they would receive for it a substantial reward from Cardinal Beton. As an outrage it was perhaps well-calculated to serve Beton's purpose, and make reconciliation between James and Henry impossible. Whether or not he was guilty cannot be proved, but in answer to the following letter the council arrested and surrendered the murderers, and sued for a six months' truce in order to conclude a treaty of peace.

XIV. To James V

[*Dec.* 10, 1542.]

Right excellent, right high, and mighty Prince, our good brother and nephew, we commend us unto you in effectual manner. Letting you wit, that we have received your letters of the last of November, whereby you require our safe-conduct for Mr. James Leyrmouth, Sir John Campbell, and others, to repair hither unto us to declare the verity of the unhappy and cruel murder of Somerset one of our heralds-at-arms, done, as your letters purport and specify, by William Leach[1] and John Priestman, fugitives of England, whom, as you write, you have caused to be put in sure keeping. Nephew, this slaughter is so cruel,

[1] Leach of Horncastle was one of the individuals implicated in the northern rebellion who was definitely excluded from the King's pardon. See, e.g. *L.P.* XI, 1062.

so abominable, and so barbarous, as, howsoever other things stand between us, we cannot choose but most heartily wish and desire that it may appear both to us and [to] the world, that it had been committed against your will, and that you do no less detest and abhor it, than the importance of the case requireth. But, nephew, where you desire to have this declaration made here by the said Leyrmonth and others, to the intent punishment might after follow according to the quality of the crime; to that we have thought meet frankly to signify unto you that there can be no such declaration made here, as can either satisfy us, whose honour the matter most toucheth, or purge the attemptate clearly to the world, which must needs have it in extreme detestation, unless you shall first deliver the persons, whom your said letters declare to have committed the murder, to the hands of our Warden, that they may be conveyed hither, and here receive condign punishment for their most cruel and detestable enterprise. For, if you should take the punishment of them yourself, it might not only be thought to us, who hath received the displeasure of it, and is not now, as you know, in the terms of amity with you, but also to the whole world, that to cover the act, whereby it should not appear from whence it had his ground and original, though you show yourself displeased with it; yet having the matter still in your own hand, you might cause other malefactors to be executed in the lieu of the very offenders, and suffer the offenders to escape unpunished; which suspicion were in any wise to be eschewed and avoided. Wherefore, seeing the matter cannot be cleared by any mean of declaration here, but only by the deliverance of the said persons named in your said letters, we have written to our said Warden, that if it shall like you to deliver them to him or to his deputies, he shall receive them, and see them conveyed surely unto us. Right excellent, right high, and mighty Prince, our good brother and nephew, we beseech God to send you health, and to direct your proceedings to His pleasure. Given under our Signet, at our honour of Hampton Court, the 10th of December, the 34th year of our reign.

A similar protest was sent to Paget, English ambassador at Paris,[1] to be conveyed to Francis, to prevent him, if possible, from aiding the Scots.

XV. To Paget

[*Dec.* 4, 1542.]

TRUSTY AND RIGHT WELL BELOVED, we greet you well. And herewithall we send unto you the copy of a declaration, which we have caused to be made and published to the world touching the grounds and causes of the war now open between us and Scotland; the discourse whereof being well noted and imprinted in your mind, albeit you shall be well able to declare and prove that this war was first procured and moved by the Scots, and how we were enforced to the same, before we would in any wise enter in it; yet, forasmuch as the Scots have sithens sought all ways and means possible how to heap and amass injury upon injury against us, and, like most cruel and barbarous people, have not only refused to render for ransom such prisoners as they took when we were in treaty of peace with them, but also have most cruelly and pitifully, *contra jus gentium*, and against all laws of arms and order used amongst Princes, to the most pernicious example and extreme danger of all ministers, slain and murdered Somerset, one of our heralds at arms, being sent with letters to the King of Scots from our Lieutenant for delivery of the said prisoners, as he was returning homewards, with their answer of refusal of the same, as by certain copies sent unto you herewith you shall perceive; we have thought meet to will and command you upon the receipt hereof to make your access to our good brother the French King, and after our most hearty commendations to declare to the same, both how the said Scots did provoke and enforce us to this war at the beginning, and how they have since in the refusal to render our prisoners for ransom, contrary to the order ever used in wars between England and Scotland till this day, as themselves do confess, and in this

[1] b. 1505, d. 1563. A man of ability, who rose steadily, and became a member of the Privy Council in 1543. During the last years of the reign he and Hertford were probably Henry's most trusted advisers. Henry's will appointed him one of the governors of Edward VI.

most cruel murdering of our messenger and herald-at-arms having his coat on his back, and also a pursuivant of Scotland appointed to conduct him, to the intent as it doth evidently appear they might be the more sure to have him in the way at such place as it appeareth they had determined for that purpose; the like treachery being never before heard of amongst the most cruel and barbarous people of the world. Wherefore you shall on our behalf most heartily desire and pray our good brother the French King, that, seeing we have been thus used by the said Scots, he will, in respect of our amity and of the treaty between us, take order that none of his subjects shall in any wise directly or indirectly favour, aid or assist them, but that he will for his part deal with us in this matter uprightly, as we do, and have done, in this time of trouble between him and the Emperor. And if he shall allege that the Scot is his old confederate, and that he is bound by treaty to aid and assist him for defence of his own; to that you may answer, that if he so do, he shall not do with us as we have done with him in this trouble between him and the Emperor. For we might have given the Emperor aid when he was now invaded, which we did not, but kept ourself indifferent, and so we trust he will do now with us, and not give aid to the Scot, seeing that all this matter hath his original of him, and also that he hath sithens used himself as is declared. And further you may say, it is specially provided by treaty, that, in case the Scot enter into England with above one hundred men, he shall not be taken as a comprehens in their amity. And seeing he hath not only entered, both at the beginning, and now lately, with many thousands, but also used himself thus barbarously towards us, you may say we have such a trust and opinion that, both for his own honour, and also in respect of our friendship, and of our proceedings with him, he will in no wise make himself any party with him. And what his answer shall be hereunto, and what you can further learn of his inclination in this and all other occurrents, our pleasure is you shall give us advertisement with all possible diligence.

To Henry the death of James seemed an assurance that the opportunity for which he had always schemed had at last arrived, and that union between England and Scotland was now within his grasp. On January 4, 1543, he wrote to the Scots Council.

XVI. To the Council of Scotland

We greet you well. Letting you wit that we have received your letters dated at Edinburgh the 20th of December, containing your determination for such punishment of those malefactors that murdered our herald, as may be to the world the purgation of your innocency for the same, and moreover the death of your late master our nephew, whose soul God pardon, with your suit and desire to send ambassadors unto us for the appointment of great matters as ye write, such as might tend to the wealth of that realm and the surety of our said nephew's daughter, which he hath left in very tender age, and further a request for an abstinence of six months as in your said letters is contained. For answer whereunto, you shall understand that in doing that ye intend for your purgation to the world of that detestable act in the murder of our herald, ye shall show for so much to have regard and respect to your own reputation : And as touching the death of our nephew in this time of enmity, whatsoever our worldly quarrel was towards him and that realm, we cannot for our natural conjunction and proximity of blood but be sorry for his death, and love the daughter he hath left, being our proniece, as kindred should of congruence require us to do, which we intend so to declare both to you and the world as we shall discharge our honour in that behalf. Wherein if you show that towardness in deeds, whereunto wisdom and her wealth ought to persuade you, conforming yourself to the mind and opinion of those that earnestly mind the wealth of both these realms, it shall shortly appear, without tract and delay of time unfruitfully consumed in the ceremony of ambassades, that we both love our said proniece, the wealth of that realm, and hate no one of you further than your particular practises and doings shall deserve. In which matter we, upon humble suit of such as were here prisoners with us, were content to hear such overtures as they for the wealth of the realm made unto us, who with our licence, upon hostages and pledges given, repair now unto you. Wherefore agree you shortly together to make jointly such special suit and in certain and plain terms unto us, as we with reason and honour may accept, whereupon we shall for our part do as becometh us, and use our proniece and you in such sort as you shall have no cause to repent. But think not that we will waste time in communication of words, ne upon trust of fair language, pretermit the opportunity offered of God to unite these two realms in one govern[ment], if not by conformity as we most desire, otherwise as it shall please God to aid and assist us; and therefore, referring the opening of this matter to such of our prisoners and other of your country as now repaireth thither, we shall conclude this our letter with these few words: that as you use yourself towards us jointly or apart, and declare in your deeds that you mean earnestly the wealth and preservation of our proniece, and of the good government of that realm, so shall we use you for your wealths, commodities, and particular advancements; and ye doing the contrary, we shall prosecute you and use you as your deserts in this case shall justly require. For albeit our proniece cannot, as you write, neither offend God nor man, yet under a feigned pretence of her, and not searching that may be to her certain preservation, ye may offend both God and man, which you shall do wisely to avoid and eschew, and do so as you may obtain rest, peace, tranquillity and favour. And therefore what ye will do herein by one whole consent or the consent of such as will agree in reason, signify unto us or to our lieutenant the Duke of Suff(olk), who now repaireth to the Borders, with speed your resolution, in special, absolute, and certain terms, to the intent upon knowledge thereof we may condescend upon your suits to such an abstinence as shall be requisite for the further conclusion and perfection of the same.

To all such as take upon them the government of Scotland, and to all others either of the nobility or of the Council there.

Orders were sent to Lord Lisle[1] on the Border to be in readiness to support any active measures that might have to be taken.

[1] John Dudley, afterwards Duke of Northumberland.

XVII. TO LISLE

[*Jan.* 9, 1543.]

RIGHT TRUSTY AND RIGHT WELL BELOVED COUSIN, we greet you well. Letting you wit that considering with ourself how that we do at this time stay our sword and force lying on the Borders, and that we be not yet by any certain mean assured that the borderers of Scotland shall do the semblable: we have thought that it should much confer both the surety of our Borders, and to the advancement of the strength and force of our party, to have a proclamation made upon all our Marches, that whatsoever borderer will come in to you within 15 days next after the making of the same, and promise to stand with us in the first article concerning the getting of the child into our hands, and the government of that realm, subscribing his hand to the same, and also that he shall not attempt any displeasure to our realm and subjects, the same so coming in and promising as aforesaid, to be taken as our friend and to be so used; and he that will not so do to be reputed as an enemy to us and our purpose in that behalf, and to be used as an enemy as opportunity shall serve for the same. In which matter we have written to our trusty &c. Sir Richard Southwell Knight &c., to feel the opinions of the Scottish Lords now at Darneton,[1] and to advertise you of the same; willing and requiring you, in case you shall perceive by his advertisement that they shall think the same good and convenient to be put in execution, you will cause such a proclamation to be incontinently made upon all our Borders, to the intent you may see who will conform themselves to it, and who will not, that every man may after be used according to his deserving. Furthermore, you shall understand that, albeit it is specified in our former letters and instructions to Mr. Southwell, you, and Sir Thomas Wharton, that the special cause of the enterprise to be now made, upon the consultation had amongst them at Darneton, is to get the child, the person of the Cardinal, and of such as be chief letters of our purpose, and also of the chief holds and fortresses, into our hands; yet no mention is made, to whom the said castles and fortresses shall in that case be delivered. Wherefore, like as we have also written

[1] i.e. Darlington.

to Sir Richard Southwell therein, and willed him to signify our pleasure in the same to the Lords at Darneton, and of the whole to give you advertisement; so we have thought meet to require you that, in case our 4000 men shall enter, upon the resolution of this consultation, you will instruct all our chieftains and counsellors that shall enter to have special regard to that point. And when it shall come in question amongst them, to whose custody any of the said fortresses shall be delivered, albeit they shall in no wise seem to mistrust the Scots, yet they shall bend as much as they may that the same may indeed be appointed to some English man, having also special regard that before they depart out of the country they see the said hold furnished with victual, munition, ordnance and all things necessary, according to the purport of our letters written to the said Richard Southwell accordingly. . . .

At Solway Moss the Earls of Cassilis and Glencairn, together with five barons and some five hundred lairds and gentlemen, had been taken prisoners. Cassilis and Glencairn and other important individuals Henry now bound by pledges—and hostages—to support the union with England. The following extracts from a letter to Sir Richard Southwell make it quite clear just what Henry was demanding.

XVIII. To Sir Richard Southwell

First, for the better information and instruction of the said Sir Richard Southwell, the same shall understand that the Scots prisoners at their being here have all condescended and agreed to an article subscribed with their hands, wherein they require the King's majesty to take into his hands and government the young daughter of Scotland, and also of the whole realm, with promise to serve the King's highness to that intent, as the said Sir Richard by the copy of that article sent unto him herewith shall perceive, unto which article also the Earl Bothwell hath likewise subscribed; so as this article is taken among the prisoners and also the Lord Bothwell as an open matter not to be kept secret of them, but to be openly knowledged and avowed as a thing tending to the high wealth and benefit of all the realm of Scotland.

Moreover ten of the prisoners, that is to say the Earls of Cassilis, Glencairn and the Lord Maxwell, the Lord Fleming, the Lord Somervile, the Lord Grey, Robert Erskine, Oliver St. Clair, the Lord Cragge and Kerse, these ten as men pretending a more near and earnest devotion to the King's majesty, have subscribed an article that in case of the death of the daughter, the King's highness will take upon him the crown and government of the realm of Scotland, they will serve his Majesty to their powers in that behalf, as by the copy of that article sent herewith may appear; and so this is a secret article, known only to these ten, and not opened hitherto to the Lord Bothwell nor any other of them; for albeit the Lord Bothwell hath heretofore promised more largely to the King's majesty, yet nevertheless the same hath not been spoken of unto him, lest the secrecy promised to the other ten should be percase impaired; which the said Sir Richard shall show to the said ten, devising with them not to be a known of it to the Lord Bothwell, to the intent he shall not be miscontent or conceive suspicion that all the proceedings here hath not been opened unto him, and also because it is to be feared that he should be something addict to the Earl of Arran.

Enclosed with the letter to Southwell were the following secret articles.

(fol. 59) The copy of the Secret Article whereunto the ten only named in the instructions have subscribed.

Where it was proponed unto us by his Majesty and his most noble council that if the said daughter were deceased what we thought then most necessary to be done for the wealth of the realm of Scotland? To that we answer that for the wealth of the same, if it would please his Grace to take the whole rule, dominion, and government of that realm upon him that the same may be governed in peace, tranquillity, and justice to be furtherborne in the said realm; we now, his Grace's prisoners, shall to that purpose, when we shall be at our liberty in Scotland, serve his Majesty after our powers with bodies, puissance, and hearts to our uttermost.

(fol. 60) [The Article to be signed by Angus.]

First: where I have been advertised that the King of Scots is deceased, having left a daughter now alive, I think it most expedient and humbly beseech the King's majesty that he will vouchsafe to take into his hands the government and keeping of that daughter to the intent that his Highness may marry the same to my lord prince his Grace's son, and by means thereof to clear all titles and to unite both realms, seeing to the good rule and administration of justice as well of the realm of Scotland as of the realm of England, for the quietness, tranquillity, and common wealth of them both; whereunto I shall aid and serve his Majesty to the uttermost of my power according to my bounden duty.

And whether the said daughter shall chance to come to his Majesty's hands or not, or shall fortune to die hereafter or otherwise be exployed, I think it shall be highly for the wealth of Scotland if it will please his Grace to take the whole rule, dominion, and government of that realm upon him, that the same may be governed in peace, tranquillity, and justice to be furthborne in the same realm; whereunto I shall also serve his majesty to the uttermost of my power, according to my most bounden duty.

These pledges exacted from his prisoners, Henry then sent them back to Scotland, in the wake of Angus and his brother Sir George Douglas. In much of the correspondence they are alluded to as the 'assured Scots', and their task was to form an Anglo-Scots party in the government, to ensure the carrying out of Henry's plans. Just how entirely his will was set upon their accomplishment may be gauged from the fact that, contrary to the universal custom of the time, he exacted no ransoms at all from any of his prisoners.

For the moment it looked as if he would succeed. Beton was imprisoned, and the second Earl of Arran who, as next heir to the throne after the infant queen, had been appointed Regent, threw in his lot with the English party. In March, 1543, the Scottish Parliament passed an Act which permitted the use in Scotland of the English Bible, and in the following letter Henry did his best to urge on the good work, sending detailed instructions for the dissolving of the Scottish monasteries and the confiscation of their revenues. Alterations in his own hand testify once again to the care with which he scrutinized the document.

XIX. To Sadler

[*April* 4, 1543.]

Trusty and right well beloved, we greet you well. Letting you wit that having received your letters of the 27th of March, and perceiving by the contents of the same how the Governor of Scotland hath showed himself to be of good inclination to favour our affairs, having specially declared the zeal he hath to the advancement and setting forth of the Word of God, with his desire to the extirpation of hypocrisy and superstition maintained in the state of monks and friars, and the reducing of the clergy to such good order and reformation as they may abandon the usurped authority of the Bishop of Rome, and knowledge such obedience to their prince as they ought by God's laws, and thirdly, the affection of the said governor which he allegeth to have to prefer the marriage of the young princess to our son, rather than to his own, which he allegeth he might have obtained by parliament, if he had so minded: forasmuch as in these three points there hath not been hitherto on our behalf anything particularly spoken whereby to declare how we accept and embrace the same, we have thought good to instruct you amply, sithens as by your letters we perceive he hath desired our advice and help in that behalf, how to devise and commune with the said governor in the same. . . .

First, as concerning the setting forth of the Word of God, we think requisite to admonish him of that which by experience we know to be true, that it shall be necessary to foresee that in publishing to the people the Scripture, he causeth them therewith to be admonished to receive the same reverently and humbly with a desire TO LEARN BY IT HOW[1] they may direct their manners, living, and true worshipping of God, AND NOT BY[2] carnal fancy to frame themself such vain and evil opinions as hath by seditious persons been raised in the heads of unlearned people, tending to the subversion of policy and the confusion of good and godly order in the Church. For eschewing whereof, all such books must be forbidden and defended as be printed in the English tongue beyond the seas, and also all such other books from whence soever they come, which tend to that purpose, and the only Scripture to be permitted among the people for the first, till other books may be set forth by public authority containing a pure true doctrine, neither swerving to the left hand of iniquity, ne to the right hand with other pretence of holiness than is agreeable to God's truth. Wherein ye may say we have taken labour and pains, and with God's grace shall shortly bring them to perfection, and establish such a certain doctrine as is maintainable by the mere truth, and such as no man shall be able to impugn and disallow. Which as soon as it shall be perfect we shall send unto him to be there published, for the conjunction of these realms in one unity of the true understanding of God's Word, whereby to eschew the frenzies[3] and dreams of the inferior people on the one side, and the corruption of hypocrisy and superstition brought in and persuaded by the Bishop of Rome and his adherents on the other part.

As concerning the second point, for the extirpation of the state of monks and friars, the enterprise whereof requireth politic handling, it shall be first necessary that the governor send substantial and faithful commissioners, as it were to put a good order in the same, and to provide that they may live the more honestly without wasting of such things as they have in their possession belonging to their churches, or the letting or alienation of those lands and farms which be most commodious for them. Which commissioners must have secret commission most secretly and

[1] *Thereby to be instructed and learned of the will and pleasure of God according whereunto* deleted.

[2] *Without any* deleted.

[3] MS. *fransyes*. *L.P.* read *fancies*.

groundly to examine all the religious of their conversation and behaviour in their livings, whereby if it be well handled, he shall get knowledge of all their abominations; and that once gotten, he with the chief of the noble men, agreeing with them for the distribution of some of the lands of the abbeys to be divided to himself and among them, which shall be to their great profit and benefit, we think good that the governor should treat thereof; and then, with the bishops apart, or some such of them as be most tractable, and making unto them as assurance of their estate, should also offer unto them some augmentation by annexing to their small portions some of such small houses as lie conveniently for them, and also to devise with them for the alteration of certain other abbeys to the state of secular priests, with finding[1] of poor lame men, of scholars to the university, as their portion may serve, whereby the state of the clergy shall be better preserved and in a more decent order than it is now in. And then with both parties, both bishops and temporal lords, to devise how necessary it is to allot a good portion of those lands of the abbeys to the augmentation of the state of the king and the[2] young queen, and their heirs and successors, so as they may be able to maintain their estate upon the public revenues, and not enforced in times of peace to seek such ways as their late king did, whereby to grieve and annoy his people. And it is to be thought that the platform of the disposition of those abbeys being in this wise made and known before, particularly to what uses they should be employed as afore, with a reasonable provision for the entertainment of the religious men now being in them, and for term of their lives, the proceeding to the execution in the suppression of the same, will be the more easy and facile among such as will understand the truth, and knowledge the abominable life continued among those which now in diversities of sects usurp those places, not only to the high displeasure of God, but also as a great deformity in the commonwealth, spending their time in all idleness and filthyness with such face of hypocrisy and superstition as is intolerable.

[1] *Hamilton Papers* and *L.P.* read ' sending '. To ' find ' is the usual phrase in the sixteenth century for ' to keep ' or to support any one with an allowance of money.

[2] I have corrected this passage from the fair copy.

Thirdly, ye shall say that whereas the said Earl hath said that for declaration of his affection towards us, he hath forborn to practise the marriage of the Princess of Scotland with his son, and procured the same to be agreed unto by the parliament there to be concluded with our son—albeit the appearance thereof is not great, for that it is to be thought that they would not so disparage their Queen as to marry her to an Earl's son in her own realm—yet you may show unto him that we have in such wise accepted his demeanour hitherto in all the affairs of Scotland, that we have in our own breast devised such ways and means for the advancement of the reputation of his blood as he may have cause to rejoice and take comfort in his conformity to our proceedings. For ye may say that whereas we have a daughter called the Lady Elizabeth, endowed with virtues and qualities agreeable with her estate, whom we esteem and regard, as natural inclination, with respect of her place and state, doth of congruence require: we have determined in our heart, if we shall see him sincerely to go through with us in all things, to condescend to a marriage to be celebrate between his son and our said daughter, if he shall think it for his honour and advancement to desire the same, and thereby to take his son so conjoined with our daughter as our son-in-law, being content according to that estate to bring up and nourish him in our court with us. By reason whereof, all other commodities not counted, the governor may perceive that by means thereof he shall with the estimation of our authority be able to retain and keep the place he now occupieth quietly and peaceably without interruption; which else percase might be very dangerous, for doubtless if he make a secret and due search what was minded by their lords and bishops that would not come in to him at the first, we think he shall perceive a combination to his destruction, with the Earl of Angus and all that party, and the putting of the Cardinal to liberty, and the taking of the young Queen into their hands, and mayhap not without the consent of the Dowager. Which thing, though they now could not bring to pass, yet be they sworn one to another to prove it and not to desist at some one time or other to bring it to pass; which if they by their own policy cannot find the means shortly to bring to light, we doubt not, they proceeding with us according to our expectation, to bring it to their knowledge. And ye may say that ye doubt not but even at this day the governor may perceive that all draw not by one line, and that the parliament matters have no greater authority than power can uphold them; and albeit there is now nothing openly said against him, there hath been privy mutterings and whisperings specially against him, which upon occasions might burst out and be greater. And forasmuch as we perceive him that he is specially affected to the setting forth of God's word, and the advancement of God's glory in the extirpation of hypocrisy and usurped authority by the Bishop of Rome, in the execution whereof may arise amongst carnal men grudge and displeasure, we think that he joining with us in this marriage and the education of his son, shall be great stay and assistance to his proceedings, so as he may the more boldly proceed in that godly enterprise, and the adversaries the more afraid to resist and withstand him or to enterprise anything to his disquietness. And what honour, what reputation, what worldly glory, it shall be to him otherwise, for his son to marry a King of England's daughter, and to be nourished up thereafter in a King of England's court, we doubt not but[1] he can consider! And ye may say ye have commission to break this matter secretly unto himself, by whom it is to be handled with his most trusty friends, and not many, in such sort as other may not have opportunity to let it; which percase diverse would do, and not be content that the governor's son should be here, knowing that then the governor himself could suffer no displeasure in his estate, but with his son in our hands, should have commodity to revenge it, which we would not fail to do, being his son married to our daughter. And this is the only way and mean for the governor to keep his place and establish his blood in surety; whereas else many practises may be excogitate, and devices contrived upon occasions, much to his unsurety and danger of his blood, which by this device may be preserved. And whereas the governor hath now but an office there for a time among them until their young queen come to age and then she living and coming to age, his authority of government to be extinct, he shall by this marriage obtain both to himself and his son and

[1] MS. *be*.

their posterity, a root and foundation of a certain perpetual honour and surety. For if this marriage take effect with our daughter, whatsoever otherwise befall of the young princess, both he and his son remain so provided for, as he could hardly have wished or desired the better. And with these and such like reasons ye may set out this general overture as proceeding from us to be opened unto him secretly, fashioning the matter so as the reasons to enforce the overture may seem to proceed from you, as of yourself, lest he should think that we, in the pressing of him to embrace it, should mean otherwise our own commodity, where indeed it is such as he should embrace upon a word spoken. And yet because he is a man that seeth not deepliest in these matters, it shall be good ye lay all thing before him, and set forth such reasons as we have written, and other such as ye can devise for that purpose, binding always upon him to send his son hither if the marriage shall take effect, whatsoever allegation of aught or other matter he would allege. For that is a special point not to be omitted, and without which there could grow unto him no reputation. For if his son come not, it shall be called but a worldly practise and a talk : if he come, it shall be truly taken for a thing done, and be terror to his evil-willers and a plain declaration of his benevolence towards us. Wherefore ye shall press him to know what answer he will make unto you and signify the same unto us with diligence.

The Act permitting the use of the English Bible was an earnest of success in more vital matters; but the letter that follows suggests that the 'assured Scots' were not as assured as might be wished, and there were still many difficulties to be overcome if a settlement was to be reached. Incidentally it names the leaders of the rival French and English parties and calls our attention to the return from France of the Earl of Lennox, of whom more is to be heard.

XX. To Sadler

By the King

Henry R. [*April* 14, 1543.]

Trusty and right well beloved, we greet you well. And by the continue of your letters of the 6th of this present do perceive such conference as you have had with the Earl of Angus, the Lord Maxwell, and Sir George Douglas, touching the effect of our letters addressed unto you the 30th of March; wherein we specially note how the said Douglas affirmeth he is free of all such promises, as the rest, like men, as he sayeth, which knew not what they did, ne were able to perform the same, have promised unto us; which words he hath used to you and others in sundry communications heretofore, and was yet never answered to them: and also how they would excuse themselves of their slack dealings towards us by that there was a Governor named before their coming home; joining therewithal how they be there divided into two parties, naming the Earls of Argyle, Murray, Huntley, and Bothwell, with all the bishops and clergy of the realm, and their part-takers, to be of the one; which be all given to the cast of France: and the Governor, with the Earls of Angus, Glencairn, Cassilis, and the Lord Maxwell, with their friends, to be of the other party; which, the said Douglas sayeth, be given to the cast of England.

Second, the fickleness and inconstancy which they note to be in the Governor, whereby they seem to fear his revolt to the adverse party being for France, in case he should be any thing pressed for our purpose: considering how the Earl of Huntley, being a chief fautour of that party, and others of that sort, have liberty to insinuate themselves unto him, and to put in his ear, what he and his band shall think for them expedient.

And finally, the arrival of the Earl of Lennox, with his words and the fashion of his proceedings, sithens his coming home, as Sir George Douglas reporteth the same.

For answer whereunto you shall understand, that, considering in what incertain terms those matters stand at this present, and minding, as you may perceive by our former letters, to decipher the ground of their intents, to the end we may thereupon direct our affairs as appertaineth; our pleasure is that you shall, upon the receipt hereof, take opportunity to confer eftsoons with the said Douglas and the rest signified in our said former letters, touching the state of the matters between us and Scotland.

And first, when you shall take occasion to provoke the said Sir George Douglas to repeat the words by him so often spoken, touching his liberty and freedom from all the promises made by his brother, and those which were here our prisoners, whereupon he shall eftsoons utter the same; you shall, as it were of yourself, tell him plainly and in a frank manner that you have been sorry to hear him so often speak of that sort as he hath done, implying in effect as though he owed us neither suit nor service, but at his pleasure; where indeed yourself knoweth that no man (his brother excepted) hath made so large promises unto us as he hath done, who hath heretofore bound himself, without condition, to be and remain for ever our true and faithful subject. And you may say that you have heard credibly that even at his last repair into those parts, when he spake with us in the lodge in the park at Windsor, he did not only repeat unto ourself his bond and promise in that behalf, but also spake unto us many other things as touching the Crown of Scotland, with such like things which be of too great importance to be now so far out of his memory, that he may conveniently say that he hath not promised so largely as the rest, where indeed his promises be far larger. And therefore you may tell him, that your advice and counsel is that he leave that kind of language, and that he apply himself to accomplish that which he hath promised, and specially whilst he is in that place and authority that he may do what he list, which hath no such certainty of continuance but it may alter or he be ware, unless he weigh things otherwise than he doth yet, and prevent the dangers, by getting the holds into their hands, and the following and setting forth of our purposes in such sort, (wherein consisteth his honour and surety) as we may see both he and the rest mind indeed that they have said and promised unto us.

Second, where they labour all to excuse themselves unto us concerning the omitting of their said promises, by the election of the Governor before their return and entry in to Scotland, declaring therewithal that they rest at this present divided in the two parties before specified; to that you may answer, that the naming of the Governor before their entry can be none excuse to them, if their proceedings hereafter should not redubbe that which hath been omitted. For, like as they cannot be charged with those things which were done before their return, howsoever the same weigh for or against our purposes; so it cannot be avoided but the establishment of him to be Governor and second person of the realm by act of Parliament, whereunto they gave their voices, was directly against their promise. Nevertheless you may say, that you perceive we take that excuse in good part, having a certain opinion that their doings hereafter shall declare that it was indeed against their minds to consent unto it, if it might have been at that time otherwise framed.

And, as to their division into two parties, you may say that, as they speak it, so we know it to be such indeed as they had need to have special regard to it. For if their adverse party may by any means, fair or foul, prevail against them, let them make a sure account and reckoning that they shall shortly so smart for it as shall be to their confusions; which, if they be wise men, having this warning, they will foresee and prevent in time, having now the place and authority to do it; which not taken in season may be forethought when it shall be too late to repent it. And where they all note inconstancy in the Governor, you may tell them that, if he be a man of that disposition, they had the more need to have a good eye to him, and to give him the better advice and counsel, what is expedient for him also to consider in that part; wherein they may use this division of parties for France and England, with the difference between him and the clergy and others in religion, and for a mean to induce him both to stand fast to our party, and to beware how he shall trust those which be given to the contrary faction. And upon this ground they may devise with him, that what face soever the said Governor shall make outwardly, as though he made them all privy to all his proceedings, it shall be most necessary for him that he shall elect only five or six sure persons to be used in his secret matters. For it may be inculked to him, that if he should chance to revolt to the other party, he may be sure that the bishops and clergy, with their part-takers, knowing his disposition and opinion as they do, will shortly dispatch him, yea, percase when he shall think himself most assured amongst them; which shall also follow at length, though he relent not to them, if he make those which be assured of their party privy to his secret intents and proceedings: which two things, well impressed in his head, shall not only confirm him in his good disposition towards us, but also shall cause him to give less credit to the Earl of Huntley, and those which, for the only achieving of their own purpose, would seem now for the time to be most assured unto him. . . .

Furthermore you shall understand, that the Ambassadors of Scotland had access to our presence on Wednesday last, and delivered unto us letters from the Governor, containing generally the overture of the contract of the marriage and the perpetual peace, with further credence, as by the copy of the said letters, which you shall receive herewith, you shall perceive. And forasmuch as they pressed not to make any further declaration unto us, but only stood with good words upon the said two points expressed in the letters, we dismissed them, and referred them for their further conference in the particularities of their matters to our Council, with whom they dined on Thursday last. And after dinner our said Council declared unto them the effect of the letters which they presented unto us, and how it had pleased us that the further opening of the matters should be amongst them; requiring them therefore that it might like them to proceed in the same with us accordingly. Whereupon they produced two commissions made in the Queen's name, and sealed with her great Seal, and also with the Governor's seal, and subscribed with his own hand; the one containing power and authority to contract the marriage, and to determine of the custody of the Queen's person; the other to conclude the peace, with a blind clause of liberty to renounce all other leagues contrary to this which they desire. Upon the reading of which two commissions, it was told them by our said Council that they well perceived whereunto the said commissions tended; nevertheless for that the same were long, and such as were not in all things conceived after the accustomed form, and could not therefore thoroughly and in every point be well conceived at the first reading, they put them in remembrance how their letters contained credence besides the points contained both in the letters and the said commissions; requiring them, in case they had any special credence besides, that it might like them first to declare unto them the same, to the intent they might advertise us of it. Whereunto they answered, they had none, but such as depended upon the two points contained in the said letters. And then Sir James Leyrmouth made a certain declaration of the Governor's good will towards us, and how of his humanity (as he called it) he had left the marriage of their young Queen which he might have had for his son, if he would have followed it, to satisfy us, and in respect of the common wealth of their realm. And after him Mr. Balnaves made a certain discourse of their desire to this alliance and amity, framing his tale nevertheless as though it had been desired by us; wherein was some altercation amongst them, and the matter plainly opened, how it was moved by the prisoners upon the hand of God which happened upon their apprehension. And, being these things brought to silence, our Council began again, and required them to declare frankly the particularities of the two points contained in their commissions, to the intent they might in like manner advertise us of the same. Whereunto they answered, first, that they had power to contract the marriage, and to capitulate that it should not only be confirmed by their Parliament; but also that all the nobles of Scotland shall give their seals for the performance of the same, with this condition, that their Queen shall not depart out of their realm, till she be of full age to consummate her matrimony. And as to her education, they offered that we should at our pleasure appoint two knights and two ladies of England to be about her person; adding hereunto that they would have the Governor that is now, to be Governor of that realm during her minority, and also after for term of his life, and that they would have a Governor of the birth of that realm ever after at their own election, with the free use of their own laws and customs, and also the chief holds of Scotland not be delivered till she had issue by our son.

Second, they said they had power to contract the peace, till she should come of lawful age, or for forty, threescore, or one hundred years, or to make it perpetual, and in the same to leave out the provision for France, which in the last treaty they would not consent to have in any wise omitted. To this it was answered by our Council that they were sorry to perceive their commission to be so slender; for as to the first, they said they saw small surety in the bare contract without other assurance than they spake of, and that it was too absurd, and might not stand with the office of a King, either to have any man placed in his realm as a

Governor, but such as he should appoint under him, or to have any part of his dominion appertaining to him, in other hands than he should appoint and think convenient. And as to the second, our Council asked them, whether they would not renounce their leagues with France, and become friend to friend, and enemy to enemy. Whereunto they answered, that they would not meddle with France, but they might not enter such a pact as should testify that they determined plain enmity against them. Which things heard, our Council told them they would inform us of the same; and so for that time they departed.

And being the premises immediately signified unto us by our Council, we resolved that they should yesterday meet again with the said ambassadors at Westminster, and declare unto them plainly that, being informed of their purpose holden on Thursday, and considering well the points and effect of the same, we were sorry to perceive that they proceeded no more frankly with us. And, to advertise them resolutely to what point we would grow in these matters, first, it was told them that we can be well content to accept the contract with the assurance of their Parliament and noble men's seals upon the same, so as we may have the child delivered at convenient time after into our hands. At which point we stood awhile with them. And perceiving them to stick sore at that, then came we to this point, to have pledges in the mean season delivered unto us, both for the same, and for the peace; and such personages, both of England and Scotland, to be about her person as we should think for her better education and surety convenient. For it should not be convenient for us to put the marriage of our son in suspense, who is a Prince to be desired for the daughter of any king in Christendom, unless we might have better assurance than bare words and writings, that this agreement should, God willing, take certain effect. Neither shall it be meet that he be matched with any personage but such as may before have some knowledge of the nurriture and fashion of this realm. And as to the Governor, it was answered, that we having a regard to his towardness and good will towards us, with his zeal to the wealth of that country, could be content that he, continuing in the same good sort, should have the rule and government of the country during her minority, and also after under us and our son, if he use himself as appertaineth. And likewise we could be content to elect such a Scottishman to have the government after, under us and our said son, appointing to him such counsellors as we should think convenient; which is as much as can in this case be desired, unless they would in deed prescribe a government to their king and governor, which the nature of his place and office can in no wise admit or suffer: ne we will in any wise be otherwise bound unto them than is specified. And likewise we can be pleased that they shall continue their laws and customs. And this we resolved for the first point; and that their chief holds should by consent be committed to such Scottishmen's keeping as we should think meet for the same.

To the second it was answered that, if they would contract a perpetual peace, and in the same bind both parties to be friend to friend and enemy to enemy, we would gladly go through with it; which, howsoever this thing should chance, must needs be most beneficial unto them, being our amity the most propice for them of any in Christendom; and yet by this pact they shall not seem specially to covenant against France, ne to do any thing but, the cause of this league considered, must needs appear most honest, and for them most beneficial and necessary. And thus we resolved for the second point. Whereunto they answered that they could not conclude thoroughly in all these things without advertisement, desiring respite to write home for that purpose; which was granted them, so as the certain answer might be accelerated.

There was some reasoning between them and our Council, in the debating of this matter, touching our title to Scotland, which was spoken of by reason of a request they made that, if she should die without issue, the realm should remain to the next heir of blood there, whereby they would have had us made an entail, which should have implied a grant that there rested in us no right to that realm. But it was so quickly cast off, and our title so vively repeated, that that matter fell, and finally they desired to have our resolution in writing, offering to go with it, or to send it, for the more expedition and better framing of all things to purpose. Which we granted, and thereupon delivered them a schedule, the copy whereof you shall receive, to the intent you may in express words join with them in the matter of the same.

The real triumph of the year, however, was the signing of the Treaty of Greenwich on July 1. It was a reasonable treaty. By it a peace was made between the two countries, which was to last till a year after the death of either of the contracting parties. Further, a marriage treaty between Prince Edward and Mary Stuart was finally agreed on. Mary was to remain in Scotland with her mother till the age of ten, and six Scots nobles were to be her hostages at the English court. In the event of there being issue from the marriage, and of the uniting of the two crowns, the name, laws and ancient liberties of Scotland were to be preserved. England had yielded on both points that the Scots demanded—namely, the keeping of the Queen in Scotland, and the inclusion of France in the peace treaty.

On July 1 Henry must have felt that the aim of a lifetime had been accomplished. Before the month was out he knew it was all to do again. The Scots as a nation were still hostile to England, and viewed Henry's manœuvres with the deepest suspicion. His claim of suzerainty, and the terms which he had originally proposed, had been ill-advised. Sure, at last, of success, he had incautiously dropped the mask, demanding that Mary should be at once handed over to his keeping, and that the Scots alliance with France should be forgone. Though the demands had been given up, their mere formulation had meant playing into the hands of the pro-French party. Arran possessed neither ability nor strength of character, and finding himself up against an outstanding personality like Beton, against the clergy, and against national feeling, was only too ready to be deflected from loyalty to Henry's plans. Beton was released: the French sent a fleet to Scotland: and before July was out the Cardinal had besieged the palace of Linlithgow in order to capture the Queen. Arran came to terms at once, and by agreement Mary was removed to Stirling, to be safe from any attempt that might be made by Henry. Henry exclaimed indignantly to Sadler in a letter of September 30, 'It was told us that if we would bear a little with them at the first all should succeed after as we would have it. And now we see the Queen at the order of the Cardinal, we see one man and he our enemy, to direct and determine all together at his own arbitre!' He protested to Arran, he offered help, and he gave advice: and the progress of events in July and August can be followed in these two letters.

XXI. TO SIR RALPH SADLER

[*July* 22, 1543.]

TRUSTY AND RIGHT WELL BELOVED, we greet you well, and by your letters of the 16th of this present, we have at good length perceived the perplexed state of the affairs of Scotland, with the determination of the governor touching the same. And to the intent he may now, in this time of trouble, receive some comfort at our hands; like as we have already written to our cousin of Suffolk to send unto you 1000 pounds to be delivered unto him by way of a present, or token from us; so we have now written unto him such letters as you shall perceive by the copy sent herewith unto you, willing you for your credence to declare unto him as followeth.

First, you shall declare unto him, that where we perceive by your advertisement, how the Cardinal with his complices and part-takers, labour to make a revolt and rebellion against him: we be right glad (standing things between us as they do) to understand how prudently he prepareth both to withstand and refell the same, and also to put in surety the person of the young Queen, which is the mark they shoot at; thinking, that if they might once get her into their hands, they should thereby make such a party, as they should be able to dispose of the government of the realm as to them should seem for their own purposes most expedient.

Secondly, where he seemed, in his last conference with you, to desire some aid of money of us for his supply in this trouble, you shall tell him, that, over and besides the token which we sent him, if the case so require, giving us warning in time, we shall so help him and consider his case, as he shall have good cause to say, we be an assured friend towards him and the commonwealth of that realm, as our amity now requireth. But you shall here tell him, that, seeing all the nobles of Scotland have chosen him to be their governor by a common consent, and have subscribed to the same; our opinion is, that he should not only make their doings therein mani[fest] to the whole world, whereby their inconstancy and disloyalty may appear; but also that, being now well learned by the example and experience of the Cardinal and others, what it is to give scope and liberty to such as be bent and determined against him, in case any of them come in his hands, he should bestow them where they should do him nor the realm no hurt; and, in the mean season, upon their open attemptate, proclaim and use such of them as he shall think good as rebels and traitors to the Queen and the realm accordingly.

Third, where it appeareth, that he mindeth to meet the rebels on the other side of the water, and so to give them battle, if they will abide it; you shall say, we think it not meet that he should pass the said water, ne put himself in hazard at his enemies' call; but we think it most expedient and necessary for him to take Stirling into his own hands, whereby he may be master of the passage; and then, as he may be sure to be master of all that is on this side the said water, so he may take his advantage of his enemies, and fight with them, or leave them, as shall be most for his own commodity.

Fourth, where he desireth us to take in good part for a time, though the Borderers do not as becometh them; you shall to that tell him, that if he will be so content, we shall so chastise those Borderers, as, with our advice, he may plant others in their places; for which purpose, we have written to our cousin of Suffolk, and to the Lord Warden of our Marches, to put all our Borders in order for the same, willing you to advertise our lieutenant and Warden of his determination in this behalf.

Fifth, where it appeareth by your letters, that eleven of the French ships, which have kept that coast this long season, lie now in the May: you shall understand that being lately the whole number of sixteen, in their return towards France, there encountered with them six of our ships, which took two of them, and had undoubtedly taken the admiral, and moe of the best of them, if they durst have tarried it; but perceiving themselves at the last too weak, after a sore fight between them, they share off, and these eleven plied again towards Scotland, though there we cannot yet certainly hear what is become of them. And if the governor think it good, we will send our navy to the May, where they be, to take them, which shall be a great surety to Scotland, and a great discourage to all that depend upon France. But, in that case, the governor must permit our ships to take them, though they should fly into the Leith for succour, and also help them with victuals and other necessaries, if they shall need the same; willing you to know his mind herein, and to signify the same unto us with all diligence, doing what you can to cause him to stay them till our ships come: and if that will not be granted, then we would you should have a diligent eye upon them, that you may advertise us a seven-night at the least before they shall be ready to depart, that we may provide and lay for them, in such place for the taking of them by the way as shall be most convenient. . . .

Seventh, our pleasure is, that if this matter grow to such a garboil and extremity, as the young Queen shall be removed from Linlithgow, you shall do what you can, by all good means and persuasion, both with the governor, the Earl of Angus, and Sir George Douglas, to get her removed to Tantallon; but whether that shall be granted or no, you shall travail that the old Queen may be secluded from her, and left at Linlithgow, or where it shall please her. Which the governor may, and hath good cause to do, seeing this conspiracy for her surprisal could not be made but by her consent; the like whereof she will undoubtedly attempt hereafter by all means, so as the young Queen cannot be sure in her company; foreseeing that he put most trusty and sure folks about her, both for her sure keeping and preservation of her health accordingly.

Eight, our pleasure is, that you shall also advise the governor, the Earl of Angus, and our sure friends there, before they shall join with their enemies, to put all the strong holds in such sure hands and custody, as, whatsoever should chance, they may be preserved and kept against the conspirators, and to the benefit of the party which be obedient, and have concluded upon this peace with us. And if it shall come to the fight, you shall require the governor on our behalf, that albeit it be their manner to light all on foot when they join in battle, yet he will, at our desire, preserve one thousand good men, with a good captain, still on horseback, so as the same may stand still in a wing, or stale, till the forces be joined, and then to enter freely upon the rebels: which, if he follow, he shall find shall be much to his benefit, and to the great discomfort of his enemies. [Given under our signet, at our manor of Oatland, the 22nd of July, the 35th year of reign, &c.[1]]

XXII. To Ralph Sadler

[*Aug.* 4, 1543.]

Trusty and right well-beloved, we greet you well, letting you wit that we have received your letters of the last of July: by the contents whereof we perceive such conference as you lately had with the governor, the Earls of Angus and Glencairn, the Lords Maxwell and Somerville, touching the overtures made by the Bishop of Orkney and the Lord Fleming on the behalf of the Cardinal and his complices, being the said Lord Fleming and Bishop of that party; and also, concerning such aid as the said governor, and the rest before named, do desire of us for their defence and surety, with a repetition of their offers unto us, in case the governor shall not be able so to daunt the cardinal and his part-takers, as they shall agree to the ratification of the treaties passed between us, or that the Queen shall be conveyed away, whereby they shall not be able to deliver her at the time by the said treaties appointed and prescribed. For answer whereunto, our pleasure is, that immediately upon the receipt hereof you shall make your repair to the governor, and making unto him our hearty commendations, with condign thanks for his honourable proceedings and friendly offers made unto us, you sh[all] declare unto him that we be of such mind and determination again towards him, as he may be well assured that neither now

[1] This is now cut off in the MS.

nor hereafter we shall suffer him to receive any such damage or dishonour, as he shall not have good cause in the end to say that he hath had a most constant and faithful friend of us. And for his present relief at this time, we have, according to his desire, appointed our lieutenant in those parts to put in order five thousand men, to be addressed unto him when he and you together shall by your letters desire the same. Which five thousand men shall enter in two parties; the one from the west marches, in the conduct of Sir Thomas Wharton, till he shall arrive with the Lord Maxwell; and then the said Lord Maxwell to be chief captain of that number: the other by the east and middle marches, in the conduct of Sir Ralph Evers, knight, Brian Leighton, Robert Collingwood, and Robert Horsley, esquires, till they shall arrive with the Earl of Angus; and then the said Earl to be their chief captain; accounting the said Earl and Lord Maxwell, with all the rest of our friends there which adhere surely to him, to be of such honour and truth, as we dare well commit the leading of our people to them. . . . And where the governor desireth to have such as we shall send for his aid, bring some victual with them; we have, for his satisfaction therein, not only taken order that they shall bring as much victual with them as can conveniently be prepared in the short time of their assembly, but also that plenty of corn shall be sent into the Firth, both from Newcastle and from Berwick; not doubting but the governor, with the rest of the earls and others our friends, and specially those which shall have the chief charge of our subjects, will take order that when it shall arrive it may be employed for the victualling of the same, as appertaineth.

And our further pleasure is, that you shall also declare to the said governor, and to the rest of the lords our friends there, that in case the number now sent shall not so daunt the said Cardinal, as he and his complices shall be glad and fain to consent to the ratification of the treaties, the laying in of pledges and all other things convenient, or that the said Cardinal shall convoy away the young Queen's person, we will prepare a greater furniture to repress their malice; not doubting but the governor will (in case of that necessity) deliver unto us the holds which he hath promised to deliver; assuring the said governor that in case they take away the person of the young Queen, and dispose her marriage otherwise than by our consent, we will, by force of our title and superiority, make him king of the rest of Scotland beyond the Firth, aiding him with our power by sea and by land to recover the same, so as he go through with the overture of marriage between his son and our daughter the Lady Elizabeth, which is of such sort, and shall be such an honour and establishment to his son after him, as he could not recover the like party in Christendom.

And being now in such terms with the governor and the rest of our friends there, that we must and do account our affairs all one; we can do no less but to remember unto them, how they have been heretofore abused by the Cardinal and his part-takers, and what inconveniences have ensued of the same, to the intent they may hereafter beware of the craft and falsehood of him and his angels, and utterly stop their ears to any thing that can be said on his behalf. Wherefore you shall desire and pray both the governor and the rest of the said lords our friends, and specially the Earl of Glencairn and the Lord Maxwell, to weigh their greater affairs more deeply, and to consider how they have been now twice deluded by the crafty means of the said Cardinal; once in his deliverance, and now again at the delivery of the young Queen; requiring them, at the contemplation of our advice and counsel, and also in respect of their own honours and estimations, which shall be much defaced in the world, if he should eftsoons deceive them the third time, to beware of him, and utterly to close their ears, as is aforesaid, against him and his complices. Which advice and counsel if they follow not, but shall percase tolerate many things in hope of better, whereby he shall get the upper-hand and victory of them, what scruple soever they have of an honest zeal, which would be loath to have any slaughter in their native country; they may be assured in that case that he will spare no one of them, but dispatch them, either together, or one after another, as he shall have his most opportunity. And therefore, seeing the said Cardinal is now at Stirling, and travelleth secretly to assemble again his army, to the intent he may both depose the governor, and of all the rest dispose at his pleasure; considering his force, being so lately disparkled, will not soon or easily be brought again together, our advice and counsel is, that the governor shall secretly and suddenly, in any wise, send a good band of his men to Stirling, and either there to take him and bring him to the castle of Edinburgh, or at the least to drive him over the water, and then to set such an assured order for the safe keeping of the bridge, as neither the Queen shall be conveyed away, though the barons having the keeping of her would consent thereunto at the said Cardinal's request and desire, ne that the Cardinal, or any of his complices, be permitted to pass the bridge, or that any of them on this side do resort to him, but at the governor's will and pleasure.

But it was too late. By September Arran was regent in name only: all the fortified holds in the country were in the Cardinal's keeping: and the real power had been vested in a Council, composed largely of the clergy favourable to French interests, and dominated by Mary of Lorraine and the Cardinal. To Arran Henry protested in dignified terms.

XXIII. To the Earl of Arran

By the King

HENRY R. [*Oct.* 27, 1543.]

Sithence the arrival here of this bearer sent from you unto us, while you occupied the place of governor there, to be here in place of an ambassador from that realm, we have heard that you, author of his message, forgetting your duty to that realm, your honour and estimation to the world, and your private and secret promises unto us, have revolted unto your adverse party, submitted yourself to the government of your enemies, and surrendered the state, which, you bare us in hand, was given you by parliament; which well appeareth by that, as, when the cardinal, your new reconciled friend, in the presence of our ambassador, plainly affirmed in your own hearing, that our covenants, passed with Scotland, were passed by private authority: in which few words, you, holding your peace without any denial, seemed to consent to the same, and suffered yourself not only to be accused of untruth to that realm, and also to us, to send ambassadors in the name of the whole realm otherwise than you ought to do if that were true, but also therewith he did you to understand, that he esteemed for no parliament such convention in Scotland as wherein you were made governor; by which parliament the said ambassadors were also ordained to come unto us, and authorized to treat, bargain, and conclude with us. And so finally you have in such wise used and behaved yourself, as such covenants as hath been by your mediation passed by the authority of that whole realm with us, be now infringed and broken. And, if you could then, without contradiction, in a public audience keep silence, whilst you were thus charged and touched, and would, for defence of your doings, say nothing; you must much more be content to hear of us your blame on the other part, and so much the rather, that we speak to you the truth which you ought to consider, and the cardinal powdered his tale with lies, which you ought to have then refelled, if truth, if honour, if nobleness had been regarded of you. We have proceeded with you princely, minding the conservation of your young Queen, the wealth of that realm, and your own particular benefit and advancement. Upon confidence of your loyalty we did give ear to such covenants, as else we would have hardly been persuaded unto; which when we see so evidently fail, and that, as you sent this bearer unto us in the time of your well-doing, so by your frailty and inconstancy you have in such wise swerved, as it appeareth that you be governed otherwise than were convenient. We esteem and repute, that as with fair and pleasant words you sent this bearer unto us, so with your unseemly deeds you have revoked him. According whereunto as one whose message is by you frustrate and disappointed, we have thought good to remit unto you the same, referring unto his declaration of what disposition and inclination we were of, if you had continued according to his credence, and how your doings have altered us, unto whom we doubt you will give credence.

Given under our signet at our manor of Ampthill, the 27th day of October, the thirty-fifth year of our reign.

Fearing for the safety of his ambassador Sir Ralph Sadler he had previously threatened the citizens of Edinburgh in the following letter.

XXIV. To the city of Edinburgh

[*Sept.* 9, 1543.]

We greet you well. And being advertised that our ambassador resident in that town, whose chief charge consisteth to solicit the accomplishment of such treaties, pacts and covenants as by the Governor and three states of that realm are concluded with us, hath of late by certain of your town been menaced and threatened to be violently and extremely handled, contrary to all law of reason, nature and humanity, only upon pretence, as they noise abroad, that we have here caused to be stayed certain ships of Scotland, the doing whereof, upon such grounds and intents as we did, we are always able to justify and maintain: forasmuch as the injury done to an ambassador hath been ever accounted among all Christian men of so high a nature as it was never left unpunished and revenged, and cannot therefore without great diminution of our honour be pretermitted and neglected, but prosecuted with more cruelty than we would gladly have cause to exercise against you: we have thought good to admonish you to beware, and eschew that outrage, whereby ye might provoke worthily our extreme displeasure and indignation, and to forbear that attemptate, not only for the detestation of it in all men's ears, but also for fear of the revenge of our sword to extend to that town and commonalty, and all such p[ersons] as shall by any means hereafter come in to our hands, to the extermination of you to the third and fourth generation; persuading unto yourself that, as we have, of a special zeal to the rest and quietness of both realms, condescended to agree to such treaties and covenants as have been concluded, so we be minded for our part to continue the same with such as shall in all their doings show themselves by public testimony content therewith, and shall handle them from henceforth with all favour, friendship and humanity, and also restore the ships and goods of all those which shall declare themselves towards us and the maintenance of the treaty accordingly. And on the other part, such as shall show themselves to be of a contrary faction, who shall either misentreat our ambassador, or otherwise use themselves than the treaties will, those we intend to use as enemies to both realms and shall handle them accordingly. Wherefore, considering we be thus good unto you to declare our affection and intent so plainly towards you, it shall be wisely done of you to foresee the dangers, and to be of such behaviour towards us, as ye may continue our good determination towards you; and ye that be well minded, to dissever yourself from the rest of the worst sort, and joining together to expel and repress the malicious sort, to give us thereby knowledge, whom we may favour as well disposed to the conservation of the treaties, and whom we shall prosecute as misdoers and offenders; so as one do not bear the fault of an other; whereof we would be loath; and yet for want of such knowledge will not fail to revenge and punish your outrages, if any be committed, as it shall chance any of you to come into our hands, besides the execution of our force against that town and the whole country; whereunto ye may in that case assuredly trust.

The Privy Council also sent Sadler Henry's assurance that 'in case your finger should ache by their means all Edinburgh shall rue it for ever after, His Majesty is so earnestly determined to revenge it with all extremity'. (September 9, 1543.)

By December the treaty of Greenwich had been repudiated, and the alliance with France renewed. As early as September, when threatened with check-mate, Henry had laid his plans, as witness the following letter to the Duke of Suffolk.

XXV. TO SUFFOLK

[*Sept.* 14, 1543.]

RIGHT TRUSTY AND RIGHT ENTIRELY BELOVED COUSIN, we greet you well. Since the depeche of our former letters unto you, signifying what we wrote to the Earl of Angus concerning an enterprise to be made by him and other our friends for the surprise of the Cardinal and Governor, which we fear they will not so earnestly execute as we have willed them to do, yet we doubt not but they will be induced by your good dexterity and handling in part to follow our advice in those letters comprised, that is to say, in assembling themselves in a place of surety as nigh to Edinburgh as they may, and there to stay and parliament with the said Governor and Cardinal, touching both our affairs and their surety, till such time as they shall know further of our mind and pleasure. Wherefore, remembering your advertisement of the number of horsemen put in areadiness in the countries within your commission, amounting to 15,000 spears and archers on horseback and moe, who have by you already commandment to repair to you within 24 hours warning, and that it is reasonably to be judged that 8,000 of that number, suddenly assembled by you upon pretence to make a road upon the Humes and Carrs, might shortly and with speed pass through to Edinburgh, with such provision for victual as we doubt not you will make for eight or ten days, in which time the matter shall be faict or faille, without any resistance to be made by the power of Scotland not warned thereof before, and being so lately dissevered: we have debated this matter with our Council here and think it feasible, they having dismissed the rest of their men, saving a few besides their household servants, that you may either surprise the town of Edinburgh and the Governor and Cardinal within the same, with this number of eight thousand horsemen under your conduct and leading, with such captains as you shall appoint to have charge under you, whereof my Lord Warden to be one if you think it so convenient; or else to burn the town and as much of the rest of the countries of such as be our enemies, sparing as nigh as you can our friends and their adherents, as you can coming homeward. Which enterprise as we judge, speedily set forth by your foresight, dexterity, and wisdom, can have no let or impediment to hinder the same or any part thereof, unless they shall fly by sea; for which purpose we would that you shall immediately rig out five or six ships out of Newcastle and Berwick, to enter in to the Firth, and there to stay their passage, and also all such as would come to their aid; or else shall fly away by Stirling, which they that be of our part may easily then let if they list. And as touching the chief and principal ground, which is our honour: the Scots, and specially the Governor, having deluded our expectation as he hath done, and the treaty not observed on their part, we may well, our honour saved, with force cause them to know how they use us not accordingly as their duty and as our proceeding towards them requireth.

And being these 8,000 men already by you put in such areadiness, the same may be easily put in order and also furnished with victuals to make this small journey, not being forty miles if you depart from Wark, as we think you should do. And further, if ye set forth in the evening, and sending for Sir George Douglas before, make a pretence to him that your purpose is to harry the Humes and Carrs, and when you shall have passed the first night, and rested the day following, so as you may in the evening set forth again to be at Edinburgh the next morning, and then only to disclose your whole enterprise to him, and then to cause him to give the rest of the lords on our part advertisement to have the better eye to the Cardinal and Governor, lest they should steal away by Stirling bridge, and at the least do endeavour themselves in that part to serve us. Whereby they in Edinburgh shall be surprised or ever they mistrust any such matter, so as they having then none other way to escape, shall be fain and compelled to enter in to the castle with such number as they have in the town, which if they so do shall be compelled for lack of victual to yield both castle and town within, as we think, four days. Or if they fortune any other way to escape, at the least we think you may burn the town in spite of the castle, by day or by night. Which effect only of burning the town, if the other two fail, with the damage you shall do to our enemies in your return, shall be worth the charges of this enterprise; which besides the small expenses thereof, can have no danger at all, being Scotland as it now is divided, or at the least their forces so laid down of late, that they shall be the more unready to be shortly levied, seeing that there is some trust between them of accord and agreement. As touching ordnance and munition, considering the small abode to be made there, though we think it not necessary that you carry with you any great abundance, yet we think meet you shall carry with you a convenient proportion of culverins, d(emi) culverins, and faucons, providing such shifts of draughts and carriages for the same, as it shall be none or small impediment to this intended enterprise. . . .

He had persevered with his diplomacy, as witness the two letters that follow, the second with many alterations in his own hand. One thing favourable to his plans, however, is to be noted in No. XXVII—' the towardness of the Earl of Lennox '. Lennox was as near as Arran in the succession, and Beton had used him by letting him hope that he might oust Arran as Regent and even marry the Queen dowager. Having obtained possession of the Queen, Beton made it plain that Lennox need expect nothing. In consequence, he turned to the English party for his revenge.

XXVI. INSTRUCTIONS TO SIR ANTHONY BROWNE, KNIGHT, MASTER OF HIS HIGHNESS'S HORSES, WHOM HIS MAJESTY DOTH SEND AT THIS TIME IN THE NORTH PARTS, FOR THE PURPOSE ENSUING[1]

[*Sept.* 1543.]

Where the King's Majesty hath been many ways provoked and constrained by the late King of Scots to enter the war with Scotland, in the heat whereof, and when God had given His Majesty great victory and advantage, it pleased Almighty God to call the said King of Scots to His mercy, leaving behind him one only daughter the King's Highness pronepte, whereupon His Majesty was not only content, of his own most gracious and godly nature and disposition, to suspend and stay his sword, but also to harken to the suits of the nobles of Scotland, and after to the suits of the Governor and the nobles of the realm labouring for peace, and for the marriage of the young Princess to my Lord Prince's Grace, which peace and marriage was sithens concluded by the consent of the Estates of their Parliament authorizing certain personages, which repaired hither as Ambassadors from their whole Parliament for that purpose: forasmuch as, sithens the conclusion of the said peace and marriage, and the ratification of the same solemnly made by the Governor, the same, being seduced by the Cardinal and his complices, hath not, conform to the purport thereof, put in hostages by the said treaty required,

[1] Browne was a half-brother of Fitzwilliam, Earl of Southampton.

ne hath kept such other promises as he hath made to His Majesty, but hath broken the same after so light and ungentle a sort as ought justly to provoke His Majesty's indignation against them: His Highness, most prudently considering that, where words and writings confirmed solemnly by oath will not serve, the force of the sword is to be extended, thereby to constrain such unfaithful people to know their duties and to give place to reason, hath thought it more than necessary, unless the said Scots shall, with all humility, and without desire of any alteration of any point of the said treaties, make petition to His Majesty, with the present offer also of such assurance as His Majesty shall be contented to accept, so it may please His Highness to pardon their remissness and to accept their offer and suit, that His Majesty should so daunt them by force, as they may be compelled to know their ungentle and lewd proceeding with His Majesty in this behalf.

Browne is instructed to consult with Suffolk and others of the Council of the North

to whom he shall address himself with all convenient diligence, and at his first arrival cause the said Duke and other of the Council, upon consultation had within what time the 8,000 horse men and 2,000 footmen may be assembled, to signify to the King's Majesty with speed, within how many days the entry in to Scotland may be actually made, after knowledge of the King's Majesty's absolute pleasure to put the same in execution.

And, forasmuch as it is to be supposed that at his repair to the said Duke he shall find with the same Sir George Douglas, His Majesty's pleasure is, that he the said Duke, Lord Parr, the said Sir Anthony, and Bishop of Durham shall frankly enter with the said Sir George to know certainly of him what he, and his brother the Earl of Angus, with their friends, will now do for His Majesty: expressing plainly unto him, how that first his brother the Earl of Angus, a little before his going in to Scotland, said he durst undertake to set the crown of Scotland upon His Majesty's head before midsummer then following; how that he, the said Sir George himself after, and also diverse others, have continually sued to His Majesty to bear and tolerate, alleging that with sufferance all things would succeed better and better to His

Majesty's purpose, where as in deed nothing hath yet succeeded, but contrariwise evermore from worse to worse, whereby His Majesty hath not only spent much money, but also lost much advantage otherwise: putting him also in remembrance therewith what promise and bond he and his brother, with other noblemen, have made and put to His Majesty, for doing of service, in case the Governor should revolt, as he now hath done, or that the young Queen should be taken out of the hands and order of such as be appointed by Parliament to keep her, who is now at the order of her mother and of the Cardinal, the copies of which bonds the said Sir Anthony shall carry with him: pressing him the said Sir George hereupon to declare what may be trusted to of them: and tasting[1] him, whether he will consent that his brother, he and the rest should make such a proclamation in Scotland, as the said Sir Anthony, having a draft thereof with him, shall declare unto him, and whether he will solicit the speedy proclaiming of the same or no, and cause the same effectually to be put in execution: declaring finally unto him, if the said Sir Anthony see him slack and full of casting perils, that His Majesty will no longer feed them with money, as he hath done, unless he see some more fruit thereof than he hath done hitherto.

And if it shall chance that the said Sir George shall in his answer allege that himself, his brother, and some noblemen, and others their friends, will do their duties in refusing to come in to the Cardinal, and shall be ready to do any other service that His Majesty shall think expedient and command them; then the said Duke &c. shall demand of him what friends they have that they think will surely adhere and stick unto them, and shall cause him to give the names of as many as they be perfectly sure of in writing. And if he shall seem to doubt of any of those that he shall call his friends, then be plainly told him that it shall not be expedient he put any one man in as his friend that he is not most sure of; and so they shall cause him to make his book of no more than may be accounted sure for their part, and if they use themselves otherwise, then to be taken as no friends. And when they shall have thus searched the said Sir George, whereby they may know what is to be trusted of him and that sort, and that he

[1] Examine, test.

shall be departed from them, then shall the said Duke &c. devise to put in order as secretly as they can eight thousand horsemen and two thousand light footmen, to be ready to enter suddenly into Scotland with all the victuals prepared at Berwick and such further furniture as every particular man can bring with him, and to devast all the country of the enemies even to Edinburgh gates if it may be, or make further enterprise of the town of Edinburgh, as upon their arrival there they shall see feasible. And thus the said Duke, the Lord Parr, Bishop of Durham and Sir Anthony Browne, consulting together as afore, and having a foresight of the provisions of victuals and the assembling of the men, with description of the captains, and order to be observed and kept with as much diligence as may be, they shall forbear the actual execution, and remain in expectation of knowledge of the King's Majesty's pleasure, whether they shall proceed to the said enterprise or no. In which enterprise His Majesty will that the said Lord Warden enter in person, as chieftain, and the said Sir Anthony shall also enter in person with him, as His Majesty's Counsellor, and one who can in that matter, by the reason of his experience, give the said Lord Warden good counsel and help to direct all the proceedings; not doubting but they will so endeavour themselves together as they shall give the enemies a notable buffet.

And the said Duke &c. shall take order that such garrisons be laid from time to time on the Borders as they shall think sufficient for the defence of the same.

The said Sir Anthony shall also remember to devise with Sir George Douglas for the conveying of Master Sadlier to Tantallon, to the intent he may there be in surety from the malice of such as be adversaries to the King's Majesty.

The following letter again shows the minute care that Henry lavished on his diplomatic correspondence.

XXVII. To Angus, Cassilis, and Glencairn

[*Oct.* 19, 1543.]

. . . We greet you well, and have received your letters of the 12th of this present, whereby we do perceive much to our contentation your good inclinations and minds to continue and persevere for the advancement of our affairs in those parts WHEN TIME AND OPPORTUNITY MAY SUFFER. And whereas we have been advertised as well from our ambassador there as now by your last letters of the towardness the Earl of Lennox showeth himself to have to do us service, and to declare himself FOR OUR PARTY, conformable to such BANDS AS YOU AMONG YOU ARE BOUND TO, WHICH IF THE DEEDS OF the said Earl BE in the effect correspondent to his promises, the same shall in the end find at our hand great KINDNESS and commodity; so we have ALSO thought good, for the affection we bear to your assurances, to desire and pray you to consider and weigh THE EVENT OF THESE THINGS in your proceedings more prudently and with greater foresight than you have done in some things heretofore. You do now see, we are sure, how much you have been abused with giving too great credit to the fair dissimuling words and promises of him that occupieth the place of the Governor. Fairer behests than he made, greater devotion than he pretended to bear to all such things as we and you would have had advanced, never man could make or show in words; but now what his heart was, his deeds do plainly declare unto you! Wherefore let him be your example, and beware that fair semblant OF SUCH LIKE do not too much attrape you, and having heretofore by the false craft of the Cardinal, by the inconstant and untrue dealing of him that occupieth the place of Governor, been deceived, show now your selves sufficiently [an]d in this your new confederacy with the Earl of Lennox AND ALL OTHER THERE, work so substantially, as your affections and good wills to the advancement of our affairs, WITH WISE FORESIGHT TO your own assurances, may plainly in effect appear to the world. For your better proceedings wherein, albeit we doubt not but that according to your former advertisements hither, there be many noble men and gentlemen addict and given to our party, yet we think it best that four or five of you, that is to say you THE EARL OF ANGUS, LENNOX, CASSILIS, AND GLENCAIRN, WITH THE ADVICE OF SIR G. DOUGLAS, do take upon YOU SOME MORE PAIN TO DIRECT AND FRAME THE

AFFAIRS MORE READILY TO THE HANDS OF THE REST, MAKING (WHEN THE AFFAIRS HAVE BEEN WELL FRAMED BY YOU) SUCH OF them REST PRIVY TO THEM OR YOU CONCLUDE, AS SHALL BE THOUGHT BY YOU AMONGST YOU MOST CONVENIENT: for where many be of counsel things can neither be k[ept] so secret nor yet so well wrought as they may be by fewer. Consider IT NOW AMONGST YOU I PRAY YOU, how necessary it shall be for your assurances AND COMMODITY to provide now, that this money and munition brought out of France, WHICH IS NOW in the cas[tle] of Dumbarton, BE SUBSTANTIALLY LOOKED TO SO THAT IT MAY SERVE FOR YOUR COMMODITIES, AND NOT TO PUT IT IN TRUST OF ONE MAN ALONE, WHICH WHEN HE LUST MAY MAKE Y[OU] REPENT AND THEN TOO LATE. THEREFORE WE THINK IT WERE CONVENIENT THAT YOU AMONGST YOU SHOULD APPOINT such as you know to be men of trust and fidelity towards you TO have the charge and oversight of the said money and mu[nition], ALTHOUGH IT BE WITHIN THE FORESAID CASTLE; [and] by fair means and persuasions to induce thereto the said Earl of Lennox to BE CONTENT WITH THE SAME, and to say unto him, among other reasons that you may allege for your purpose, that in case he should leave the government of the castle in the hands of any one man as he hath hitherto, now that such money and munition is within the same, he might peradventure have an evil account of it, AND rather by that means put weapon in his enemies' hand to his own confusion, AND YOURS AMONGST YOU. FOR DOUBTLESS THE CARDINAL, KNOWING IT TO BE THERE, will work by all means possible to get into his hands THE PLACE or at the least [the] money and munitions that is come out of Fra[nce]. You see many men now a days be of such inconstancy and unfaithfulness, as yourselves have specially experimented many times in THE FORESAID Earl of Arran AND OTHER. . . .

Preparations, warnings, protests and diplomacy were of no avail. In December, 1543, the Scots Parliament declared the English treaties null and void, and in January, 1544, the 'assured Scots' came to terms with Beton, after a half-hearted attempt to stand by their promise. They pledged themselves to abandon the English alliance, and by the spring even the Douglases and Lennox had fallen away. Henry knew now that he had been tricked once again, and that all his planning was likely to come to nothing. He was at war with France, which made the reaffirming of the old Franco-Scottish alliance a real danger. He had some genuine grounds for resentment, to reinforce a passionate rage at the thwarting of his aim; and in consequence he proceeded to vent the exasperation of a lifetime in what can only be described as a policy of wasteful and unparalleled vindictiveness. At the beginning of May, Edward Seymour, Earl of Hertford and brother to Queen Jane, sailed up the Firth of Forth with an English fleet. His orders were to

burn Edinburgh town, so razed and defaced when you have sacked and gotten what ye can of it, as there may remain forever a perpetual memory of the vengeance of God lightened upon (them?) for their falsehood and disloyalty. Do what ye can out of hand, and without long tarrying to beat down and overthrow the castle, sack Holyrood House and as many towns and villages about Edinburgh as ye may conveniently; sack Leith, and burn and subvert it and all the rest, putting man, woman and child to fire and sword, without exception, where any resistance shall be made against you; and this done, pass over to the Fifeland and extend like extremities and destructions in all towns and villages whereunto ye may reach conveniently; not forgetting, among all the rest so to spoil and turn upset down the Cardinal's town of St. Andrews, as the upper stone may be the nether, and not one stick stands by another, sparing no creature alive within the same, specially such as either in friendship or blood be allied to the Cardinal.

Hertford wrote, on May 9, that he had made 'a jolly fire and smoke upon the town', and had left it and Holyrood 'in manner wholly burnt and desolate '. Then he wasted the country-side, as ordered, firing every village through which he passed. ' And so ', he wrote on May 18, ' this journey is accomplished to your Majesty's honour, in such sort as we trust your Majesty shall hear that the like devastation hath not been made in Scotland these many years.'

Though he read the Scots this grim lesson in the summer Henry had not been neglecting his more diplomatic methods. The Earls of Glencairn and Lennox were still attached to the English interest, so Henry dangled before the latter an attractive bait—marriage with his own niece, the Lady Margaret Douglas, daughter of Margaret Tudor and the Earl of Angus.[1] The following extract is also of interest, in that it shows Henry as still willing to pour out money in order to win individual Scots nobles and achieve his aim.

XXVIII. To Wharton and Bowes

[*March* 26, 1544.]

. . . And, whereas the Earl of Lennox hath lately by his Secretary made suit unto us to have in marriage the Lady Margaret our niece, in case the said Scottish Commissioners shall renew the said suit on the behalf of the said Earl, the said Lord Wharton and Sir Robert Bowes shall say, that albeit we for our part, if the said Earl shall perform the said covenants which for his part are to be performed, and in his doings and proceedings towards us shall use himself according to our expectation, we could be contented that the said marriage do take effect between him and our said niece : yet forasmuch as we have promised unto our niece never to cause her to marry any but whom she shall find in her own heart to love, and that, they having never one seen another, we know not how they shall like one another when they see together : and for that also, though we were never so well pleased with the matter, and they also like each other never so well, yet the thing cannot be perfected with the honour of all parties, until also it be agreed on either side, both what shall be given with her, and also what she shall have again assured unto

[1] The marriage actually took place in July, 1544, and the son born of it was Henry Darnley, the future husband of Mary Queen of Scots.

her by the said Earl for her dower: it is a covenant that cannot be easily now treated, the state of the rest of things being as they be, and all other matters standing as they do yet. And therefore they shall say unto them that hereafter, when the said Earl shall have done some notable good service unto us, and shall, upon the sight of our niece, like her, and she again like him, we shall, upon his overture in that matter, make him such a reasonable answer, as he shall have cause to be contented.

And finally, forasmuch as the Lord Dunlanrik, who it is thought shall be one of the said Commissioners, may peradventure show himself scant well pleased that he hath not some portion of money appointed to him at this time when he shall know of the rewards, which of our liberality we be determined to give to the Earls of Cassilis and Glencairn upon the conditions aforesaid; the said Lord Wharton and Sir Robert Bowes, putting the said Dunlanrik in remembrance, with gentle words, of the reward of £100 which we lately sent unto him, with the yearly pension also of 500 crowns, which we have promised unto him, shall say unto him that, albeit we do not reward him now at this time, yet he had of us when they had nothing, and continuing good servant unto us, as we trust he will, shall have also again peradventure when they shall not; advising him in gentle manner not to mistrust our goodness, and to think, that serving us according to our expectation, we will have such consideration of his good service from time to time, as with reason ought to content him. . . .

By themselves Lennox and Glencairn were not strong enough to create a party that would balance or defeat the Cardinal's, and in consequence the destructive English raids were continued into the autumn. Early in 1545, however, a Scots army under Arran and Angus encountered the Warden of the Middle Marches, Sir Ralph Eure, near Jedburgh, and inflicted a severe defeat on the English forces at Ancrum Moor. To Arran their victory was an assurance of the loyalty of the erstwhile 'English' lord, Henry's former pensioner, Angus. To Francis I it was an assurance of the stubborn and unconquerable resistance in Scotland, upon which he could calculate for help in his war against Henry. To Henry it was a warning. He took it as such, and in April made once again his old offers of peace and alliance. Relying on French help, and on the rumour of the projected French invasion of England, the Scots rejected the offer; and in May the French fleet landed a considerable force, which in August joined with the Scots army and marched towards the Border.

The French invasion and the Scots incursion were both signal failures. Methodically ruthless Henry took his revenge in the autumn. Hertford's second mission of destruction was even deadlier than the first, and the list of his burnings and devastations makes terrible reading. It includes the destruction of 243 villages, five market towns and seven monasteries. Nevertheless, the shrewdest blow struck on Henry's behalf was struck by the Scots themselves. It was nothing less than the murder of Cardinal Beton.

That Henry himself and the English Council were either concerned, or prepared to be concerned, is quite evident from various letters, of which the following extract is a sufficient and typical example. The letter, addressed to Hertford, and written in Paget's hand, is signed by him and by Suffolk, Russell, Essex, Gardiner, Wriothesley and St. John. The King has seen certain letters sent from the Earl of Cassilis to Sadler, 'the one containing an offer for the killing of the Cardinal, if his Majesty would have it done, and would promise, when it were done, a reward'. To this amiable proposition 'His Majesty hath willed us to signify . . . that His Highness, reputing the fact not meet to be set forward expressly by His Majesty, will not seem to have to do in it; and yet, not misliking the offer, thinketh good that Mr. Sadler . . . should write to the Earl of the receipt of his letter containing such an offer, which he thinketh not convenient to be communicated to the King's Majesty: marry, to write to him what he thinketh of the matter, he shall say that if he were in the Earl of Cassilis' place, and were as able to do His Majesty good service there, as he knoweth him to be, and thinketh a right good will in him to do it, he would surely do what he could for the execution of it, believing verily to do thereby not only acceptable service to the King's Majesty, but also a special benefit to the realm of Scotland, and would trust verily the King's Majesty would consider his service in the same, as you doubt not, of his accustomed goodness to them which serve him, but he would do the same to him.'[1]

It is a case of one of the letters that Henry himself did not write—an eloquent silence. Nevertheless, although his would-be complicity is beyond doubt, circumstances played into his hands. Beton, hated as a persecutor in his own country, had, in March, 1546, burnt an eminent and zealous preacher of the reformed faith, one George Wishart. It was a blunder, made at a critical moment. Protestantism had been gaining ground in Scotland, nor was the cause of union with England without its adherents—real but more far-sighted patriots than those who supported the disastrous policy of league with France. On May 29 a band of determined Scots, who saw in the Cardinal's policy ruin for their country, forced their way into his castle of St. Andrews, stabbed him to death, and hung the lifeless body over the castle walls for all to see. Of England's complicity there can be no doubt whatever. Rewards of £50 each, authorized by the Privy Council, were given to several of the lairds concerned. One of the most interesting comments is that of Bishop Thirlby, in the postscript of a letter written to Paget from Ratisbon: 'I had almost forgotten to tell my gladness of your tidings of the Cardinal of Scotland. It is half a wonder here that ye dare be so bold to kill a Cardinal!'[2]

The assassination removed the most powerful obstacle that lay between Henry and his desire. The Scots were, at the last minute, comprehended in the peace treaty which Henry signed with France on June 7, 1546 (see p. 416). Friendly overtures were also made in the following letter, as well as an effort on behalf of Beton's murderers, who had shut themselves up in the castle of St. Andrews, and were being besieged by the government. Eventually some of the murderers were rescued by English ships and brought to London.

[1] As far as is known, this particular scheme was not the one actually responsible for Beton's death. P.R.O. S.P. 49, vol. 8, no. 28. *L.P.* XX, i. 834 (1).

[2] *L.P.* XXI, 1070.

XXIX. To the Governor and Council of Scotland

[*Dec.* 20, 1546.]

My Lords, we greet you well. And having perceived by the ambassadors lately arrived here, by your advices in the name of our dear cousin your mistress, the desire which you have to be reconciled in friendship and amity unto us; albeit you have heretofore on her behalf and in her name confirmed by the Great Seal of that realm, and with the assent of the Parliament, passed certain covenants with us, which were not accomplished according to your promises, whereby we have good cause to refuse to treat no more with you in her affairs; yet, being of our own disposition given to peace and tranquillity, when we may enjoy the same with honour, and be not provoked to the contrary, we could be contented to give ear to such offers as with honour and of reason were to be accepted, so as ye would give to the world to understand by deeds that ye are no less desirous of our love and friendship, than often times you have showed yourselves to be by words. And for the first degree thereunto, if you can be contented to withdraw the siege which you have laid to the castle of Saint Andrews, for our sake and at the contemplation of our request, until the matter of displeasure against them within were further debated, we would take it for a token of love and kindness towards us, and the rather think you esteemed somewhat the more our friendship, wherein we pray you to satisfy our desire. For having found the gentlemen within the same ever ready and glad to advance to the best of their powers the matter of marriage between our dearest son the Prince and your mistress, we have born them therefore our favour, and made them promise to help them in their necessities, whereof as they have need, being thus straightly put at by you without desert, all things weighed, so we have thought it expedient to make means for them in this wise unto you, which we eftsoons pray you to consider, for otherwise we shall be enforced of honour to provide that they be not oppressed, and to relieve them in such wise as we may conveniently. And thus requiring your answer herein by this bearer Richmond, one of our heralds, we commit you to God. From our manor of Nonsuch, the 20th day of December, the year of Our Lord God 1546, and of our Reign the 38th.

Between them the two Betons had stood for continued and skilful opposition to Henry's aim in Scotland. Both men of powerful intellect, as ruthless and unscrupulous as Henry himself, focussing the national feeling for independence, representing and commanding all the power and resources of the ancient church, they had successfully foiled his diplomacy; and though he lived to see the death of the Archbishop and the murder of the Cardinal, his victory came too late. The Cardinal's death in no way altered the general determination of the Scots to preserve their national independence, and by January, 1547, Henry himself was dead.

The letters collected in this chapter give a vivid impression of the unyielding and rooted determination, and of the fixity of purpose inherent in Henry's character. They show too, very clearly, the kind of men with whom he had to deal. Henry's own description of the Scottish nobles and clergy as 'a sort [i.e. set, pack] of wolves' was all too apt. There was not one disinterested patriot among them. One and all, they used the struggle for Scotland's national independence as the opportunity for selfish ends—personal power, gains, family interests. The story which these letters do not tell, however—unless, perhaps, by implication—is the tragedy of James V. Of the popular 'King of the Commons', affectionately nicknamed the 'Red Tod' (fox), we see nothing at all; nor yet of the monarch who founded Scotland's College of Justice. We realize next to nothing of the almost wholly disastrous circumstances of his upbringing. Equipped neither by training nor discipline, called to rule an uncivilized and semi-barbarous nation, the utter hopelessness of his struggle is epitomized by the anecdote which tells how the first Earl of Arran, on his death-bed in 1530, warned James that his most hated enemy Angus was the only Scots lord who was true to him. Doomed from the start, it is symbolic of his whole frustrate and unhappy career that in these letters he should hardly appear as a personality, but only as the victim of the unrelenting Tudor purpose.

CHAPTER V

DIPLOMACY AND WAR—LAST ROUND (1540-1547)

'We be so occupied, and have so much to do in foreseeing and caring for everything ourself, as we have almost no manner rest or leisure to do any other thing.'

HENRY VIII TO KATHARINE PARR: 1544.

BY 1540 it might have looked to the superficial observer as if Henry had played a number of losing rounds. He had lost in Cromwell a finance minister of genius. He had achieved nothing by the Cleves alliance, and had been involved by it in an episode that had been to him personally both distressing and distasteful. And he had got nothing out of the elaborate diplomacy of his negotiations with the Emperor in 1538 and 1539. Actually, however, the last years of the thirties had been by no means barren of gain. Religion was now settled very much as Henry wished it to be. Protestant and Catholic alike had been warned: there was the Act of Six Articles for use, if and when necessary. The strength of the Crown had been amazingly well demonstrated by the complete failure of the Pilgrimage of Grace. And if the King had lost the financial genius of Cromwell, he had to some extent exhausted his utility, and had also sacrificed—in his own good time, and when no suspicion of popular compulsion could be imagined—the most unpopular of his ministers to a popular, though engineered, vengeance. In the domain of foreign policy he had again tried and proved his strength. As the Chancellor could boast to Parliament in 1542, the country, though threatened, had suffered no invasion for thirteen years. Henry had reined in his unruly reformers in time, so that the breach with Rome had taken him just as far as he meant to go and no further. And all the time he had been steadily improving and consolidating the defensive and offensive equipment of the realm, more particularly his beloved navy.

In 1541 an event analagous to the murder of Somerset Herald precipitated war on the continent. Two French envoys, passing through Italy, were murdered by order of the governor of Milan, an Imperialist. Francis, in his determination to regain Milan, still dreaming of the conquest of the whole of northern Italy, was prepared to go to any lengths—or rather, at this precise moment, to the length of making an alliance with the Turks. His messengers, in fact, had been on their way to Constantinople, when the governor of Milan interfered, in the interests of Christendom. In August the Turks overran the whole of Hungary: and in October, when Charles attempted to capture Algiers—the headquarters of the Sultan's irresistible pirate fleet—his navy was destroyed by a storm and his troops almost wiped out in their forced retreat. By 1542, therefore, Francis, 'confederated with the Turk,' was ready for war. Venice was on his side, also the Pope, and some of the Lutheran states of Germany; and Solyman had promised two hundred thousand troops to attack Germany. Things looked black for the Emperor, and he turned, unwillingly enough, to Henry as a possible ally. That the French, already provided with allies, should also have turned to England at this moment, speaks even more for the general estimation of Henry's strength.

For Henry the clash between Charles and Francis meant yet another chance to enrich himself at the expense of one or other. His own inclination was towards the Emperor—Flemish trade meant much to his subjects—but in the meantime the usual marriage negotiations with France, and preliminary conversations with Charles, gave him an opportunity to remain conveniently neutral. He had his own affairs to settle in Scotland: and it was apparent that the longer he took in making his decision the more he might expect to get out of a treaty with the Emperor. In July the French invaded the Low Countries, and as the months went on the Emperor grew more accommodating. He had brought himself to accept the idea of alliance with his excommunicated uncle, but Henry was determined that in any treaty he signed, when accepting each other's enemies as their own, the adjective 'spiritualis' should be added in the specification thereof. Only one interpretation was possible: 'spiritualis' meant, quite simply, the Pope—an embarrassing situation for the orthodox Charles. In September he was obviously tempted—so much so, that Henry's ambassador, Bonner, went so far as to write to England that he thought, if the war went on, the Emperor would be bound to break with Rome, in which case he would be to the Pope 'acerimmus hostis'. Against this Henry wrote in the margin 'bene'! He also underlined the whole passage, and against Bonner's statement that the Emperor had told the Pope not to trouble to send him a Cardinal to mediate between him and Francis he wrote a satisfied 'N. bene'. By February, 1543, a compromise was arrived at: the stumbling-block was cast aside, and in the secret treaty signed on the 11th both princes agreed that neither would accept any ally or confederate who was an enemy of the other.

The progress of events can be gathered from the following letters, which are more or less self-explanatory.

1. To Francis I

[*July* 23, 1542.]

RIGHT EXCELLENT, RIGHT HIGH AND MIGHTY PRINCE, our dearest brother, cousin, and perpetual ally: we commend us unto you in our most hearty and effectual manner; advertising you that we have received your letters addressed unto us by the bearer, one of your secretaries: and have heard the credence committed to the same, containing specially two points: the one, the injuries and meschantes, as he called them, done unto you by the Emperor, not only in the detaining and keeping from you of certain your possessions, but also in the killing of sundry your ambassadors, as the said Secretary said, *contra jus gentium*; whereby you were determined to proceed to the revenge of it, as your honour enforced: the other, that you have made a league, both offensive and defensive, with the Dukes of Saxony and Cleves, and the Kings of Denmark, Sweden and Scotland, wherein you have reserved an honourable place for us, with six months' space for the knowledge and determination of our mind, whether we shall think meet to enter into the same, or no: desiring therefore to knowledge our intent in that behalf.

Right excellent, etc.; it shall like you for answer to understand that we be not a little sorry, by this and other means, to perceive and see that by the dissensions of you two, being great princes in Christendom and our friends, the state of Christendom should be in such perturbation, and such an entry made to the common enemy of the same, the Turk, as must undoubtedly redound to the great ruin and desolation thereof, unless God of His infinite goodness shall provide for some agreement between you, or some other remedy for it. Touching which agreement, we doubt not but you do well remember how we have heretofore offered ourself to be a mean, at which time you seemed rather to put your confidence in the Bishop of Rome, so as the sequel declareth the matter to be nothing amended, but in worse terms than it was before. Nevertheless, if our wit, power, authority or friendship might do anything in it, and you both so contented, we would yet be glad to employ it to both your commodities, and the benefit and quiet of Christendom, with the repulse of the common enemy of the same.

Second, we do right heartily thank you for your overture touching your leagues made with the princes before-named. But forasmuch as we have ever determined to keep our amities as our honour requireth, and not used to enter into any treaty before we saw and considered the articles of the same; we have thought meet to desire and pray you to deliver a copy of the articles of your said leagues to our ambassador resident with you, to be by him sent unto us. Which if it shall like you to do with some diligence, we shall, upon the sight of them, make unto you such our answer, before the six months shall be determined, as shall be reasonable. Right excellent, right high,

The following letter to Paget, ambassador at the court of Francis, gives a good idea of the negotiations Henry was carrying on with France, and also of the degree of secrecy attached to his 'secret' treaty with the Emperor.

II. To Sir William Paget

[*Oct.* 24, 1542.]

Trusty and right well beloved, we greet you well. Letting you wit that by the continues of your sundry letters lately addressed unto us we have not only perceived your dexterity and diligence in the execution of the charge committed unto you, which we take in very good and thankful part, but also how the French King and his Council seem to fear, and to take it in manner for a thing certain, that we have concluded a new league with the Emperor, having of late tasted[1] you therein both by La Planche and by the Admiral himself, and therewithal assayed what hope they might gather of the continuance of our good will and amity towards them, by the mean of some new overture to be made of the marriage between our daughter Mary and the Duke of Orleans, or otherwise that might serve for that purpose. For answer whereunto you shall understand that, knowing by experience the practices of the world, and perceiving how men do now days bruit things for their commodity, declaring them sometimes to be of other sort than indeed they were ever meant or intended; we have thought convenient by these our letters to instruct you how you shall proceed there, both to give them some inkling how we stand with the said Emperor, and also what you weigh[2] in that matter of the amity lately in communication between us; to the intent that, taking your occasion upon some other ground and matter to commune with the Admiral or such other of the Council as you shall think meet, you may of yourself so touch those matters as they may gather of our words that yourself is of a good affection towards them, and that you think and doubt not but we be also clear from any new amity with the Emperor, and, as you think, of good inclination towards them, if they would minister any reasonable and friendly matter whereupon to experiment the same.

And first, touching the Emperor, you may say of yourself that, forasmuch as they have been in hand with you sundry times to know whether we had entered any league or new amity with him, at which times they have also showed themselves desirous of the entertainment of our amity, you wrote home to some of your secret friends here to give you advertisement how things stood, and what you might be bold to say touching both those matters; and you have received an answer again from your said

[1] Tested.
[2] Consider, make estimation of.

friends, that, whatsoever bruits and noises be spread abroad, or whatsoever overtures have been made unto us, there was neither new league made with him the day of writing hereof, nor any marriage concluded with him, neither that we have lent him any money; only it is written to you, that certain matters touching the merchants on both parties, which were in controversy, and bred to the said merchants on both parties no small incommodities, be discussed and ordered; which is all that you can learn is done with him, albeit it is written to you that the Imperials have much pressed a straiter amity between us; and therefore you may say, it shall not be well done that they give credit to any light reports, for you dare be bold to say that, when these were written, the date whereof you may allege of yourself, all is untrue that hath been affirmed to the contrary.

Second, you shall say that as touching our affection to our good brother the French King, you think assuredly it hath been, and yet is, you doubt not, of such sort as would prefer his amity before all others, so as it might be established in such sort as should declare as hearty love and affection to be in him towards us as we have born to him, and that our honour were so considered in the same, as appertaineth. And you may say that, if they would weigh deeply how necessary this amity and this perfect knot between both realms should be for them and their posterities, you doubt not but they would work more earnestly and reasonably for the conclusion of it, and the removing of all doubts that might in any wise breed any quarrel hereafter; which they might easily do, if that matter of the pension, and the arrearages due of the same, were so entreated with us and provided for, as you think it might be, if they would earnestly and reasonably set in hand with it. For you may say, you think assuredly there is in us such a rooted love and affection towards our good brother, as in respect of the same we could be content to grow to some reasonable moderation of our pension, so as we might have any reasonable and honourable recompence for the same. But how far it varied from reason and all friendly equality to ask that which they asked when the matter was last in communication, you may say you doubt not but, if the French King would change parties with us in it, and indifferently weigh it, himself would judge and think that it required a much further consideration and recompence than was offered. And surely, if the matter had been anything friendly, and with any manner of reasonable conditions treated with us, you think we would not have refused it. It was bare tallage that Princes might grant what they would in respect of marriage, where the demand was such as the like was never heard of; and yet His Majesty was then content, and as you think would yet be, to give a greater portion in respect of that marriage than ever was given in a like or a far greater case; so as we might have some reasonable way devised for the rest that should not be remitted in respect of the same, either by stalling[1] the remnant of the arrearages to days of payment and the moderation of the pension, or by the giving of some lands to us in recompence of it, which might be done without any their great lack or damage; yea, and in your opinion much to their surety: as, to utter your own fantasy, if they would presently give us Ardres, with the confines, which is but a small matter, with the country of Brednerd,[2] which they have but lately overrun and devasted, and Turneham and Mountory, which they have not yet in peaceable possession, with some other such corner or piece of ground as might be commodious for us, and be a mean of establishment of such meets and bounds between us, as should for ever abolish all cause and occasion of contention and quarrel between both realms: and for the rest, that should not with these things be countervailed, to covenant that if hereafter he should chance to get any other things meet for us, to give us the same in full and clear recompence of all matters now between us.

By this or some like devices you may say they might, as you think, be most assured of our friendship, which might stand them, if they weigh it well, in no small stead; as, if they consider things well, you may say of yourself that they give pensions to many, which might better be withdrawn than this, and cannot stand them in any such stead as we may. For if we two were once thus surely knit and conjoined together, and all these matters

[1] Fixing the days for making payments by instalments.

[2] Brednerd is Bredenard, a district in Flanders; Turneham is Tourneham in Artois, and Mountory the castle of Montoire between Audruick and Tournehem.

for ever extinguished, we might work great things, both for the benefit of Christendom, and also for both our own private commodities; specially having joined with us some of the Princes of Almayn, whom we doubt not to bear good will unto us. Willing you of yourself to open this discourse to them, and as received from a friend of yours here, and in no wise from us; that by their answer, which our pleasure is you shall send to us with all diligence, we may perceive how they be inclined, and whether they do indeed so much desire our amity as hath been pretended.

One of Henry's causes of complaint against France was that his life-pension of 100,000 crowns, originally granted in 1525 (see p. 39) was in arrears to the extent of a million crowns. This was bad enough, but a worse insolence followed, when it came out that what the French would expect by way of dowry with the Princess Mary was nothing less than the cancellation of all arrears, and the transfer of the French pensions to the Duke of Orleans. In the next letter yet another cause for complaint is set forth—namely, the arrest by France, early in 1543, of all English merchant ships in French ports, as a retaliation for Henry's capture of French pirate ships in the channel.

III. To Paget

[*Feb.* 9, 1543.]

Trusty and right well beloved, we greet you well. Letting you wit that we have received your sundry letters, as well those of the second and fourth of this present as also your last of the 6th of the same; and by the continues thereof do perceive your conferences both with the French King and the Cardinal of Tournon, wherein you have used yourself in such sort as is much to our contentation. And forasmuch as the Frenchmen make their ground and foundation of these last injuries in the arresting of our ships and merchants goods in France upon the matter of the French ships here stayed at the Wight; our pleasure is that, upon the receipt hereof, you shall repair to the French King's Council, and on our behalf declare unto them that we much marvel of this their unkind manner of proceeding towards us, which is not only most contrary to the amity contracted between us and our good brother their master, but is also void of all pretence and colour of reason and justice. For, to compare the proceedings of both parties together, you may say that the French ships stayed here gave just occasion of it themselves, as well by their presumptuous attemptate in the open taking of one of our subjects in our own port, contrary both to friendship and all humanity, seeing they were entered in to the same for their safeguard, and had the commodity of it, and by the conveying away and aiding of him with their boats which did the said attemptate, as by their refusal after to speak with our officers coming in gentle sort to them, and the putting of themselves in order as enemies, without suffering any man to come near, till our said officers were fain to arm out ships and boats, and therewithall to take them perforce. On the other side the English ships arrested there offended not, ne gave any manner of occasion wherefore they might by any colour be troubled, so as their doing in that behalf is merely contrary to the amity. Wherefore you shall desire them to see the said ships and also all our merchants goods arrested in France undelayedly delivered, according to reason and the amity between us; considering they have no ground to detain them, for it is no reason to detain them that have not offended, for those which offended, and did what in them was to violate the amity, which they cannot, as is aforesaid, detain, but contrary to the league, and with rupture of the same: or else we must needs think that they intend not the observation of the said league, and will take order for the preservation and safeguard of our subjects, and for the requittal of their injuries accordingly; praying them to ascertain us with speed of their determination in that behalf, for we had much liefer they declared themselves open enemies, than under pretence of amity thus to deceive our expectation and injuriate our subjects. Requiring them, therefore, that they will put undelayed redress to these matters, as to the leagues do appertain; and for our part they may be assured that, they handling us as their friend, their subjects here shall be used accordingly with justice. Signifying further unto you, that by the next post we shall address our letters to the French King for your return accordingly.

As soon as the 'secret' of the Anglo-Imperial alliance came

to the ears of Francis he tried to buy off Henry by promising to pay all his debts and pensions, and to cease interfering in Scotland. Henry and Charles, however, had bound themselves, in the event of war with France, not to treat separately either for a truce or for peace; and in spite of this tempting offer, Henry kept solemnly to his pact, recalled his ambassador from Paris, and on June 23 declared war. The only action in which the English were concerned during 1543, however, was the siege of Landrecies in Flanders. A small force of some five or six thousand men, under the command of Sir John Wallop, served with the Emperor's army from July till November, when according to the ancient habit of armies in Gaul, they went into winter quarters.

Henry himself crossed to France in July, 1544, and the progress of events can be followed in the next three letters.

The first is a sign manual warrant issued in order to raise a forced loan. It had been preceded in 1542 by a similar one, from the repayment of which Henry had been released by Parliament in 1543. Moreover, in 1543, subsidies had been raised from both clergy and laity. To these indications of the enormous cost of the war must also be added a benevolence of two shillings in the pound which was raised in the following year.

IV. To the Privy Council, and Others

[*Aug.* 11, 1544.]

Trusty and well beloved, we greet you well. And whereas being entered into league and amity with our good brother, the Emperor, and having covenanted with the same to invade presently, this year, the realm of France, as well for the preservation of the state of Christendom, as for sundry our just and lawful quarrels against the French King, for the which purpose, and for the better conducting of our affairs in that behalf, we have already passed the seas in our own person with our puissant army; forasmuch as by the entry of the said wars, which (thanks be to Almighty God) we have hitherto passed to our honour, with good likelihood of better success, we see manifest occasion of much greater charge than was at the beginning considered; as well for the tarrying longer forth, upon sundry respects other than was determined before our going, as also for the leaving of some mass of money for the furniture and keeping such holds and places of strength, as we have already gotten, and shall, by the grace of God, get hereafter: we have thought expedient to foresee, that for want of a sufficient furniture, we be not enforced, leaving undone things necessary to be done, to retire ourself sooner than either sha[ll be] meet for our honour, or convenient for the advancement of our affairs; and therefore, considering the time so near at hand, as we cannot use any other present means for the supplement hereof than with being bold of such our assured loving subjects as we know will not stick to press themselves to satisfy our desire herein, as well in regard of the common weal of their natural country as of their particular obedience and singular affection towards us. And reputing you one amongst the rest, of that sort, so well dedicated unto us, as will and can gratify us in this behalf, we have thought good to desire and pray you, and in consideration of the present state, as well of Christendom, as of the common weal of this our realm, earnestly to require you to show yourself, now at this time specially, so loving a subject unto us, as you will make mean, either of your self, or your friends, to lend unto us the sum of sterling, and to provide so therefore that the same may be delivered at London, unto our trusty and right well-beloved Councillor, [Sir John Williams Knight, Treasurer of the augmentations of our Crown,][1] within days next ensuing the date hereof; whereby as you for your part, following the steps of divers of your degree and quality who have already right honestly and frankly declared their love towards us, upon this our like request made unto them, shall give us good cause to take the same at your hands very thankfully, and kindly, as an argument of the good affection you bear unto us, and the benefit of the common weal of this your natural country, so we promise you assuredly, by these presents, to cause the same to be repaid unto you, within after the date hereof; heartly praying you in no wise to fail us herein at this time, but lovingly and frankly to strain yourself to satisfy our expectation of you, as ye tender our favour and the advancement of the affairs and common wealth of this our Realm.

[1] Supplied from S.P.I., §190, f. 243v, except for *Williams*.

The second letter shows Francis at work trying to separate the allies. Charles had been unsuccessfully besieging St. Dizier since the beginning of July: Henry had been equally unsuccessful at Boulogne and Montreuil; so Francis wrote to each of them privately to suggest how profitable it would be to make peace with him. Henry sent his letter on to Charles, and answered Francis as follows.

v. To Francis I

[*Aug.* 3, 1544.]

Monsieur my good brother, I have received your letter by this bearer the Sieur de Framozelles, and have understood his credentials, but marvel not the less at the beginning of this your last letter than at that which formerly you wrote me: because as this overture for peace was, as you know, first proposed by the Sieur de St. Martin, your subject, and, after I had shown myself averse to give ear thereunto, was again renewed by Monsieur le Marechal du Biez, and the Seigneur de Vervins your captain at Boulogne: yet in this your said last letter you speak as if the matter had been first set forth by us, wherein you greatly touch our honour, the which, as you are aware, having always guarded inviolably to this present, I will never consent in my old age that it shall be anyway distained. As for the proposal that the said Sieur de Framozelles has made me for peace, praying me on your part to know the intent of our good brother the Emperor in this matter: I am glad, as much for respect to the tranquillity and universal good of Christendom, as for the friendship which has hitherto been between us, to be a mediator with our said good brother the Emperor, so that you will make him by us such sufficient offers as he shall have good reason to accept them; beseeching you to be content with this answer for the present, for until we shall have sent him word of this matter, it is not possible, neither on my part nor on his, honourably to give you any more precise answer. In that, by your fault, or at the least the fault of your counsellors, having been constrained to take up arms against you, I cannot (with mine honour) renew our friendship, without that our said good brother the Emperor be advertised thereof, and be as fully considered, as to him appertains.

Wherefore at your request I am sending post haste to him, to know his disposition in this matter, trusting within 15 or 20 days at the utmost, to have answer from him; about which time, if you will send to us, we will let you have more ample reply in this matter, the which may find good issue if you will show yourself as well affected to the weal of Christendom as you write you are, and as conformable to reason as behoveth.

The third letter is particularly interesting. Although the greater part of it was written by a secretary, it was obviously all dictated by Henry. Addressed to his wife, Katharine Parr, it is one of the very few personal letters written by Henry in his later years, and its simpler and more familiar style is very noticeable. It gives a most characteristic glimpse of the King, 'caring for everything ourself', summing-up very succinctly the position of affairs and appraising with equal shrewdness the motives of his ally.

VI. TO KATHARINE PARR

[*Sept.* 8, 1544.]

MOST DEARLY AND MOST ENTIRELY BELOVED WIFE, we recommend us heartily unto you, and thank you as well for your letter written unto us by your servant Robert Warner as for the venison which you sent then by him, and now last by Fowler, servant unto our dearest son the Prince, for the which we give unto you our hearty thanks, and would have written unto you again a letter with our own hand, but that we be so occupied, and have so much to do in foreseeing and caring for everything ourself, as we have almost no manner rest or leisure to do any other thing.

The cause why we have detained here so long your said servant hath been upon hope to have sent you by him good news of the taking of the town, which no doubt we should have done, by the grace of God, before this time, but that our provision of powder is not come out of Flanders as we thought it would. Within two or three days we look for it here, and then shortly after we trust to write unto you some good news. And yet, in the mean season, we have done somewhat of importance, for we have won, (and that without any loss of men) the strongest part of the town, which is the bray[1] of the castle—such a piece, and of such strength, as now that we have it in our hands we think four hundred of our men within it shall be able to keep it against four thousand of our enemies, and yet it is much weaker to the castle side than it was outward to us.

It lieth afore the castle, which hath no loop or flank to beat it, so as our men be in it in safety in some part thereof, but not in all, having the dyke at our commandment but not with sure biding in it, both for the top of the castle and a ring that goeth about it; for which ring there is good hoping, for we would fain have it, and they be loath to lose it: so sometime it is ours and another time theirs; but yet we trust to set them by it. But hitherto they have hardily defended it, and fought hand to hand for it, much manfuller than other Burgundian or Flemings would have done; for such as we have of them will do no good where any danger is, nor yet abide there with their will. This, and lying in another place within their first dyke, and almost as well entered the second, is hitherto as far forth as hath been done, saving that we lie so nigh them round about the town that we take more hurt with stones than ordnance.

Further, the French King is very desirous of a peace, and maketh much suit unto us for the same, insomuch as he hath sent unto us a letter of his own hand, desiring by the same a safe-conduct for certain notable personages to repair unto us from him in ambassade: that is to say, the Cardinal of Bellay, the premier president of Rouen, the premier Treasurer of all the finances of France, the Captain of the Guard to the Dauphin, being a Gentleman of his Privy Chamber, and one of his principal Secretaries, who be come hitherward on their way to Abbeville, attending for our safe-conduct, which we have sent to them, and have appointed our castle of Hardelow, (whereof you have been advertised heretofore,) for them to repair unto, and fifty horses in their company, twenty to be lodged within our said castle and the rest abroad in other places at our appointment.

And for because the said French King hath promised to use our advice for the making of his appointment with the Emperor, we have of late written to our ambassador with him to know

[1] Outwork.

what things he will demand, which he hath sent to us in certain articles touched somewhat with the extremist; and we again have, upon his desire to know our demand in case the French men would sue to him for peace, sent to him for our demands certain articles containing to have satisfaction of the arrearages due unto us for our pension, with all manner damages and interests which we have sustained by reason of the wars, and also the realm of France, with the duchies of Normandy, Aquitaine and Guienne, which demands we have made to meet with the extremity of the Emperor's demands, which be so sore, as it should appear, that either he mindeth to have no peace, or that, if any peace should be treated, he would pluck the honour of the compounding of it out of our hand, notwithstanding that the matter was committed to us by the French King's suit, and that also, as the French King sayeth, he never made means to the Emperor for a peace; all which these our advertisements we pray you communicate unto our Council attendant upon you there.

And whereas you desired to know our pleasure for the accepting into[1] your Chamber of certain ladies in places of others that cannot well give their attendance by reason of sickness; albeit we think those whom you have named unto us as unable almost to attend by reason of weakness as the[2] others be, yet we remit the accepting of them to your own choice, thinking, nevertheless, that though they shall not be meet to serve, yet you may, if you think so good, take them into[1] your chamber to pass the time sometime with you at play, or otherwise to accompany you for your recreation.

As touching your request made unto us for Archer's wife, we are content, at your desire, to stay the giving from her of those things you wrote for, and so may you do there until you hear further of our pleasure, in case any person would sue to have any of them.

At this point Henry took the letter and added a short postscript in his own hand.

At the closing up of these our letters [the bysyzing of] the castle afore-named, with the dyke, is at our comman[d]ment, and

[1] Rymer *unto* [2] Rymer omits.

not like to be recovered by the Frenchmen again, as we trust; not doubting with God's grace but that the castle and town shall shortly follow the same trade, for as this day, which is the eighth day of September, we begin three batteries, and have three mines going, besides one which hath done his execution in shaking and tearing off one of their greatest bulwarks. No more to you at this time, sweetheart, both for lack of time and great occupation of business, saving we pray you to give in our name our hearty blessings to all our children, and recommendations to our cousin Margaret[1] and the rest of the ladies and gentlewomen, and to our Council also.

Written with the hand of your loving husband,

HENRY R.

The mining that Henry speaks of was almost immediately successful. On September 11 a mine was exploded under the castle, and on the 14th the town surrendered. The siege of Montreuil, however, had to be raised on the 26th; and on the 30th Henry himself returned to England, leaving Norfolk to occupy the heights behind Boulogne, in order to prevent it being retaken by the Dauphin.

The letter that follows shows Henry dealing openly and fairly with his ally, and informing him of the French overtures. Dr. Nicholas Wotton, to whom the letter was addressed, was his ambassador with the Emperor.

VII. To Wotton

By the King

[*Aug.* 5, 1544.]

TRUSTY AND RIGHT WELL BELOVED, we greet you well. Letting you wit that we have received your sundry letters, and give unto you our hearty thanks for the advertisements contained in the same. Nevertheless, we would be glad to hear from you more particularly, if ye can get the knowledge of it, what number of horsemen, footmen, pioneers, ordnance, and munition there is in that army, and what you hear also of the Emperor's marching to Paris. And whereas a gentleman of France, called St. Martin, hath heretofore been made by Monsieur de Bies and Monsieur

[1] i.e. Margaret Douglas, his sister's daughter.

de Vervins, Captain of Boulloyn, (at the appointment, as it should seem now, of the French King) a mean to practice with certain gentlemen of Calais and Guisnes for an overture to be made unto us for peace, and brought the matter so far forward that the French King himself was glad to write to us in that behalf; to the which practice the Emperor's late Ambassador here with us was ever from time to time made privy, and our Secretary, Sir William Paget, sent from us unto our good brother, as you know, to declare unto him among other things the whole continue of the said practise, showing to him both the original letter sent to us from the French King, and also the copy of our answer unto him again; these shall be to signify unto you, the French King now of late hath eftsoons renewed the said request for a peace, and sent hither to us a gentleman of Boullonnoys called Framozelles with letters of credence, as such offers, as you shall perceive by the copy thereof, which, together with the copy of our answer you shall receive, to the intent you may show the same at your next access unto the Emperor, which we require you to make as soon as you can conveniently; and then with our most hearty commendations declaring unto him the renewing of the said practise as aforesaid, you shall say that, considering the earnest request and desire the French King showeth himself to have to make his peace, as well with us as with our said good brother, and his offer to be advised by us concerning the matters of difference between them twain; and that also in case the said French King indeed come to reason for the satisfaction of us both, there must needs ensue a singular benefit to the common weal of Christendom, being by these wars amongst ourselves not only so devasted, as in many years it cannot be recovered, but also so over-run by the Turk our common enemy, as, if God put not shortly an order and quietness among Christian Princes, our religion shall greatly decay, and Christendom thereby brought shortly in to thraldom; and considering also that the war cannot endure always, but once there must an end be had: we have thought good to confer hereupon with our said good brother the Emperor, and to devise with him for such a bargain to be made with the French King, in case he shall eftsoons sue earnestly for the same, as may be most beneficial unto us both.

For likeas we have only heard, and that not without the consent of our said good brother the Emperor, who hath himself done the semblable, so you may say he may be assured we will never consent or agree to any accord with the said French King, without such a regard be first had for his satisfaction as our amity doth require. Whereunto if the said French King shall refuse to agree, our said good brother may be assured that we will never take peace with him, although he would for our particular satisfaction make us never so large a proffer. Wherefore, seeing the said French King hath now offered unto us to be advised by us concerning the satisfaction of our said good brother, we, minding in no wise to work without him, and thinking we shall the better proceed in this matter with his advice and counsel, desire to be informed what things he will be contented withal, and to signify unto us by degrees what he will first ask; and secondly, to what point he will resolve to come to at the last, to the intent we may work for him thereafter accordingly; praying him to send the same unto us in writing signed with his hand, like as we for our part will use the semblable manner of proceedings with him touching the declaration of our mind for such things as we would have brought to pass for our satisfaction, in case the French King shall upon occasion enter to practise with him, and that our good brother doth advertise us of the same. By this mean, the one of us knowing what the other would desire, may make our bargain the better with our adversary, and provide for another's benefit and commodity as occasion shall require, and yet in the mean season to let nothing of our enterprises: nothing doubting but, as we will have such a regard of his honour and profit as becometh one perfect friend to have of another, so he will use himself towards us in semblable manner. Requiring you for the obtaining of his said demands, with a perfect answer in the premises, to use such dexterity as we may have the same from you within these 15 or 20 days at the furthest, and so to handle the matter with the Emperor and Monsr. de Granvelle as they conceive no sinister opinion of our proceedings in this behalf, as indeed we mind in no wise to give them any occasion to the same, but have utterly determined with ourselves to preserve our honour, and to use ourselves towards him in the handling of this matter as the friendship between us doth require, whereof you may assure them on our behalf. . . .

The Emperor's reply, inspired by Granvelle, while suggesting that the offers made to England were inadequate, proposed terms for himself that obviously could not be granted. Henry, apparently perplexed by these exorbitant demands, made answer in the following letter. He finds the demands 'couched in such extremities . . .

VIII. To Wotton

[*Sept.* 1544.]

. . . and so far out of the limits of the treaty, as we cannot a little marvel, and have occasion to think that either our said good brother mindeth in no wise to fall to any reasonable composition, or at the least that, if any be made, we should not have the handling of the same. The treaty bindeth us at the most no further than that the Emperor may have the Duchy of Burgundy, and certain towns here in Picardy; and the articles, which the Ambassadors have delivered unto us as the articles whereupon the Emperor will rest, contain demands that himself, the Empire, the King of Romans, the States of Italy, the Commonalty of Sienna, may have restitution of their damages by reason of these last wars; that the Duke of Savoy be restored to all such lands as the French King withholdeth of his, as well on this side as beyond the mountains; that the treaties of Cambrai and Madrid be entirely performed by the French King; that restitution be made unto him of the Duchy of Burgundy and the Viscounty of Ausonne, with all the mean profits perceived by the French King sithens his first possession of them; that Estanay be delivered unto him as a forfeiture; and that all other places, wheresoever they be, which the French King hath taken from him sithens the beginning of this last war, be restored unto him, with the interests. Which demands be such, as, if our said good brother stick to them in treating with the Admiral, when he cometh unto him, the French King neither will, we suppose, take upon him to perform them, nor can be able, we be assured, although he would never so fain; which albeit we write unto you in the terms aforesaid, to the intent you may know how we take the same, yet we mind not that you should declare to the Emperor or Granvelle that we mislike the same, unless that any of them first find fault with ours, as demands too extreme; and then our pleasure is you shall with good terms answer that we require nothing more than is in our treaty; whereas a great sort of his demands be not contained in the same, like as you may perceive by the perusing over of the said treaty.

As touching the demands which we require to be made by our said good brother the Emperor for our part in his treaty with the French King, we send unto you in articles herewith the same, being correspondent to that we may ask by our treaty, and containing nothing more; which our pleasure is you shall present unto our good brother the Emperor, first without subscribing the same, and afterwards, in case you shall be required to the subscription, say you have no commandment or commission so to do, and yet you will take upon you to subscribe them, so as they will there let you have a copy of the articles sent hither from thence for your better instruction; for that manner of proceeding the Ambassadors here used with us, refusing to sign their said articles until they were promised a copy of those which we send now unto you; saying also they did subscribe on their own heads, having no commission or commandment to do the same, which by the way you may note unto Granvelle and the Viceroy, because they promised unto you otherwise. . . .

At the beginning of September Charles began to advance on Paris, deliberately leaving the Dauphin in his rear to cut off his supplies. As Charles was no fool it is to be presumed that he was deliberately getting himself into a position in which he would be 'forced' to make a separate peace, having first by secret negotiations assured himself that whatever happened to Henry he himself would secure what he wanted out of the war. The position of affairs, and Henry's attitude, are clearly indicated in the following. Professor A. F. Pollard considers that in the race between Charles and Henry to see who could make peace first and extract the greater profit, 'Charles proved the nimbler'. He describes the Emperor's duping of Henry as a 'masterpiece of unscrupulous statecraft'.

IX. To Wotton

[*Sept.* 15, 1544.]

. . . And to the first, whereas the Admiral hath offered (as the said Monsr. d'Arras hath informed us) to restore unto the Emperor and the Duke of Savoy, incontinently, all such places as the said French King hath taken from them sithens the last wars, and also furnish the Emperor against the Turk of 600 men of arms and 10,000 footmen, or to give him the soulde[1] of the same; and that, for a further increase of amity between the Emperor and the French King, if the Emperor will be contented to give either the Princess of Spain in marriage to the Duke of Orleans with all the Low Countries, or else the second daughter of King Ferdinand with the Duchy of Milan, the French King will restore to the Emperor and the Duke of Savoy all that ever he holdeth of theirs, both beyond and on this side the mountains; and for our satisfaction hath offered only to pay us our arrearages, part in hand, and part at reasonable days, and for payment of our said pension hereafter to be ordered therein by the Emperor's advice: you shall say, that having no less regard unto the Emperor's honour for the conclusions of these matters than we have unto our own, we have thought good not only to signify unto him our friendly opinion touching his own matters, which we take to be common unto us, but also, notwithstanding the said French King hath sent the Cardinal of Bellay, the Premier President of Rouen, and the Secretary L'aubespine, the Chief Treasurer of his Finances, as special commissioners to treat with us for a peace, yet to advertise him by you, as we have partly done by Monsr. d'Arras, in what sort we mind to agree to the peace, and what thing we desire to have for our satisfaction, without the which we would not willingly agree to a peace.

And to the first, we think surely that, considering the great charges and defrays the Emperor hath been enforced to make by

[1] Soldiers' pay.

reason of these wars, and what damage and trouble his subjects have sustained by the same, and likewise what great things he is content to give in a marriage to made with the second son of France, the eldest son having issue male alive; this party, if it be concluded, shall scant be so beneficial and honourable to the Emperor as we would wish it; and yet that overture least beneficial, which is made for the marriage of his daughter, she being Princess of Spain, and if it should chance the Prince to die, which God forbid, the heritor to the Emperor of all that he hath, besides that the forgoing with her in marriage of the Low Countries should be so great a detriment to all the rest of the Emperor's dominions, as all his posterity after him should repent the same. And therefore surely our advice is, which we give unto him of our friendly and amicable love and affection, that he neither marry such an heir in likelihood of so many seignories unto a Duke of Orleans, nor yet give with her so great and profitable a jewel as the Nether Country is.

And as for the overture of the marriage of the King of Romans' daughter, albeit we think too large a dower proferred with the same, yet we esteem it rather to be embraced than the other : for as for the Duchy of Milan, being a thing appertainant to the Empire, may, after the decease of the Emperor, come into some controversy, to whom it shall descend, and yet cannot, when it is had, be kept without inestimable charges; whereas the Low Country, being the certain inheritance of the Emperor's succession out of all doubt and question, and guardable without any great charges, if it should be given from his son in marriage with the daughter, may hereafter grow to some inconvenience : which our said good brother can of his wisdom well consider, and seeth that the one of the two overtures is much rather to be embraced than the other.

And as touching the offers for our part that is made there, we doubt not but the Emperor himself findeth the same so meagre, and we know them so far under that which hath been offered unto us already, that neither he, we think, would counsel us, nor we can be contented of our honour to receive. They have offered here already to pay unto us our arrearages out of hand, to make us satisfaction for our damages of our wars, to continue our pension, and for the accomplishments of these pourtes to give us good and sure hostages, to remit Arde with the territory to our disposition, and to cause the Scots to be ordered in reason by us, or else to abandon them; wherewithall if they shall also renounce all the claim they can make to Boulogne and Boullougnois (which we have now in our possession), and also surrender unto us the whole County of Guisnez, we will be contented to condescend to an agreement: or else, in case the continual payment of the said pension shall seem a perpetual burden unto the French King, and therefore he would be loath to condescend to the agreement of the peace with our said good brother upon that condition, we shall be contented if the said French King will, instead of our pension, render unto us the County of Ponthieu and Montreuil with the territory (notwithstanding we be indeed like very shortly to win the same), to embrace it, and to renounce our claim to the said pension; desiring our good brother to stick to us to one of these two overtures, unless the state of his affairs at this present be such as he shall think it expedient to have peace, and that the French King will not agree unto the same, if he should be bound to pay all such sums of money as we demand to be paid unto us of him for our domaiges; and in that case we are pleased, to the intent our good brother the Emperor may the better make his bargain, and the sooner to induce them to his contentation, albeit our said domaiges have been unto us very chargeable, for his sake yet to remit the same, having good and substantial hostages for the performance of the rest; advertising our said good brother that by all likelihood of conferences of our Commissioners and the said Cardinal of Bellay and the others from the said French King, there is appearance that they will incline to the same, and more.

And, whereas our said good brother would be glad, in case the peace go not forward, that our army should march towards Paris, ye shall say to him, that no man would be gladder it should so do than we; but, considering that as it hath been necessary for him to take up such towns as have lain in his way, without the which he could not well have passed, so we have been enforced to do the semblable; by reason whereof, as he saith, the time of the year is now so far spent as it will not serve to go thither, much less to go and come again, besides that the country is so devasted on every side as we shall not find sufficiently of victuals; our carriages here so few, and those out of Flanders likewise so few, for we could never have from thence a competent number; and therewithall so weak as they have been scant able in summer to travel to and fro for our victuals, and would be less able to go in winter to Paris. Our horsemen of Almayn, both those at our solde and at his, be so ill-willing to lie any longer abroad as they make their count to return home again soon upon Michaelmas. We cannot see, all these things considered, our armies can in any wise join, nor one of us come to the relief of another, though we would never so fain; and yet indeed (which you shall not utter, unless ye see the Emperor not satisfied with the foresaid considerations) we are not bound by our treaty to continue any longer our invasion than four months, the which expiring now shortly after Michaelmas, our said good brother, we doubt not, would consider the time we be too short for our said voyage. . . .

Having crushed his troublesome Lutheran subjects in Germany, and broken their alliance with France before he started on his march of invasion, Charles did not want a very great deal. Moderate as always, if he could secure Milan and keep Francis from interfering in Germany, he was willing to make peace. He was not anxious to preserve the alliance with Henry, into which only a difficult combination of circumstances had forced him. Nor did he wish to declare the Scots his enemies, as to do so would have interfered with the trading of his Flemish subjects. Realizing that Henry had no intention of marching on Paris, even if it had been possible, he at once proceeded to accept the 'necessity' of his position and to make a separate peace. The Bishop of Arras, Granvelle's son, had been sent by Charles to Henry to ask, either that Charles should be allowed to make peace to extricate himself, or else that Henry should raise the sieges of Boulogne and Montreuil and march to his assistance. The Bishop did what he was doubtless required to do, and gave his master the answer he wanted—that Henry consented to Charles making peace. Actually Henry had attached conditions

—that Charles must insist on the conceding of Henry's aims, as he himself had so recently insisted on behalf of Charles, which is made clear in a subsequent letter (No. xv) to Thirlby, first and only Bishop of Westminster, and one of Henry's ambassadors to the Emperor. As a result, however, of Arras's dissembling, Charles on September 19 signed the Peace of Crespy, by which Francis was detached from the Turks and from the Lutheran cause in Germany. England was not included, but the Emperor undertook to preserve his pact with Henry, and to arbitrate between him and Francis. In the first round Charles had undoubtedly got the better both of his enemy and of his ally.

In the negotiations that followed between England and France all might have been well but for Boulogne. Henry was determined to keep it, at all costs: Francis, prepared to yield on most points, was equally adamant on this. In October it was nearly recaptured by the Dauphin, Norfolk having retired to Calais and left it defended only by a small garrison. Had not the stupidity of this move been retrieved by the resource and gallantry of the defenders things would probably have gone hard with Norfolk, as is evident from the beginning of the next letter. Henry did not easily forgive the mistakes of his servants.

x. To Norfolk, Suffolk, and others of the Privy Council at Calais

By the King

HENRY R. [*Oct.* 14, 1544.]

Right trusty and right entirely well-beloved Cousins, right trusty and right well-beloved, and trusty and right well-beloved, we greet you well. Letting you wit that we have seen your letters of the 11th of this instant, and as well by the same as by your other letters addressed to our Council attendant upon our Person do well understand your humble submission with your like suits unto us to forget your late proceedings. For answer whereunto you shall understand, that, like as we think these suits and submissions to proceed from you being indeed penitent for that is past, so not doubting but this shall be a warning for you from henceforth, and that your meaning was for better purpose than that declared; considering also that God hath so wrought the thing as the inconveniences which might have ensued be now past, the enemies being retired, the victuals and ordnance at Boulogne being also set in good order; we are contented both to take this your humble submission partly for a recompense of that which is past, and also to remit and forget the same; trusting verily that for a fuller recompence of your offences you, like men of honour and courage, will not suffer our enemies, being so small a number, to be lodged in such places, as by Monsr. de Liques advertisements doth appear; but, as shortly as possibly may be, remove them from their lodgings, and totally ruinate and burn the same, so that from henceforth they may be no succours to our enemies: for the accomplishment whereof we would wish that, after as secret a manner as you may possibly, you, my Lords of Norfolk, Suffolk and Privy Seal, or such others as you assuredly trust, will execute the same, (having first good advertisements of the retire of the enemies, and taking with every of you or them such convenient furniture of men and munition as you shall think meet for that purpose) do all three, at one or divers times as you think best, secretly give the assay to those places, which being before reported unto us not to be tenible for our men, shall, we doubt not, be of as little force for the enemies; and so to use this matter as you may discomfit or take as many as you may of our enemies, and after raze and utterly waste the places, so as the enemy may have no more succours there; which enterprise we think shall not only be much to our honour (the enemies being put to the worst in all places, and we last in the field), but also a great quiet for our subjects there this winter, a continuance of our possession in Boullonoyes, and no small honour to you. And therefore we would you went merrily and courageously to this thing, the good achievement whereof we shall accept to redub things by-past, and further shall take the same in right good and thankful part towards you. And this thing being by you done, our pleasure is, that you, our Lieutenants, appointing two thousand of our men to pass to Boulogne, either by water or by land, as to you shall be thought most convenient, with such proportions of victuals as shall remain and may well be spared at Calais, and may conveniently serve them for three or four days at the least; and taking order also for such numbers to be left for the defence of our pieces and pales there as you shall think requisite, do put yourselves in order with the rest of our whole army to return home to us, having, nevertheless, before your transportation, good respect to your sure passage, with forsight of the strength of the enemies upon the seas: and if it shall be so thought to you expedient, you may stay unto such time as you shall hear that our other ships, which be already vailed,[1] and shall pass to the seas as soon as the wind will serve, be also joined with our navy there, and after to come in one conserve, if you conveniently may, togethers, whereby you shall be the more strong to withstand the enemies in all events.

And where it appeareth by your said letters that certain Italians and Spaniards have rendered themselves to serve us in the wars, we pray you to take such order as they may be honestly entertained, whereby you shall not only encourage them the better to serve us, but also learn both some part of the enemies proceedings, and also what captains or noblemen of theirs hath been slain; for the knowledge whereof we require you to travail, and after advertise us accordingly. Given under our Signet, at our Palace of Westminster, the 14th of October, the 36th year of our Reign.

After the French failure to recapture Boulogne a conference was arranged at Calais. English interests were represented by Hertford, Paget and Gardiner, the Empire by the Bishop of Arras, and France by Cardinal du Bellay. The French, having made their peace with Charles, were not prepared to yield the two things on which Henry had set his heart. They would not let England keep Boulogne, and they would not pledge themselves to non-interference in Scotland. England yielded upon other points, but here she was immovable, and in consequence the conference broke up in October, leaving England nominally supported but actually deserted by the Emperor, and at war with both France and Scotland. Annoying as it was to have been out-manœuvred by Charles, however, Henry had learnt the

[1] Having already dropped downstream.

value in diplomacy of the reiterated assertion that, whatever might be their temporary misunderstandings, he and the Emperor were always the best of friends and allies. The refusal to accept as a fact the Emperor's desertion, and the bland assumption that the Emperor would honour his agreements, are nicely illustrated in the following letter, which contains a number of alterations and insertions made by Henry himself.

XI. To Norfolk, Suffolk, and Privy Council at Calais[1]

By the King

Henry R. [*Oct.* 20, 1544.]

Right trusty and right entirely beloved Cousins, right trusty and right well-beloved, Right Reverend Father in God, and trusty and right well-beloved, we greet you well. And have received your sundry letters of the 18th of this instant, the one from you all and the other from you that were in the former commission; and by the contents of the same do perceive as well the haulte proceedings of the French Ambassadors, as the cold and unfriendly doings of the Bishop of Arras and his colleagues, with some of your advices and counsels for sending to the said Emperor. For answer whereunto, you shall understand that if we of ourself would be so fondly disposed to leave Boulogne, we think that you and all the rest of our realm neither would nor could take the same in good part, considering the great commodity of it for this realm; and would therefore rather advise us of fresh to employ all our forces to the defence of it, and to the further annoyance of our enemies. And thinking your counsel good in the sending to the Emperor to know what may be trusted to at his hand, we have thought good that YOU, ACCORDING TO YOUR ADVICE, pretending yet to have none answer from us, AND DOUBTING GREATLY WHEN YOU SHALL, by reason of the uncertainty and danger of the passage, in case the Frenchmen shall remain in the same terms at the receipt hereof that they were at the writing of your said letters, you, my Lords of Hertford and Winchester, MAY DECLARE TO THE EMPEROR'S AMBASSADORS THAT, SEEING THE

[1] Printed from the signed copy, P.R.O., S.P.I., §194, f. 6, with the King's corrections indicated, as shown in the draft, §194, f. 10.

FRENCH AMBASSADORS AND YOU AS YET CAN NO BETTER AGREE, AND THAT IT WILL BE A PRETTY WHILE, BY THE FORESAID REASONS, OR YOU MAY HEAR FROM US, THAT YOU HAVE IN COMMISSION ALREADY[1] IN that[2] CASE TO REPAIR to thc Emperor's person, like as our pleasure is INDEED YOU SHALL DO BY CONVENIENT post, leaving you, the Dukes of Norfolk and Suffolk, the Lord Privy Seal, Sir John Gage, Sir William Paget, and Sir Richard Riche to entertain both the Emperor's and the French Ambassadors till our answer may arrive with you. And at your coming to the said Emperor you shall present unto him our letters of credence, which we send unto you herewith, with the copy of the same; and, after our most hearty commendations, shall say, that at such time as it pleased us to address you to Calais, to treat with the French Ambassadors, our further pleasure and commandment was, that in case you should not find the said French Ambassadors conformable to grow to such an amity and peace as reason would, you should immediately make your repair to the said Emperor, and declare unto him on our behalf the full discourse and state of your proceedings with them, not doubting but that according to the good amity between us and the said Emperor, we shall find him always ready either to press the said French King to agree to such reasonable conditions of peace as we have been contented to condescend unto in respect of the common quiet of Christendom, being the same less than hath been heretofore offered unto us by his Ambassadors; or, if the said French King shall refuse to agree thereunto, that in that case the said Emperor will declare himself enemy, and join with us, as the said treaty bindeth; in the expressing whereof WE DOUBT NOT BUT THAT you, the Bishop of Winchester, SEEING YOU BE SO WILLING TO GO IN THIS COMMISSION, WILL plainly AND MANIFESTLY declare to the said Emperor such parts of the said treaty as do enforce AND BIND HIM TO the same, AND YOU BOTH TO PRESS HIM as much as you conveniently MAY, ACCORDING TO OUR EXPECTATION OF YOU, to do HEREIN AS IT becometh him IN THAT BEHALF, SO AS we may either obtain that

[1] Omitted in final version. [2] SUCH

we desire, or AT the least see what may be at his hand trusted to, in case we shall continue the war wherein he hath now THUS left us in; and thereupon to advertise us WITH ALL DILIGENCE, and so return to Calais AGAIN by CONVENIENT post, AND TO PERSUADE THE AMBASSADORS OF THE EMPEROR AT THE LEAST TO ENTERTAIN THE FRENCH AMBASSADORS STILL THERE TILL YOUR RETURN, OR ANSWER HAD FROM US, WHICH WE MIND NOT TO SEND, OR AT THE LEAST NOT TO HAVE IT DECLARED TO THEM, TILL YOUR REPAIR AGAIN.

And where you write of the numbers of the French army yet remaining about Montreuil, we cannot think it to be true, the reports as well of such gentlemen as were at the camp, the advertisements of the trumpets and other espialls, the scarcity of the victuals, the famine and death of horses, considered.

And understanding that the number of our men at Calais doth daily diminish, by reason of the death now being there; forasmuch as we think it necessary, and therefore intend to make certain fortifications at Base Boulogne, without the which, and the keeping of the same in the mean season, we shall not be able to keep the haven, the lack whereof would be such a maim for the victualling of that town, as, what pain soever we take for it, we must provide that our purpose therein may be accomplished; we would be very glad to have the number of two thousand of our best men now being at Calais to be sent to Boulogne, if you may by any means see them furnished of sufficient victuals for twelve or fourteen days, whereunto we pray you to have a diligent and an earnest respect: and doubt you not but, by the grace of God, we shall within that time cause the passage so to be opened as both you and they at Boulogne shall want no victuals, but have sufficient furniture of the same, and have also taken order that, howsoever the passage be stopped, some refreshing shall come unto you. . . .

Given under our Signet, at our palace of Westminster, the 20th of October, the 36th year of our Reign, at midnight.

The final breaking-off of the conference was precipitated by Henry's refusal, in a letter of October 26, of the Articles proposed by the French.

XII. Answers to be made by the King's Majesty's Commissioners

To the Cardinal's saying that touching the renunciation of the amity with Scotland, or the foregoing of Boulogne, Ardres, or Guisnes, the final resolution was his master would none of them, and thereto he said the King's Majesty might trust: His Highness pleasure is, that you shall answer that this article is so unreasonable, so unjust, and so far discrepant from both the contents of the French King's own hands, and also the Cardinal's credence, declared to His Majesty in the camp, after Boulogne was won, that His Highness cannot think the said Cardinal to be so much his friend as he did before, seeing he now returned with so unjust and peremptory answer; and His Majesty is sorry to see his great kindness, not a few times showed to his master, so suddenly forgotten: and therefore seeing reason ruleth not will on their behalf, reason willeth that *clavus clavo trudatur.*[1]

To the Cardinal's saying that his master would have Boulogne rendered unto him again by this treaty, for else, if he won it by force, he would pay neither pension nor arrearages: you shall answer thus;—Thinketh he that the King's Majesty is so inferior to his master, that His Highness dare not contrary his will? and that His Majesty is so feared with his threats, that His Highness would obey thereto? He may stand so in his own conceit, but by all the journeys which His Majesty, or His Grace's Lieutenants, have made hitherto into France, it hath never showed so, nor His Majesty trusteth never shall; and that His Majesty wondereth that, since the French King hath lost it, why he should now set so much by it, and would not in three months space rescue it when His Majesty lay before it, trusting it shall be a dear Boulogne to him, or he recover it from His Majesty, for all their great bragges.

To the Cardinal's saying, how the Bishop of Rome laboured to his master to have dissuaded this assembly, offering to spend

[1] One nail be knocked out by another.

in his quarrel all the jewels he hath, *et triplicem coronam*:[1] you shall answer;—What matter is it to His Majesty for the assembly he speaketh of? for His Majesty is none of it. He meaneth the assembly of the Emperor and the French King, by which the said Bishop of Rome feareth loss of his See, and hath good cause so to do, if it be true that the Cardinal said, and for the breach of that purpose he would spend *triplicem coronam*, and yet speaketh it so *in duplicem sensum*,[2] that he would blear the French men's eyes, as they with fair words have done to many other.

To the Cardinal's saying to Mr. Paget in secret, that the Emperor went already about the calling of a General Council: You shall answer;—*Quid ad Regiam Majestatem?*[3] As for His Highness' part, whensoever it be, His Majesty prayeth God it may be, as it should be, both begun and finished.

To the Cardinal's saying that the French King had put himself to the Emperor's arbitrage for the pension and the arrearages, *et ces aultres choses*, and that though they break off now, he would be contented to send his Commissaries to the Emperor hereafter to treat, so as the King's Majesty would make like submission and send Commissaries, and that within a month, for else he thought himself discharged of the submission he had made to the Emperor: and if it were deferred any longer he thought himself discharged of the offer touching the pension and arrearages: You shall answer;—What and how he hath submitted himself to the Emperor, the Emperor can best tell, and His Majesty trusteth will so look on it that his former bond made unto His Majesty, which both the Bishop of Arras and the said Emperor also hath always declared to be except, be in no wise broken by this, specially seeing will ruleth them, and no reason. As touching their breaking off now, if they so do, it proceedeth of their unreasonableness, and no default in His Majesty. And as for new meetings and assemblies for treaty of peace, since, from the first overtures proceeding from them, they have and do still diminish, and now at the last come to a self will: His Majesty

[1] And his tripled crown: i.e. the papal tiara.
[2] In double sense.
[3] What is that to the King's Majesty?

can conceive no great expectation like to ensue of it; wherefore if they come not off otherwise now, than hitherto they have, His Majesty purposeth no longer to hearken to those ways, not doubting with God's grace, ere long time, to hear them sing another song.

To the Cardinal's private talk with Mr. Paget touching the French King's forces, &c.: You shall answer;—As touching his forces by land, His Majesty doubteth not but that it is known how shamefully they ran their way from their enterprises both of Baseboulogne and Guisnes; and yet with no small loss both of many gentlemen and other, whose weapons and bodies remain with His Majesty. And as for the seas, though they stole on His Majesty or His Highness were aware, and thereby took some poor sick men and horses, His Majesty doubteth not, by God's grace, if they dare abide it, to make them spin as fast away with sails, as by land they did with horse and heels; and yet, when they were in their chief pride on the sea, His Majesty's poor fishermen took up a 100 ton of their wine for Montreuil, and His Majesty hath victualled both Boulogne and Calais, and this all their gain they have had hitherto, thanked be God, and we trust daily shall have less.

Henry then proceeded to put the Emperor's good faith to the test. The French, after their failure to take Boulogne, had attacked Guisnes and been effectually repulsed. This attack gave Henry a pretext, and he wrote accordingly to Charles.

XIII. To Charles V

[*Nov.* 14, 1544.]

Most high, most excellent and most mighty Prince, our very dear and well beloved good brother and Cousin, as much and as affectuously as is possible we give you greeting.[1] Having understood from our ambassadors now resident with you the difficulties and doubt made for them by certain of your counsellors, not crediting that the French, since the peace made latterly between you, have hostilely and with a main army invaded our

[1] The address is added from the draft, as is the envoy on p. 386.

countries, territories and possessions, as much on this side of the sea as on the other, it has seemed good to us, to the end that the truth of it may be palpable to you, to inform you by our letters that the said French, having first enterprised the taking of Basse Boulogne, have been since within our marches of Guisnes, and there having destroyed certain churches and strongholds, have done their utmost to surprise our castle of Hampnes and our town of Guisnes, from whence every time, thanks be to God, they have been shamefully repulsed. And not content with having attempted to the uttermost of their power to injure and endamage us by land, have further engaged us by sea, and having surprised some poor soldiers, who because of sickness had been sent home from our town of Calais,[1] landed within our realm about our town of Dover, and endeavoured in every possible way to injure us, in which everytime they failed, and to their own hurt were forced to return to their ships; wherein they continued, lying in wait to surprise our ports, havens and roadsteads, until such time as our army, which we have been forced to equip and send to sea for the defence of our subjects, forced them to retire, thanks be to God. All which things our said ambassadors shall severally declare unto you more plainly, to whom we pray you, most high, etc., to give credence as if we were there in person, and to give them good and brief answer, as is required by the treaties and the long and continual amity between us. May the Creator have you in His Holy keeping. Written from our palace of Westminster, the fourteenth day of November 1544.

Hertford and Gardiner tackled Charles and Granvelle in person at Brussels. Both fell back on the message of the Bishop of Arras; and before the month was out had formally repudiated the treaty. Charles would not again declare war upon France: he had had Henry's consent to the peace, and nothing could move him from his position. Gardiner even went so far as to tell the Bishop of Arras exactly what he thought of him:[2] but

[1] 'ont este envoyes au pais dehors de nostre ville de Callais' ? had been sent into the country outside our town of Calais.

[2] Gardiner was no mean master of dignified invective, and this letter is as fine a specimen as any. It is in Latin, and has been printed in *S.P.* X, p. 193. Froude has translated half of it. (See *History* IV, p. 379.)

the facts were plain. The Emperor did not mean to support Henry.

The peace between France and the Empire was as pleasing to Pope Paul III as the alliance between England and the Empire had been displeasing: and Henry, faced with the prospect of a renewal of the Catholic league against England, once again opened negotiations with the Protestant states of Germany.[1] In spite of advances from both sides, however, the proposed Protestant alliance came to nothing, and although the war between England and France still continued Henry and Charles managed to avoid an open breach. An affair which might have precipitated it was eventually adjusted. English privateering vessels had captured some sixteen ships from Antwerp that were endeavouring to run the blockade into French ports with food supplies. The Netherlands retorted by seizing English ships and property, and arresting English subjects within their borders. This, again, was a violation of the treaty, which had expressly forbidden reprisals. The Emperor refused to release Henry's subjects until his subjects had received complete redress, which Henry considered ' strange and unkind '.

XIV. To Paget[2]

[*Feb.* 20, 1545.]

(f. 122) . . . the said Sir William, with our condign commendations, shall say that whereas we addressed lately our ambassador resident with him to open and read unto him certain matters of importance, with request not only to have answer again unto the same, but also that the arrest of our subjects and goods there might be discharged; for as much as we neither have yet any answer touching the said purposes, and that also the said arrest remaineth in such sort as it did, being importuned with the dolances of divers and many of our subjects complaining of the great losses and damages they do sustain by reason of the said restraint, and also to know what thing it is that he saith he hath so often willed his ambassadors to move us in, and get none answer; we thought good to address unto him our said Secretary,

[1] See particularly *S.P.* X.

[2] Sent as a special ambassador to the Emperor.

both to declare unto him how much his proceeding ever sithens his peace taken with France hath grieved us, being of a strange and unkind sort towards us, his ancient and well approved friend in all his necessities from the beginning; and also to require him, seeing that both himself and his principal ministers and ambassadors doth from time to time signify and say unto us and our ministers and ambassadors, that he intendeth and meaneth to observe the treaty and amity between us, to show some deeds correspondent to his words, in case he mean indeed, as he hath said, the observance of the treaty between us, that things may then pass and be done in such order as the treaty doth prescribe unto us; which, when it was made first, was thought so plain and evident, and with such an agreeable consent and uniform meaning of us both and of both our Councils, as could not ne ought to have any other understanding or interpretation than by the very words of the said treaty is comprehended; and so was it esteemed and articled, howsoever some folk list to wrest it at their liberty. And here our said Secretary shall pause, to hear what he will say; . . .

(f. 124^v^) . . . Our said Secretary shall reply, that he cannot but marvel much to hear them say that they will keep their amity and treaty, when that their deeds in all things declare the contrary. For besides this point of the arrest, the intercourse and traffic between the subjects, the provisions of victuals and munitions for our money, should not be empeched, his subjects should be suffered to serve us, and our men of war to have passage through his country: of all which things no one point is observed by the treaty. Whosoever is enemy to one should be enemy to the other, and so we have required him to be to our enemy the French King; which he delayeth to do. By his words he sayeth he is our friend, but by his deeds he will declare no one point of friendship. And we are not so ignorant but that we see the cause of this his proceeding. We know that he having to do, as he hath, with the Turk, he would be glad to be in peace elsewhere. He would be loath to fall out with the French King, of whom he trusteth to have some aid against the Turk, and so we see he seeketh all his own commodity, and careth little for his friends: and having now himself gotten peace (with what honour the world judgeth), he is contented that we, which needed not to have entered the war but for his sake, for we might have had an honourable end if we had listed to have left him in the briars, which we never went about, and that did the French ambassadors testify in the presence of his own ambassadors Chappuis and Currieres, do remain still in the wars, without using any manner of mean or making any manner of overture to bring us either to a peace or truce. . . .

(f. 125ᵛ) Ever sithens that time, which is now four months passed and more, notwithstanding that we have pressed him to enter with us the war again, as we think by the treaty he is bound to do, what one way hath he used to bring us to any manner of appointment with our enemy? which, if he had gone about, might have been both to his quiet, and somewhat to our satisfaction. If he had been of so friendly a mind, as he sayeth he is unto us, seeing that our enemy dependeth so much upon him, as by their treaty it seemeth he doth, he should either have driven him to have offered us reasonable conditions, and to have sent ambassadors to have come immediately unto a peace; or, at the least, to have taken a truce with us, whereby in the meantime there might arise further overtures and communications for a peace: but he, contrarywise, forgetting all friendship and kindness, taketh his rest and careth little for his friend, and his dear and old friend, as all the world knoweth. Whereunto if it shall be answered that he would be glad there were a peace between us and our enemy, or a truce, if he thought we would be contented he should labour for the same; to that our said Secretary shall answer that we never minded to refuse any reasonable offer, and that if either honourable conditions for an immediate peace were proponed, or an overture made for a truce, so as Boulogne be not touched, he knoweth us to be a Prince of that reasonable equanimity, that he doubteth not we would be contented to accept the same; . . .

The year 1545 began with the announcement that by the advice of his Council the King had 'determined to practise a benevolent loan'—in other words, that he would for the moment spare the mass of the people, and pay for the war at the expense of the wealthier classes. It was hoped in this way to raise some sixty thousand pounds to finance the campaign for the first half of the year. In the meantime the French were making every effort to recapture Boulogne, and at the end of January Marshal du Biez took up a position opposite the town and endeavoured to erect a fort, to command the entrance to the harbour, and to prevent Hertford getting supplies from England to the garrison. The plan proposed by Francis was that while the Scots crossed the Border with an army, the French, with two other armies, should simultaneously deal with the English forces in France and invade England with the help of the French fleet.

The first part of the plan failed hopelessly, du Biez and his army being routed by the English garrison in a night attack early in February. The Scots' plan was more successful, and resulted in the English defeat at Ancrum Moor (see p. 348). The decisive blow was timed for the summer; but Henry was ready for it, with a mustering of some hundred thousand men in arms, and a fleet of about a hundred sail. John Dudley, Lord Lisle, was in command, and Henry himself went down to Portsmouth in July to supervise arrangements.

With an army on board, the great French fleet of 150 sail, besides pinnaces and rowing galleys, arrived in the Solent on July 18. There was much manœuvring, and an initial skirmish. French troops were landed on the Isle of Wight and repulsed with losses. All attempts to draw Lisle out into the open, where their numerical advantage would have told in favour of the French, failed. By July 24 the French admiral d'Annebault had decided not to attempt anything further in the Solent, and the fleet sailed away to anchor behind Selsey Bill. Threatened by an attack from Lisle, it hurried across to Boulogne, got rid of 3,000 pioneers and 4,000 troops, and then recrossed the Channel to make another attempt. On August 15 they were sighted off Shoreham. There was another indecisive engagement, and in the morning the French fleet were sighted on the horizon, speeding back to France. The invasion scare was over, the English still commanded the Channel, and Lisle took his fleet across to France and burnt Tréport—'just to show 'em,' as one might say! Had d'Annebault struck decisively when he landed troops in the

Isle of Wight affairs might not have turned out so satisfactorily for the English. Losing this advantage, however, and being kept at sea by Lisle's tactics for nearly a month, the French admiral found his crews and soldiers dying from the plague in their hundreds, and so was forced to give up the lavishly-planned enterprise, defeated by his own mistake, and his misfortunes almost as much as by his enemies' carefully restrained defensive tactics.

In the preceding chapter we have already seen the final result of the Scottish plan, in the ravaging of the country carried out in the late summer by Hertford in revenge for Ancrum Moor. At Boulogne there was still hope. While d'Annebault had held the Channel the invading garrison had been virtually blockaded, and du Biez had been able to build up his fort at the entrance to the harbour. Once the French fleet had dispersed, however, food supplies were run in daily, and the garrison still held out, till at the end of September the French raised the siege. In consequence, the year closed with England in an infinitely more advantageous position than when peace negotiations had failed the previous autumn. Moreover, during the year, Henry had again by judicious reprisals made it quite clear to Charles that he would not put up with injuries to his subjects in the Emperor's dominions nor yet to repeated violations of the treaty. During the summer, as the strength of Henry's position became more and more evident, the Emperor became more and more ready to honour his obligations under the treaty. In July, in the middle of the 'invasion', Henry sent the following 'strong' letter to his ambassador with Charles.

XV. To Thirlby

[*July* 28, 1545.]

Right Reverend Father in God, &c. Signifying unto you that the Emperor's Ambassador hath been here with us to declare that upon occasion of our letters lately written to his master for the sending of the aid, which he is bound to furnish us by virtue of the treaty, he had commission to commune with us or our Council for the ecclarcissement of the treaty, and thereupon desired to know whether that by the asking of this aid we meant that the Emperor should declare himself against France, or no. Whereunto, likeas we have answered the said Ambassador, so our pleasure is, that desiring access unto the Emperor, and at your coming to him taking occasion of the said purpose set forth unto us by the said Ambassador, you shall say, that the treaty having been well digested and couched in such plain and sincere words, terms and sentences, as the same is most easy to be understanded, and ought not to be intercepted or construed to other sense or purpose than the words of the same doth purport and express, for so by a special article in that self treaty it is covenanted, to the intent that all cavillations or wrastings should be excluded and have no place, there can be no other ecclarcissement than is already, and needeth not to have any glose, when that the text of itself is plain enough.

The treaty, as it appeareth, is divided in two parts; the one provideth for invasion, and extendeth only to the French King at the time of the said invasion; the other part extendeth to the French King and all others. For the first part we said that by the treaty the Emperor might not make peace with France, without that we first did consent and were satisfied, as is expressed in the nineteenth article of the said treaty. Whereunto if the Emperor answer that we have consented, alleging the untrue report of his own servant the Bishop of Arras; to that he shall answer, that whatsoever d'Arras hath said, or any of his own servants that were present with him, they are no meet personages in a case of their masters, wherein themselves also be workers, to make any prove against an act passed before by the solemn oath of their master, and confirmed in writing under his sign and great seal; and how dangerous an example, and how prejudicial this act shall be to the faith of all Princes, let the Emperor consider. We doubt not but whatsoever personages of equity heareth, or shall hear, that the Emperor standeth bounden unto us, by his oath, sign and seal, to do a thing, they will think the testimony of the Emperor's own minister is no sufficient proof to discharge him of the same. And, albeit we should consent (as d'Arras sayeth), yet being not satisfied in such form, and with such things as the treaty determineth, the Emperor hath not liberty to make peace without us; and that we neither did nor meant to consent without satisfaction; it appeareth by our letters sent at that time to the Emperor, wherein we referred the further declaration of our answer touching those matters to our Ambassador Mr. Wotton, to whom also at thas instant we wrote both letters, commission, and instructions for his proceedings there on that behalf. But presupposing that we had indeed consented, and were also satisfied to our contentation, whereby that part of the treaty, which for this present war and the invasion of the French King were taken away; yet the other part, which bindeth either of us to other in amity and part-taking against the French King, and all other that shall invade, for what cause so ever it be, remaineth still; and thereby, whensoever the French King or any other shall invade either of us, the other is not only bound to give him aid, being invaded (as in the 7th article of the treaty is expressed), but also to be enemy to his enemy (cf. p. 355), as plainly appeareth in the 6th article of the said treaty; and so plainly, that it needeth no other eclarcissement.

And in case the Emperor shall say that, we not keeping our journey to Paris, as was agreed, he was enforced and might make the peace, and so charge us with the breach of treaty; to that you shall say, that if we would have taken advantage of not keeping of covenants, and thereupon used a pretence to have entered bargain with France, we had good and just cause, for that the Emperor neither kept upon the sea the army he was bound to keep, nor yet entered into France by the day appointed between us; but, laying siege to other places before his entry into France, to prepare way for his victuals, as he said, tarried a month well near after his day of entry, whereas we kept our day of entry in to France, albeit we were ill served, and had great lets, by reason of want of victuals and carriages, which for our money the Emperor was bound to furnish us of, and as wisdom and the reason of war requireth: and, taking example at the Emperor, thought it not expedient to leave any place behind us that might empeach our conduct of victuals. Wherein as we did nothing but that we might do lawfully, and agreeable with our covenants, so the same appeared wisely handled to the Emperor's Ambassadors, and to the Regent, who, as the said Ambassadors declared unto us, did commend and allow our doings and siege at Boulogne. And therefore the said Bishop shall say that, if the Emperor do desire that the treaty may be eclarcised, to the intent that each of us may know what he ought to do for the other, and will enter disputations of the treaty, we cannot talk otherwise with him than as the treaty leadeth, nor admit any other eclarissement or interpretation than the words of the treaty do purport; which contain expressly that the Emperor, without our consent and satisfaction, could not make peace with France; and, when we were in peace also, and satisfied that the invader, whatsoever he be, and though he were his own brother the King of Romans, ought to be a common enemy to us both, whensoever and as often as he did invade any of us, notwithstanding any other treaty that he hath or shall make with any other man; for that it is covenanted that this treaty shall prejudice and derogate all other treaties made or to be made with any other.

Mary, if the Emperor shall take another way with us, and by means of friendship declaring how loath he would be to enter into the war, for such considerations as seemeth good unto him, and therefore desire us not to press him for this time to declare himself, and yet, being loath to see us oppressed or bragged thus with our enemies, do send unto us for some relief the aid due by the treaty; offering also, which he without offence of his treaty with France (for that by the old treaties and amities between our two houses it hath been always used), to suffer such horsemen and footmen to pass, as will come through his country to serve us, governing themselves by the way honestly, and to permit such munition to pass through his country as we provide for our necessary service, and also mutual concourse and traffic of victualing of our frontiers, the one the other; we can be contented to forbear for a time to require of him this declaration. And with this manner of proceeding, being friendly, reasonable and honourable for both parties, we think the Emperor ought to be satisfied and contented. And what answer the said Bishop shall have herein he shall advertise us with all diligence. And forasmuch Monsr. Granvelle hath the chief place and authority about our said good brother the Emperor, the said Bishop shall take opportunity to make unto him our hearty commendations; and further say that howsoever his son hath dealt in the misreport of this matter, yet we cannot but have a good opinion of his good affection and zeal to the continuance of the amity between his master and us. And therefore not doubting but, being in place and authority, he will travail as much as in him lieth, both for the continuance and increase of the same; we require him, in all such things as the said Bishop shall have to do there on our behalf, to give unto him his favourable address, counsel and furtherance for the advancement of the same.

And finally, the said Bishop shall employ himself and travail by all the means he can devise, to know as well the state of the said Emperor and of his Court, with the mutations of the same from time to time, as also of his proceedings with the French King, the Scots, the Bishop of Rome, Turk, Venetians, and other states and occurrences, and with diligence to advertise us of the same accordingly.

In August, once the French fleet had dispersed, Charles went so far as to offer Henry money for the aid required of him by England, though he still refused to do anything to violate the treaty of Crespy. In October, France made overtures for peace, to the acceptance of which Henry was urged not only by his Lutheran friends in Germany, but also by those of the cabinet—notably Norfolk and Gardiner—who realized the financial difficulty. The Germans sent an embassy under Bruno and Sturmius to urge the necessity of peace, their arguments being that the war, if prolonged, would so weaken England as to give the Emperor sufficient power to do what he pleased for the subduing of his Lutheran states. Henry's attitude—which was not that of his Council—can be gathered from the two letters to Paget which follow. Paget found Bruno frank and genuine—too much so for a diplomat. Sturmius he regarded as French in his sympathies, and a 'practitioner'. Practitioners or not, Paget was instructed to warn them 'in the way of friendship' that 'it should be wisdom for them and their masters, in this busy world, to suspect the worst, and not to think but that the French King's council is crafty enough to mind to deceive them'.

One of the most striking things about these negotiations, however, is the way in which, from motives of policy, Henry kept even his own ambassadors in the dark. 'We be very well pleased', he writes to Paget,

> that you alone shall give ear unto Sturmius, or any such other as shall hereafter make the like overtures unto you; all which overtures we would have you keep secret to yourself, ***without declaring the same to my lord of Winchester, or to your colleagues***, unto such time as ye shall both see more to what end the same will tend. (*Nov.* 29, 1545.)

The end he had in mind was simply to wring better terms from the Emperor by continuing negotiations with the Protestant mediators, and so threatening him with the prospect of an undesirably strong combination against him should their mediation succeed. If he could force the Emperor to meet his treaty obligations, he could then afford to drop the Protestants and demand better terms from France.

XVI. To Paget

[*Westminster, Dec.* 4, 1545.]

Trusty and right well-beloved, we greet you well; and let you wit that having received your letters of the second of this present, by the which we do both perceive such further conference as hath lately been between you and Sturmius, and also your desire to know our final resolution for your further proceedings there, we have thought good, for answer, to signify unto you that, where Bruno, the chief and most grave of those Ambassadors, did by the way touch an overture, and wished that, for the acquittal of all debts and pensions, Boulogne and Ardres with their whole counties might be rendered unto us by the French King &c.; we would that you, taking some occasion to bring that overture again in communication, should by all ways and means devise to search out the foundation thereof, and to get out, if you may, what ground he had for the proponing of this overture; whereof as you shall see any fruit like to ensue, so we would you should enter and proceed further, using such good means in the treating and debating thereof, as ye may make our best bargain.

For your more ample instruction wherein, you may declare unto them, that albeit, being Boulogne with the great part of the country of Boulognois already in our possession, the town of Ardres with the county of Guisnes and the residue of Boulognois seemeth a very small thing in respect of the great sums of money already due unto us; yet, for that we would do them to understand that we have nothing more at heart than a good pacification of all such things, as now be in controversy between us and France, specially because by these means a great likelihood might be of the clear extinguishment of all occasions of contentions and strives between us and our and his successors for ever; we can be contented, the rather for that this overture hath proceeded from them, whom we account to be men of good faith and well dedicate to our affairs, to remit all the arrearages due unto us, all our charges and expenses sustained in these wars, so as we may have for the same the town and country of Boulognois, the town of Ardres with the county of Guisnes, wholly and freely released, to be quietly had possessed and enjoyed of us and our heirs for ever. In debating of which point, like as our pleasure is, you shall extend all your dexterity to set forth the great sums we shall in this case depart withal, the smallness of that we shall receive again, and employ yourself wholly to persuade the reasonableness of this offer unto them; so, if you shall in the end see that they shall not like it, nor will by no means assent to the same, our pleasure is, you shall descend to another degree, viz. to offer them not only the acquittal of all our costs and expenses in the wars, but to discharge also the pension perpetual, so as they do, from the time of this treaty concluded, pay unto us truly our pension viager during the time of our life, with the arrearages thereof. Wherein albeit they shall have no great cause to stick, yet because we would it were wholly deciphered what they shall mean in this overture, rather than fail, if the French King will leave to us and our successors for ever the towns and territories abovesaid, we shall be pleased to remit the whole arrereages, the whole charges, the pension perpetual and the half of the pension viager; or if they shall, in lieu thereof, be contented to pay us in hand one million, to remit also the whole pension viager. These degrees we would were so opened unto them, as upon a refusal of the first, ye do always proceed to the next, and so from degree to degree, unto such time as ye shall see their final resolution in this matter; remembering unto them, if they shall come to any agreement with you, that, for lack of performance of that shall be promised on their behalf, we and our successors shall remain in the same state we are at this present to all respects and purposes. And in your travailing with them in the points aforesaid, you must stick earnestly with them, and in no wise descend to the second degree, but upon a manifest appearance that they would rather break up than assent to the first; and in that case you may, as of yourself, propone the second degree, asking them, what they will say, if you might attain at our hands to assent to that. And the like order ye may observe in the rest of the degrees aforesaid.[1]

Touching the Scots, you may say unto them, that you marvel what moveth the French man to stick so earnestly to their comprehension, who can serve France to no purpose, but only to set bogges and matters of new variance betwixt us and them. And forasmuch as we (if they shall be contented to come on with us roundly) can be contented to show ourself willing, yea, with the forbearing of great things due unto us, that, all occasions of new contention being taken away, this peace and amity between us and France might be so established, as the same may have a continuance, and endure between us and our successors for ever, you think ye may say that they, if they mind the conclusion of amity indeed, should have the like consideration to take away all occasions of any variance hereafter, and be glad that all matters that might by any means minister matter to the breach of this amity were clearly taken away. They have not been so precise to have the Scots comprehended in other treaties in times past with us, and in their late treaty with the Emperor they left them out. You know that, at the being of the Ambassadors with us at Boulogne, they said they desired nothing but to have some good ground whereby they might honourably declare to the world that they should leave then upon some good cause; and being at that time showed how the Scots had, by treaty before

[1] cf. the seven alternative commissions in the 1525 letter.

made and concluded with us, expressly abandoned France, the French Commissioners seemed satisfied in that point; wherewith they ought to be satisfied in reason, considering that the Scots were not comprehended in the treaty between us and France heretofore, but with conditions which the Scots have not observed. And therefore, if they leave them out now, they shall leave them in the self same state they found them in before the beginning of these wars. Which thing as they may do without any touch of their honour, and ought to do by their old treaties; so they will do (you may say) in deed, except they mean to patch up an agreement for the time, and yet to keep in the deck such matter as shall breed new variance, when they list, or may see their best advantage. And therefore, seeing this treaty is for a peace, you would wish (ye may say) that it may be concluded with such conditions, as it might continue a peace in deed for ever. These points you must set forth unto them as earnestly and vehemently as ye can, travailing by all ways possible to induce them to leave out the comprehension of the Scots; but if in the end, if they will by no means assent thereunto, you shall then declare unto them the treaty which hath passed between us and the Scots for the marriage of the young Queen to our son: the performance whereof if the Scots shall offer unto us, and be contented with the alteration of such matters of no great weight, as are to be changed in that treaty, the substance thereof remaining in force, and will also deliver unto our custody their said young queen, to be kept after such sort as was proponed unto you this other day by Sturmius; in that case we will be pleased the Scots shall be comprehended with the like qualification as was made in the treaty, the copy whereof we commanded to be sent unto you. And for the better conducing of these things you may secretly travail with the said Bruno, declaring our good inclination towards him, and feel him, whether he can be contented to owe his service towards us, and to receive our pension, as Sturmius hath, of the French King. Whereunto if you shall perceive him well affected, our pleasure is you shall secretly inquire what pension the said Sturmius hath of France, to the intent upon knowledge thereof we may appoint the like for him.

Finally, where they have eftsoons moved you for an abstinence during this treaty, we be very well pleased to grant the same during that time, for the land only, so as they begin not in the mean time any new fortification in Boulognois, nor the county of Guisnes.

XVII. To Paget

[*Hampton Court, Dec.* 26, 1545.]

. . . First, you shall understand that having perused the articles or capitulations which you sent unto us, and having altered and added certain points of importance therein, we do now remit the same unto you to be concluded upon in such form as they be now conceived, if you may induce the French Ambassadors thereunto; or otherwise to be altered and qualified by your common agreement in some words and terms, so as the substance of the matters do remain.

And touching the comprehension of the Scots, our pleasure is that you shall travail as earnestly as ye may to have this truce concluded without any comprehension of them, whom we would most gladly, and think it necessary, to be left out; for without that, this truce, serving the French King to many purposes, should be to us every way overmuch prejudicial. And therefore, like as we for our part can be pleased to conclude this truce generally with them without comprehension of any States or Princes, so we think it reason that they shall conclude with us after the like sort. For it hath not been seen in any treaty of truce that we have made with any Prince in all our time, that any other Prince hath been comprehended. And further you may also declare to the Ambassadors, as well French as of the Protestants, how that by such treaties of amity as be between us and our good brother the Emperor, we may not in any wise comprehend the Scots in this or any other treaty of truce or peace.

As for the time of commencement of the said truce; although we see not how we may give assured notice thereof to all our subjects, being, as we have heretofore signified unto you, dispersed in sundry places and companies, before the first day of March, and therefore think the day appointed in your former instruction to be a very meet time for the beginning of the same; yet, if they shall show themselves much desirous to have the truce begin rather,[1] we shall be pleased to assent thereunto. Mary, you must tell them withal, that we cannot assure them to give perfect notice to our men before the said day; and therefore, if for want of knowledge of the truce, which nevertheless shall be published with as much speed as may be, any prejudice shall ensue to any of the French King's subjects, we doubt not they will of their wisdoms impute the same to their own hasty abridging of the time, and not to those which shall then be found ignorant of the same. And therefore, for the avoiding of all such occasions of new quarrels, and to the intent all things might be fully observed according to the agreements, we thought the first day of March to be a meet day for beginning of the said truce, the end whereof you must always forsee to be agreed upon the last of October according to your former instruction, notwithstanding you shall perchance at their instance somewhat prevent the commencement of the same.

Thirdly, touching a further meeting of the Protestants and other Commissioners for us and the French King primo Maij or other such time as shall be agreed upon, except we saw a greater appearance of some conformity in the French King than hath yet been shown hitherto, we neither think it meet to trouble the Protestants with any other resort to a new assembly nor mind to make now any appointment for the time of any such new convention, whereof (the French King being so much wedded to his own will, as he is) there is no likelihood of any fruit to ensue. And yet, if in the mean time we may by any means perceive that the French King will relent in his obstinacy, and come on more roundly to some reasonable and honourable conditions for a peace, we would not only be very glad to use the mediation of the Protestants in the mayning of the same, but also give them well to understand that we do both repose a more ample and fuller confidence in them than the French King either doth or will do, whatsoever he pretendeth and would make them believe, and would also in the concluding thereof use their advice before any others; not doubting but we shall find them as much addicted to the advancement of our affairs as of the French King's.

[1] Earlier.

Fourthly, as touching Bruno, we will ye shall allure and procure him to serve us earnestly, as much as shall be possible for you to do. And as for his pension, for this beginning we be pleased to grant unto him 5 or 600 crowns by year, the less or the more to be at your discretion; and as his service shall appear hereafter acceptable unto us, so peraventure to increase it. And for the first payment thereof, we will you take one year's pension of such our treasure as remaineth in our Treasurer of Calais' hands, or is or shall be brought from our servant Thomas Chamberlain to our said Treasurer; which, taking his oath if it may be, otherwise his promise in writing, to do us service, you may, if he condescend thereunto, secretly deliver unto him, with a cipher to advertise us of the state of things in Almayn from time to time, as occasion shall serve; giving him such good words withal, on our behalf, as may both encourage him to serve us truly and diligently, and minister hope unto him of more ample benefit at our hands, if he shall show himself no less willing to the advancement of our affairs and diligent in our service than we have conceived good trust of him.

Finally, if in the end of this your long conference the French Commissioners will neither come on more roundly in the conditions of peace, nor assent to a truce in such sort as we have prescribed unto you, but will break off; our pleasure is, that you shall both give immediate notice thereof to our Ambassadors with the Emperor, and also give knowledge of the same to our officers at Boulogne, Guisnes and Calais, to the intent every of them may see the better to the guard of their pieces, and consider also by what means and with what numbers the enemy may be most troubled; advertising us of their opinions therein, to the intent we may further dispose, as to us shall be thought convenient.

In spite of these negotiations, however, the war continued to be waged in a desultory fashion throughout the winter of 1545. Henry would not yield Boulogne, and was adamant on the question of Scotland. The Council were only too anxious to give up Boulogne, Norfolk, the treasurer, being convinced that a continuance of the war would ruin the realm. His son, Surrey, who was in command there, urged Henry to keep it; and one of

Surrey's servants writes: 'As to Boulogne, every Councillor saith "Away with it", and the King and your Lordship say "We will keep it".' By March, 1546, Henry's pertinacity had its reward. The time element, once again, had done its work. The country's credit, in reality nearly exhausted, appeared inexhaustible: and in March the Emperor threw in his lot with the winning side. He signed a ratification of the treaty, promising to intervene if England or the Calais Pale should be invaded. In consequence, peace negotiations were begun again in April, and the following letter sets out Henry's demands.

XVIII. To Hertford, Lisle, Paget, N. Wotton

[*April* 27, 1546.]

Right trusty and right well-beloved Cousins and Councillors, and trusty and right well-beloved, we greet you well.

. . . First, where the said Monluke[1] making a long rehearsal of the old friendship between us and his master, how necessary and expedient peace is for both parties, what great devastation and wasting of the poor people of both sides hath been &c., concludeth that his master is very desirous to have peace, so as the same might be had honourably, and his realm not excorsed[2] and fleen to the bones; our pleasure is that, at your next meeting together with the French Commissioners, you shall declare and set forth plainly unto them that albeit the occasion of the rupture of that old amity between the French King and us (for the assured continuance whereof we have heretofore ministered in deeds good occasion) hath proceeded only of them, yet have we at all times been very willing, and yet be well pleased, that all things may be well and honourably compounded, and have been contented heretofore to send our Ambassadors, men that we do specially trust, for the debating and concluding of the same, the stay whereof hath proceeded only of the wilful unreasonableness and want of conformity of their part, being their Commissaries in their conferences so much wedded and addict to their own

[1] i.e. Jean de Montluc.

[2] This quotes Paget's 'escorsed and fleen' (i.e. skinned and flayed), his literal translation of Montluc's phrase. 'Excorsed', *lit.* fr. Fr. écorcher, to skin an animal, hence *fig.* 'to skin' by making extortionate demands.

wills, as without satisfaction of their own will and appetites they would always break off, and nothing might be concluded. Wherefore it shall be necessary that you do tell them, as it were for an introduction of the matter, in plain terms, that if they shall mind the conclusion of this peace earnestly indeed, as they pretend, they must set apart all wilfulness, and think that they have to do with a Prince of such honour, as with froward dealing will not be drawn to their appetites, and yet can be well contented to give ear to friendly and honourable conditions.

And here it shall be well to put them in remembrance that we are not ignorant in what state their master standeth presently, both touching his subjects, men of war, penury of victuals, decay of his navy, &c.; what attemptates they have made without any success or fruit of the same; how we shall at all times be able to victual our pieces of that side without danger; how difficult and almost impossible it is, and shall be, for them either to do us any annoyance upon the same, or to victual their own; how hard it shall be for the French King to continue any navy upon the seas, being always in such danger for want of ports, if any storm arise; that we, without any our charge, shall at all times be able not only to victual our pieces, but to annoy also them at our pleasure; which things we do but touch unto you, whom we know, for your experience in our affairs, to be so well acquainted with every part thereof, as you may set forth the same at full unto the said Commissioners, and withal to tell them that, like as we do know their doings in Almayn, Italy, and everywhere, so have we, and mind by the grace of almighty God, to provide accordingly. And that notwithstanding, both for God's sake and in respect of the wealth of Christendom, and for that old hearty good will that of long time hath between us and their master, we shall be right glad that peace be concluded, and our old amity and friendship renewed again, so as they will abandon their will, make friendly and round offers, and in the debating thereof consider that reason and indifferency would we should have no less respect to our honour than their master hath to his. And here you may touch again to them the unreasonableness of their request to have Boulogne, which we have royally conquered in our just wars. They neither have used so to leave any piece won by them in their wars, as may appear by Hesding and Piemont, nor in our first wars with them the keeping of Tournay and Turwin was any let to a conclusion of a peace at that time.

As for the matters of your instructions, albeit we think that the same be already for the effect thereof so qualified, especially for the first, as, if they mind to come on *bona fide*, they ought in reason condescend unto; yet, if you shall see that frankness in them that Monluke pretendeth, forasmuch as it appeareth by his talk with you, Mr. Secretary, that besides the payment of our pension, they will be contented willingly to leave to our hands some part of Boulognois for our surety of the payment of our arrearages, charges and expenses; our pleasure is, that you shall travail as much as ye may to cause them to declare what parts of Boulognois they will agree of their own good wills to leave unto us; and if you shall see them coming toward any conformity, then, assaying first whether you can bring them to be contented that all Boulognois, from the water a' this side Étaples, do remain still in our hands, you shall in the end come to this, that, their new fort being razed, and left to us as a fisher town, we may have in our quiet possession all Boulognois from Hardelow, or at the least from the river coming by Porthyll, by such limits and bounds as upon view of the ground shall be thought meet, and accorded between you and them.

And where it seemeth to you, our Secretary, by your conference with Monluke, that they will not come to such a sum to be paid for our costs and expenses as is contained in your instructions, we shall be pleased to moderate the same and to abate one million of the crowns, so as they will assent that the whole county of Guisnes may quietly remain to us and our heirs for ever, whereby occasions of bogs and variances may well be taken away, and this amity, which we would have so made as the same might endure, have his continuance accordingly.

And for the better inducing of the French Commissioners to a conformity in this point, you may remember unto them how small a commodity their master hath at this present of the said county of Guisnes, the profit whereof remaineth almost all to other men; so as, if they mean a perfect and final establishment of an amity indeed, there is no cause why they should in reason refuse to assent to the same.

In the setting forth of which things, and beating into their heads what advantage we have presently over them, (and that we have greater advantages over them they do know,) how expedient and necessary the conclusion of this peace and amity shall be for them, we require you to employ all your good dexterities; travailing also to beat out as near as ye may to what points they will finally grow; and advertising us from time to time of all your proceedings, upon knowledge whereof we shall signify our certain pleasure further unto you as any occasion shall so require accordingly.

The letters that follow show the progress of the negotiations during May, and take us up to the moment of the signing of the actual treaty on June 7, 1546, showing how very nearly, once again, the whole thing came to an abortive end.

XIX. To Lisle, Paget, &c.

[*Greenwich, May* 9, 1546.]

RIGHT TRUSTY AND RIGHT WELL-BELOVED COUSIN, AND TRUSTY AND RIGHT WELL-BELOVED, we greet you well. And let you wit that we have seen your letters of the 7th of this instant, and by the same do understand at good length your proceedings at this your first meeting with the French Commissioners. . . . We have also thought good to signify our pleasure unto you as followeth.

First, because in your last conference with them they seemed to esteem Boulogne and that part of Boulognois which we have justly conquered to be a thing of such small importance as 100,000, or at the most 200,000 crowns, might countervayle the redemption of the same, and therefore did offer no more but 200,000 crowns for the redemption of that town and other our lands; you shall declare unto them that, besides the great expenses done by us upon the fortification and building of the said town since the conquest thereof do declare to the world that we have another estimation of it than they seem to have, we can be contented, in respect of the weal of Christendom, and for the good of peace, to grant unto them a great deal more for the quiet keeping of it, being already by all laws our own, than they offer to depart withal for the redemption of the same; and will be pleased to remit to the French King all the arrearages, debts, charges of the war, and the recompense of the fortifications already done, so as the French King, for him and his successors, will leave to us and our heirs for ever Boulogne, and from Boulogne along the sea coasts to the top of the hill beyond Hardelow, and so from the top of that hill along as the hills lieth, continuing the height of the hills beyond Leekes, until ye come to that part of the County of Guisnes next adjoining to the hills which we have in our possession, and all the ground between the said hills and the sea side. And in case, having set forth the greatness of this offer by all such ways and means as ye shall think best and meetest for that purpose, and having conferred the same with the small and meagre overtures made by them heretofore, you shall in the end perceive that they do mislike this condition, and will not accept the same, you shall finally in the treaty of this branch, rather than fail, offer unto them the remission for ever of our pension perpetual, wherewith and with the arrearages and other things aforesaid we can be pleased to depart frankly withal, so as the French King will give, grant, release and surrender in to our hands, to the use of us and our heirs for ever, that small portion of ground aforesaid. And here you may set forth unto them what a great benefit and likelihood of our continual friendship for ever should ensue by the concluding of the peace after this sort; for by this means all bogs and occasions of new quarrels might be fully extinguished, and this amity being once agreed upon have his continuance for ever.

When you shall have travailed with them in this branch as earnestly as you may, after such sort as is aforesaid, if in the end they will not accept the said conditions, our pleasure is you shall descend to one other offer. And, repeating unto them what great sums of money we have been and be pleased to remit unto them, besides the remission of our pension perpetual, for the only keeping of that which is our own, you shall say that ye doubt not but (if they mean good faith in the treaty and debating of this matter) they will make a more large, or at the least as great, an offer to us for the redemption of that which is none of theirs, and now out of their possession. Wherefore, if they be not willing to leave Boulogne and such part of the land as is aforesaid, but will stick precisely to their former request that the same may remain in the case of redemption; then, besides the payment of our pensions perpetual and viager,[1] with the salt, from henceforth according to the former treaties, which must begin at Midsummer next the first payment thereof, and besides the payment of the arrearages of our said pensions and other debts due unto us, the payment whereof we can be contented shall be stalled[2] at some reasonable days, so as the first payment thereof be at Midsummer next, they must leave to our quiet possession Boulogne and such part of Boulognois and the county of Guisnes, as shall be signified unto you by a plat,[3] as soon as Rogers, who is already sent for, may come and go unto you, the same to remain quietly to us and our heirs, without any their let, disturbance, claim or empechment,[4] until after the payment of the said arrearages and debts, they shall present and pay upon one day to us or our heirs two millions of gold, and truly perform in the mean time the pacts and covenants agreed upon. Which sums of two millions they ought not in reason to account over great, seeing they were bound unto us upon the agreement, after our last wars with them, to pay unto us as great a sum as this is, and yet had then no town nor possessions rendered unto them, whereas now they shall have a town, which hath cost us more than twice two millions, and is with our great charges now made a town impregnable for ever.

If you shall see that after the coming of the said plat, and debating of this matter, they will agree with you upon the conditions aforesaid touching the redemption; our pleasure is that you shall remember and provide that it may be specially covenanted that the limits and bounds of our pale between Boulognois and our county of Guisnes for ever shall be from the river at Marguison as it passeth from Leekes to the sea side, which being

[1] i.e. the one granted for Henry's lifetime.
[2] Paid by instalment.
[3] Plan.
[4] Hindrance.

the old limits of our pale in very deed, and now eftsoons reduced to our possession again, we require to be so provided for, as all occasions of any other strife for limits may be appeased and taken away hereafter.

You shall also understand that we have seen the articles devised by the French Commissioners touching the matters of the Scots, which appeareth unto us so strange, and so far both from common reason, and from that friendly compounding of things which they would seem to declare, that we cannot but think they mind not indeed the perfecting of this amity so earnestly as hath been pretended. Which thing, as it may appear by all the rest of their doings and conferences at this time, being all the same grounded more upon their own wills than upon any indifferency, so in this point of the Scots the same is most manifest. For heretofore, when the other French Commissioners treated this matter of the comprehension of the Scots with you, our Secretary, they seemed then contented to leave the Scots uncomprehended, and to pass them over in silence, upon your promise only that we would forbear to extend our force by invasion of their country without new occasion ministered unto us. And therefore you shall declare unto them that in this matter, if their master mind now indeed to have the old amity between us and him renewed, there is no more cause not to agree now than there was at that time when they offered that offer to you, nor greater cause to stick so much at this matter of the Scots now than there hath been at the concluding of other treaties heretofore. And seeing we require nothing of the Scots but only the performance of their own pacts and covenants, we think they ought in reason be well contented with such order touching the matter of the Scots as we have heretofore signified by our former instructions unto you. And in case they shall come to no conformity in none of the ways aforesaid, then to declare plainly unto them that they be so much wedded to their own wills that they can blame no man else for the let of the peace but themselves; and that they be the only occasions, not only of disturbance and great expense of money of both sides, but also by this means hinder themselves from doing of other enterprises of more valour to them, peradventure by six times, than this is. And let them take good heed that for refusal to give two millions for so strong and goodly a hold as that now is, they be not occasions to themselves to spend six.

Finally, if they in the end shall perchance make a motion or overture to have a truce agreed upon, we can also be pleased you shall assent thereunto and conclude a truce, so as it be not under two years, and they to cease to disturb us in the mean time in Boulogne, leaving it to our quiet possession, with such other quantity of Boulognois and the County of Guisnes as shall be signified unto you with all speed possible by another plat which we mind to send by Rogers unto you.

XX. To Lisle, Paget, &c.

[*Greenwich, May* 22, 1546.]

Right trusty and right well-beloved Cousin, and trusty and right well-beloved, we greet you well. And let you wit that, having seen your letters with the plat addressed unto us by Sir Richard Lee, and understanding by the same as well that the matter not yet agreed upon resteth much upon the limits, as also to what resolution the French Commissioners, as it appeareth, mind finally to descend unto; wherein ye seem also desirous to know our pleasure: we have thought good to signify unto you, if ye shall not be able to bring them to agree to such limits, as be set forth in our former instruction, we be pleased that you shall finally agree upon the said limits as followeth; but, if you may possibly, you shall please us well to bring them to the limits signified by our former instructions, especially for the limits of the haven.

First, that the haven be agreed upon to be ours, so far as the water overfloweth at the high water of both sides from the sea to Pont Brick.

Second, that from the Pont de Brick upward, the river coming into the said haven shall be the limit on the other side, and remain common unto us and the French King, so as they neither do ne attempt any thing in the said river, whereby the same may be turned any other way from the accustomed way by which it now runneth into the haven.

Thirdly, where they claim three villages lying between the head of the said river and Guisnes, for that, as they say, they have as yet the possession of the same, ye shall declare unto them, that their possession (if any such be) hath been and is but *precaria possessio*,[1] and such as rather hath been suffered of the contempt of our men, than otherwise enjoyed of any force; and seeing we have (as they know) had possession of some of their towns as far as Turwin, be nevertheless pleased now to depart with the same again, they cannot by any reason stick with us at so small a trifle as these three villages, the attaining whereof may be to our pale an occasion of some unquietness, and to them no commodity. And if they shall reply unto you again that those villages be necessary for the conduct of their victuals, and for their way to Ardres, we be also pleased, if they shall show themselves conformable in the residue, that by your discretion such parcel of ground shall be appointed unto them, whereby they may have an honest way by sufferance, as one friend hath with another.

Ye must herein travail earnestly, and set forth unto them how much we be pleased to remit of that we might otherwise reasonably require of them; and if, things being thus framed, they shall not show themselves now conformable, the world must think that they have not indeed (whatsoever they swear and pretend) minded to deal friendly *et bona fide* with us, and that the fault of the continuance of these wars is only in their wilfulness, and nothing at all in you, whatsoever hath been said by them in that behalf: remembering unto the Admiral (whom you take to be a wise man) how much the conclusion of this peace may be for the common profit of Christendom; and, although they shall perchance relent in some things, to consider withal that we be pleased to do the same in greater things, and that sticking in small may turn both us and his master to such expenses as may perchance be hereafter repented, and yet they never like to come to so good conditions as they may now.

Finally, where they are contented to covenant that, after the declaration of this peace, no new fortification shall be commenced of either side; we be also pleased ye shall assent on our behalf to

[1] Possession on sufferance.

the same, and put that also amongst your capitulations of this treaty accordingly.

XXI. To Lisle, Paget, &c.

[*Greenwich, May* 26, 1546.]

Right trusty and right well-beloved, and trusty and well-beloved, we greet you well. And where we have heretofore signified our pleasure unto you, that we were pleased you should covenant with the French Commissioners, that, after the declaration of this peace, no new fortification shall be commenced of either side; having now sithens that time considered that matter with ourself, we can see no reason why we should be so bound for our part, for we think that they have none occasion why they should bind us not to fortify, seeing that we have none other surety but the sure keeping of our country there till the time of deliverance. And for their part we think they should be bound not to fortify any new fortifications, according to the pact, because they should leave our country quietly unto us unto the time agreed upon; at which time the fortifications and all Boulognois shall be theirs. And therefore we desire you to travail as earnestly as ye may to procure some moderation of this point, and to obtain that we may have liberty to fortify within the country remaining with us at our pleasure, for the sure keeping of the same, seeing they give us none other pledge. For the better conducing whereof to good purpose you may do your best, and use also Francisco Bernardo[1] to join with you as a minister, who (we doubt not) will show himself well willing to further the same to the best of his power. And in case you can obtain that by no means, we think good you do assay whether you may induce them to be contented that we shall except any one place within their frontiers, in the which they shall begin no new fortification, leaving them full liberty to fortify in all other places at their wills. Whereunto if you may induce them to assent, we be pleased you shall promise the like on our behalf again, that, they accepting any one place within our limits, we may fortify in all other parts of the same. And if you shall be able to bring them to agree to either of the

[1] A Venetian, acting as an intermediary for peace.

said conditions, you shall (we assure you) minister right thankful pleasure unto us, and yet, rather than you should break off for this point, we be pleased (if you can bring them to no other conformity) that you shall finally in the end agree, according to our former instructions and letters heretofore addressed unto you in that behalf.

XXII. TO LISLE, PAGET, &C.

[*June* 2, 1546.]

RIGHT TRUSTY AND RIGHT WELL-BELOVED, AND TRUSTY AND RIGHT WELL-BELOVED, we greet you well. And let you wit that we have seen your letters addressed unto us by this bearer, together with such capitulations as the French Ambassadors delivered unto you, so unreasonably framed in sundry points as it may appear manifestly by the same that they have in this treaty rather meaned to win time by their accustomed manner of practices than to conclude *bona fide* that which they have pretended, going about to win from us by craft and fraud those things which by sword and force they neither be, nor ever shall (we trust) be able to recover. Nevertheless upon the perusing of their articles we have yet once again devised others; in the penning whereof, like as in sundry points we have been pleased to yield to their desires, so in some other points we have omitted certain parts of their said articles and altered some other parts to more reasonable conditions, as by the said articles, which we at this present do send unto you, you shall perceive at more length.

Before the opening of which articles unto them our pleasure is, you shall first declare the great unreasonableness of their requests touching the restitution of the old owners and inhabitants of Boulognois, and touching their device for the use of the haven, wherein besides those considerations which we have caused to be put in pen, and do send unto you herewith, you may also add such others as you shall think expedient; declaring and showing unto them how much they have been addict to their own wills against all reason from the beginning in this treaty; how much we have been pleased to relent to their satisfaction almost in all things, for the good of Christendom, and sparing of the effusion of Christian blood; and now, things being so near a good conclusion, let them consider whether it be expedient for their master's affairs and their own estate to break the towardness of this amity between two such Princes for a few peasants, or other such men's causes as they now stick upon. And here travail, as much as you may, to bring them to agree to the former instructions heretofore sent unto you; whereunto if they will by no means assent nor agree unto, then our pleasure is, that you shall say, as of yourself, that you are sorry to see these things frame after this sort; and because you have been ministers so long in this affair, you would be glad to see the same conduced to a better conclusion, and therefore require them to devise yet once again; and so (ye may say) you will do also. And so, after promise made to that effect, you may then, as of your [selves, show these articles,][1] and say, that being desirous to see some good end of this long treaty, you have yet once again devised more reasonable conditions than may with indifferency be required. Whereunto if they will assent upon sight of the same, we be very well pleased you shall conclude a peace with them. Otherwise, if you shall see that they will by no means assent thereunto, because by these their proceedings it appeareth manifestly that they mean nothing less than to conclude a peace indeed, we think it very expedient for our affairs, for sundry respects, that, by your good policies and wise handling, some such means were used; as, this treaty [being de][2]ferred for a while, we may in the mean season win so much time, as our things, as well for the seas as other ways, may be put in order to meet with them in all events. For which purpose we mind to take such speedy and substantial order as shall appertain.

And for the better mean to conduce this to good purpose, we think it shall be very well, that you, as of yourselves, showing these our said capitulations unto them, do require to have the same sent to their master, from whom you doubt not, (ye may say) to receive a more reasonable answer than you have received at their hands; and seeing you have at their desires sent their capitulations unto us, you think they will not deny to show you

[1] MS. damaged: lacunæ supplied from Calig. E. IV, f. 163v.
[2] Supplied from *S.P.* XI, 192.

the like gratuity again, in sending of your articles to the French King; whereof (you may bear them in hand) you look undoubtedly for good success, seeing things be reduced to so narrow points as they be, and so many things remitted and yielded unto on our behalf as have been. But if, before any sending, they will perchance agree with you upon the articles which we do now send unto you, you must consider, before the full ending of this matter, that the river from Pont de Brick to the head of the same, and the head itself, be more certainly set forth than they were by their capitulations, and [that the limits][1] also from the head of the said river to Guisnes be likewise set forth by good and sure bounds and limits. For which purpose, if you shall agree so far, our pleasure is you shall send for Rogers our servant to peruse the whole of the said limits, and to make a plat thereof to be sent unto us, whereby we may the more certainly see what portion of ground is appointed to remain with us accordingly.

As for the comprehension of the Emperor, the article which we do now send unto you touching his comprehension, is framed after like sort as the Emperor comprehended us in his late treaty with France, [as appeareth by][1] the copy of the said treaty, which we have of the Emperor's delivery. And where the French Commissioners have affirmed unto you that there be more words in the said comprehension than appear in our copy, you may tell them that at the late being of the Admiral, Chancellor and Bochetel with the Emperor, the said Bochetel then said openly to our Ambassadors, in the presence also of divers of the Emperor's Council, that the Emperor would by no means agree with them without a full and special [comprehension of us.][1] And therefore seeing he then affirmed so, we must think that our comprehension was and is after the like sort as he then said, and as we have also been advertised other ways. Nevertheless, if they whom we take to be men of honour shall send us the very true and whole copy of that clause of the comprehension, as it is conceived in deed, subscribed with their hands, we may be induced the better to credit the same, and proceed thereafter accordingly.

Finally, if the French Commissioners will not assent to any

[1] Supplied from Calig. E. IV, ff. 166, 166v.

of your requests aforesaid, but wilfully mind to break off, because in their late conference with you upon these matters they [have][1] said that, if the peace should now break off, being brought to so narrow points, they would charge you before God and us, for the same; you may tell them again, that if now they shall, as they have hitherto, continue their wilfulness, and will allow nothing for reason but that which shall proceed from themselves, they must think to go as they came, and withal consider that they shall never have so much reason offered again at our hands, whereof they may be well assured. And if things shall not now come to an end, we having in so many things followed their desires, you must and will (as the truth is) declare [before (the) world,][1] that their only obstinacy and wilful proceedings be the cause thereof. And in this case you may tell them plainly and roundly also, that the coming of their men to our frontiers, and the staying of all the hulks and other preparation to the seas, sithens the commencement of this treaty, make declaration to the world what good faith they have meant at this time; whereof like as we have had continually certain knowledge, so have we, and shall also more amply by the grace of God, provide for the same accordingly.

And in this case of their obstinate and wilful breaking off, our pleasure is that you, our Admiral, returning first to your charge upon the seas, and setting such order in the same as shall be requisite, do, after order given there, return to our presence for a few days according to your desires, and you, our Secretary and Mr. Wotton, to return to us immediately upon your breaking off, with diligence.[2]

The actual treaty finally included Scotland, with the proviso that she must be bound by the treaty of Greenwich. It is perhaps not without significance that it was on May 29 that Cardinal Beton was murdered at St. Andrews (see p. 350). For the rest, it was agreed that England should keep Boulogne and the Boulonnais for eight years, at the end of which time they should

[1] Supplied from Calig. E. IV, f. 166v, 167.
[2] For note on text see App. I, Notes.

be redeemed by France for a sum of 2,000,000 crowns—Henry's claim for the expenses incurred by him for the war and the fortifying of Boulogne, and for the sum owing to him as pension arrears. The old pensions were again guaranteed—a perpetual tribute of 50,000 crowns, and a pension for the King's life of 100,000 crowns.

Boulogne, useless as a possession, symbolized military prestige, national honour. The Scots clause meant good statesmanship, and a final assertion of the aim for which Henry had striven all his life. And 2,000,000 crowns, as well as the pensions, made quite a satisfactory sum. The treaty, in fact, makes a pretty conclusion to the juggling of a lifetime—a good concrete instance of what might be gained by upsetting the European equilibrium.

CHAPTER VI

EPILOGUE

'His Majesty . . . being by God's sufferance born by just and most certain title and succession to such a kingdom as knoweth therein no superior, his crown being close, and his progenitors afore him Emperors in their own realm and dominions, doubteth not but, with God's help, he will so prepare himself as he shall be able to leave it in as good case to his son as his father before left it unto him, and better.'

—HENRY VIII TO THE DUKE OF NORFOLK: 1540.

HENRY VIII served a twenty years apprenticeship in the art of ruling. His career as a statesman began with the fall of Wolsey and the summoning of Parliament in 1529; and one of the most remarkable and memorable characteristics of that career is the use that he made of Parliament. He dealt with it in person, he debated questions with it, he was constantly present in both houses during the conduct of business. As head of the Government and his own Prime Minister he initiated most of the legislation which Parliament carried through, but he both respected and protected its privileges, including that of free speech.

All too little of this appears in Henry's letters. Here therefore, in conclusion, it is fitting that he should speak once again for himself, in the words of his last address to Parliament, delivered in 1545. Professor A. F. Pollard regards it as 'his last political will and testament'. It was delivered, according to a contemporary report, 'so sententiously, so kingly, or rather fatherly, as peradventure to you that hath been used to his daily talks should have been no great wonder (and yet I saw some that hear him often enough largely water their plants) but to us, that have not heard him often, was such a joy and marvellous comfort as I reckon this day one of the happiest of my life'.[1]

1. HENRY'S LAST SPEECH

[*Dec.* 24, 1545.]

Although my Chancellor for the time being hath before this time used very eloquently and substantially to make answer to

[1] Quoted from *L.P.* XX. ii. 1030.

such orations as hath been set forth in this high court of Parliament, yet is he not so able to open and set forth my mind and meaning, and the secrets of my heart, in so plain and ample manner as I myself am and can do: wherefore I taking upon me to answer your eloquent oration, master Speaker, say that where you, in the name of our well beloved commons, hath both praised and extolled me for the notable qualities that you have conceived to be in me, I most heartily thank you all that you have put me in remembrance of my duty, which is to endeavour myself to obtain and get such excellent qualities and necessary virtues, as a Prince or governor should or ought to have, of which gifts I recognize myself both bare and barren; but of such small qualities as God hath endued me withal, I render to his goodness my most humble thanks, intending with all my wit and diligence to get and acquire to me such notable virtues and princely qualities as you have alleged to be incorporate in my person. These thanks for your loving admonition and good counsel first remembered, I eftsoons thank you again, because that you considering our great charges (not for our pleasure, but for your defence, not for our gain, but to our great cost) which we have lately sustained, as well in defence of our and your enemies as for the conquest of that fortress which was to this realm most displeasant and noisome, and shall be, by God's grace hereafter, to our nation most profitable and pleasant, have freely of your own mind granted to us a certain subsidy, here in an act specified, which verily we take in good part, regarding more your kindness than the profit thereof, as he that setteth more by your loving hearts than by your substance. Besides this hearty kindness I cannot a little rejoice when I consider the perfect trust and sure confidence which you have put in me, as men having undoubted hope and unfeigned belief in my good doings and just proceedings for you, without my desire or request, have committed to mine order and disposition all Chantries, Colleges, Hospitals, and other places specified in a certain act, firmly trusting that I will order them to the glory of God, and the profit of the common wealth. Surely if I, contrary to your expectation, should suffer the ministers of the Church to decay, or learning (which is great a jewel) to be minished, or poor and miserable people to be unrelieved, you might say that I being put in so special a trust, as I am in this case, were no trusty friend to you, no charitable man to mine even Christian, neither a lover of the public wealth, nor yet one that feared God, to whom account must be rendered of all our doings. Doubt not, I pray you, but your expectations shall be served, more godly and goodly than you will wish or desire, as hereafter you shall plainly perceive.

Now sithence I find such kindness on your part toward me, I cannot chose but love and favour you, affirming that no prince in the world more favoureth his subjects than I do you, nor no subjects or commons more love and obey their sovereign lord than I perceive you do me, for whose defence my treasure shall not be hidden, nor, if necessity require, my person shall not be unadventured: yet although I with you, and you with me, be in this perfect love and concord, this friendly amity cannot continue, except both you, my lords temporal, and you, my lords spiritual, and you, my loving subjects, study and take pain to amend one thing which surely is amiss, and far out of order, to the which I most heartily require you; which is, that charity and concord is not amongst you, but discord and dissension beareth rule in every place. St. Paul sayeth to the Corinthians, in the xiii Chapter, Charity is gentle, charity is not envious, charity is not proud and so forth in the said chapter: behold then, what love and charity is amongst you, when the one calleth the other, heretic and Anabaptist, and he calleth him again Papist, hypocrite, and Pharisee. Be these tokens of charity amongst you? are these the signs of fraternal love between you? No, no, I assure you that this lack of charity amongst yourselves will be the hindrance and assuaging of the fervent love between us, as I said before, except this would be salved and clearly made whole. I must needs judge the fault and occasion of this discord to be partly by negligence of you the fathers and preachers of the spirituality. For if I know a man which liveth in adultery, I must judge him a lecherous and a carnal person: if I see a man boast and brag himself, I cannot but deem him a proud man. I see and hear daily that you of the clergy preach one against another, teach one contrary to another, inveigh one against another without charity or discretion. Some be too stiff in their old Mumpsimus, other be too busy and curious in their new Sumpsimus. Thus all men almost be in variety and discord, and few or none preach truly and sincerely the word of God, according as they ought to do. Shall I now judge you charitable persons doing this? No, no, I cannot so do. Alas how can the poor souls live in concord when you preachers sow amongst them in your sermons, debate and discord: of you they look for light, and you bring them darkness. Amend these crimes, I exhort you, and set forth God's word, both by true preaching and good example giving, or else I whom God hath appointed his Vicar and high minister here, will see these divisions extinct, and these enormities corrected, according to my very duty, or else I am an unprofitable servant and untrue officer.

Although, as I say, the spiritual men be in some fault, that charity is not kept amongst you, yet you of the temporality be not clean and unspotted of malice and envy, for you rail on Bishops, speak slanderously of priests, and rebuke and taunt preachers, both contrary to good order and Christian fraternity. If you know surely that a bishop or preacher erreth or teacheth perverse doctrine, come and declare it to some of our Council or to us, to whom is committed by God the high authority to reform and order such causes and behaviours: and be not judges yourselves of your own phantastical opinions and vain expositions, for in such high causes ye may lightly err. And although you be permitted to read holy scripture, and to have the word of God in your mother tongue, you must understand that it is licensed you so to do, only to inform your own conscience, and to instruct your children and family, and not to dispute and make scripture, a railing and a taunting stock against priests and preachers (as many light persons do). I am very sorry to know and hear how unreverently that most precious jewel the word of God is disputed, rimed, sung and jangled in every alehouse and tavern, contrary to the true meaning and doctrine of the same. And yet I am even as much sorry that the readers of the same follow it in doing so faintly and coldly: for of this I am sure, that charity was never so faint amongst you, and virtuous and godly living was never less used, nor God himself amongst Christians was never less reverenced, honoured or served. Therefore, as I said before, be in charity one with another, like brother and brother; love, dread and serve God (to the which I, as your supreme head and sovereign lord, exhort and require you) and then I doubt not but that love and league that I spake of in the beginning shall never be dissolved or broken between us. And the making of laws, which be now made and concluded, I exhort you the makers, to be as diligent in putting them in execution, as you were in making and furthering the same, or else your labour shall be in vain, and your commonwealth nothing relieved. . . .

The next document is little but a note, but it shows us Henry consistent to the end, occupied in the last moments of his life with the succession to the throne and the protection of the Tudor line. On December 12, 1546, the Duke of Norfolk and his son the poet Surrey were arrested on the charge of treason. Henry himself investigated the whole affair. Buckingham and Katharine of Aragon, the Pope, and the unfortunate family of the Poles, had all found Henry utterly ruthless when the question of the succession was or even seemed to be involved. Surrey was to find him equally so. His alterations in the following notes are written in a hand as firm and unfaltering as it had ever been. Surrey's offences sound trivial enough: he had quartered the royal arms with his own; his sister bore witness that he had advised her to become the King's mistress for the benefit of her family; he had said that if the King died his father Norfolk ought to be Protector. Trivial or not, Henry knew that Norfolk was a possible claimant to the throne; and he had no mind to leave a legacy of trouble to his nine-year-old son.

II. Charges against the Duke of Norfolk and Earl of Surrey

If a man coming of THE COLLATERAL LINE TO THE HEIR OF the crown, who ought NOT to bear the Arms of England BUT ON the second quarter, with the difference of THEIR ancestry, do PRESUME TO change his right place, and bear them in the first quarter, leaving out the true difference of the ancestry, and, in the lieu thereof, use THE VERY PLACE only of the Heir Male Apparent; HOW THIS MAN'S INTENT IS TO BE JUDGED; AND WHETHER THIS import any danger, peril, or slander to the title of the Prince or very Heir Apparent; and how it weigheth in our laws.

If a man PRESUME TO take into his arms an old coat of the Crown, WHICH HIS ANCESTOR NEVER BARE, NOR HE OF RIGHT OUGHT TO BEAR, [ ] and use it without difference; whether it may be to the peril or slander of the very Heir of the Crown, or be taken to tend to his disturbance in the same; and in what peril they be that consent that he should so do.

If a man compassing WITH HIMSELF TO GOVERN THE REALM, DO ACTUALLY GO ABOUT TO RULE THE KING, AND should, for that purpose, advise his daughter, or sister, to become his harlot, THINKING THEREBY TO BRING IT TO PASS, AND SO WOULD RULE BOTH FATHER AND SON, AS BY THIS NEXT ARTICLE DOTH MORE APPEAR; WHAT THIS IMPORTETH.

If a man say these words, 'If the King die, who should have the rule of the Prince, but my father, or I,' what it importeth.

The depraving of the King's Council.

If a man shall say these words of a [nobleman] or woman of the Realm, 'if the K[ing] were dead, I should shortly shut him up'; what it importeth.

If a man provoked and compelled by his duty of allegiance, shall declare such matter as he heareth touching the King, and shall after be continually threatened by the per[son] accused, to be killed or hurt for it; [what] it importeth.

If a man take upon him to use [liberties] in his Lordship, or to keep pleas [or to make] himself free warren in his groun[ds, without] licence; what it importeth.

If a subject presume without li[cence to][1] give arms to strangers; what it imp[orteth].

Early in the new year Surrey was found guilty and beheaded. Norfolk was also condemned; but that 'fell sergeant Death' was swifter in his arrest than the officers of the King, and it was Henry, not Norfolk, who passed to his final account on January 18, 1547.

[1] Lacunæ supplied from original draft.

In the last document of all, which is a brief extract from his will, Henry determines the succession to the throne according to the powers conferred on him by Parliament by the Act of 1536, and by the later Acts which amplified these powers by entailing the succession upon Mary and Elizabeth, unless such entail should prove contrary to his desires.

III. Henry's Will

[*Dec.* 30, 1546.]

(f. 7) And as concerning the order and disposition of the Imperial crown of this realm of England and Ireland, with our title of France, and all dignities, honours, pre-eminences, prerogatives, authorities and jurisdictions to the same annexed or belonging, and for the sure establishment of the succession of the same. . . .

(f. 7v) We will by these presents, that immediately after our departure out of this present life, our said son Edward shall have and enjoy the said imperial crown and realm of England and Ireland, our title to France, with all dignities, honours, pre-eminences, prerogatives, authorities and jurisdictions, lands and possessions to the same annexed or belonging, to him and to his heirs of his body lawfully begotten.

And for default of such issue of our said son Prince Edward's body lawfully begotten: We will the said Imperial crown and other the premises, after our two deceases, shall wholly remain and come to the heirs of our body lawfully begotten of the body of our entirely beloved wife Queen Katharine that now is, or of any other our lawful wife that we shall hereafter marry.

And for lack of such issue and heirs we will also that after our decease, and for default of heirs of the several bodies of us and our said son Prince Edward lawfully begotten, the said imperial crown and all other the premises shall wholly remain and come to our said daughter Mary and the heirs of her body lawfully begotten, upon condition that our said daughter Mary, after our decease, shall not marry ne take any person to her husband without the assent and consent of the Privy Councillors and others appointed by us to our dearest son Prince Edward aforesaid to be of counsel, or of the most part of them, or the most of such as shall then be alive, thereunto, before the said marriage, had in writing and sealed with their seals; all which conditions we declare, limit, appoint and will by these presents shall be knit and invested to the said estate of our said daughter Mary in the said imperial crown and other the premises.

And if it fortune our said daughter Mary to die without issue of her body lawfully begotten; we will, that after our decease, and for default of issue of the several bodies of us, and of our said son Prince Edward lawfully begotten and of our daughter Mary, the said imperial crown and other the premises shall wholly remain and come to our said daughter Elizabeth, and to the heirs of her body lawfully begotten.

Elizabeth's marriage was limited by similar provisions to those already made for her sister's; and in default of her issue the Imperial crown

> (f. 9) shall wholly remain and come to the heirs of the body of the Lady Frances our niece, eldest daughter to our late sister the French Queen lawfully begotten;

After Frances, her sister Eleanor was named, and in the event of failure of issue by her the crown

> shall wholly remain and come to the next rightful heirs.

It is noteworthy that the heirs of his eldest sister Margaret of Scotland are not only passed over in favour of the younger sister Mary, but that they are never named.

In this brief extract is the final assertion of Henry's ' imperial theme '—the real and unquestioned authority of the sovereign within his state. Here, at last, is the entire fulfilment of his dream of power, and the triumph of his own deliberately conceived policy. There is nothing one can add to Stubbs's comment: ' Here was a " lex regia " indeed; a dictatorship which, with all conceivable limitations, left the " king master and only master " in his own house.'

In 1522 Sir Thomas More, communicating Henry's comments to Wolsey, wrote: ' which consideration his Grace would have planted into the instructions with his own hand, saving that he said your Grace could, and so he requireth you to do, better furnish it and set it forth '.[1]

In 1529 Erasmus, describing to Cochleius the appearance of Henry's letters, wrote: 'In these there were manifest signs of comment, addition, suppression, correction and alteration. You might recognize the first drafting of a letter, and you might make out the second and third and sometimes even the fourth correction: but whatever was revised or added was in the same handwriting.'[2]

At thirty Henry was still prepared to learn, and to admit that others might do better than he could. In the forties it is the King himself who plants and furnishes and sets forth his precise intentions. At fifty he is still submitting everything to the closest scrutiny. Instructions for the fortification of Hull, in 1542, have additions throughout made in Henry's own hand. He deals with the most minute points. To the order that the master-mason and master-carpenter are to sit with the paymaster at every paying of wages Henry adds 'if they be not sick'. When it is laid down that the paymaster shall receive sixpence a day for a clerk, Henry adds 'to help to write his book'.[3]

As a young man Henry told the Venetian ambassador that he was content with his own, and sought only to command his own subjects; adding, however, that on the other hand 'I do not choose that any one shall have it in his power to command me.' The young man who spoke these words had not begun to understand the significance of what he was saying. While Wolsey's brilliant mind dominated his, Henry made little or no effort to 'command' his own subjects by commandeering the sources of power in his own kingdom; and his foreign policy danced to the papal tune, even, at one period, to the tune of his nephew Charles. In his forties and fifties Henry, the mature ruler, might with truth have repeated his youthful boast as the keynote of his policy, and this is the Henry to whom the letters introduce us—the man who could conceive a policy of 'imperial' independence

[1] *S.P.* I, p. 110.
[2] Quoted from F. M. Nichols, *Epistles of Erasmus*, I, p. 424.
[3] *L.P.* XVII, 140.

for England, who could realize the necessity for uniting the British Isles under one government, the man who, standing between the old world and the new, could realize the full and practical implications of the fact that imperial power admits of no dividing of allegiance between Church and State. In his letters we can follow the broader concept and sweep of the fundamental idea of his policy: we can see him steadily consolidating his position by concentrating all the real sources of power in his own hands, until to the legislative authority of the King in Parliament he has added the control of the vast wealth confiscated from the Church, as also such spiritual authority as can be conferred by ecclesiastical supremacy. We can also appreciate his amazing grasp of the importance of detail. The man who adds and alters, cancels and expands in the letters and other documents, is the man who in Wales works towards unification by getting rid of the Welsh language, and in Ireland by getting rid of the national dress. A poet in our own time has written of Henry's true daughter—

> '. . . not a keel
> Grounds on the Cornish pebbles, but the jar
> Thrills through all English earth home to my feet.'

It may well stand for an expression of the deeper truth and of the importance that lies behind Henry's concern with master-masons and carpenters in Hull.

Every human being sets his fellows the eternal riddle of human personality. How we read it depends on ourselves; 'and that's the truth, if you think it is'. Given a reasonable equipment of knowledge of fact and event; and some touch of that gift of 'the sense of the past', without which the study of history is a dead thing; it is, I believe, possible to draw near in his letters to some understanding of the man that was Henry VIII. To find it set forth to perfection the reader must turn to Professor A. F. Pollard's magnificent last chapter. Here, in conclusion, it must suffice to say that the explanation of his success as a ruler is to be found in the nature of the man that the letters reveal—typical of the age and the nation to which he belonged, typical of much that was worst and much that was best in his fellow-countrymen, and yet at the same time, by virtue of his natural and induced egotism, and by the accident of inherited position, transcending the type. Physically, mentally, morally and spiritually he typifies the materialistic outlook of his day. Learning, in time, what he wanted and why he wanted it, he was able to pursue his aim with complete singleness of heart, because it began and ended in his own being, which was at the same time, paradoxically, the national being. Henry the King is Henry the man, who, in the words of his most recent biographer, ' stands like a vast shadow thrown on the screen of history by England's self '.[1] There is no cleavage, no inner conflict, no psychological struggle—hence the terrific force of the continual and effective expression of the will to power.

[1] Helen Simpson: *Henry VIII.*

APPENDICES

APPENDIX I

SOURCES AND REFERENCES

Number	Correspondent	Date	Source	L.P. reference
			PART I	
			CHAPTER I	
I.	Erasmus	Jan. 17, 1507	Latin; *Erasmi Epistolae*: ed. P. S. Allen, I, p. 436	
† II.	Philip, King of Castile	April 9, 1506	French: Addit. 21404, f.9	
† III.	Margaret of Savoy	June 27, 1509	French: Addit. 21404, f.10	I.84
IV.	Ferdinand of Aragon	Nov. 1, 1509	Latin: *Span.Trans.*, I, 5, f.59. P.R.O. (mod. fr. Simancas)	I.220
			CHAPTER II	
I.	Cardinal Bainbridge	May 6, 1512	Latin: Sanuto, *Diarii*, XIV, p. 267	I.1182
II.	James IV	Aug. 12, 1513	Calig. B.VI, f.56 (contemp. copy)	I.2161(5)
III.	Duke of Milan	Sept. 16, 1513	Latin: *Ven.Trans.* 195, f.169. P.R.O. (mod. fr. Milan)	I.2270
* IV.	Wolsey	1514	Calig. D.VI, f.121, and Rymer, XIII, p. 403	I.2956
* V.	Wolsey	? 1521	Vesp. F.XIII, f.138	III.1814
† VI.	Tunstall and Wingfeld	March, 1525	S.P.I., §34, ff.89-107	IV.1212
			PART II	
			CHAPTER I	
* I.	Wolsey	July, 1518	Vesp. F.III, f.73	II.4279

(*)	I.	Anne Boleyn	1527	French: Crapelet: Vatican 1	IV.3221
(*)	II.	Anne Boleyn	1527	French: Crapelet: Hearne 5	IV.3325
(*)	III.	Anne Boleyn	1527	French: Crapelet: Vatican 2	IV.3326
(*)	IV.	Anne Boleyn	1527	French: Crapelet: Vatican 4	IV.3218
(*)	V.	Anne Boleyn	1527	French: Crapelet: Vatican 10	IV.3220
(*)	VI.	Anne Boleyn	1527	French: Crapelet: Vatican 8	IV.3219
(*)	VII.	Anne Boleyn	? 1527	French: Crapelet: Vatican 11	IV.4537
(*)	VIII.	Anne Boleyn	Feb., 1528	Crapelet: Vatican 14	IV.3990
DD	IX.	Clement VII	Feb. 10, 1528	Latin: Halliwell, *Letters of the Kings of England*, I, p. 293	IV.3909 and 3901
(*)	X.	Anne Boleyn	June, 1528	French: Crapelet: Vatican 3	IV.4403
(*)	XI.	Anne Boleyn	June 22, 1528	French: Crapelet: Vatican 12	IV.4383
(*)	XII.	Anne Boleyn	June 22-30, 1528	Crapelet: Vatican 9	IV.4410
(*)	XIII.	Anne Boleyn	early July, 1528	Crapelet: Hearne 13	IV.4477
	XIV.	Wolsey	July, 1528	Fiddes' *Life of Wolsey*: I: *Collections*, p. 174: ed. 1724	IV.4507
	XV.	Wolsey	July, 1528	Herbert: *Life of Henry VIII*: *History of England*, II, p. 67	IV.4509
(*)	XVI.	Anne Boleyn	mid July, 1528	Crapelet: Vatican 15	IV.4539
*	XVII.	Wolsey	July-Aug., 1528	Vitell. B.XII, f.4, and Burnet, I, ii, 55	IV.4360
(*)	XVIII.	Anne Boleyn	Aug.-Sept., 1528	Crapelet: Vatican 16	IV.4597
(*)	XIX.	Anne Boleyn	Aug., 1528	Crapelet: Vatican 7	IV.4648
(*)	XX.	Anne Boleyn	mid Sept., 1528	Crapelet: Vatican 6	IV.4742
(*)	XXI.	Anne Boleyn	end Oct., 1528	Crapelet: Vatican 17	IV.4894

All Cotton and Additional MSS. are in the B.M.: MSS. with classification numbers S.P.I., S.P. 49 and E. 36, are in the P.R.O. The location of any other MS. used has been given in the reference table.

Holograph letters are marked *

Signed letters are marked †

Holograph letters, located and still extant, but not printed from directly, are marked (*)

Letters signed with a stamp are marked S.

Drafts are marked D; copies are marked C. 'Copy' means the fair copy made when the letter was written.

	Number	Correspondent	Date	Source	L.P. reference
		CHAPTER III			
†	I.	Bryan and Vannes	Dec. 1, 1528	Vitell. B.X, f.163	IV.4977
†	II.	Gardiner, Bryan, Casale and Vannes	Feb., 1529	Vitell. B.XI, f.67	IV.5270
†	III.	Benet, Casale and Vannes	June 23, 1529	Vitell. B.XI, f.169	IV.5707
S	IV.	Lord Dacre	March 28, 1530	Calig. B.VII, f.160	IV.6295
†	V.	Ghinucci, Benet and Casale	March 21, 1532	Latin: *S.P. VII*, p. 360, fr. P.R.O. original	V.886
D	VI.	Cranmer	April 12, 1533	Harl. 283, f.97	VI.332
S	VII.	Lady Cobham	April 28, 1533	Harl. 283, f.96	VI.395
	VIII.	*Proclamation*	(See *List of*	*other Documents*.)	
D	IX.	?	Sept., 1534	Nero B.VI, f.85	VII.1209
D	X.	Clement VII	? 1530	Vitell. B.XIII, f.168, and Burnet IV, p. 169	IV.iii.App.260

PART III

	Number	Correspondent	Date	Source	L.P. reference
		CHAPTER I			
D	I.	Lincolnshire rebels	Oct. 19, 1536	E.36, Vol. 118, f.98	XI.780(2)
D	II.	Duke of Suffolk	Oct. 24, 1536	S.P.I., §109, f.62	XI.850
D	III.	Duke of Norfolk	Oct. 27, 1536	S.P.I., §109, f.214	XI.884
C	IV.	Yorkshire rebels	? Nov. 2, 1536	E.36, Vol. 118, p. 150	XI.957
D	V.	Ellerker and Bowes	Nov. 27, 1536	E.36, Vol. 121, p. 23	XI.1175
D	VI.	Norfolk	(Dec. 2) 1536	S.P.I., §112, f.88	XI.1227
D	VII.	Fitzwilliam and Russell	Dec. 8, 1536	S.P.I., §112, f.184	XI.1271
D	VIII.	Norfolk	Feb. 22, 1537	S.P.I., §116, f.92	XII.i.479
D	IX.	Norfolk	June 12, 1537	S.P.I., §121, f.96	XII.ii.77(1)

†	I.	Wyatt	Oct. 10, 1537	Harl. 282, f.34	XII.ii.869
†	II.	Wyatt	Jan. 22, 1538	Harl. 282, f.15	XIII.i.123
†	III.	Wyatt	Feb. 15, 1538	Harl. 282, f.23	XIII.i.281
C	IV.	Wyatt	Feb. 22, 1538	Harl. 282, f.1, contemp. decipher fr. †cipher orig. f.17	XIII.i.329
†	V.	Wyatt	April 5, 1538	Harl. 282, f.26	XIII.i.679
†	VI.	Wyatt	?June 3, 1538	Harl. 282, f.68	XIII.i.1133
†	VII.	Wyatt and Hoby	Oct. 16, 1538	Harl. 282, f.73, Vesp. C.VII, f.71, Vitell. B.XXI, f.168	XIII.ii.622
C	VIII.	Wriothesley, Vaughan and Carne	Dec. 23, 1538	S.P.I., §140, f.152	XIII.ii.1127
†	IX.	Wyatt	Jan. 19, 1539	Harl. 282, f.43	XIV.i.92
†	X.	Wyatt	Feb. 13, 1539	Harl. 282, f.47	XIV.i.280
D	XI.	Charles V	Feb. 13, 1539	French: Harl. 282, f.67	XIV.i.279
†	XII.	Wyatt	March 10, 1539	Harl. 282, f.50	XIV.i.487

CHAPTER III

	I.	*The Ten Articles.*	(See *List of*	*other Documents.*)	
	II.	*Proclamation.*	(See *List of*	*other Documents.*)	
	III.	*Proclamation.*	(See *List of*	*other Documents.*)	
	IV.	*Act of Six Articles.*	(See *List of*	*other Documents.*)	
*	V.	*Two notes* (theological).	(See *List of*	*other Documents.*)	
*	VI.	Tunstall	*c.* March, 1539	Cleo. E.V, f.131	XIV.ii.App.29

CHAPTER IV

†	I.	Francis I	Aug. 20, 1515	French: Addit. 19649(3)	II.826
D	II.	Duke of Albany	Dec. 10, 1522	Calig. B.VI, f.254	III.1854
C	III.	Earl of Surrey	Oct. 5, 1523	Calig. B.VI, f.350	III.3394
C	IV.	James V	July 21, 1524	Addit. 24965, f.138	IV.524
C	V.	Queen Margaret	July 21, 1524	Addit. 24965, f.140	IV.525

SOURCES AND REFERENCES

Number		Correspondent	Date	Source	L.P. reference
D	VI.	Lord William Howard	Oct., 1534	S.P. 49, Vol. 4, f.57	VII.1350
D	VII.	Lord William Howard	Jan.-April, 1536	Addit. 32646, f.59	?
†	VIII.	James V	Dec. 22, 1536	Addit. 19401, f.31	XI.1351
C	IX.	Earl of Angus	Aug. 25, 1532	Calig. B.I, f.134	V.1254
C	X.	Ralph Sadler	1540	National Library of Scotland, Advocates MSS. 33.3.10	XV.136
D	XI.	Lord Audeley	Aug. 29, 1541	S.P.I., §167, p. 8	XVI.1125
D	XII.	Scots' ambassadors	Feb. 6, 1542	Addit. 32647, ff.7^v and 8^v	XVII.88(1)
	XIII.	*Declaration.*	(See *List of*	*other Documents.*)	
D	XIV.	James V	Dec. 10, 1542	S.P. 49, Vol. 5, f.110	XVII.1187
D	XV.	Paget	Dec. 4, 1542	S.P.I., §174, f.174	XVII.1166(2)
D	XVI.	Council of Scotland	Jan. 4, 1543	Addit. 32649, f.6	XVIII.i.7
D	XVII.	Lord Lisle	Jan. 9, 1543	S.P.I., §175, f.7	XVIII.i.25
C&D	XVIII.	Sir R. Southwell	Jan. 8/9, 1543	Addit. 32649, f.49, f.59 and f.60	XVIII.i.22
D	XIX.	Sadler	April 4, 1543	Addit. 32650, f.123	XVIII.i.364
†	XX.	Sadler	April 14, 1543	Calig. B.VII, f.311	XVIII.i.402
D	XXI.	Sadler	July 22, 1543	Addit. 32651, f.124	XVIII.i.935
D	XXII.	Sadler	Aug. 4, 1543	Addit. 32651, f.188	XVIII.ii.9
†	XXIII.	Arran	Oct. 27, 1543	Addit. 32091, f.136	XVIII.ii.313(2)
D	XXIV.	City of Edinburgh	Sept. 9, 1543	S.P. 49, Vol. 6, f.119	XVIII.ii.154
C	XXV.	Duke of Suffolk	Sept. 14, 1543	Addit. 32652, f.88	XVIII.ii.184
D	XXVI.	Sir Anthony Browne	Sept., 1543	S.P.I., s.181, f.149	XVIII.ii.198(1)
D	XXVII.	Angus, Cassilis and Glencairn	Oct. 19, 1543	Addit. 32652, f.228	XVIII.ii.289
D	XXVIII.	Wharton and Bowes	March 26, 1544	S.P. 49, Vol. 7, f.26	XIX.i.243(2)
D	XXIX.	Governor and Council	Dec. 20, 1546	S.P. 49, Vol. 9, f.33	XXI.ii.580(1)

D	I.	Francis I	July 22, 1542	S.P.I., §171, f.164	XVII.523(1)
D	II.	Sir William Paget	Oct. 24, 1542	S.P.I., §174, f.11	XVII.980(2)
D	III.	Paget	Feb. 9, 1543	S.P.I., §175, f.176	XVIII.i.134(1)
D	IV.	Privy Council	Aug. 11, 1544	S.P.I., §190, f.241	XIX.i.1032
D	V.	Francis I	Aug. 3, 1544	French: S.P.I., §191, f.25	XIX.ii.19(2)
†	VI.	Queen Katharine Parr	Sept. 8, 1544	Calig. E.IV, f.55, holograph p.s., f.56v, and Rymer XV, 50	XIX.ii.201
D	VII.	Dr. N. Wotton	Aug. 5, 1544	S.P.I., §191, f.42	XIX.ii.32
D	VIII.	Dr. N. Wotton	Sept., 1544	S.P.I., §192, f.1	XIX.ii.180(1)
D	IX.	Dr. N. Wotton	Sept. 15, 1544	S.P.I., §192, f.86	XIX.ii.234
†	X.	Duke of Norfolk and others	Oct. 14, 1544	S.P.I., §193, f.154	XIX.ii.436(1)
†	XI.	Duke of Norfolk and others	Oct. 20, 1544	S.P.I., §194, f.6	XIX.ii.463(1)
C	XII.	Privy Council at Calais		S.P.I., §194, f.78	XIX.ii.484(3)
D&C	XIII.	Charles V	Nov. 14, 1544	French: S.P.I., §195, ff.101 and 103	XIX.ii.609(1)&(3)
†	XIV.	Paget	Feb. 20, 1545	S.P.I. s.198, f.122	XX.i.227(2)
D	XV.	Thirlby	July 28, 1545	S.P.I. s.204, f.148	XX.i.1292
D	XVI.	Paget	Dec. 4, 1545	S.P.I. s.211, f.153	XX.ii.925(1)
D	XVII.	Paget	Dec. 26, 1545	S.P.I. s.212, f.117	XX.ii.1037(2)
D	XVIII.	Earl of Hertford and others	April 27, 1546	S.P.I. s.217, f.109	XXI.i.685
D	XIX.	Lord Lisle and others	May 9, 1546	S.P.I. s.218, f.18	XXI.i.775
D	XX.	Lisle and others	May 22, 1546	S.P.I. s.219, f.18	XXI.i.877
C	XXI.	Lisle and others	May 26, 1546	S.P.I. s.219, f.82	XXI.i.926(2)
D	XXII.	Lisle and others	June 2, 1546	S.P.I. s.219, f.146	

Chapter VI

I. *Last speech to Parliament.* (See *List of other Documents.*)
II. *Charges against Norfolk and Surrey.* (See *List of other Documents.*)
III. *Henry VIII's Will.* (See *List of other Documents.*)

Other Documents

	Number	Source
	II, 3, No. VIII.	*Proclamation for the abolishing of the usurped power of the Pope.* June 9, 1534/5. Society of Antiquaries. *Proclamations* I (78). *L.P.* VIII, 848.
	III, 3, No. I.	*The Ten Articles.* [July] 1536. Cleo. E.V, f.62. *L.P.* XI. 59(1).
D	No. II.	*Proclamation for bringing in Seditious Books.* Nov., 1538. Cleo. E.V, f.357. *L.P.* XIII. ii. 848(2).
	No. III.	*Proclamation for Uniformity in Religion.* April, 1539. Cleo. E.V, f.312 *L.P.* XIV. i. 868(1).
D	No. IV.	*Act of Six Articles.* 1539. Cleo. E.V, f.327. *L.P.* XIV. i. 868(9).
*	No. V.	Two theological notes. ?1539. Cleo. E.V, f.143v. *L.P.* ?
	III, 4, No. XIII.	*Declaration of the causes of the Scots War.* 1542. Hall's *Chronicle*, p. 846. *L.P.* XVII. 1033.
	III, 6, No. I.	Last speech to Parliament. Dec. 24, 1545. Hall's *Chronicle*, p.864. *L.P.* XX. ii. 1031.
D	No. II.	Charges against Norfolk and Surrey. Dec., 1546. S.P.I., §227, f.123. *L.P.* XXI. ii. 555(14).
†	No. III.	Henry's Will. Dec. 30, 1546. P.R.O. Royal Wills, E.23(4). *L.P.* XXI. ii. 634(1).

NOTES

I. I, No. II.

The text has been taken from a contemporary copy, Calig. B.VI, f.56. (*L.P.* I. ii. 2161(5)). Hitherto this letter has been printed from Harl. 787, f.58, described by *L.P.* I. ii. 2161(i) as a 'contemporary copy'. Actually, however, it is written in a seventeenth century hand, and cannot be earlier than *c.* 1650. It has the advantage over the Caligula copy in that it gives the correct date, July 26, at l. 3. Moreover, it corresponds fairly closely with Rymer's printing. On the other hand, the Caligula copy and another almost identical contemporary copy in the P.R.O. are equally 'authentic' in point of style, and give the impression of being slightly more carefully done.

The text has been taken from the unique printed copy in the collection of the Society of Antiquaries, *Proclamations* I. 78; (*L.P.* VIII. 848; R. Steele, *A Bibliography of Royal Proclamations of the Tudor and Stuart Sovereigns*, I, No. 153.) The year is not given by the original, but Wilkins' *Concilia*, III, 772, dates it 1534, printing from Foxe's *Book of Martyrs* and Bonner's *Register*. Steele and *L.P.* date the original 1535, on the evidence of an MS. note, An. 27, H. 8, on the proclamation. This would appear to be confirmed by the unusual opening line, 'Yet once again . . .' There are differences between this text and the one given by Wilkins, which suggest that Foxe printed from a version issued in 1534, now not known.

III. 3, No. II.

Printed from MS. draft Cleo. E.V, f.357, with corrections in Henry's own hand. It is not identical with the only known printed copy in the collection of the Society of Antiquaries (*Proclamations*, II, 96) from which it is dated. The wording differs slightly, and the printed version has an extra paragraph at the end, embodying the measures for the disgrading of Becket from Saint to Bishop, and for the destruction of his pictures and images.

III. 5, Nos. II, III, XVI, XVII, XIX, XX, XXI, XXII.

These eight items have been printed from the original drafts, as the actual letters in Calig. E.IV (ff.95, 109, 120, 129, 151, 157, 163, 165) are too badly burnt. These letters are all addressed, and were presumably signed at the head. From them I have supplied dates, a few (silent) corrections of simple miswritings, and in No. XXII the lacunæ caused by injury to the draft.

APPENDIX II

BIBLIOGRAPHICAL LIST

THE student who intends to do any intensive work upon the reign of Henry VIII should refer straightaway to

Bibliography of British History. Tudor Period, 1485-1603. Edited Conyers Read. Clarendon Press. 1933.

The ordinary reader who wishes to pursue in further detail either the general history of the reign or any of the aspects treated in the various chapters of this book will find the following list helpful for preliminary guidance.

(i) GENERAL

(*a*) PRIMARY SOURCES AND AUTHORITIES OTHER THAN MSS.

Letters and Papers, Foreign and Domestic, of the Reign of Henry VIII, 1509-1547. 21 vols. J. S. Brewer and J. Gairdner. (With a second revised edition of Vol. 1, edited R. H. Brodie, 1920.) 1862-1910.

State Papers of Henry VIII. 11 vols. Record Commission. 1830-52. (A selection of letters from Henry, his ministers and others, printed *in extenso*, dealing with foreign, Scottish and Irish policies, the Pilgrimage of Grace, etc., etc.)

Lord Herbert of Cherbury: *The Life and Reign of King Henry VIII.* 1649.

(*b*) MODERN AUTHORITIES.

The Cambridge Modern History. Edited Ward, Prothero and Leathes. (Vols. 1-3.)

H. A. L. Fisher: *History of England from the Accession of Henry VII to the Death of Henry VIII.* 1906. (Vol. 5 of *The Political History of England.* Edited Hunt and Poole.)

J. A. Froude: *History of England, from the Fall of Wolsey to the Defeat of the Spanish Armada.*

A. F. Pollard: *Henry VIII.* 1902 (with illustrations); 1905; latest edition 1934.

A. F. Pollard: *Wolsey.* 1929.

See also

Introductions to 21 vols. of *Letters and Papers.*
Dictionary of National Biography.

(ii) SPECIAL SUBJECTS

(*a*) THE DIVORCE.

Lord Acton: *Wolsey and the Divorce of Henry VIII* in *Historical Essays and Studies.* Collected and edited Figgis and Lawrence. 1907.

Stephan Ehses: *Romische Dokumente.* 1893. (See also *English Historical Review*, XIX, 632-45.)

J. Gairdner: *New Light on the Divorce of Henry VIII: English Historical Review.* (Vols. XI and XII.) 1896-7.

Paul Friedmann: *Anne Boleyn.* 2 vols. 1884.

N. Pocock: *Records of the Reformation: The Divorce.* 2 vols. 1870.

See also under *General* (*b*); and for foreign affairs at the time, E. Armstrong: *The Emperor Charles V.* 2 vols. 1913.

The Anne Boleyn Love-letters require a special note. The originals, with the exception of those here numbered II and XIII, are in the Vatican. They were first printed in London in 1714 as

> *Love Letters from King Henry VIII to Anne Boleyn.* London. For J. Churchill. 1714.

Thomas Hearne, the antiquary, is generally regarded as the editor, and the Preface states that the letters were printed from a copy of the originals made by Dr. Fall, a Precentor of York, and given to Bishop Burnet for his *History of the Reformation*, for which, however, the Bishop decided that certain expressions made them unsuitable. Translations of all those written in French were made for this 1714 edition, which includes the two already mentioned which are not now in the Vatican. They were published again in 1720 as Appendix IV in

> *Robertus de Avesbury Historia de mirabilibus gestis Edwardi III.* Edited T. Hearne. Oxford. 1720.

They are here described as 'faithfully transcribed from a copy taken from the originals, which are kept in the Vatican at Rome. The copy taken 1682.' No translations are given, and there are slight differences, chiefly of spelling, between this and the 1714 text. In 1745 the letters were reprinted from the 1714 edition in the *Harleian Miscellany*, Vol. 3.

At the beginning of the nineteenth century the originals were taken as Napoleonic spoil and remained for some years in the Bibliothèque du Roi at Paris. While there they were carefully copied by M. Meon, and after the return of the originals G.-A. Crapelet printed an edition from the copies:

> *Lettres de Henri VIII à Anne Boleyn.* Edited G.-A. Crapelet. Paris. 1826. Second edition 1835.

This edition of Crapelet's is now regarded as the standard text, and includes the two letters which are missing from the Vatican collection, taking the text from Hearne. In 1902 Professor A. F. Pollard reproduced a facsimile of the letter here numbered IV in the first (illustrated) edition of his *Henry VIII.* Comparison of Crapelet's text with this facsimile reveals only one or two minute errors. If Hearne's text of the same letter is checked by the facsimile it will be noticed that there are decidedly more errors, and that at one point nearly two lines are omitted.

In this present selection all the Anne Boleyn letters are printed, and the text is taken from Crapelet, with occasional emendations from Hearne; e.g. *Cocke* for *Corke* (No. XIII, l. 2).

The text used for *Letters and Papers* was taken from a periodical called *The Pamphleteer*, which published in 1822-3 (Vols. 21 and 22, Nos. XLII and XLIII) *The Love Letters of Henry VIII to Anne Boleyn*, edited with an introduction by the editor of *Historia Brittonum*, who states that he copied the letters from the originals (part of Codices Vaticani, No. 3731) in the belief that they had not previously been published. He mentions ' occasional interlineations ', and states that, with two exceptions, each letter is written on one side only of a sheet of paper measuring 10½ ins. by 7½ ins. In No. I, l. 8, he undoubtedly gives the correct reading *Juors* (i.e. iuors = jours = days) where the other texts, including Crapelet, have *Mores*, i.e. Moors.

(*b*) RELIGION.

See first under *General* (*b*).

Gilbert Burnet: *History of the Reformation of the Church of England.* Edited N. Pocock. 7 vols. 1865.

R. W. Dixon: *History of the Church of England.* 6 vols. 1878-1902.

J. Gairdner: *The English Church in the Sixteenth Century.* 1902. (Vol. 4 of *A History of the English Church.* Edited Stephens and Hunt.)

F. A. Gasquet: *Henry VIII and the English Monasteries.* 2 vols. Second edition. 1906.

Charles Lloyd: *Formularies of Faith.* 1825. (Reprints Ten Articles, Bishops' Book and King's Book.)

A. F. Pollard: *Thomas Cranmer and the English Reformation.* 1905. New edition 1926.

J. Strype: *Ecclesiastical Memorials.* 3 vols. 1721. (Valuable for documents.)

(*c*) SCOTTISH POLICY.

P. Hume Brown: *History of Scotland.* (Vols. 1 and 2.) 1899-1909.

Before turning to MS. sources the reader will find an amazing wealth of material in letter form in the following:

State Papers of Henry VIII. (Vols. 4 and 5.)

Hamilton Papers. Edited Joseph Bain. 2 vols. 1890-92.

State Papers and Letters of Sir Ralph Sadler. Edited A. Clifford. 3 vols. 1809.

(For Henry's work of unification in Ireland and Wales see particularly

R. Bagwell: *Ireland Under the Tudors.* (Vol. 1, Chs. 9-15.) 1885-90.

C. A. S. Skeel: *The Council in the Marches of Wales.* (1904.)

(*d*) Foreign Policy.

See first under *General* (*a*) and (*b*) all items.

Calendars of State Papers. (These are more or less covered by *Letters and Papers*, but reference can be made to *Spanish*, Vols. 1-8; and *Venetian*, Vols. 1-5.

Correspondance Politique de MM. Castillon et de Marillac. Edited J. Kaulek. 1885. (Correspondence of French ambassadors, 1537-41.)

(*e*) Books and Articles Published Since 1950

The following supplementary selection covers some of the more recent trends in studies dealing with the reign and the King's character. The only full-length biography of recent years is John Bowle's *Henry VIII* (1964), which has a number of very desirable illustrations.

S. T. Bindoff: *Tudor England*. Pelican. (1950.)

A. G. Dickens: *Thomas Cromwell and The English Reformation.* (1959.)

G. R. Elton: 'Thomas Cromwell's Decline and Fall', *Cambridge Historical Journal* X. (1951.)

The Tudor Revolution in Government. (1953.)

'King or Minister?' *History*. (1954.)

England under the Tudors. (1956.)

Henry VIII. An Essay in Revision. (1962.)

P. Hughes: *The Reformation in England.* 3 vols. (1950-4.)

J. Hurstfield: 'Was there a Tudor Despotism after all?' *Transactions of the Royal Historical Society*. Ser. 5. Vol. 17. (1967.)

T. M. Parker: *The English Reformation to 1558.* (1950.)

J. F. D. Shrewsbury: 'Henry VIII, a medical study'. *Journal of the History of Medicine* VIII. (1952.)

FF

APPENDIX III

EXAMPLES OF CORRESPONDENCE IN LATIN AND FRENCH

To the Duke of Milan

(See Part I: Ch. I: No. 4)

Ex quo Galliam sumus ingressi omnibus certaminibus superiores communibus hostibus extitimus: magnum eorum numerum et ex nobilissimis coepimus, Marinum ipsorum munitissimam urbem aquisivimus. Illinc Tornacum versus castra movimus: ad quam urbem, die hujus mensis XX pervenimus eamque absedimus ac tormenta nostra ad oppugnatione locari jussimus et in ea aliquot ictibus oppidanas adsalutavimus, eisque bidui inducias ad nobiscum [de] deditione agendum petentibus concessimus: et de rebus nostris Gallicis hactenus. De anglicis vero cum Rex Scotorum affinitatis necessitudinis, et foederis inter nos sanctissimi per (prorsus) oblitus, in partes Gallorum, quas pluris quam omnia divina atque humana jura facere videtur, se contulisset, et Scotorum X millia in nostrum regnum Angliae permisisset omnesque a non amplius quam mille ex nostris partibus (   ), partim capti et profligati fuissent, ipsemet Scotorum Rex cum ingenti exercitu dictum nostrum Regnum Angliae invasit et primo vetustum quoddam opidulum sua sponte pene collapsum ac minime munitum et idcirco prope modum derelictum quod ad Episcopum Dunelmensem pertinet, cepit, tum intra nostrum Regnum ad iiij miliaria perrexit. Ibi Illustris Dominus Comes de Surre, cui eam provinciam arcendi Scotos demandaveramus, ipsis obviam factus, die viij dicti mensis cum illis conflixit, diuque utrimque acriter est pugnatum. Tandem vero Deo optimo maxime violati foederis ultore, meliorem causam juvante, nostri superiores evaseunt, et magnum hostium numerum multosque eorum nobiles ceciderunt, reliquos in fugam verterunt, tormentaque eorum omnia coeperant, castrisque demum universis ipsos spoliarunt; nullo ex nostris optimatibus, quod adhuc sciatur, desiderato.

De ipso autem Rege Scotorum, quid fortuna in ea pugna habuerit, certum nondum habetur. Atque dictus dominus Comes de Surre Serenissime domine Reginae consorti nostrae carissime quam totius nostri Regni Angliae gubernatricem relinquimus, properanter et de longa pugna fessus significavit, ac exactius paulo post se scripturum pollicetur. . . .

Ex castris nostris apud Tornacum Die xvj Septembris MDXIII

HENRICUS.

PS. His scriptis, certum nuntium accepimus Regem ipsum Scotorum in supradicta pugna fuisse peremptum, ejusque cadaver repertum et agnitum, ac ad proximum templum elatum: ita graviores quam voluissimus suae perfidiae poenas nobis dedit.

To Anne Boleyn

(See Part II, Ch. II, No. 5)

Toutefois, ma mestres, qui'l ne vous pleu de souvenir de la promesse que vous me fites quant je estoy dernirrement vers vous, c'est à dire de savoire de vous bones novelles, et de savoire response de ma dernirre lettre; nenmoins il me semble qu'il appertient au vray serviteur (voyant que autrement il ne peut rien savoir), d'envoiere savoire la salute de sa mestres, et pur me acquitre de l'office de vray serviteur, je vous envoye cest lettre, vous suppliant de me avertire de vostre prospérité, lequel je prye à Dieu qu'el soite ausi long comme je voudray la mien, et pur vous faire encorps plus sovent sovenire de moy, je vous envoye per ce porteur ung bouke tué hersoire bien terde de ma main, esperant que quant vous en mangerés, il vous sovendra du chaseur, et ainsi à fault de espace je fray fin à ma lettre escripte de la main de vostre serviteur qui bien sovent vous souhait où lieu de vostre frere.

APPENDIX IV—GENEALOGICAL TABLE

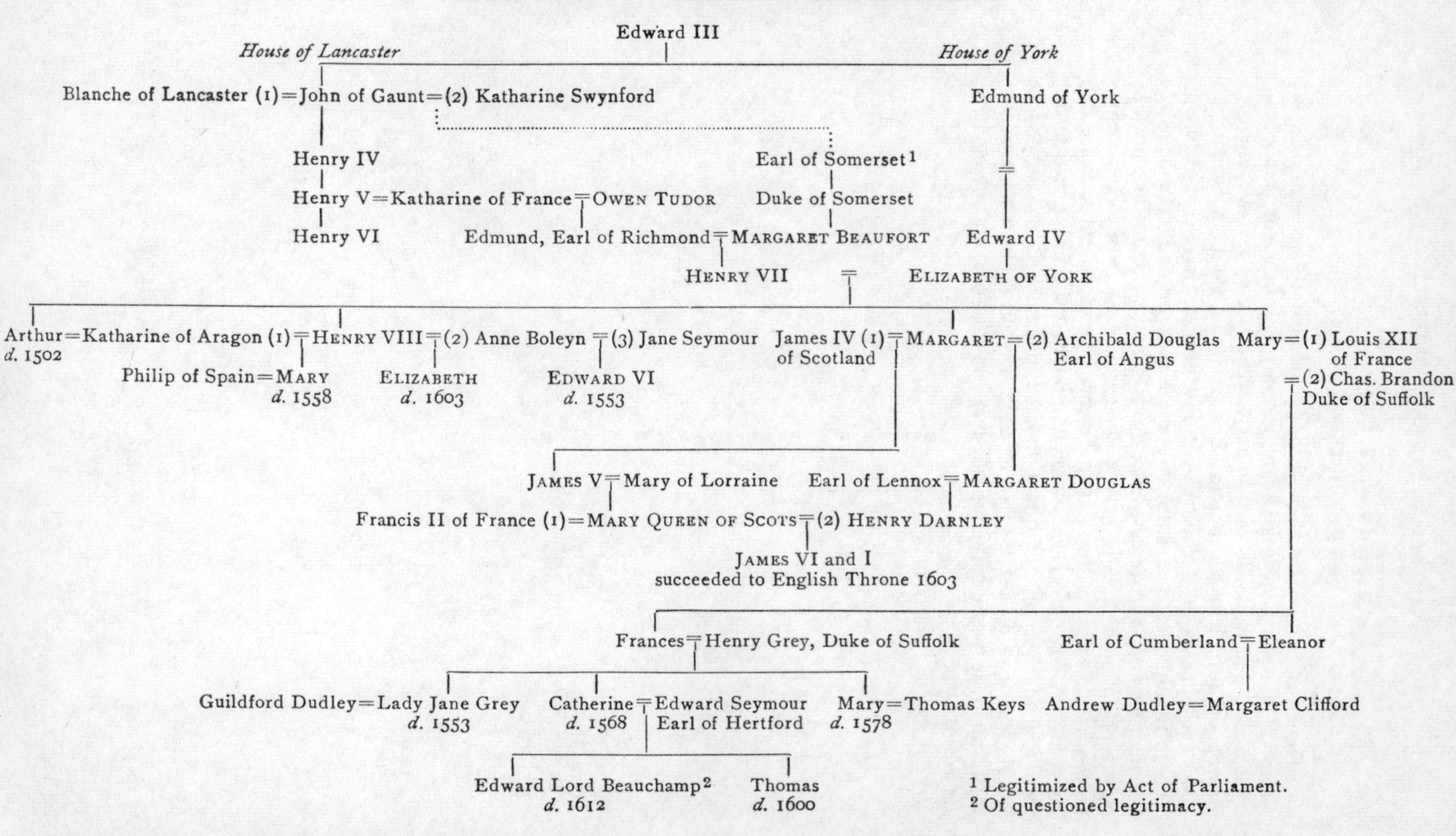

[1] Legitimized by Act of Parliament.
[2] Of questioned legitimacy.

INDEX